PETER DE RIVO ON CHRONOLOGY AND THE CALENDAR

ANCIENT AND MEDIEVAL PHILOSOPHY

DE WULF-MANSION CENTRE
Series I

LVII, 1

Editorial Coordinator

Russell Friedman

The "De Wulf-Mansion Centre" is a research centre for Ancient, Medieval, and Renaissance
philosophy at the Institute of Philosophy of the KU Leuven,
Kardinaal Mercierplein, 2, B-3000 Leuven (Belgium).
It hosts the international project "Aristoteles latinus" and
publishes the "Opera omnia" of Henry of Ghent and the "Opera Philosophica et Theologica" of
Francis of Marchia.

PETER DE RIVO ON CHRONOLOGY AND THE CALENDAR

Edited and introduced by
Matthew S. Champion,
Serena Masolini, and
C. Philipp E. Nothaft

LEUVEN UNIVERSITY PRESS

© 2020 by the De Wulf-Mansioncentrum – De Wulf-Mansion Centre
Leuven University Press / Presses Universitaires de Louvain/ Universitaire Pers Leuven
Minderbroedersstraat 4, B-3000 Leuven / Louvain (Belgium)

ISBN 978 94 6270 244 8
eISBN 978 94 6166 347 4
https://doi.org/10.11116/9789461663474
D/2020/1869/44
NUR: 732

Cover: Geert de Koning

GPRC
Guaranteed
Peer Reviewed
Content
boekenvak.be/gprc

Contents

ACKNOWLEDGEMENTS

This volume would not have been possible without the support of friends and colleagues across multiple continents and institutions. The authors would like to express their particular gratitude to John Arnold, Barbara Bartocci, Joe Canning, Paul Cavill, Rebecca Darley, Consuelo W. Dutschke, Russell Friedman, Gian Carlo Garfagnini, Alastair Hamilton, Kat Hill, Suzanne Paul, Eyal Poleg, Andrea A. Robiglio, Pietro B. Rossi, Miri Rubin, Chris Schabel, Violet Soen, Miranda Stanyon, Laura Stewart, Michiel Verweij, Brodie Waddell, and Alex Walsham. Our particular thanks, too, to Cambridge University Library, Columbia University Library, the Warden and Fellows of All Souls College (Oxford), Birkbeck College, University of London, KU Leuven, and the Institute for Religion and Critical Inquiry, Australian Catholic University. The wheel diagrams reproduced on pages 68 and 106–107 were kindly constructed for us by Alfred Lohr, to whom we are much obliged. Finally, each of the authors would like to thank each other for the great pleasure of learning together while drafting and editing this volume.

Abbreviations

BAV	Biblioteca Apostolica Vaticana
BMaz 300	MS Paris, Bibliothèque Mazarine, 300
CCCM	*Corpus Christianorum Continuatio Mediaevalis*. Turnhout, 1966–
CCSL	*Corpus Christianorum Series Latina*. Turnhout, 1953–
CSEL	*Corpus Scriptorum Ecclesiasticorum Latinorum*. Vienna, 1866–
EpApol	Paul of Middelburg. *Epistola apologetica ad doctores Lovanienses*. Leuven: Johannes de Westfalia, [not before 27 Feb.] 1488. ISTC: ip00184500.
GCS	*Die griechischen christlichen Schriftsteller der ersten [drei] Jahrhunderte*. 60 vols. Leipzig/Berlin, 1897–1989.
ISTC	http://data.cerl.org/istc/_search (Incunabula Short Title Catalogue)
KBR	Koninklijke Bibliotheek van België/ Bibliothèque Royale de Belgique
MGH	*Monumenta Germaniae Historica*
OpRes	Peter de Rivo. *Opus responsivum ad Epistolam apologeticam M. Pauli de Middelburgo de anno, die et feria dominicae passionis*. Leuven: Ludovicus Ravescot, [1489]. ISTC: ip00534000.
Paulina	Paul of Middelburg. *Paulina de recta Paschae celebratione et de die passionis Domini nostri Iesu Christi*. Fossombrone: Ottaviano Petrucci, 1513.
PL	*Patrologiae cursus completus, series Latina*. 221 vols. Paris, 1844–1865.
TerTra	Peter de Rivo. *Tercius tractatus de anno, die et feria dominicae passionis atque resurrectionis*. Leuven: Johannes de Westfalia, 1492. ISTC: ip00534100.

PREFACE

Over the course of the fifteenth and sixteenth centuries, debates over the chronology of Christ's life and the reform of the ecclesiastical calendar exercised some of Europe's foremost intellectuals. A particularly original intervention in this ongoing discussion was the *Dyalogus de temporibus Christi* ("A Dialogue on the Times of Christ") written in 1471 by the Leuven philosopher and theologian Peter de Rivo (*c.*1420–1499). Known from a single manuscript exemplum, copied in Leuven in the year of writing and now held in the Rare Book and Manuscript Library of Columbia University, the *Dyalogus* takes the form of a discussion between a Jew, Gamaliel, and a Christian, Paul. The text begins with Gamaliel evincing his readiness to acknowledge the truth of Christianity, were it not for the bizarre multitude of conflicting views concerning the dates of Christ's birth and death. In the course of the dialogue, his interlocutor Paul manages to resolve these contradictions through subtle and carefully deployed chronological arguments, thereby paving the way for Gamaliel's conversion. On the way towards this conclusion, the *Dyalogus* offers a lively historical examination of the calendrical cycles used by the Roman Church as well as a wealth of incidental discussions, including references to contemporary bell-ringing practices, theories of perfect numbers, and an original proposal for a calendar reform. The correction of the ecclesiastical calendar and the calculation of Easter is an issue Peter returned to in 1488, the year in which he committed to writing a short and pithy reform proposal to be implemented in the year 1501. This work, the *Reformacio kalendarii Romani*, had been considered lost until it was located bound together with printed works by Peter in an incunabulum held at the University Library in Cambridge. In this volume, we present the first critical edition of these two texts, together with a substantial historical introduction setting out the context of Peter's works and their significance for a wider understanding of fifteenth-century intellectual and religious culture.

Peter de Rivo was one of the most renowned figures of the early University of Leuven. He was professor of philosophy and rhetoric at the Faculty of Arts, professor of theology, and served three times as rector of the University. Interest in Peter has traditionally been limited to his role in the so-called 'Quarrel' over future contingents at the University of Leuven. Recent studies, however, have shed light on other significant aspects of his multifaceted oeuvre, which includes commentaries on Aristotle as well as other writings related to his activities as a theologian, cleric, and 'university man' involved in the political and social life of the Duchy of Brabant. From the earlier years of his career at Leuven until the very last, Peter showed a keen interest in the study of chronological and calendrical questions, composing a Gospel Harmony (the *Monotesseron*) and engaging in a heated dispute on the date of Christ's crucifixion with Paul of Middelburg. The authors of this volume have all been involved in writing some of the first detailed studies of Peter de Rivo's life and works: Serena Masolini's recent study of de Rivo's biography has charted the career and wider connections of this influential Leuven master;[1] the first substantial contribution on Peter's chronological work was offered by Philipp Nothaft;[2] and Matthew Champion has considered these texts, together with Peter's *Monotesseron* and the *Reformacio kalendarii Romani*, in the wider framework of fifteenth-century perceptions of time.[3]

Research on Peter de Rivo is clearly having a moment. His *opera* and *persona* can provide new perspectives on the intellectual, institutional, spiritual, and political history of late fifteenth-century Europe. More specifically, the texts and debates presented in this volume are capable of illuminating the roles calendars and chronological questions played in shaping various strands of pre-modern religion, public life, and scholarship. In addressing these questions, this volume seeks to add to a growing literature on the history of chronology, time reckoning, and temporalities.

On Paul and Gamaliel

One of the most immediately striking aspects of Peter de Rivo's *Dyalogus* is that the text takes the form of a dialogue between a Christian and a Jew: Paul and Gamaliel. The immediate reference here is to the Apostle Paul and his one-time teacher Gamaliel, mentioned in the Acts of the Apostles (5:34–39 and 22:3). But the prologue to the *Dyalogus* that introduces the characters makes it clear that there is a difference between the historical Paul and Gamaliel and the figures who play out Peter's arguments in relation to the chronology of Christ's life: "thus, just as Paul had once learned the Law from Gamaliel, in this little work Gamaliel will be seen to be taught by Paul about the things of the faith."[4] In choosing the dialogue form to play out these questions Peter de Rivo was perhaps influenced by his knowledge of the works of the Spanish converso bishop Paul of Burgos (also known as Pablo de Santa María, c.1351–1435).[5] Paul had used the dialogue form famously in his *Scrutinium scripturarum* (c.1432), an influential work of anti-Judaic polemic that reflects complex debates between conversos and Iberian Jews earlier in the century.[6]

By specifically using the name Gamaliel, de Rivo potentially drew on a seam of associations with Gamaliel current in Christian intellectual culture. The biblical Gamaliel had by this time long been fused with the later Rabban Gamaliel II (late

---

[1]   Masolini, "Petrus de Rivo."
[2]   Nothaft, *Dating the Passion*, 231–240.
[3]   Champion, *The Fullness of Time.*
[4]   *Dyalogus*, prologue [ll. 27–29].
[5]   For Peter's knowledge of the works of Paul of Burgos, see below, xxxviii and lv–lvi. For an anonymous twelfth-century dialogue between Paul and Gamaliel, which Peter appears not to have known, see below, cxiii.
[6]   For a recent study of Paul's *Scrutinium scripturarum*, see Yisraeli, "From Christian Polemic to a Jewish-Converso Dialogue."

first, early second century), who appears in the Mishnah and Talmud as an authority on the Jewish calendar and later even had calendrical texts ascribed to him.[7] Since Gamaliel played a prominent role in rabbinic literature, so much so that his name could even at times be used as a short-hand for the Talmud itself,[8] it is possible that Peter was trading off a general contrast between the followers of—to his mind—the Old Law and the Talmud, and the new broom of the Gospel, symbolically aligned with the Apostle Paul. But there was a different Gamaliel tradition, too, that was also widespread by the later Middle Ages. We encounter it in one of the most famous dialogues to deal with Jewish-Christian relations, Petrus Alfonsi's *Dialogue against the Jews* (1109/10). In a passage relating to questions of chronology, we find Gamaliel appearing as a crypto-Christian:

> Petrus: In reality, sometimes you [the Jews] even change the day of the Passover and defer it until the day following, because you never celebrate it on Monday, or Wednesday, or Friday. I want you to explain to me why you do this.
>
> Moses: I do not know why, other than that our sages ordained it so, and Gamaliel above all.
>
> Petrus: And do you know why Gamaliel did so?
>
> Moses: No.
>
> Petrus: Indeed, Gamaliel was a holy man and a faithful Christian. And because he knew that on Monday the Jews initiated a plan by which Christ could be condemned, and, moreover, on Wednesday the silver was given for the betrayal of Christ, and that on Friday Christ was fixed to the Cross, because, I say, he knew this and did not want any joy to be expressed on those days, for this reason he forbade them from celebrating the Passover on those days and enjoined that it be deferred until the day following. He did not want to reveal this secret, however, to everyone.[9]

Here, then, we find a way in which the pairing Paul and Gamaliel might be used to signal that Jewish and Christian accounts of Christ's life end up singing from the same hymn sheet. In this tradition, Gamaliel could even become a saint. In the *Legenda aurea* of Jacobus de Voragine (*c.*1229–1298), the most widely read and circulated compendium of saints' lives in the fifteenth century, Gamaliel appears as a prominent figure in the legend of St Stephen the Protomartyr. According to the *Legenda*, "St Gamaliel, and Nicodemus who stood up for the Christians in all the councils of the Jews, buried [Stephen] in a plot of land that belonged to Gamaliel, and made great mourning over him."[10] So while in one sense pointing to divisions between Jews and Christians over the chronology of Christ's life, in another sense

---

[7] Nothaft, *Medieval Latin Christian Texts*, 72, 340, 606–607.

[8] Van Liere, "Gamaliel"; De Visscher, *Reading the Rabbis*, 113–119.

[9] Alfonsi, *Dialogue against the Jews*, trans. Resnick, 263–264. See also Nothaft, *Medieval Latin Christian Texts*, 53–54.

[10] Jacobus de Voragine, *The Golden Legend*, trans. Ryan, 1:48.

the choice of Gamaliel as Paul's dialogue partner potentially defuses debate, moving the discussion into a safe contemporary space where no real Jews exist. This was, in fact, very much the social situation in fifteenth-century Leuven. Although Jews had been present in the city from at least the thirteenth century, the fourteenth century saw their persecution in the wake of the Black Death and eventual expulsion following an accusation of host desecration in Brussels in 1369–1370.[11] Peter de Rivo's *Dyalogus* is, then, very much a conversation played out in the sphere of the imaginary.

Plan of the volume

Our editions of Peter de Rivo's *Dyalogus* and *Reformacio* are prefaced by an introduction comprising five chapters.[12] The first chapter offers a biography of Peter that situates his chronological and calendrical works in the context of his wider oeuvre. Next, we trace Peter's argument in the *Dyalogus*, setting it in the context of the medieval debate surrounding the chronology of Christ's life (Chapter 2). This is followed by an account of the subsequent controversy that Peter entered with Paul of Middelburg, as documented by Peter's own *Opus responsivum* (1488) and *Tercius tractatus* (1492) as well as Paul of Middelburg's *Epistola apologetica* (1488) and a string of unedited letters written by him between 1492 and 1497 (Chapter 3). Focussing on the later *Reformacio kalendarii Romani*, the fourth chapter is an analysis of Peter's two proposals for a reform of the ecclesiastical calendar, issued respectively in 1471 and 1488. The fifth and last chapter turns from the content of Peter de Rivo's treatises to their possible receptions, by addressing the question of Peter's readership and the place of his work within broader strands of fifteenth-century religious reform. As a professor of theology and *plebanus* of St Peter's in Leuven, Peter was in contact with the major religious communities in Leuven and Brabant, where his works were known and read. Both of the manuscripts reporting Peter's *Reformacio* and *Dyalogus* were originally preserved and produced at two priories of Augustinian canons affiliated to the Congregation of Windesheim—the priory of Bethleem in Herent and the priory of St Martin in Leuven. Meditation on time and chronology played crucial roles in these communities, where the liturgical calendar was the chief frame for social and devotional life. In addition, the chapter reveals that the manuscript containing the *Dyalogus* had a curious afterlife in mid-seventeenth-century England that casts light on a wider history of manuscript transmission and the reception of conciliarism in the context of the troubled reign of Charles I (1600–1649).

---

[11]   For a further discussion and literature, see Champion, "The Presence of an Absence."

[12]   Each chapter of this introduction was first drafted by an individual and then worked on as a team. Serena Masolini was responsible for Chapter 1 and for the section on "The Codices," Philipp Nothaft for Chapters 2–4, and Matthew Champion for Chapter 5. The "Notes" on the two editions were prepared by Philipp Nothaft.

Note on citation practices and terminology

The bibliography at the end of this volume lists all literature cited (in abbreviated form) in the footnotes as well as the source editions used in the *apparatus fontium* of the two editions, excepting only those sources that are cited according to their series-abbreviation (CCCM, CCSL, CSEL, GCS, or PL). A full listing of all passages referenced in the *apparatus fontium* is supplied in a separate source index.

As is common practice in scholarship on pre-modern astronomy, we reproduce the sexagesimal fractions in astronomical parameter-values by using a semicolon to mark the start of a sequence of sexagesimal fractions and commas to delimit individual sexagesimal places. Hence, 29;31,50d is equivalent to 29 + 31/60 + 50/3600 days.

In discussing chronological arguments, we frequently use the term 'weekday' in its old-fashioned sense of 'day of the week' (i.e., including Saturday and Sunday).

Unless otherwise noted, all translations of Latin passages into English are ours.

INTRODUCTION

CHAPTER 1
PETER DE RIVO: A UNIVERSITY PROFESSOR IN FIFTEENTH-CENTURY LEUVEN

> Here, whoever casts his eyes, I beg you, pray for me.
> If you ask who I am: I am Peter, and my surname is
> de Rivo. If you seek to know where I was born: in Aalst
> in Flanders. If you should inquire what my occupation:
> human and—although undeservedly—divine wisdom.
> If you demand my status: the burden laid upon me is the care
> of this church and chapter of Leuven.
> What the end of my life will be: someone else shall reply.[1]

Peter de Rivo, alias Pieter vander Beke, was born in the early 1420s in Aalst, a city of the County of Flanders belonging to the diocese of Cambrai.[2] According to his epitaph, found at the end of the letter he wrote to an anonymous Augustinian canon of the priory of Groenendaal in the Zoniënwoud, he devoted his life to the study of philosophy and theology, and to the duties connected to his ecclesiastical offices at the collegiate church of St Peter in Leuven.[3]

Peter's life witnessed the development of the early University of Leuven, founded in 1425 by Pope Martin V at the request of the Chapter of St Peter, the municipal authorities, and John IV, Duke of Brabant.[4] Initially limited to the faculties of Arts, Medicine, Canon Law and Civil Law, the first *studium generale* of the Low Countries built upon the heritage of the nearby universities of Cologne and Paris, from which it took inspiration for drafting its statutes and drew recruits for its teaching staff. The permission for the institution of the Faculty of Theology arrived in 1432, when Pope Eugene IV agreed to the request of the city authorities—supported by

---

[1] *Epitaphium magistri Petri de Rivo egregii in alma Universitate Lovaniensi doctoris*, MS Stuttgart, Württembergische Landesbibliothek, HB I 10, fol. 305v: "Huc quisquis flectas [flectes MS] oculos pro me precor ora. / Quis sim si rogites, Petrus, cognomine dictus / De Rivo. Si nosse petas ubi natus, Alosti / Flandrensis. Si que michi sit professio queras, / Humane licet immerito diveque sophie. / Si statum postas onus impositum michi cure est / Istius ecclesie sinodi quoque Lovaniensis / Quid [quis MS] michi limes erit vite respondeat alter."

[2] Short accounts of Peter's life are reported in Molanus, *Historiae rerum lovaniensium*, vol. 1, 507; Andreas, *Fasti academici*, 93–94; Id., *Bibliotheca Belgica*, 758; Foppens, *Bibliotheca Belgica*, vol. 2, 1004–1005. For an intellectual biography of Peter de Rivo, see Masolini, "Petrus de Rivo," and Masolini and Schabel, "Peter de Rivo."

[3] The letter is edited in Masolini, "Petrus de Rivo," 88–89.

[4] On the first years of the University of Leuven, see, among others, Van Eijl, "The Foundation of the University of Louvain," and Lamberts and Roegiers, eds., *Leuven University 1425–1985*.

the Duke of Burgundy, Philip the Good—to complete the foundation by inaugurating the last and highest faculty.[5] Peter de Rivo matriculated five years later.

Like all aspiring students in theology who were not members of the regular orders, Peter started his studies within the halls of the Faculty of Arts, attending classes in the *trivium* and *quadrivium*, as well as in a considerable portion of the *corpus Aristotelicum*. In 1442 he received a canonry at the collegiate church of St Rumbold in Mechelen and was promoted to Master of Arts. One year later, he started teaching as professor of philosophy at the 'pedagogy' of the Castle (*paedagogium Castri*), one of the four residential colleges where the greater part of education in the Arts took place at the time. Immediately after the foundation of the university, all classes of the Faculty of Arts had been held at the *Vicus* or *Schola artium*. Within a couple of decades, however, the courses on logic, natural philosophy, and metaphysics were transferred to the four pedagogies—the Pig (*Porcus*), the Falcon (*Falco*), the Lily (*Lilium*), and the Castle (*Castrum*)—, while the *Vicus* remained the main center for the teaching of eloquence (*Rhetorica*) and moral philosophy (*Ethica*). Peter remained connected to the Castle until his death, as is witnessed in his final will, in which he bequeathed his house to the pedagogy.

As a professor of philosophy, Peter commented on Porphyry's *Isagoge*, along with Aristotle's *Categories, On Interpretation, Prior Analytics, Posterior Analytics, Topics (I–II), Physics, On the Heavens, On Generation and Corruption, Meteorology, On the Soul*, and *On Sense and the Sensible*.[6] He also composed a *Lectura* on the *Metaphysics (I–IX)*, but the only known copy of this work, which was preserved in a codex in the Magdeburg Domgymnasium (MS 165), was destroyed during World War II.[7] The list of texts commented on by Peter mirrors quite faithfully that of the required readings (*libri audiendi et legendi*) that a fifteenth-century student of the Leuven Faculty of Arts was asked to prepare in order to obtain his licence.[8] It is therefore highly probable that these commentaries were the outcome of the lectures that Peter gave at the Castle during the first ten to fifteen years of his career. However, it is not possible to date these works more precisely, since the manuscripts that we possess are later witnesses, copied in convents of the Dominican province of Saxony belonging to the Congregation of Holland (Magdeburg, Halle/Saale, Kalkar,

---

[5]   On the Faculty of Theology of Leuven, see de Jongh, *L'ancienne faculté de théologie*; Van Eijl, "Louvain's Faculty of Theology"; and Claes, "Changes in the Educational Context."

[6]   For an overview of Rivo's commentaries, see the two-part article "Reading Aristotle at the University of Louvain" (Bartocci, Masolini and Friedman, pt. I; Bartocci and Masolini, pt. II). Provisional editions of a number of Rivo's commentaries are available at https://hiw.kuleuven.be/dwmc/peterderivo (last accessed 12 August 2020).

[7]   The content of the manuscript is described in Dittmar, *Die Handschriften und alten Drucke des Dom-Gymnasiums*, 32–34.

[8]   On the *curriculum studiorum* that was in force at the fifteenth-century Leuven Faculty of Arts according to the early statutes, see Geudens and Masolini, "Teaching Aristotle at the Louvain Faculty of Arts."

and Rostock) between 1467 and 1480.[9] Peter's *Lecturae* consist of synthetic exposi-
tions of Porphyry's and Aristotle's texts, which are then discussed through a set of
brief objections and replies. To judge from a first general survey and selected case
studies, Peter seems to have followed the directives prescribed by the early statutes
of the Leuven Faculty of Arts, committing to the path of the *via antiqua* against
nominalism. Since its foundation, the University of Leuven had indeed taken a side
in the *Wegestreit*, promoting the reading of Aristotle through the interpretation and
doctrines of Albertus Magnus, Thomas Aquinas, Giles of Rome, and Averroes ("ubi
contra fidem non militat"), and banning the teachings of John Buridan, Marsilius
of Inghen, and William of Ockham.[10]

Besides the commentaries on Porphyry and Aristotle, another philosophical
work authored by Peter de Rivo has survived. In a manuscript preserved at the
Maurits Sabbe Library in Leuven, one can find a partial witness of a treatise on the
will, undated, which was copied and annotated in the margins by Adrian of Utrecht
(later Pope Adrian VI), who studied at the Faculty of Arts of Leuven from 1476.[11]

In 1456 Peter served as the official letter writer of the University, and from September 1457 to March 1458 he was appointed for the first time as rector. Two years
later, Peter received the canonry at the collegiate church of St Peter, which was
connected to the chair of rhetoric, succeeding Johannes Block and Hugo de Rimen
in the first (albeit not always happy) attempts to introduce the study of the *litterae
humaniores* in the Low Countries.[12]

Among Peter's literary production, one should mention the *Libellus quo modo
omnia in meliorem partem sunt interpretanda*, a dialogue in verse between man and
reason on how the dramatic events of the history of salvation should be considered
as a way toward the greater good.[13] The text was published in Leiden by Jan Seversz
on 20 March 1509 in a volume including the works of Engelbert Schut of Leiden,
a representative of the generation of writers who, despite their questionable Latin

---

[9]   MS Greifswald, Bibliothek des Geistlichen Ministeriums, 34.D.IX, and MSS Berlin, Staatsbibliothek, Magdeburg 201, 220, and 227. On the history of the manuscripts and their copyists, see
Masolini, "Petrus de Rivo," ch. 3.2.1.

[10]   For further discussions of the anti-nominalist regulations at the early University of Leuven
and on cases of deviation from those regulations, see Geudens and Masolini, "Teaching Aristotle at
the Louvain Faculty of Arts"; Geudens, "On the Logical Topics"; and Geudens, "Louvain Theories of
Topical Logic."

[11]   MS Leuven, Maurits Sabbe Library (GBIB), 17, fols. 423v–424v, incipit (fol. 424r): "Ex tractatu
Rivo in quo tractat an voluntas producit in se actum volendi per se, contra maximam Aristotelis,
quod impossibile est idem esse in actu et potentia." Among the recent contributions on Adrian VI, see
Verweij, *Adrianus VI (1459–1523)*.

[12]   Both De Vocht (*History of the Foundation*, 117–127) and IJsewijn ("The Coming of Humanism,"
217–235) are quite critical with respect to the quality of the teaching of rhetoric at the early University
of Leuven. IJsewijn, however, makes a modest and hypothetical allowance for Peter by maintaining that
the first holders of the chair of rhetoric were "all Netherlanders and all—except perhaps De Rivo—no-
torious failures in the field of eloquence" (235).

[13]   Leiden: Jan Seversz, 1509. A manuscript copy is preserved, with the title *Colloquium inter
hominem et rationem*, in MS Ghent, Universiteitsbibliotheek, 658, fols. 1r–10r.

skills and attachment to scholastic traditions and forms, fostered the rise of the new learning in Northern Europe.[14]

A further text composed by Peter de Rivo as a rhetorician was the *Relatio seu propositio coram Maximiliano Lovanii reserata in primo introitu terrarum sponse sue*, an encomium written in 1477 on the occasion of the first entry into Leuven of Archduke Maximilian of Austria, son of the Emperor Frederick III and future husband of Mary, Duchess of Burgundy.[15] The two surviving witnesses of Peter's *Relatio* circulated together with four other works dedicated to Maximilian of Austria around 1477–1478. The first was composed by Thierry van Thulden, abbot of the Abbey of Park in Heverlee. The other three were authored by two Italian humanists enrolled at the University of Leuven: Antonius Gratia Dei and Ludovicus Brunus. The presence of these last texts should be connected to the consolidation of the influence of Italian humanism in the Low Countries at the end of the fifteenth century.[16]

While teaching at the pedagogy of the *Castrum* and undertaking the role of professor of rhetoric, Peter commenced and pursued his studies in theology. But his *cursus studiorum* did not run smoothly. In 1448–1449 he lectured on Peter Lombard's *Sentences* as a *baccalaureus sententiarius*, but after that date his theological career appears to have drastically slowed. According to the statutes, he should have been able to obtain his *licentia* in the span of five or six years. The *Dyalogus de temporibus Christi*, however, states that in 1471 Peter was still a *baccalaureus formatus* (i.e., the stage that immediately followed that of *baccalaureus sententiarius*). Moreover, he did not obtain his doctorate until 1477. This delay seems largely due to his involvement in the dispute over the truth-value of future contingents that pitted him against the theologian Henry of Zomeren, a controversy that emerged in the mid-1440s, and then exploded in 1465.[17]

Behind this controversy lies an age-old dispute over the proper understanding of Aristotle's *De interpretatione* chapter 9, in which it is argued that if future-tense statements of facts are either true or false, then the future is completely fixed and everything that happens would happen of necessity. If this were the case, Aristotle claims, then human beings will be powerless to change the course of events, rendering the notions of human free will and moral responsibility problematic. Given its focus on the truth-value of statements about the future, the discussion called into

---

[14]   See Coebergh-van den Braak and Rummel, *The Works of Engelbertus Schut*, 2; IJsewijn, "The Coming of Humanism," 220.

[15]   MS Brussels, KBR, 17320–17330, fols. 77–79, and MS Glasgow, University Library, Sp Coll Hunterian Bf.3.15, fols. 98v[k8]–99r. For an edition and study of the *Relatio*, see Masolini, "Petrus de Rivo," 47–79.

[16]   See, for instance, Vanderjagt, "Classical Learning"; Jodogne, "L'Umanesimo italiano"; and Tournoy, "Gli umanisti italiani."

[17]   On the 'Quarrel,' see Baudry, *La querelle des futurs contingents* (in English as Baudry, *The Quarrel over Future Contingents*, trans. Guerlac); Schabel, "Peter de Rivo and the Quarrel" (pts. I and II). For an updated account of the texts produced in the context of the controversy and their editions, see Masolini, "Petrus de Rivo," 229–236.

question the truth of future-tense statements contained in scripture and liturgy, most importantly prophecies, as well as divine foreknowledge and providence.

During the quodlibetal disputation of December 1465, Peter was asked to discuss "whether it was in Peter's power not to deny Christ, after being told by Christ, 'You will deny me three times.'"[18] In response to this question, Peter defended the position on divine foreknowledge and future contingents that had been held by Peter Auriol (†1322) more than a century earlier.[19] Following in the footsteps of Auriol, Peter claimed that future-tense propositions are neither true nor false, but neutral, and that divine knowledge cannot be understood as preceding the occurrence of future events in an "intervening line of succession." God does indeed have knowledge of the particular things of the world, but he is "indistant" to them, having an intuitive knowledge of events as present, not as future; thus, no divine knowledge, strictly speaking, can be called foreknowledge. Peter maintained, moreover, that one should distinguish between two senses of truth: a "popular" sense—i.e., the truth faithfully expected by the believer on the basis of the trustworthiness of he who says that something will occur (veritas popularis or veritas secundum fidem); and the logical truth that inheres in propositions (veritas secundum logicam aut philosophiam). In this respect, prophecies are true according to the "Uncreated Truth" that Holy Scripture makes them signify, however they cannot be said to be true in a philosophical sense.[20]

Peter's response elicited a severe reply from the theologian Henry of Zomeren, triggering a debate that would last more than ten years. An altercation that began in the classrooms of Leuven gradually expanded throughout Europe, involving local authorities, the faculties of theology in Paris and Cologne, and, finally, Rome and the papacy. At the request of Pope Sixtus IV, Peter left for Rome on September 1472 in order to present his positions to the Roman curia. Peter was forced to retract his position in 1473 and formally condemned in 1474 with the bull Ad Christi vicari. But Peter did not let the condemnation stand without an attempt at positive spin—an attempt that resulted in a further investigation.[21] As a result, Peter had to sign a new retraction in 1476 and was allowed to resume his activities in 1477, when he was re-elected rector of the University. In the same year he was finally promoted to doctor and professor of theology, being appointed to the chair connected to a prebend at St Peter's, which had been previously held by his former mentor Johannes Varenacker (†1475).

---

[18] This quotation and the following are taken from Baudry, The Quarrel over Future Contingents, trans. Guerlac, 36–45.

[19] For an overview of Peter Auriol's positions on future contingents and their reception, see Schabel, Theology at Paris.

[20] On this point, see Bianchi, Pour une histoire de la double vérité, 69–85.

[21] New light on this final phase of the quarrel is shed by a series of texts contained in MS Leuven, Universiteitsbibliotheek, 1635, composed between 1473 and 1476 in opposition to Rivo's doctrines by an anonymous Thomist theologian active in Leuven at the time.

Among the texts that Peter wrote during the last decades of his life, a major role is played by works that are related, in one way or another, to chronology. The most famous were those composed in the context of the controversy with Paul of Middelburg concerning the year and date of Christ's death:[22] the *Opus responsivum ad epistolam apologeticam Magistri Pauli de Middelburgo de anno, die et feria dominicae passionis* (1488),[23] and the *Tertius tractatus de anno, die et feria dominicae passionis atque resurrectionis* (1492).[24] Peter's treatise on the reform of the ecclesiastical calendar—entitled *Reformacio kalendarii Romani* and edited for the first time in the present volume—also dates from this period. The text of the *Reformacio* had been considered lost until 2012, when Matthew Champion discovered it in an incunabulum preserved in Cambridge University Library.[25]

But Peter's interest in chronology dated back to his student years. In the prologue of the *Opus responsivum*, Peter narrates that, during a quodlibetal disputation when he was young, he had proposed the controversial theory that Christ was not crucified on the same date as the Annunciation; he was then guided back to the path of truth by his teacher Varenacker.[26] In 1471, when the debate over future contingents was at its height, Peter returned to this topic and composed the *Dyalogus de temporibus Christi*. In this work Peter addressed the different opinions concerning the dating of the year of Christ's birth, that of the Passion, and the day and hour of his death. On this occasion, Peter defended the traditional opinion that Christ's Passion occurred on 25 March—as he would do almost twenty years later during his dispute against Paul of Middelburg. The *Dyalogus* has survived in only one manuscript, today preserved at Columbia University.[27]

A remarkable witness to Peter's interest in chronology is, finally, the *Monotesseron evangelicum de Verbo Dei temporaliter incarnato*.[28] This work, whose title recalls the Gospel harmonies by Jean Gerson and by Johannes Varenacker (now lost), presents the events of Christ's life and preaching recorded by the four evan-

---

[22]   On the controversy, see Nothaft, *Dating the Passion*, 222–240, and below, Chapter 3.

[23]   Leuven: Ludovicus Ravescot, [1489]. ISTC.: ip00534000.

[24]   Leuven: Johannes de Westfalia, 1492. ISTC: ip00534100.

[25]   The text is found in Cambridge, University Library, Inc 3.F.2.9 [3294]. These pages were originally part of a manuscript coming from the priory of Bethleem (MS Brussels, KBR, 11750–11751), preserving other chronological works of Peter de Rivo; see Champion, *The Fullness of Time*, 134–135, and below, Chapter 5.1 and the section on "The Codices" § 2.

[26]   Petrus de Rivo, *OpRes*, sig. a3r–v (prol.). No written version of that early disputation has survived.

[27]   MS New York, Columbia University, Rare Book and Manuscript Library, Western 31, pp. 313–429.

[28]   The *Monotesseron* has been studied by Champion, who analyzed its correlation with Peter's treatises on chronology and calendar reform within the framework of fifteenth-century perceptions and thinking about time, especially with regards to the spiritual communities linked to the Modern Devotion (*The Fullness of Time*, 137–149, and "'To See Beyond the Moment'"). For the relationship between Rivo's *Monotesseron* and Gerson's Gospel harmony, and its reception in the *Concordia evangelica* by Cornelius Jansenius of Ghent, see Masolini, "How to Order Four into One."

gelists united into one chronological sequence.[29] Unlike his predecessors, Peter elected the Gospel of Luke as the backbone of his reconstruction of Christ's life, claiming that Luke was the evangelist who explicitly intended to write his Gospel according to the historical sequence of events (*ordo naturalis*). The other evangelists often imposed a different narrative flow (*ordo artificialis*), sometimes anticipating what would occur later (*anticipatio*) and at other times recollecting what occurred earlier (*rememoratio*).[30] In order to explain the criteria behind his synopsis and its features, Peter resorted once more to the dialogue format, including as a preface to his *Monotesseron* a conversation between two characters: on the one hand, Symon, the disciple who expresses his doubts about the utility and functionality of this brand-new harmony of the Gospels; on the other hand, Petrus, his friend and preceptor, who dismisses his reservations by explaining the structure of the work and clarifying specific difficulties.[31]

Two reworkings of Peter's *Monotesseron* have survived, both transmitted with the title *Monotesseron Luce cum tribus*. Both appear linked to Thierry Bezudens and the priory of St Paul in the Red Valley (*Domus sancti Pauli in Rubeavalle*, hereafter referred to as the Rood-Klooster) in Auderghem.[32] It is worth noting that in each of the manuscripts containing Peter's *Monotesseron* or its reworkings, the layout and paratexts differ according to the intents and needs of the author himself, of the copyists, or of the readership. In at least two cases (MSS Brussels, KBR, 11750–11751, and BMaz 300), the readership can be closely connected with the milieu of Brabantine religious communities influenced by the *devotio moderna*, where Peter's synopsis may have been instrumental to devotional practices linked to the liturgy and to personal meditation on the Scriptures.

Besides the *Monotesseron*, only two short works survive as evidence of Peter's activity as a theologian. The first is a brief explanation of Ambrose of Milan's commentary on Ps. 118:154 ("Judge my judgment and redeem me: quicken thou me for thy word's sake"), presented as an appendix to Ambrose's text in a manuscript in the Bibliothèque Mazarine in Paris.[33] The second is the aforementioned letter to a *frater professus* of the priory of Augustinian canons of Groenendaal, which is followed by Peter's epitaph. In the letter, Rivo addresses three doubts on matters of confession that had been raised by his interlocutor.

---

[29] The work is preserved in three manuscripts: MSS Brussels, KBR, 129–130, 11750–11751, and 5570. The latter contains only the last part of the *Monotesseron* and is accompanied by a commentary.

[30] In the mid-sixteenth century Peter's choice to use Luke as a baseline for his synopsis was mentioned and harshly criticized by Cornelius Jansenius Senior in his own harmony of the Gospel, the *Concordia evangelica*. See Masolini, "How to Order Four into One."

[31] For further comments on the use of the dialogue format, see below, xxvi and cxiii.

[32] MSS BMaz 300 and Vienna, Österreichische Nationalbibliothek, ser. nov. 12890; see Champion, "'To See Beyond the Moment.'"

[33] *Explanatio verborum Ambrosii in versiculo secundo vicesimi octonarii psalmi CXVIII*, in MS Paris, Bibliothèque Mazarine, 567, fols. 218ra–220rb.

If one excludes the dispute with Paul of Middelburg, the last two decades of Peter de Rivo's life passed quite smoothly. The papal condemnation of Peter's doctrines on future contingents did not prevent him, after his final revocation in 1476, from spending the rest of his life as a respected member of the Faculty of Theology and of the town. Outside the university halls and far from the doctrinal controversies, Peter was a man involved in the political, social, and religious life of his region.

Besides being a teacher, Peter served three times as rector of the University (1457, 1477, and 1478). In this role he had to look after the practical aspects of the life of the University as well as that of the town, and so we find him acting as testamentary executor, ambassador, and political intermediary.[34] The panegyric that he was appointed to write, as rector of the University and professor of rhetoric, for the first entry of Archduke Maximilian into Leuven was not the only time that Rivo had to resort to his subtle diplomatic skills—skills that he must have tested and improved during the years of the debate over future contingents. After the death of Charles the Bold on 5 January 1477, the Burgundian Low Countries endured a period of political instability, scarred by dynastic uncertainty and urban revolts. During the years of Mary of Burgundy's problematic succession and her marriage with Maximilian, Leuven was not untouched by riots. In this regard, the name of Peter de Rivo is found in archival documents among those who had taken charge of tempering the insurrections, mediating first between internal city factions, and then between the city and Maximilian.[35]

As a professor of theology, cleric, and man of faith, Peter de Rivo was in contact with several religious communities within and beyond Leuven. Evidence coming from chronicles and library catalogues reveals that Peter was known and read outside the halls of the University, especially within the Brabantine houses of Augustinian canons affiliated with the Congregation of Windesheim.[36] As we have seen, the Rood-Klooster in Auderghem possessed a codex containing Bezudens's revision of Peter's *Monotesseron*. The same volume includes a printed copy of the *Opus responsivum* and a series of texts composed in the context of Paul of Middelburg's disputes with Thomas Basin and Peter de Rivo.[37] Similarly, the priory of Bethleem in Herent owned a copy of the *Monotesseron* that was originally bound in a manuscript containing Peter's *Reformacio kalendarii Romani* and his works against Paul of Middelburg.[38] Peter, moreover, was remembered for his role in the quarrel over future contingents by Petrus Ympens (†1523), historiographer and prior of Bethleem, in his famous *Chronicon Bethlemiticum*.[39] As we will see, the only

---

[34] Masolini, "Petrus de Rivo," 36–46.

[35] Ibid., 47–58.

[36] Ibid., 80–89.

[37] See Chapter 3.5 below.

[38] See Chapters 5.1, 5.3, and "The Codices" § 2 below.

[39] The passage of the *Chronicon* mentioning Petrus de Rivo and the Quarrel is cited in Molanus, *Historiae rerum lovaniensium*, 507; Andreas, *Fasti academici*, 93–94; and Foppens, *Bibliotheca Belgica*, vol. 2, 1005. For more on Ympens' chronicle, see Chapter 5.3 below.

surviving witness to the *Dyalogus de temporibus Christi* comes from the priory of St Martin in Leuven,[40] which was also in possession of a (now lost) copy of Peter's *Relatio* in honor of Maximilian of Habsburg. Based on Peter's letter on confession to his anonymous friend, one can assume that he was quite familiar also with the community of canons at the priory of Groenendaal, which he had probably visited more than once.[41] Finally, Peter probably maintained a close connection with Leuven's new Carthusian community, as witnessed in Johannes de Thymo's chronicle, which includes him in the list of its benefactors and even provides the date of his death. According to Thymo's testimony, Peter died on Septuagesima Sunday, 26 January 1499, after serving as *plebanus* of St Peter for almost twenty-four years. He bequeathed his house to the students of the Castle and donated his books of theology and canon law to the Charterhouse of Leuven.[42]

The date provided by Thymo has puzzled scholars, who have opted to set Peter's death in the year 1499, in 1500, or to leave the matter undecided. This uncertainty is in part caused by the different dating styles which were in use in Leuven during the fifteenth century. The most common starting dates for the calendar were Christmas, 1 January, and Easter Sunday, although other versions of the year proliferated.[43] 26 January fell on Saturday on 1499 and on Sunday in 1500. However, in 1500 Septuagesima Sunday fell in mid-February, and it seems improbable that the chronicle made such a large error. But Septuagesima fell closer to the date recorded by Thymo in 1499: Sunday, 27 January. The most likely possibility is therefore that Peter died on Saturday, 26 January 1499 after sunset, when, according to the liturgical division of the day, Sunday had already begun. This is also consistent with the fact that obituaries usually set 1 January as the beginning of the year. It is a fitting historical irony that the date of Peter's death should give rise to a chronological riddle, given his life's work enquiring into, and quarrelling over, time, chronology, and the calendar.

---

[40]   See Chapters 5.1–2 and "The Codices" § 1 below.

[41]   On the priory of Groenendaal, see Peersons, "Prieuré de Groenendael"; Dykmans, *Obituaire du monastère de Groenendael*; and Verhelst, "Domus beatae Mariae Virginis."

[42]   Reusens, "Chronique de la Chartreuse de Louvain," 249: "Anno [m]cccc xcix°. Obiit hoc anno in Lovanio, xxvi januarii, que fuit dominica Septuagesime, venerabilis vir magister Petrus de Rivo, doctor sacre theologie eximius, vir sancte vite et honestissime conversationis, qui pedagogiam Castri multo tempo laudabiliter rexit, et postmodum plebanus ecclesie sancti Petri Lovaniensis fere anni xxiiij annis exemplariter rexit; qui magnus fautor et promotor fuit hujus nove plantationis. Sepe refrigeravit nos; quum non habebamus denarios ad necessaria emenda, ipse liberaliter et letanter contulit nobis necessaria. Hic legavit nobis libros suos omnes, qui ad theologiam et ad jus canonicum pertinebant etc. Vide in libro elemosinarum, qualiter hij debent accommodari Castrensibus, etc." On the Charterhouse of Leuven, see Delvaux, "Chartreuse de Louvain"; Timmermans, "Chartreuse Sainte Marie Madeleine." On the chronicle, see Champion, "Emotions and the Social Order of Time."

[43]   See Champion, *The Fullness of Time*, 66.

Chapter 2
The Chronology of Christ's Life in Peter de Rivo's
Dyalogus de temporibus Christi

1. Background and Sources

The *Dyalogus de temporibus Christi*, written in 1471,[1] occupies a unique place in medieval scholarly literature for the way it uses the format of a dialogue treatise to frame a technical investigation into the chronology of Christ's life. Previous to the *Dyalogus*, the last noteworthy effort to deploy the dialogue format in the field of historical chronology had been made by the monastic historian Sigebert of Gembloux in his *Liber decennalis*, written in 1092. Sigebert, whom Peter de Rivo knew as the author of a popular catalogue of ecclesiastical writers (*De viris illustribus*),[2] had pitted a student against his master in a wide-ranging, if somewhat meandering, discussion that sought to establish how the date of the world's creation and the years of Christ's birth and death might be joined together in one coherent chronological system.[3] When Peter sat down to write the *Dyalogus*, he had an even more specialized investigative goal in mind, which was to establish, to the highest attainable degree of certainty, the year of the nativity and the year and date of the crucifixion, as well as to resolve the contradictions that existed between written authorities on these matters.

Peter's decision to discuss these questions in a separate work, let alone in a dialogue between a Jew and a Christian, was not an obvious choice. Although it is true that the chronology of Christ had been broached a good number of times in Latin literature before 1471, most of these discussions took place in the context of larger works on chronography, *computus* (Easter reckoning), or calendar reform. Perhaps the first work to problematize the chronology of Christ's life on a comprehensive scale was the massive three-book *Chronicon* by Marianus Scottus, completed *c.*1073, whose midsection (Book II) was devoted exclusively to Jesus and the apostles.[4] A vaguely similar structure is on display in the *Summa de temporibus* written in 1260–1264 by the Dominican philosopher Giles of Lessines, where the years of Christ's birth and death, as discussed in Book II, form a bridge between Giles's treatments of historical chronology (Book I) and calendrical astronomy (Book III).[5] An exclusive focus on questions pertaining to Christ's life is suggested by the title

---

[1]   As revealed by the colophon in the only extant copy, the text was completed before 8 July 1471.

[2]   Peter cites the work in *Dyalogus*, tr. 1, c. 1 [ll. 101–118].

[3]   See Verbist, "Een elfde-eeuwse dialoog"; Verbist, *Duelling with the Past*, 173–237, in addition to the critical edition and detailed introduction in Wiesenbach, ed., *Sigebert von Gembloux*.

[4]   Verbist, "Reconstructing the Past"; Verbist, *Duelling with the Past*, 85–146.

[5]   Nothaft, *Medieval Latin Christian Texts*, 135–136, 199–200; Nothaft, "'With utmost certainty'," 336–341.

of a *Tractatus de tempore dominice annunciationis, nativitatis et passionis* that the Swabian astronomer Heinrich Selder completed between 1378 and 1385. In reality, more than half of the text preserved under this rubric was devoted to anti-astrological arguments, while the scope of the chronological questions discussed in the remainder of the *Tractatus* went considerably beyond the dates of Christ's life.[6]

Other than in the lengthy works just mentioned, medieval readers would have had the chance to encounter discussions of Christ's chronology in short epistolary treatises, for example those written in 1037 and 1065 by Oliba of Ripoll on the weekday of the nativity,[7] or in the context of scholastic disputations and *quaestiones*.[8] An example of the latter type is the "notable question on the year, month, date, and age of the Moon of Christ's Passion and his age [at that time]," extant in a fifteenth-century manuscript from England. Its anonymous author remained very guarded in his conclusions on the matter, admitting that the problem resembled the "dragon called Hydra, which is imagined by the poets to have many heads, and once one is cut off several more will grow."[9]

In order to see more clearly why medieval authors considered the question of Christ's precise dates and years such a difficult one, we can start with the data points they regarded as relatively uncontroversial. According to one (almost) universally accepted assumption, which can be traced back to the third or fourth century, Jesus was born in Bethlehem on 25 December, the date of Christmas.[10] As early as the fifth century, this date had become one of a tetrarchy of fixed points in the liturgical year, which also included the Annunciation (i.e., Christ's conception) on 25 March and the conception and birth of Christ's precursor, John the Baptist. According to a widely cited interpretation of Scripture, John's utterance "He must increase, but I must decrease" (John 3:30) had to be read as a reference to his own birth on 24 June and the relative length of day and night. In the same manner as John's day of birth coincided with the summer solstice and hence marked the beginning of a

---

6   Nothaft, "*Vanitas vanitatum et super omnia vanitas*"; Nothaft, "'With utmost certainty',"
341–347.

7   See Villanueva, *Viage literario*, vol. 8, 222–226 (transcriptions of both letters); Junyent i Subirà, *Diplomatari i escrits*, 336–338 (edition of the letter of 1037); Cordoliani, "Inventaire," 119–120. Other letters touching on the matter of Christ's chronology were written by Heriger of Lobbes in c.995 and by Abbo of Fleury in 1003 and 1004. See Abbo of Fleury, *Miscellanea de computo, de astronomia et de cosmographia*, c. 29–30 (ed. CCCM 300, 131–143); Cordoliani, "Abbon de Fleury"; Verbist, "De Epistola ad Hugonem"; Verbist, *Duelling with the Past*, 15–33, 57–84.

8   See Nothaft, "Nicolas Trivet," for the discussion and edition of a quodlibetal *quaestio* on the date of Christ's Passion determined by Nicholas Trevet in Oxford c.1303.

9   MS Oxford, Bodleian Library, Rawlinson G.40, fols. 50v–52r (s. XV), at fol. 50v: "Dicendum quod ista questio summe difficultatis est [...] nec aliquis mihi ventus est qui sciret eam dissolvere quantum ad omnem difficultatem, quin soluto uno dubio emergunt multa dubia in modum ydre draconis, qui fingitur a poetis habere multa capita et uno absciso plura creverint." Ibid., fol. 52r: "Explicit questio notabilis de anno, mense, kalendis, luna passionis Christi et de etate eiusdem."

10   See, for example, Lazzarato, *Chronologia Christi*, 173–197; Nothaft, "Early Christian Chronology"; Schmidt, "Calculating December 25."

gradual decrease of daylight, Jesus's birth on 25 December was supposed to have heralded its increase.[11] Similarly, the Annunciation on 25 March was thought to have been accompanied by the vernal equinox and hence with the astronomical beginning of spring. That this was no longer the case in the fifteenth century was readily explained by an astronomical flaw in the Julian calendar, whose intercalation cycle implied an average year length of 365 1/4 days. This was known to exceed the length of a tropical year by close to 11 minutes of an hour, with the result that over time the dates of the equinoxes and solstices receded towards the beginning of the respective month. By 1471, Peter's year of writing, the vernal equinox could fall as early as 11 March, fourteen days ahead of the Annunciation.

Peter's *Dyalogus* made no secret out of the fact that this calendrical regression impaired the calculation of Easter, where the vernal equinox was assumed to reside perpetually on 21 March.[12] According to the standard calendrical definition, Easter was the Sunday following the paschal full moon, which in turn was defined as the first fourteenth day of the lunar month to fall on or after the vernal equinox. The lunar component contained in this rule was a consequence of Easter's historical and theological ties to Passover, which began with a communal meal on the eve of the 15th day of Nisan, the first lunar month of spring in the Jewish calendar.[13] A conventional reading of the four Gospels suggested that Christ had celebrated such a meal with his disciples on the evening before his death. In principle, this should have put the crucifixion on 15 Nisan, yet medieval commentators were also aware of some irritating passages in the Gospel of John (18:28, 19:14, 31), which seemed to imply that Christ and his disciples anticipated Passover by a day and that the crucifixion had really taken place on the afternoon of 14 Nisan.[14]

Attempts to determine the Julian equivalent of these dates in the year of the crucifixion are traceable back to the beginning of the third century. Our key source in this regard is an Easter table for the years 222–333 carved into the plinth of the so-

---

[11]   For early examples, see ps.-John Chrysostom, *De solstitiis et aequinoctiis*, ed. in Hamman, *Patrologiae Latinae Supplementum*, cols. 561–563; Augustine, *De diversis quaestionibus octoginta tribus* 58.1 (ed. CCSL 44A, 104, ll. 13–17); Augustine, *Enarrationes in Psalmos* 132.11 (ed. CCSL 40, 1934, ll. 14–19); Augustine, *In Iohannis Evangelium* 14.5 (ed. CCSL 36, 144, ll. 23–26); Augustine, *Sermones* 192.3, 194.2, 287.3 (ed. PL 38, cols. 1013, 1016, 1302); Augustine, *Sermo Frangip.* 8.3 and *Sermo Guelferb.* 22.5 (ed. Morin, *Sancti Augustini Sermones*, 229, 515); Caesarius of Arles, *Sermones* 216.2 (ed. CCSL 104, 859); McCluskey, *Astronomies and Cultures*, 26–27; Warntjes, *The Munich Computus*, 106–107.

[12]   See Chapter 4 below.

[13]   On the ties between Easter and Passover, see Leonhard, *The Jewish Pesach*, with references to further literature. On the history of Easter reckoning, see Schmid, *Die Osterfestberechnung*; Jones, *Bedae Opera de temporibus*, 6–122; Peri, "La data della Pasqua"; Lejbowicz, "Des tables pascales aux tables astronomiques"; Mosshammer, *The Easter Computus*, 40–316; Mosshammer, ed., *The Prologues on Easter*; Stern, *Calendars in Antiquity*, 380–424.

[14]   For literature on this complex of questions, see Ogg, *The Chronology*, 208–242; Brown, *The Death of the Messiah*, 2:1350–1378; Finegan, *Handbook of Biblical Chronology*, 353–369; Humphreys, *The Mystery of the Last Supper*; Saulnier, *Calendrical Variations*; Pitre, *Jesus and the Last Supper*, 251–373.

called 'statue of Hippolytus', which assigns the 14 Nisan of Christ's Passion to Friday, 25 March AD 29.[15] This calendar date, 25 March, remained a firm part of the Latin Christian tradition for many centuries, to the extent that medieval *kalendaria* and martyrologies frequently assign to it not only the Feast of the Annunciation, but also the death of Christ.[16] It was not so with the year AD 29, which could not be reconciled with the year of Christ's nativity implied by the commonly accepted *Annus Domini* era. This era was bequeathed to the medieval Church by the sixth-century monk Dionysius Exiguus, who in the introduction to his influential 95-year Easter table told readers that he preferred numbering the years in this table "from the incarnation of our Lord Jesus Christ" rather than from the beginning of the reign of Diocletian, whose regnal era had been used for this purpose in previous Easter tables.[17]

According to Dionysius, Easter of the 248th year of Diocletian, which in the Egyptian calendar would have run from 29 August AD 531 to 28 August AD 532, fell in the 532nd year from the incarnation. In the absence of further instructions from Dionysius, it remained unclear whether (a) the incarnation itself was supposed to have occurred in AD 1 or (b) the first Year of the Lord was the first year *after* the actual incarnation, which thus would have taken place in 1 BC. Whichever reading one preferred, the Gospel according to St Luke stated that Jesus was already "about thirty years of age" when he was baptized in the river Jordan (Luke 3:23), while the internal chronology of John's Gospel, according to which at least two Passovers intervened between the baptism and the crucifixion (John 2:13, 6:4), strongly suggested that he preached in public for a minimum of two years and some months.[18] According to Eusebius of Caesarea, whose fourth-century *Chronicle* provided the starting point for most medieval forays into biblical chronology, Christ's ministry

---

[15]   de Rossi and Ferrua, eds., *Inscriptiones Christianae*, 7:412 (#19933). For discussion, see Nothaft, *Dating the Passion*, 38–56.

[16]   To name but a few relevant examples: ps.-Jerome of Stridon, *Martyrologium Hieronymianum* (ed. PL 30, col. 449); Rabanus Maurus, *Martyrologium* (ed. CCCM 44, 32); Piper, *Die Kalendarien*, 17–21, 88; Stokes, ed., *Félire húi Gormáin*, 62; Stokes, ed., *Félire Óengusso Céli Dé*, 100; Lowe, *Die ältesten Kalendarien*, 16; Wilson, ed., *The Calendar of St. Willibrord*, 5; Best and Lawlor, eds., *The Martyrology of Tallaght*, 27; Wormald, "A Liturgical Calendar from Guisborough Priory," 15; Wormald, ed., *English Kalendars before A.D. 1100*, 4, 18, 46, 60, 74, 88, 102, 116, 130, 144, 172, 186, 200, 214, 228, 242; Wormald, ed., *English Benedictine Kalendars after A.D. 1100*, 1:4, 21, 36, 53, 70, 86, 102, 119, 135, 151, 170, 2:10, 29, 46, 65, 81; Munding, ed., *Die Kalendarien von St. Gallen*, 1:46, 2:45–46; Kotzor, ed., *Das altenglische Martyrologium*, 2:43–48; Kuithan and Wollasch, "Der Kalender des Chronisten Bernold," 501; Borst, *Die karolingische Kalenderreform*, 48, 52, 116, 200, 203, 210, 213, 222, 264, 346, 349, 372, 417–419, 642, 739–748; Borst, ed., *Der karolingische Reichskalender*, 1:713–716, 722–723; Ó Riain, ed., *Four Irish Martyrologies*, 50, 141. See in addition Loi, "Il 25 Marzo"; Lazzarato, *Chronologia Christi*, 421–423, 467.

[17]   Dionysius Exiguus, *Libellus de cyclo magno paschae DCCCII annorum* (ed. Krusch, *Studien* [1938], 64): "Quia vero sanctus Cyrillus primum cyclum ab anno Diocletiani CLIII coepit et ultimum in CCXLVII terminavit, nos a CCXLVIII anno eiusdem tyranni potius quam principis inchoantes, noluimus circulis nostris memoriam impii et persecutoris innectere, sed magis elegimus ab incarnatione domini nostri Iesu Christi annorum tempora praenotare." See Declercq, "Dionysius Exiguus"; Mosshammer, *The Easter Computus*, 319–437.

[18]   Ogg, *The Chronology*, 28–60; Finegan, *Handbook of Biblical Chronology*, 344–345, 351–353.

even lasted for a span of three-and-a half years, which was congruent with some of the numbers mentioned in the Book of Daniel (7:25, 9:27, 12:7).[19] A simultaneous acceptance of the Dionysiac incarnation era and Eusebius's "long" chronology of Christ's ministry would have mandated placing the nativity on 25 December in 1 BC or AD 1 and the Passion in AD 34 or AD 35, yet the Easter tables the medieval Latin Church had inherited from the same Dionysius Exiguus threw a massive spanner in the works. In AD 34, the data of the 19-year lunar cycle showed the 14th day of the Moon before Easter on 21 March, which was a Sunday. The rules of the *computus* demanded that Easter was postponed by a week to the following Sunday, 28 March. Good Friday hence fell on 26 March, the 19th day of the lunar month, which contradicted the common belief that Christ had died when the Moon was in its 14th or 15th day on 25 March. The situation in AD 35 was only marginally better: 25 March fell on a Friday, as required, but coincided with the 29th day of the calendrical lunation and hence almost with a new rather than a full moon.[20]

Among the Christian computists who noticed this problem early on was the Venerable Bede, who in AD 725 told readers to "give thanks to God" (*age Deo gratias*) should they manage to find the appropriate combination of data in AD 34.[21] This sardonic remark became the starting signal for an extended medieval European quest for the "true" dates of the life of Jesus Christ, which were supposed to cohere not just with each other, but with the calendrical or astronomical parameters for the assumed year of the Passion.[22] That this quest was far from trivial becomes clear from considering that the only year in the vicinity of AD 34/35 to feature the desired combination of 25 March falling both on a Friday and on the 15th day of the Moon was AD 12. To favour the latter as the probable year of the crucifixion, as was done by Abbo of Fleury at the start of the eleventh century and by Marianus Scottus in the 1070s, entailed a dramatic revision of conventional chronologies. It meant that Christ's birth no longer fell in 1 BC or AD 1, but in or near 22 BC, which according to the available patristic and chronographic sources still had to coincide with the 41st or 42nd year of the reign of Augustus,[23] the emperor who had ordered the census that brought Mary and Joseph to Bethlehem (Luke 2:1–5).

---

[19] See Eusebius of Caesarea, *Chronicon*, trans. Jerome of Stridon (ed. GCS 47, 174); Eusebius of Caesarea, *Historia ecclesiastica* 1.10 (ed. GCS 9.1, 72–77); Eusebius of Caesarea, *Demonstratio evangelica* 8.2.107 (ed. GCS 23, 389); Andrei, "Cronologia di Cristo," 178–190. On the prevalence of the Eusebian "long" chronology in subsequent Christian literature, see Ogg, *The Chronology*, 98–128; Lazzarato, *Chronologia Christi*, 287–323, 483–499; Nothaft, *Dating the Passion*, 59–60.

[20] For more on this problem and its manifestations in early medieval sources, see Nothaft, *Dating the Passion*, 69–102, as well as Warntjes, "A Newly Discovered Prologue"; Nothaft, "Chronologically Confused."

[21] Bede, *De temporum ratione*, c. 47 (ed. CCSL 123B, 431–432).

[22] The main study of these "critical computists" is Verbist, *Duelling with the Past*. See, in addition, Wiesenbach, ed., *Sigebert von Gembloux*, 63–168; Nothaft, *Dating the Passion*, 103–112; Nothaft, "Nicholas Trevet."

[23] Lazzarato, *Chronologia Christi*, 62–100; Naumowicz, "La date de naissance."

Bold attempts to rewrite Roman imperial chronology along these lines are visible in the *Chronicon* of Marianus Scottus, who stretched this chronology by the required 22 years,[24] and in a work *De decursu temporum* written in *c.*1135 by Heimo of Bamberg, who took the drastic measure of re-interpreting the familiar Dionysiac era as referring to years since the Passion.[25] Besides generating some implausible chronological consequences, their approach was ultimately doomed to be considered a failure for resting on a flawed assumption. Unaware of the vicissitudes of calendrical history, authors such as Marianus and his contemporary Gerland (who accepted an alternative date for the crucifixion, 23 March, and ended up shifting the corresponding year to AD 42) tacitly agreed that the 19-year lunar cycle that served the Latin Church in determining the date of Easter was more or less the same as the lunar calendar that had been used to calculate the Passover date in first-century Jerusalem. That this historical picture was untenable would become increasingly clear during the twelfth century, as Latin computists familiarized themselves not only with new astronomical sources that exposed the inaccuracy of the 19-year cycle, but also with the actual rules of the contemporary Jewish calendar.[26]

The upshot of this development was that Latin scholars began to step outside the framework of the Easter *computus* when thinking about the Passion problem. One of the pioneers in this regard was the Westphalian cathedral canon Reinher of Paderborn, who in 1170/71 argued that the data provided by the Jewish calendar fully vindicated the hypothesis of a crucifixion in AD 34, but instead of 25 March the correct date had to be 26 March.[27] The same conclusion was defended, albeit on different historical grounds, by a computist named Master Cunestabulus writing in 1175,[28] who in turn drew on the *Compotus Petri*, a text composed in 1171. According to the latter, the question was inscrutable owing to the plurality of different calendars and intercalation rules used in antiquity as well as the changes some of them may have undergone over the centuries.[29] Later authors would seize on this sort of diversity to argue that 25 March could well have been a Friday in AD 34, as the solar calendar of the first century may have placed the bissextile day in different years or observed a different relation to the seven-day week than the Julian calendar known to Dionysius Exiguus. Aside from the chronicler Alberic of Trois-Fontaines (d. *c.*1252), who argued that Christ's Resurrection had changed the "order of the

---

[24] Nothaft, "An Eleventh-Century Chronologer."

[25] Verbist, *Duelling with the Past*, 251–339. For the short-lived popularity of this interpretation of the Dionysiac era in high medieval sources, see Nothaft, "Victorian Survival."

[26] Nothaft, *Scandalous Error*, 80–115, 180–183; Nothaft, "Between Crucifixion and Calendar Reform"; Nothaft, *Medieval Latin Christian Texts*, 43–68; Nothaft and Isserles, "Calendars Beyond Borders," 2–15.

[27] Reinher's argument is discussed in more detail in Nothaft, *Dating the Passion*, 128–146; Nothaft, *Scandalous Error*, 90–95.

[28] Master Cunestabulus, *Compotus*, c. 39 (ed. CCCM 272, 114–124); Nothaft, *Dating the Passion*, 146–154.

[29] *Compotus Petri*, c. 65, MS Paris, Bibliothèque Mazarine, 3642, fols. 41vb–42va.

times" (*ordo temporum*),[30] one of the earliest attempts in this direction was made by Giles of Lessines, who tackled the problem of the Passion date in two versions of his *Summa de temporibus*. In a manner similar to Cunestabulus, Giles argued that the Jews of Jesus's day based their lunar months not on a fixed calendrical cycle, but on the first visibility of the new moon crescent, which in his opinion made it possible for Passover in AD 34 to have fallen on 25 March.[31]

A different strategy was tried out in *c*.1267 by the Franciscan Roger Bacon, who used computed times of the mean opposition of Sun and Moon to support the tentative conclusion that Christ had died on Friday, 3 April AD 33.[32] Bacon's date appealed to a number of subsequent Latin writers, who could base their argument either on astronomical calculations or on the Jewish calendar, which identified 3 April AD 33 as the eve of Passover (14 Nisan).[33] Among those who affirmed this 'new' Passion date during the fourteenth and fifteenth centuries were the author of the treatise *Auctores kalendarii* written in 1317,[34] Jean des Murs in *c*.1332,[35] Johannes de Termis in 1345,[36] Heinrich Selder in 1366 and again shortly after 1378,[37] Paul of Burgos in *c*.1429,[38] and Hermann Zoest in two treatises written in 1436 and 1437.[39]

It does not appear that any of these writers regarded themselves as holding a particularly risky opinion, even as they placed the crucifixion on a date not supported

---

[30]   Alberic of Trois-Fontaines, *Chronica* (ed. Scheffer Boichorst, 679). The idea that the *ordo temporum* was altered during the night of the resurrection was perhaps borrowed from Bede, *Homeliae* 2.7 (ed. CCSL 122, 226–227, ll. 43–68).

[31]   See the diverging recensions of the *Summa de temporibus* in MSS Bologna, Biblioteca Universitaria, 1845, fols. 32vb–34rb (bk. II, pt. 2, c. 8–9), and Arras, Médiathèque Saint-Vaast, 674 (722), fols. 69v–70v (bk. II, c. 12).

[32]   Nothaft, *Dating the Passion*, 178–196; Nothaft, *Medieval Latin Christian Texts*, 198–199.

[33]   For a detailed investigation of Jesus's chronology using the Jewish calendar but settling for 25 March AD 12 as the date of the Passion, see Robert of Leicester's *Tractatus de compoto Hebreorum aptato ad kalendarium* (1294), studied and edited in Nothaft, *Medieval Latin Christian Texts*, 183–203, 262–283. For another defender of this date, see Nothaft, "Nicholas Trevet."

[34]   See the discussion and edition of this work in Nothaft, "The Chronological Treatise," 16–22, 44–59. The authorship is discussed in Nothaft, "John of Murs."

[35]   See Jean des Murs's *Sermo de regulis computistarum*, which is preserved in MSS Brussels, KBR, 1022–1047, fols. 40ra–vb, 203r–204v (two separate copies); Erfurt, Universitäts- und Forschungsbibliothek, Dep. Erf. CA 4° 360, fols. 51r–52r; Erfurt, Universitäts- und Forschungsbibliothek, Dep. Erf. CA 4° 371, fols. 44v–45r; London, British Library, Royal 12.C.XVII, fols. 205va–206ra; Milan, Biblioteca Ambrosiana, H 109 sup., fols. 119r–120r; Paris, Bibliothèque nationale de France, lat. 3123, fols. 71r–72v.

[36]   See bk. II.11–12 of the *Expositio kalendarii novi et correctio veteris* in MS Vatican City, BAV, Ott. lat. 842, fols. 64v–68r. On the text and its authorship, see Nothaft, "Astronomy and Calendar Reform"; Nothaft, *Scandalous Error*, 212–223.

[37]   See the text accompanying tables for the Sun and Moon in MSS Augsburg, Universitätsbibliothek, II.1.4° 61, fols. 35r–39v, at fols. 37v–38r; Bamberg, Staatsbibliothek, Msc. Astr. 4, fols. 71ra–78vb, at fols. 75va–76ra, and the *Tractatus de tempore dominice annunciationis, nativitatis et passionis* in MS Munich, Bayerische Staatsbibliothek, Clm 18298, 1ra–34vb, at fols. 29v–33vb.

[38]   Paul of Burgos, *Additiones*, Mt 26:17, in *Biblia sacra* (ed. Antwerp 1617), vol. 5, cols. 441–446. See Nothaft, *Dating the Passion*, 215–222.

[39]   Hermann Zoest, *De fermento et azymo*, c. 4–5, MS Paris, Bibliothèque nationale de France, lat. 16404, fols. 6v–10r; Zoest, *Phaselexis* (second version), c. 2–3 (ed. and trans. Solan, *La réforme du calendrier*, 404–418). See Nothaft, *Medieval Latin Christian Texts*, 481–485.

by any patristic source. The potentially controversial nature of an astronomical dating of the Passion came to the surface only in June 1443, when the Castilian theologian Alfonso Tostado (Alfonso de Madrigal, d. 1455) spoke in favour of 3 April AD 33 and against 25 March AD 34 in the context of a public disputation at the papal court in Siena.[40] Tostado's intervention was viewed as scandalous by Pope Eugene IV and his College of Cardinals, leading to the drafting of a formal *impugnatio* by the cardinal Juan de Torquemada (1388–1468).[41] For Torquemada, it was imperative that the traditions of the Church and its foremost teachers be respected. If authorities such as St Augustine believed that the Lord had died on 25 March,[42] only the most momentous concatenation of evidence could legitimize an argument to the contrary. He reacted with scepticism towards Tostado's claims that astronomical and calendrical calculation unambiguously identified 3 April AD 33 as the date of the Passion and even cast doubt on his opponent's method, by pointing out that astronomical tables frequently failed to yield accurate predictions. More than that, he insisted that there were acclaimed computists and astronomers who could demonstrate the reliability of the traditional date.[43] One supposed example was Peter Comestor, whose twelfth-century *Historia scholastica* contained the (incorrect) assertion that a careful examination of computistical tables showed that in the year of Christ's death 1 April had fallen on a Friday and *luna* 22, which implied the same weekday and *luna* 15 for 25 March.[44] Another was Albertus Magnus, who in his commentary on the letters of Dionysius the Areopagite claimed to have reached the same conclusion by means of astronomical tables.[45] What Torquemada's comments concealed was that a Passion date of 25 March AD 34 could be upheld only on the auxiliary assumption that the solar cycle of the Julian calendar had worked

---

[40]   See Alfonso Tostado, *Defensorium trium conclusionum*, pt. 2, ed. in Tostado, *Opera omnia*, 25:91–164; Lazzarato, *Chronologia Christi*, 468–473; Nothaft, *Dating the Passion*, 203–212.

[41]   Juan de Torquemada, *Tractatus in quo ponuntur impugnationes quarumdam propositionum quas quidam magister in theologia nominatus Alfonsus de Matricali posuit et asseruit in disputatione publica in Romana curia, die Veneris, vicesima mensis Iunii anni domini 1443.* This text is preserved in MSS Madrid, Biblioteca Nacional de España, 13250, fols. 1r–6v; Vatican City, BAV, Vat. lat. 976, fols. 118r–131v; Vatican City, BAV, Vat. lat. 2580, fols. 81va–87va; Vatican City, BAV, Vat. lat. 5606, fols. 213r–239v; Vatican City, BAV, Ott. lat. 718, fols. 119v–133v.

[42]   Sources quoted by Torquemada include pseudo-Augustine (Ambrosiaster), *Quaestiones Veteris et Novi Testamenti CXXVII*, c. 55 (ed. CSEL 50, 100); Augustine, *De trinitate* 4.5, ll. 11–12 (ed. CCSL 50, 172); Augustine, *De civitate Dei* 18.54, ll. 45–46 (ed. CCSL 48, 655). See MS Vatican City, BAV, Vat. lat. 976, fols. 120v–121r.

[43]   MS Vatican City, BAV, Vat. lat. 976, fols. 121v–122r. See also the summary of Torquemada's argument in Lazzarato, *Chronologia Christi*, 465–468.

[44]   Peter Comestor, *Historia scholastica*, Historia evangelica, c. 169 (ed. PL 198, col. 1616B). Peter de Rivo refutes the claim made in this passage in *Dyalogus*, tr. 1, c. 2 [ll. 90–104], and tr. 3, c. 2 [ll. 178–204].

[45]   The reference here is to Albertus Magnus, *Super Dionysii Epistulas*, ep. 7 (ed. Simon, 509–510). As Peter de Rivo was to point out in his *Dyalogus* (tr. 3, c. 1 [ll. 114–126]), Albertus gave an incorrect date for the opposition of Sun and Moon, perhaps because he misinterpreted the beginning of the day in his astronomical tables. See Price, "The Use of Astronomical Tables"; Nothaft, *Dating the Passion*, 194–195. On Dionysius the Areopagite's report and its medieval reception, see Ritter, "Dionysius Pseudo-Areopagites"; Pompeo Faracovi, "Il tema dell'eclissi di sole," 199–202.

differently in the first century than it did in present times and that evidence of these changes had somehow been lost in the mists of time. The problem was dealt with more forthrightly by Tostado's student Pedro Martínez de Osma, who in a Salamancan disputation of 1468 despaired of finding a convincing solution to the Passion problem, even as he rejected Tostado's date for supposedly violating the requirement that Jesus must have been at least 32 years old when he died.[46]

When Peter de Rivo sat down in 1471 to pen his *Dyalogus*, he did not partake in Juan de Torquemada's facile dismissal of technical arguments, but his guiding assumptions and motivations were on the whole very similar. Like Torquemada, Peter found it difficult to accept that traditions firmly enshrined in the Latin liturgy and endorsed by the Church Fathers should be overridden by nothing more than the calculations of astronomers, who could not even guarantee that their calculations accurately represented the calendar of first-century Judaism. In spite of this similarity in outlook, however, there are no signs that he was familiar with the writings Torquemada and Tostado had produced as part of their altercation. The only hint that Peter may have had some notion of what happened in Siena in 1443 comes from his chronological *Tercius tractatus*, published in 1492, in which he mentions a report he once received from Henry of Zomeren, the theologian who became his opponent in the 'Quarrel' over future contingents (1465–1475).[47] At the time, Henry had just returned from a trip to Rome, where he had witnessed or heard of a certain astronomer who had had "silence imposed on him" for defending in a public disputation the view that Christ was crucified on 3 April. According to Peter's *Tercius tractatus*, Henry told him about this astronomer "about thirty years ago," which would place their conversation in the early 1460s.[48] It is possible, however, that Peter misremembered the year in question and that Henry's journey to Rome was the one he is known to have undertaken in 1448/49 in order to carry his university's *rotulus* to Pope Nicholas V.[49] The controversy caused by Tostado's chronological propositions would then only have been five years in the past and it is plausible to assume that it would still have been on the minds of some of the individuals Henry encountered at the papal curia. At any rate, Peter tells us that he reacted to Henry's report with a certain degree of dismay, as it appeared that the astronomer in question had simply been silenced without any attempt to refute his chronological ideas.

---

[46]   Pedro Martínez de Osma, *Disputatio de anno in quo possimus dicere Dominum fuisse passum et de quibusdam erratis in kalendario* (ed. and trans. Labajos Alonso, *Escritos académicos*, 354–369); Nothaft, "Reforming the Calendar," 525–529, 544.

[47]   For an account of the 'Quarrel', see above, xx–xxi.

[48]   *TerTra*, sig. e8r (tr. 3, c. 3, pt. 11): "Ante annos quidem circiter XXX magister Henricus de Zomeren (qui tunc ex urbe redierat) nobis retulit quod cuidam ibidem astronomo defendere volenti in disputatione publica Christum crucifixum esse tercio nonas Aprilis impositum erat silentium suis (ut ait) rationibus non solutis."

[49]   Baudry, *La querelle des futurs contingents*, 21–22.

It pained me to hear this, for in my opinion the honour of our mother Church is not sufficiently cared for if one only imposes silence on him who wants to make an assertion against her faith without having dealt satisfactorily with his reasons. From that time on, then, there grew in me the courage and a certain passion to make a more diligent demonstration as to the time when the Lord suffered. And even though there was a dearth of books at that time (for this was before books were multiplied by the art of printing), I unexpectedly, as if by some divine nod, found so many books flowing my way that they seemed to suffice. Having sweated over them for many years (as I have said), I hope to have discovered what should be believed faithfully in this matter and how one can defend it with probable arguments against any opponents.[50]

As Peter revealed in another chronological work of his, the *Opus responsivum* of 1488, his own original position had in some respects been closer in spirit to Tostado's than to that of Juan de Torquemada.[51] In the prologue to this *Opus*, Peter confesses to have once used the occasion of a quodlibetal disputation to argue against the possibility of a crucifixion on 25 March, basing himself on four seemingly uncontroversial premises: (i) Christ died between the 30th and 35th year of his life; (ii) Christ died on a Friday; (iii) Christ died on the 15th day of the Moon; (iv) the calendrical cycles were the same at the time of Christ as they were now. If (i) to (iv) were all true, or so he argued, the popular doctrine according to which Christ died on the day of his conception, 25 March, could not be maintained.[52] Peter tells us that he eventually came to reconsider this line of reasoning owing to the admonitions he received from his teacher Johannes Varenacker, who had been a professor of theology at Leuven from 1443 until his death in 1475. According to Varenacker, Peter put the cart before the horse by discarding the commonly held view merely due to its incompatibility with the four mentioned assumptions. The correct order of reasoning, as Peter himself came to agree, was to begin with the *doctrina communis* sanctioned by the Church, accepting it as a default assumption, and to be sceptical of any additional hypothesis that militated against this common teaching.[53] After

---

[50] *TerTra*, sig. e8r (tr. 3, c. 3, pt. 11): "Quod audiens dolui michi enim visum est honori matris ecclesie non satis in hoc prospectum esse, si contra fidem illius asserere volenti silentium tantum impositum fuerit et non illius rationibus satisfactum. Extunc igitur in me crevit animus et fervor quidam, ut indagarem diligentius de tempore quod dominus passus est. Et licet tunc temporis hic erat librorum penuria (nondum enim erant libri per artem impressoriam multiplicati) comperi tamen quasi nutu quodam divino preter spem michi tot affluxisse libros quot sufficere videbantur. His insudans annis (ut dixi) plurimis comperisse spero quid in dicto negocio fideliter credendum sit et qualiter idipsum probabiliter possit contra quoslibet adversarios defensari."

[51] For further discussion of this *Opus responsivum* and the *Tercius tractatus* mentioned earlier, see Chapter 3.2–3.

[52] *OpRes*, sig. a3r.

[53] Peter would have been able to find support for this view in Pierre d'Ailly's *Epistola ad novos Hebraeos* (1378), where the common position of the Church is used to defend the authority of the Vulgate. This text opens the manuscript containing Peter's *Dyalogus*. See MS New York, Columbia University, Rare Book and Manuscript Library, Western 31, pp. 1–38. On d'Ailly's stance vis-à-vis the Vulgate, see Linde, *How to Correct the Sacra Scriptura*, 67–71.

some more reading and reflection on the matter, Peter arrived at the conclusion that proposition (iv) had to be false and that the Roman calendar had undergone some change between the death of Christ and the present. He now also saw that a distinction had to be made concerning the "15th day of the Moon" in proposition (iii), as this lunar date could be interpreted either as a "true" full moon, which could only be derived from astronomical calculation, or as a "legal" full moon, which did not necessarily correspond to observable reality.[54]

The *Dyalogus de temporibus Christi* is the earliest of Peter's preserved texts to document the outcome of this thought process. At its core, the work sought to demonstrate how ecclesiastical traditions concerning the dates of Christ's life can be salvaged without running into chronological paralogisms, and without ignoring relevant historical data. As one would expect from Peter's confession in the *Opus responsivum*, this demonstration was predicated on a denial of proposition (iv), which led him to devise a wide-ranging revisionist history of the lunar and solar cycles that underpinned the Easter *computus* of the Roman Church. According to Peter, the failure of previous scholars to acknowledge 25 March AD 34 as the true and authoritative date of Christ's Passion was rooted primarily in their ignorance of the forms these cycles had taken during the first decades of the Christian era, which differed significantly from those known to modern-day computists.

Although Peter's argument forced him to engage at some length with ancient calendrical history, the range of sources he was able to exploit for this purpose appears to have been relatively limited. Apart from individual references to Suetonius (*Vitae Caesarum*),[55] Ovid (*Fasti*),[56] and Lucan (*De bello civile*),[57] Peter drew most of his information on the Julian calendar from Macrobius' *Saturnalia*, which contained a rich discussion of the history of the Roman calendar.[58] Another key source for many of Peter's assertions was the Venerable Bede's *De temporum ratione*, which also provided him with a slew of second-hand quotations, for instance from Flavius Josephus's *Jewish Antiquities* and the so-called *Acts of the Council of Caesarea*. The latter text, which put the crucifixion on 23 March, purported to be an authentic account of a second-century church council presided over by Bishop Theophilus of Caesarea, but was in fact a product of the Easter controversies of the fifth and sixth centuries.[59] Another work on Easter reckoning he had seen prior to writing the

---

54 *OpRes*, sig. a3r–v.

55 *Dyalogus*, tr. 2, c. 1 [ll. 49, 77]; tr. 3, c. 1 [l. 134]; tr. 3, c. 2 [l. 80].

56 *Dyalogus*, tr. 2, c. 3 [l. 24].

57 *Dyalogus*, tr. 2, c. 1 [l. 70].

58 *Dyalogus*, tr. 2, c. 1 [ll. 4–48].

59 *Dyalogus*, tr. 1, c. 3 [ll. 10–14]. See the diverging recensions of the Caesarean *Acta Synodi* edited in Baluze, *Nova collectio*, 13–16 (= recension A); PL 90, cols. 607–610 (= recension B); *Computus Gerlandi*, ed. Lohr, 241–244 (= recension B); PL 129, cols. 1350–1353 (= recension C); Krusch, *Studien* (1880), 306–310; Wilmart, *Analecta Reginensia*, 20–27 (= recensions C and D). A proper critical edition is being prepared by Leofranc Holford-Strevens. See also the German translation and discussion in Strobel, *Texte*, 80–95, as well as Jones, *Bedae Opera de temporibus*, 87–89; Warntjes, *The Munich*

Dyalogus was the *Epistola Cyrilli*, a pseudepigraphic work from the early seventh century based on an authentic letter Bishop Cyril of Alexandria sent to the Synod of Carthage in AD 420.[60] In addition Peter had access to an authentic letter the Alexandrian patriarch Proterius had sent to Pope Leo I in the 450s.[61]

Even though the *Dyalogus* repeatedly mentions the computist Gerland, whose work dates from the second half of the eleventh century, it appears that Peter knew about Gerland's decision to place Christ's birth in AD 8 and his death in AD 42 only from reading Roger Bacon's *Opus maius*,[62] which Peter identifies as a letter to Pope Clement V rather than to Clement IV, as would have been correct.[63] Peter's knowledge of this work also clearly influenced his understanding of what an astronomical solution to the Passion problem might look like. Towards the end of the first treatise of the *Dyalogus*, Gamaliel mentions the time of the mean opposition in the first spring month of AD 33 and AD 34, supposedly as calculated for the meridian of Jerusalem.[64] In reality, these times were derived from a table Bacon had included in his *Opus maius*, which showed the mean oppositions of March and April during 1–38 AD, the underlying meridian being that of Novara (not Jerusalem).[65]

Peter seems to have been unaware that these mean oppositions had been calculated using a thirteenth-century adaptation of the eleventh-century Toledan Tables, which astronomers in his fifteenth-century environment would have considered out of date.[66] The standard set of parameters accepted in his own day was provided by the Alfonsine Tables, which had originally been created in the thirteenth century at the court of Alfonso X, King of Castile and León (1252–1284).[67] Although Peter clearly had access to a copy of the Alfonsine Tables in their standard Latin version, he apparently lacked the training required to carry out calculations on their basis. What he did instead was to mine the chronological apparatus that appeared at the beginning of these tables, realizing that it gave valuable indications of the intervals between certain eras.[68] A similar list of eras was available to him from a copy of Gerard of Cremona's twelfth-century translation of Ptolemy's *Almagest*, which, as Gamaliel's words in the first chapter of the *Dyalogus* indicate, came with an

Computus, lxv(n. 167); Mosshammer, *The Prologues on Easter*, 100–103, 135, 141–144; Cuppo, "Felix of Squillace," 153–156; Ó Cróinín, "Archbishop James Ussher," 318–320.

[60]   *Dyalogus*, tr. 1, c. 3 [ll. 38–42]. See Warntjes, *The Munich Computus*, lxiv–lxv (n. 164); Ó Cróinín, "Archbishop James Ussher," 331–333.

[61]   *Dyalogus*, tr. 2, c. 2 [ll. 37–42]. See Mosshammer, *The Prologues on Easter*, 25; Ó Cróinín, "Archbishop James Ussher," 334.

[62]   *Dyalogus*, tr. 1, c. 1 [ll. 119–122]. Peter expressly cites Bacon as a source for Gerland in his *OpRes*, sig. a8r (tr. 1, c. 1, pt. 8). Note that Peter here wrongly describes Gerland as dating Christ's nativity to AD 7 rather than AD 8.

[63]   *Dyalogus*, tr. 2, c. 3 [l. 71].

[64]   *Dyalogus*, tr. 1, c. 3 [ll. 84–92].

[65]   See the note on *Dyalogus*, tr. 1, c. 3 below, 109.

[66]   *Toledan Tables*, ed. Pedersen.

[67]   Chabás and Goldstein, *The Alfonsine Tables*.

[68]   *Dyalogus*, tr. 1, c. 1 [ll. 63–66, 90–91].

addition to the text that expressed a single date (23 March AD 1191) through several different eras.[69] This chronological addendum—a brief note followed by a table—can indeed be found embedded in a fifteenth-century copy of the *Almagest* once housed at St Maximin's Abbey, Trier.[70] Contrary to what Peter seems to have thought, however, it was probably not the work of Gerard of Cremona, who had already died in 1187. In fact, it is found more frequently at the end of an anonymous Latin text on the Jewish calendar starting with the words *Prima erarum*.[71]

Only two of the authors Peter expressly mentions in his *Dyalogus* were recent enough to have written in the fifteenth century: the Spanish converso theologian and bishop Paul of Burgos (also known as Pablo de Santa María, c.1351–1435) and the French cardinal Pierre d'Ailly (1350–1420). He cites Paul of Burgos for his *Additiones* (1429–1431) to Nicholas of Lyra's scriptural commentary,[72] but evidently also knew Paul's *Scrutinium scripturarum* (1432), from which he derived an alternative Latin translation of Genesis 49:10, based on the Aramaic text of the Targum Onkelos.[73] Peter's references to Pierre d'Ailly concern three of his written works, namely, the *Exhortatio ad concilium generale super kalendarii correctione* (1411),[74] the *Elucidarium astronomice concordie cum theologica et hystorica veritate* (1414),[75] and the *Compendium cosmographiae* (1410/15).[76] A third work from the fifteenth century that Peter must have consulted prior to writing the *Dyalogus* is the *Phaselexis* by Hermann Zoest, who composed this treatise at the Council of Basel in 1437 in order to explicate a proposal to correct the ecclesiastical calendar.[77] Besides dealing with the reckoning of Easter, the *Phaselexis* contained two brief chapters on the Passion date in which Hermann came down on the side of those who accepted 3 April AD 33 on astronomical grounds. Peter would acknowledge his use of this text in his *Opus responsivum*, written in 1488, but remained silent on it in his *Dyalogus*.[78] That Peter was nevertheless familiar with this work when writing the *Dyalogus* is suggested by his use of the phrase *familiarissimus Dei amicus* to describe Moses, which appears in this exact form in the prologue to the *Phaselexis*.[79] It is from the same work that Peter drew the pairing *Victorius et Reynerus* as two scholars upholding a crucifixion

---

[69] *Dyalogus*, tr. 1, c. 1 [ll. 71–75].
[70] MS Berlin, Staatsbibliothek, lat. fol. 753, fol. 120v. This page had originally been left blank in order to have the star table in *Almagest*, bk. 7, begin on the following recto page (fol. 121r).
[71] Nothaft, *Medieval Latin Christian Texts*, 78–82, 124–127.
[72] *Dyalogus*, tr. 3, c. 3 [ll. 210–213].
[73] *Dyalogus*, tr. 1, c. 1 [ll. 10–11].
[74] *Dyalogus*, tr. 2, c. 2 [l. 135].
[75] *Dyalogus*, tr. 2, c. 3 [ll. 85–91].
[76] *Dyalogus*, tr. 3, c. 3 [l. 304].
[77] See below, xcvii–xcix.
[78] See *OpRes*, sig. b5v (tr. 1, c. 2, pt. 6). See also *TerTra*, sig. e5r (tr. 3, c. 3, pt. 10), where Peter mentions a treatise "de fermento et azimo (qui tempore concilii Basiliensis editus fuit)." This is Hermann Zoest's *De fermento et azymo*, written in 1436 (see n. 39 above).
[79] *Dyalogus*, tr. 2, c. 3 [l. 166].

date of 26 March.[80] The former was a fifth-century mathematician and author of a 532-year Easter table (Victorius of Aquitaine),[81] whereas the latter was none other than Reinher of Paderborn, whose *Compotus emendatus* of 1170/71 was known to Hermann Zoest, but apparently not to Peter de Rivo.[82]

And there is more: in the second part of his *Dyalogus* Peter adduces the "decree of the synod in Caesarea that was presided over by Theophilus" (*sicut liquet ex decreto synodi Cesariensis cui Theophilus prefuit*) as a source for the rule that the lunar limits for Easter are supposed to range from day 14 of the lunar month to day 21. The relevant passage does not appear among the quotes from the spurious *Acts of the Council of Caesarea* contained in Bede's *De temporum ratione*, but it can be found in the *Phaselexis*, where it is again introduced as the decree of a synod whose presiding bishop was "blessed Theophilus of Caesarea."[83] Another name Peter is likely to have known only from reading the *Phaselexis* is that of the fourteenth-century mathematician Jean des Murs, whom he correctly classifies as a supporter of the astronomically grounded crucifixion date of 3 April AD 33, but without including any quotations from Jean's polemical *Sermo de regulis computistarum*.[84] He instead refers at one point to the *Epistola super reformatione antiqui kalendarii* Jean des Murs had written in 1345 in tandem with Firmin de Beauval for the eyes of Pope Clement VI. Unaware of the text's true authorship, Peter quoted it as the *Epistola ad Clementem papam sextum* by Jean de Lignères, a Parisian astronomer and contemporary of Jean des Murs.[85] This false ascription to Jean de Lignères is indeed attested in two extant fourteenth-century copies of the text.[86]

Most of the remaining sources mentioned in Peter's *Dyalogus* were wholly conventional, in the sense that they belonged to the standard bookshelf of the late Middle Ages. Hence, we find quotes or information lifted from Augustine (*De civitate Dei*; *De trinitate*), Eusebius (*Historia ecclesiastica*), Orosius (*Historia adversum paganos*), Jerome (*De viris illustribus*), Sedulius (*Carmen paschale*), Isidore of Seville (*Etymologiae*), the *Decretum Gratiani*, Peter Lombard (*Sententiae*), and Vincent of Beauvais (*Speculum historiale*). He also cited Peter Comestor (*Historia scholastica*)

---

[80]   *Dyalogus*, tr. 1, c. 3 [l. 69].

[81]   Warntjes, *The Munich Computus*, xxxviii (n. 82); Ó Cróinín, "Archbishop James Ussher," 334–336.

[82]   Hermann Zoest, *Phaselexis* (2nd version), c. 5, 7, 9 (ed. Solan, *La réforme du calendrier*, 428–430, 446–448, 488). Peter acknowledges that he read about Victorius and Reinher in Hermann's treatise in *OpRes*, sig. b5v (tr. 1, c. 2, pt. 6).

[83]   *Dyalogus*, tr. 2, c. 2 [l. 109]; Hermann Zoest, *Phaselexis* (2nd version), c. 4 (ed. Solan, *La réforme du calendrier*, 420): "Hujus sinodi decretum beatus Theophilus Cesariensis presidens in eadem sinodo confecit, ubi in fine sic inquit."

[84]   *Dyalogus*, tr. 1, c. 3 [l. 78]; Hermann Zoest, *Phaselexis* (2nd version), c. 3–4 (ed. Solan, *La réforme du calendrier*, 410, 414).

[85]   *Dyalogus*, tr. 2, c. 2 [ll. 129–130]. On Jean des Murs and Jean de Lignères, see Poulle, "Les astronomes parisiens."

[86]   MSS Oxford, Bodleian Library, Canon. Misc. 248, fols. 23ra–27ra; Paris, Bibliothèque nationale de France, lat. 15104, fols. 114v–121v.

and Albertus Magnus (*Super Dionysii Epistulas*), but without putting stock in their claims to have confirmed the traditional Passion date of 25 March AD 34 by computistical or astronomical means.[87] In this regard, his attitude differed notably from that of Juan de Torquemada, who had used Comestor and Albertus as witnesses against Alfonso Tostado's crucifixion date of 3 April AD 33.[88]

2.   Peter's Argument

Peter de Rivo's *Dyalogus de temporibus Christi* treats the chronology of the life of Jesus Christ as a matter of solving three individual puzzles: (i) the year of the nativity; (ii) the year of the crucifixion; and (iii) the date and hour of the crucifixion. This triad of problems is mirrored by the way the first and third of the work's three treatises (*tractatus*) are each divided into three chapters. The purpose of the first treatise is to offer a survey of the confusing variety of discrepant answers to (i), (ii), and (iii) a fifteenth-century reader was likely to encounter in biblical, patristic, and later sources. In the second treatise, Peter has his protagonist Paul develop certain conclusions about the history of the Roman calendar and the 19-year lunar cycle, which hold the key to the solutions presented in the third treatise. In addition to the three treatises that make up the bulk of the *Dyalogus*, Peter furnished his work with a summary (pp. 389–397 in the manuscript) and an appendix of calendrical and chronological tables (pp. 403–429), which served to clarify certain technical aspects of his argument. The following analysis of Peter's argument reflects this order of exposition by starting, in sections (a) and (b), with an explanation of the ideas and assumptions that underlie Peter's revisionist history of the calendrical cycles familiar to the medieval Latin Church. This explanation then provides the basis for sections (c), (d), and (e), which provide a succinct account of Peter's answers to questions (i), (ii), and (iii).

a. The history of the Julian calendar

At its very core, the *Dyalogus* offered its readers a novel reconstruction of the history of the two main components of the ecclesiastical calendar—the Julian calendar and the 19-year lunar cycle—, the details of which were supposed to make it plausible that the crucifixion of Jesus Christ could have taken place on 25 March in the year AD 34. As outlined earlier, Christian scholars prior to Peter de Rivo had struggled with the fact that this widely cited date coincided neither with a Friday nor with a 15th day of the Moon in the year in question, even though the Gospels seemed to attach precisely these parameters to the day of the Lord's Passion. Peter's solution was to insist that the conundrum only presented itself for the calendrical cycles currently in use and that it disappeared as soon as one examined the history of these

---

[87]   *Dyalogus*, tr. 1, c. 3 [ll. 90–104, 164–166]; tr. 3, c. 1 [ll. 92–100, 114–126]; tr. 3, c. 2 [ll. 178–204].
[88]   See nn. 44–45 above.

cycles, which showed that they had received their present form only subsequent to the crucifixion.

In the case of the Julian calendar, Peter's jumping-off point was provided by Macrobius's *Saturnalia*, which contain a lengthy section (1.12–16) on Roman calendrical history narrated by the fourth-century pagan aristocrat Vettius Agorius Praetextatus (*c*.315–384)—or *Pretexatus*, as he appears in Peter's text. In the lengthy fragment quoted at the start of the *Dyalogus*'s second treatise (ll. 6–48), Praetextatus moves from the ancient ten-month year supposedly instituted by Romulus to Numa Pompilius's introduction of January and February and further to the calendar reform decreed by Julius Caesar. He also mentions an adjustment of Caesar's calendar carried out during the reign of Augustus, who reacted to the fact that the Roman priests had intercalated three days too many during the first 36 years of the new calendar's run. Peter's protagonist Paulus supplements the copious information in Macrobius's text with two brief passages in Suetonius's biographies of Julius Caesar and Augustus. When Peter composed the *Dyalogus* in 1471, these biographies were already available in two printed editions, both published in Rome in 1470.[89] By contrast, the *editio princeps* of Macrobius appeared only in 1472, so Peter's knowledge of the text would have necessarily been based on a manuscript.[90]

What none of these sources made very clear was when exactly Caesar and Augustus decreed their respective calendrical amendments. In the case of Caesar's reform, Peter suspected that it had taken place at the very beginning rather than at the end of his dictatorial reign. He drew one relevant clue from a passage in the *Pharsalia*, Marcus Annaeus Lucanus's famous epic poem on the Roman civil war.[91] Its tenth and final book included a scene where Caesar is shown discussing scientific subjects such as the source of the Nile and the length of the year at a banquet in Alexandria (10.172–218), which seemed to dovetail with a claim in Macrobius (*Saturnalia* 1.14.3) suggesting that Caesar's reform of the calendar was based on Egyptian wisdom. Peter knew from Suetonius that the large number of honours the Roman Senate conferred upon Caesar included the perpetual dictatorship, but his limited range of sources did not allow him to situate this title in an accurate chronology of his reign. Instead of regarding Caesar's elevation to *dictator perpetuo* as the last in a sequence of dictatorships attained between 48 BC and 44 BC, Peter arrived at the false assumption that he became perpetual dictator immediately

---

[89]   C. Suetonius Tranquillus, *Vitae XII Caesarum*, ed. Giovanni Andrea Bussi (Rome: Conradus Sweynheym and Arnoldus Pannartz, [after 30 Aug.] 1470); C. Suetonius Tranquillus, *Vitae XII Caesarum*, ed. J. A. Campanus (Rome: Johannes Philippus de Lignamine, [Aug.] 1470).

[90]   Macrobius, *In Somnium Scipionis expositio. Saturnalia* (Venice: Nicolaus Jenson, 1472). Roughly sixty of the extant manuscripts of the *Saturnalia* date from the fifteenth century. See Kaster, *Studies*, 4. For just such a manuscript at St Martin's in Leuven, see below, cxiii.

[91]   This text had been available in a printed edition since 1469. See Marcus Annaeus Lucanus, *Pharsalia*, ed. Giovanni Andrea Bussi (Rome: Conradus Sweynheym and Arnoldus Pannartz, 1469).

after his return from Egypt and that the corresponding senatorial decree marked the official beginning of his rule over Rome.

According to chronographers such as Eusebius and Bede, Caesar's reign lasted four years and six months. Since Caesar was known to have been assassinated on the Ides of March (15 March), a normal count of months would have implied an accession in mid-September. Peter came to a different conclusion, as he factored in additional information provided by Suetonius, who reported that Caesar's calendar reform involved the intercalation of two extra months between November and December. According to the chronology he developed in the first chapter of the second treatise, the four years and six months of Caesar's official reign began in November 46 BC and came to an end with his death in March of 41 BC. Peter believed he had found some supporting evidence in Macrobius's statement according to which Caesar constituted his new civil year "according to the measure of the Moon": *sic annum civilem Caesar habitis ad lunam dimensionibus constitutum edicto palam posito publicavit.*[92] This passage in the *Saturnalia* was challenging to interpret, as it seemed to conflict with the obvious fact that the Julian calendar was a solar calendar and hence not directly tied to the phases of the Moon. One way of making sense of it, however, was to suppose that Caesar selected the beginning of the first year of his reformed calendar in such a way that it would coincide with the first new moon after the winter solstice. Accepting this scenario made it possible to determine the first year of the Julian calendar on an astronomical basis, since a given date in the Julian calendar coincided with the new moon only in certain years. Relying on the 19-year cycle of the ecclesiastical *computus*, which could be treated as a reasonably accurate indicator of the dates of conjunction in the first century BC, Peter concluded that the first year of the new calendar had been coextensive with the 14th year of the 19-year cycle, and hence with 45 BC, the hypothetical second year of Caesar's reign, which had a new moon on 30 January. Since a synodic month had an average duration of *c.*29d 12;44h, the manifest implication was that the previous conjunction had occurred either on 1 January 45 BC or on 31 December 46 BC.

Still relying on the words of Macrobius, Peter further assumed that 1 January 45 BC had been the beginning of a period of 36 years during which the priests in charge of the new calendar made the mistake of intercalating the bissextile day in every third, rather than every fourth year. It was Caesar's successor Augustus who discovered this error and implemented steps to remove it by having twelve consecutive years without a bissextile day. This chronology was seemingly corroborated by the *Chronicle* of Eusebius of Caesarea, which noted that Augustus was made *pontifex maximus* in the 31st year of his reign. If this reign began immediately after Caesar's

---

[92]   Modern editions replace *ad lunam*, as found in the manuscripts, with the conjectural emendation *ad limam*. See Macrobius, *Saturnalia* 1.14.13 (ed. Kaster, 172–173), where the phrase *ad limam dimensionibus constitutum* is translated as "placed […] on a firm footing."

assassination on 15 March 41 BC, it followed that Augustus's 31st year began in the 35th year of the Julian calendar (11 BC) and ended in the 36th year (10 BC), which would have been the last year in which the priests inserted the bissextile day prematurely. Peter accordingly felt justified in concluding that Augustus's appointment to the high priesthood was connected to the discovery of the priestly error and that Augustus used his mandate as *pontifex maximus* to correct the calendar in the stated fashion (tr. 2, c. 1 [ll. 65–118]).

Based on the chronological benchmarks Peter established for the Julian calendar and the reign of Augustus, the twelve years without bissextile day began in 9 BC and ended in AD 3. The following year AD 4 should have been the first year of a regular four-year intercalation cycle ending with AD 7 as the first regular bissextile year since the introduction of the new calendar. This was the 52nd year since the beginning of the Julian calendar, the February of which belonged to the 47th year of Augustus (March AD 6–March AD 7). Peter arrived at a different result, which was in part owing to an equivocation between the 52nd year of Julius Caesar's reign and the 52nd year of his calendar. Like the 47th year of Augustus, the 52nd year of Caesar already began in AD 6, which is the year Peter ended up equating with the first regular bissextile year, ignoring the fact that the February of this 52nd year belonged to AD 7. This discrepancy aside, Peter's argument yielded the striking conclusion that the leap-year pattern that resulted from Augustus's reform did not agree with the way bissextile years were counted in the current form of the Julian calendar. According to the standard rule, which identified as bissextile each year that was evenly divisible by four, the first three leap years of the Christian era should have been AD 4, AD 8, and AD 12, whereas Peter's historical reconstruction demanded that the first regular intercalations had taken place in AD 6, AD 10, and AD 14.

The consequences of this argument for the dates of Christ's birth and death were nothing short of gratifying. If the Romans at Jesus's time used to intercalate the Julian calendar two years out of phase with the modern-day Church, this meant that AD 34, the most commonly accepted year for the crucifixion, had in fact been a leap year. As a result, February in AD 34 included one extra day not accounted for by the standard rules. According to these standard rules, AD 34 was the 15th year of the so-called solar cycle (*cyclus solaris*), a cycle of 28 years defined by the relationship between the Julian calendar and the seven-day week. The dominical letter for its 15th year was C, which meant that all dates of the Julian calendar marked by this letter could be expected to fall on a Sunday. Yet if AD 34 was a leap year, as seemed to follow from Peter's reconstruction, the dominical letter C no longer applied to all dates, but only to those that came before the bissextile day in February. For the remaining dates, the dominical letter changed to B, which implied that 25 March (a date with the ferial letter G) would have coincided not with a Thursday, as was suggested by the conventional solar cycle, but with a Friday, as demanded by the Gospels.

To Peter, this was enough to conclude that the Julian calendar had undergone some additional change subsequent to the initial correction decreed by Augustus. He found a relevant clue in the well-attested fact that the Egyptians, once they adopted the Julian leap-year rule, preferred to insert the additional 366th day at the end of their calendrical year, which ordinarily began on 29 August in the Julian calendar, but could shift to 30 August if an intercalation was made at the end of the previous year. Peter knew from the Venerable Bede that the Egyptian intercalation always preceded that in the Roman calendar, such that it took place in the August before a given bissextile February. This arrangement was advantageous for causing no disturbance in the calculation of Easter Sunday. The latter was guaranteed to fall on identical dates in Rome and Alexandria, provided Christians in both cities used the same 19-year cycle. Things would have been different if the Egyptians had inserted their leap day only *after* the Romans had inserted theirs in February. In a scenario of this type, some Roman leap years would have seen divergent dates for Easter Sunday in Rome and Egypt. Such leap years added an extra day to the lunation of February, hence causing the relation between days of the week and days of the Moon to shift relative to the Egyptian version of the calendar. In cases where a Roman leap year had the 14th day of the paschal lunation fall on a Sunday, the Romans would have postponed their feast by a week, as Easter Sunday always had to fall between the 15th and the 21st day of the Moon. The Egyptians, by contrast, would have counted one day less for the February lunation, hence placing the 14th day of the paschal lunation on a Saturday. This would have made their Easter Sunday fall on the very next day, the 14th day of the Moon according to the Romans, with the consequence that Egyptian Easter and Roman Easter fell one week apart.

Peter realized that he could use this hypothetical clash of Easter dates to explain why the modern-day leap year rule no longer lined up with the historical evidence for the early history of the Julian calendar. According to the hypothesis he developed at the end of the first chapter of the second treatise (ll. 183–239), the Romans inserted their first regular bissextile day in AD 6, whereas the Egyptians did the same only in August of the following year, AD 7. From the chronicle of Martin of Opava, he derived the information that the rule that made Easter fall on the first Sunday after the first 14th day of the Moon in spring could be traced back to the time of Pope Victor I, who occupied the chair of St Peter around AD 190. This would have been an opportune moment for the Romans to shift their bissextile intercalation by two years to avoid conflicts with the Egyptian Easter date. Retrospectively, this shift would have been equivalent to a postponement of the first regular leap year from AD 6 to AD 8, in conformity with the leap-year rule known to medieval computists.

b. The history of the 19-year lunar cycle

Peter's argument regarding the 19-year lunar cycle was in a sense analogous to the way he reconciled the weekday of the crucifixion with the solar cycle of the Julian calendar. On the one hand, he was ready to grant the lunar cycle a pre-history that reached back far beyond the first century, while on the other he argued that it had undergone certain changes explaining why the present version no longer agreed with the hypothesis that the 15th day of the Moon fell on 25 March in AD 34.

According to the sources cited at the beginning of the second chapter of the second treatise (ll. 29–50), the standard form of the 19-year cycle was first introduced by Eusebius of Caesarea and subsequently co-opted by the fourth-century Council of Nicaea as the sole basis for identifying the *terminus paschalis* or 14th day of the paschal lunation. Its accuracy, however, was compromised insofar as the predicted new moons fell behind astronomical reality at an approximate rate of one day every 304 years. By Peter's time, the actual lunar months began at least three days ahead of the date indicated in the ecclesiastical calendar, which was congruent with the fact that more than 912 years had gone by since the adoption of the 19-year cycle for the purpose of Easter reckoning.[93] As Peter explained in more detail in the third chapter, the *primatio* of the lunar month was supposed to be equivalent to the day that began on the evening following a conjunction of the Sun and Moon. If the new moon dates implicit in the 19-year cycle were still correctly aligned with the *primationes* at the time of the Nicene Council, it followed that they would have fallen very close to the actual conjunction dates at the time when Julius Caesar and Augustus created and adjusted the Julian calendar.[94] Peter added weight to this conclusion by citing the example of a solar eclipse the grammarian Servius claimed to have been witnessed on the day before Caesar's assassination.[95] It provided him with the basis to argue that the first year of Augustus's reign, which began immediately after this assassination, must have been the 18th year of the 19-year cycle (= 41 BC), in which the calendrical new moon fell on 14 March. This happened to agree very neatly with the widely held view that the first year of the Christian era, which was the second year of the 19-year cycle, overlapped with the 42nd year of Augustus's reign.

Peter deployed this sophisticated historical-astronomical argument in the context of an attempt to establish the origin of the so-called *cyclus lunaris*, which began three years later than the standard 19-year cycle.[96] Rather than following Bede in

---

[93]   See Chapter 4 below.

[94]   Contrary to what Peter sought to demonstrate in *Dyalogus*, tr. 2, c. 3 [ll. 31–67], the calendrical new moons of the 19-year cycle fell closer to the conjunctions of the third or fourth century AD than to those of the first century BC.

[95]   Modern astronomical calculations show that there was no such solar eclipse on 14 March 44 BC. See the relevant information on the *NASA Eclipse Website*, https://eclipse.gsfc.nasa.gov/SEcat5/SE-0099-0000.html (last accessed 12 August 2020).

[96]   The *cyclus lunaris* was a standard element of the Easter table of Dionysius Exiguus. See Mosshammer, *The Easter Computus*, 85–95.

treating the *cyclus lunaris* as a Roman invention, Peter preferred the explanation suggested by Roger Bacon, who correctly noted that the Jewish calendar used a 19-year cycle that resembled the *cyclus lunaris* in the sense that it started in the fourth year of its Christian counterpart (tr. 2, c. 3 [ll. 70–112]). Peter fully endorsed the idea that the lunar cycle had Jewish associations and developed it further by combining it with an original hypothesis on the history of the so-called Golden Number, or *aureus numerus*, which was there to indicate the year in the 19-year cycle in which a given date of the Julian calendar coincides with a new moon (see Table 1). Although this device became firmly established as a part of the Latin *computus* only during the twelfth century, many medieval writers believed that the Golden Numbers had ancient roots going back to Julius Caesar's reform.[97] Peter rejected this idea in favour of a different one, according to which the Golden Numbers originated as part of the Egyptian calendar. One reason why this hypothesis seemed plausible was that it chimed with the widely observed computistical convention of counting lunar years in the 19-year cycle not from the lunation of January, but from the lunation ending in the previous September. If the cycle had initially been set up for an Egyptian version of the Julian year starting on 29/30 August,[98] this explained not only the latter convention, but also why the *saltus lunae*—the omission of a day in the final year of the cycle—was commonly implemented in the lunation ending in July, or why the embolismic months associated with years 3, 6, 14, and 17 of the 19-year cycle took place during the final four months of the preceding year (tr. 2, c. 3 [ll. 116–160]).[99]

Impressed by its apparent associations with Egyptian wisdom, Peter decided to locate the origins of this calendrical system in remote antiquity. As its two most likely inventors he nominated Abraham or Moses, the biblical patriarchs. The former was believed to have brought knowledge of astronomy from Chaldaea to Egypt, which made him a plausible candidate for the invention of the lunar cycle in question, but also for the Egyptian calendar itself. Moses, on the other hand, had instructed his people to celebrate Passover during the full moon of the first spring month, which presupposed the existence of some scheme of lunar reckoning. Since Moses had grown up in Egypt, it was easy to imagine that he would have used the Egyptian calendar as the basis for his newly devised Hebrew lunar reckoning. Peter combined this historical conjecture about the biblical roots of the 19-year lunar

---

[97]   Nothaft, *Scandalous Error*, 57–60.

[98]   On the Alexandrian origins of the 19-year cycle, see Holford-Strevens, "Paschal Lunar Calendars," 187–192; Mosshammer, *The Easter Computus*, 36–37, 75–85, 95–96; Mosshammer, *The Prologues on Easter*, 1–29.

[99]   Peter puts the beginning of the embolismic month for year 17 on 1 September, which is contrary to the medieval norm of having it begin on 2 August. Similarly, the embolismic month for year 3 was commonly thought to begin on 2 December, whereas Peter puts it on 1–30 January (see *Dyalogus*, tr. 2, c. 3 [ll. 147–150] and the calendar appended to the treatise, which appears on pp. 404–415 in the manuscript). For further details, see Sickel, "Die Lunarbuchstaben," 174–190; Springsfeld, *Alkuins Einfluß*, 128–147; Holford-Strevens, "Paschal Lunar Calendars," 201–204.

cycle with the tacit assumption that the original version of this cycle distributed the Golden Numbers in exactly the same way as they were on display in the medieval ecclesiastical calendar (i.e., as shown in Table 1). What had changed since the days of Abraham or Moses was not the tableau of Golden Numbers, but merely the way the 19 years of the corresponding lunar cycle were counted.[100]

This latter aspect of Peter's reasoning was in all likelihood guided by a calendar reform proposal originally discussed during the 1430s at the Council of Basel, which showed how the ecclesiastical lunar calendar could be restored to its astronomically proper state without making any changes to the columns for the Golden Numbers found in conventional *kalendaria*. All one had to do was to shift the 19-year cycle forwards or backwards by as many years as were necessary to ensure that the Golden Numbers of the current year fell as close as possible to the actual dates of the new moon.[101] Peter applied this principle to the distant past, arguing that the *cyclus lunaris* was a relic of an ancient Hebrew lunar calendar that had once correctly assigned the Golden Number to the date of conjunction. Based on its established rate of deterioration of one day in *c.*304 years, Peter conjectured that the introduction of the *cyclus lunaris* went back to King David more than a thousand years before the birth of Christ. A certain degree of scriptural support for this idea seemed to come from a passage in Ecclesiasticus that spoke of David as the one who "added beauty to the festivals and set in order the solemn times" (47:12).

The final gambit in Peter's argument went as follows: just as the Latin Church had kept its *cyclus decemnovenalis* in use for more than a millennium, despite visible and growing discrepancies between calendrical prediction and astronomical reality, so the ancient Hebrews were likely to have maintained the *cyclus lunaris* bestowed upon them by King David for a very long time, long enough for it still to regulate the Jewish calendar in the first century AD. If this was indeed the case, then it became possible to infer the Jewish lunar dates in the year of the crucifixion from a look at the conventional tableau of Golden Numbers, provided it was interpreted through the Jewish *cyclus lunaris* rather than the Christian *cyclus decemnovenalis*. In AD 34, this *cyclus lunaris* would have been in its 13th year. As seen from Table 1 below, Golden Number 13 appears next to 11 March, indicating that this is the first day of the lunar month ending in April, which computists regarded as the paschal lunation and hypothetical equivalent to the Jewish month of Nisan. It made sense, then, to identify 25 March AD 34 with 15 Nisan, the first day of Passover.

---

[100]   Peter's hypothesis rested on the historically inaccurate assumption that the ancient Egyptian solar calendar was based on an average year length of 365 ¼ days, as would have been demanded by the structure of the 19-year cycle. In reality, the Egyptian calendar prior to the Julian reform operated with a uniform 'wandering year' of 365 days. See the discussion of ancient Egyptian calendars in Stern, *Calendars in Antiquity*, 125–166, and the criticism by Paul of Middelburg discussed below, lxxxiv.

[101]   See Chapter 4 below.

	Jan	Feb	Mar	Apr	May	Jun	Jul	Aug	Sep	Oct	Nov	Dec
1	3		3		11		19	8	16	16		
2		11		11		19	8	16	5	5	13	13,2
3	11	19	11		19	8		5		13	2	
4		8		19	8	16	16		13	2		10
5	19		19	8		5	5	13	2		10	
6	8	16	8	16	16			2		10		18
7		5		5	5	13	13		10		18	7
8	16		16			2	2	10		18	7	
9	5	13	5	13	13				18	7		15
10		2		2	2	10	10	18	7		15	4
11	13		13					7		15	4	
12	2	10	2	10	10	18	18		15	4		12
13						7	7	15	4		12	1
14	10	18	10	18	18			4		12	1	
15		7		7	7	15	15		12	1		9
16	18		18			4	4	12	1		9	
17	7	15	7	15	15			1		9		17
18		4		4	4	12	12		9		17	6
19	15		15			1	1	9		17	6	
20	4	12	4	12	12				17	6		14
21		1		1	1	9	9	17	6		14	3
22	12		12					6		14	3	
23	1	9	1	9	9	17	17		14	3		11
24						6	6	14	3		11	19
25	9	17	9	17	17			3		11	19	
26		6		6	6	14	14		11	19		8
27	17		17			3	3	11	19		8	
28	6	14	6	14	14			19		8		16
29				3	3	11	11		8		16	5
30	14		14				19	8		16	5	
31	3		3		11					5		13

Table 1: The locations of the Golden Numbers in the Julian calendar.

c. The year of Christ's birth

In tackling the year of Christ's birth Peter de Rivo remained committed to the veracity of the Dionysiac incarnation era, which put him in opposition to eleventh-century computists such as Marianus Scottus, Sigebert of Gembloux, and Gerland. According to Marianus and Sigebert, the usual calendrical cycles dictated that the crucifixion could only have taken place in AD 12, when 25 March coincided with Friday and the 15th day of the Moon, which made them push the nativity back by some 22 years. Gerland took the alternative route of subtracting seven years from the conventional incarnation era, assuming that Jesus was born in AD 8 and died in AD 42. As Peter saw it, these corrections were all based on the same erroneous methodology. Rather than recognizing that the age of the Moon in the year of the crucifixion had to be calculated using the Jewish *cyclus lunaris* then in use, they relied on the *cyclus decemnovenalis* of the modern Church, which gave them an astronomically more accurate, but historically irrelevant result.

One remaining problem with the Dionysiac era was that its combination with the Roman year starting on 1 January rendered it ambiguous with regard to the date of Christ's birth. Was this the 25 December that preceded or the one that followed 1 January AD 1? Peter settled on an interpretation that put the Lord's nativity in 1 BC. Evidence in favour of this contention came from Dionysius Exiguus, who defined the years of his 19-year cycle as beginning immediately after the *terminus paschalis* (or 14th day of the paschal lunation) of the previous year and ending with the *terminus* of the current year. Since his Easter table correlated the first *Annus Domini* with the second year of this 19-year cycle, which placed the *terminus* on 25 March, it followed by implication that the first Year of the Lord had started on 6 April 1 BC and ended on 25 March AD 1. The second year of the 19-year cycle hence contained the date of the nativity, but not the date of the conception or incarnation, which the Church commemorated on 25 March.[102] Peter went on to capitalize on this conclusion when dealing with the divergent ways of counting the Years of the Lord that his predecessor Pierre d'Ailly had associated with the prevailing customs in Italy and France. According to d'Ailly, documents signed in Italy used 25 December as the epoch of the *Annus Domini*, whereas French ones switched to a new year only on the following 25 March.[103] As Peter demonstrated at some length in the first chapter of the third treatise (ll. 220–276), it was possible to explain this divergence of customs by assuming that the French defined the *Anni Domini* as *completed*

---

[102] Peter makes this point in tr. 2, c. 2 [ll. 84–93] and again in tr. 3, c. 2 [ll. 95–109], basing himself on Dionysius Exiguus, *Epistola ad Bonifacium et Bonum* (ed. Krusch, *Studien* [1938], 82–86). In addition, he illustrated the starting and end dates of the years in the 19-year cycle in a table appended to the *Dyalogus* (p. 81 in the edition below).

[103] For divergent ways of counting *Anni Domini* in medieval charters, see Bresslau, *Handbuch der Urkundenlehre*, vol. 2.2, 428–440.

years since the incarnation on (25 March 1 BC), whereas the Italians counted them as *current* years since the nativity (25 December 1 BC).

Another relevant issue the *Dyalogus* aimed to address was the year of Augustus's reign in which Christ's nativity took place (tr. 3, c. 1 [ll. 5–30]). As far as scriptural evidence was concerned, the essential bits of information came from Luke's Gospel, which stated that Jesus was baptized in the 15th year of the reign of Tiberius (3:1) and that he was "about" 30 years old at the time (3:23). An overly precise reading of these passages could lead to the conclusion that the 30th year of Jesus's life had begun in the 15th year of Tiberius. Eusebius's *Chronicle* assigned to Tiberius's predecessor Augustus a reign of 56 years and accordingly put Christ's birth in the 42nd of Augustus's regnal years. A discrepant position was taken by Tertullian, who placed the birth in the 41st year of Augustus, presumably because he assumed that Jesus had already completed his 30th year in the 15th year of Tiberius. Peter favoured Tertullian's position, citing once again the solar eclipse that Servius's commentary on the Virgilian *Georgics* recorded for 14 March in the year of Julius Caesar's assassination. On Peter's calculation, this was 41 BC, the 18th year of the ecclesiastical 19-year cycle, making the first year of Caesar's successor Augustus run from March 41 BC to March 40 BC. The 25 December of Christ's birth hence belonged to the 41st year of Augustus's reign, which ran from March 1 BC to March AD 1, encompassing both the incarnation and the nativity. Why, then, did so many authorities put Jesus's birth in Augustus's 42nd year? Peter found the explanation in the multiplicity of ways in which different nations adjusted the years of Augustus's regnal era to their respective calendar. The Egyptians, for example, were accustomed to starting the year on the 29th or 30th of August that preceded the beginning of the Roman year, which would have put the incarnation and nativity in two different years of Augustus's reign (25 March of the 41st and 25 December of the 42nd).

A trickier case was posed by the Alfonsine Tables, which came with an extended apparatus of chronological tables that made the mean motions of the planets adaptable to different calendar systems and eras.[104] According to this chronological apparatus, an interval of 38 Julian years separated the beginning of the Christian era from the "era of Caesar" (*aera Caesaris*), which was meant to be a reference to the so-called Spanish Era (epoch: 1 January 38 BC).[105] Its misleading designation as *aera Caesaris* in the Alfonsine Tables led Peter to infer that he was dealing with a variant of the regnal era of Augustus, one that decreased the interval of complete years between Augustus's accession and the nativity of Christ. According to Peter's conjecture, this deviation from the norm could have been motivated by King Alfonso's conclusion that the crucifixion happened in the 13th rather than the 16th year of the 19-year cycle (AD 31 rather than AD 34), as the 13th year showed 25 March on

104   *Tabule astronomice illustrissimi Alfontii regis Castelle* (ed. Poulle, 107–123).
105   On this era, see Ginzel, *Handbuch*, 3:175–178; Vives, "Über Ursprung und Verbreitung"; Neugebauer, "On the 'Spanish Era'"; Blackburn and Holford-Strevens, *The Oxford Companion*, 767.

the 15th day of the Moon. If Alfonso fixed the beginning of Augustus's reign in the same way as Peter, using Servius's eclipse on 14 March 41 BC, he would have been confronted with the fact that the year of Caesar's assassination and the year of the crucifixion were separated by 71 years, that is, the 14 years from the 18th to the 13th year of the 19-year cycle plus three complete cycles ($3 \times 19 + 14 = 71$). Since Jesus was alive during the last 34 of these 71 years, the calculation would have made his birth fall in the 38th year of Augustus's reign (tr. 3, c. 1 [ll. 37–68]).

Peter's explanation of the origin of the *aera Caesaris* was flawed in two regards. Firstly, it led to an interval between Augustus and Christ that was only 37 complete years as opposed to the 38 years recorded in the Alfonsine Tables. Secondly, it clashed with the evident fact that the Alfonsine Tables assumed the standard era of Dionysius Exiguus with an epoch of 1 January AD 1. Since the first year of that era was the 2nd of the 19-year cycle, assuming a crucifixion in AD 31 would have required Alfonso to shorten Christ's lifespan by three years compared to Peter, who accepted the conventional figure of 33 years.[106] He was more successful in dealing with another recalcitrant source, a chronological appendix to the *Almagest* that made the reign of Augustus begin in 30 BC and hence eleven years earlier than expected.[107] According to Peter, the era in question counted the years of Augustus not from the death of his predecessor Julius Caesar, but from his conquest of Egypt following the Battle of Actium, which occurred in the twelfth year of his Roman rule (tr. 3, c. 1 [ll. 132–139]).[108]

Another contradiction that Peter sought to clarify in his *Dyalogus* concerned the interval between the birth of Jesus and the beginning of the reign of Diocletian. According to the Alfonsine Tables and other astronomical sources, the era of Diocletian began 283 years and 240 days after the epoch of the Christian era (1 January AD 1), on 29 August AD 284. Eusebius's *Chronicle* told a different story, insofar as it made Diocletian's reign begin with the 288th year (inclusive) since the birth of Jesus in the 42nd year of Augustus.[109] Peter came down firmly in support of the astronomers, noticing that their interval was already implicit in a fifth-century letter by the Alexandrian patriarch Proterius (451–457). The year this patriarch designated as the 89th year of Diocletian carried the calendrical markers of AD 373, hence confirming that there were only 284 years between the Dionysiac era of the

---

[106]   Peter was to offer a better explanation in his *Tercius tractatus* of 1492, where he concludes that King Alfonso must have counted the regnal years of Augustus from the moment of his reconciliation with Marc Anthony in the third year after Caesar's death. See *TerTra*, sig. e2v (tr. 3, c. 3, pt. 7).

[107]   See above, xxxviii.

[108]   Peter may have come across this solution in Roger Bacon's *Opus maius*, which locates the abbreviated version of Augustus's era in the pseudo-Ovidian *De vetula*, a metrical text Peter cites (presumably at second hand) in *Dyalogus*, tr. 1, c. 1 [ll. 78–83]. See Roger Bacon, *Opus maius*, lib. IV (ed. Bridges, 1:263–264); Nothaft, *Dating the Passion*, 166, 175–176.

[109]   On the reason behind this discrepancy, see Nothaft, "An Eleventh-Century Chronologer," 463–464.

incarnation and the era of Diocletian. Historians who put the start of Diocletian's reign at a greater remove from the birth of Jesus accordingly perpetuated a mistake, which may have first arisen from the practice of rounding up the years in the reigns of intervening emperors (tr. 3, c. 1 [ll. 145–173]).

Besides establishing that Jesus was born in the year we call 1 BC, Peter also paid some attention to the weekday of the nativity (tr. 3, c. 1 [ll. 247–277]). Authors prior to the *Dyalogus* had widely asserted that Christ's birth fell on a Sunday, the Lord's Day, which matched the calendrical situation in AD 1.[110] Peter's position seemed to commit him to a different view, as the dominical letters of 1 BC were D for dates before the *bissextus* in February and C for all dates that came after. Since 25 December had the ferial letter B, this should in principle have landed it on a Saturday, yet this line of reasoning overlooked some of the historical and calendrical facts Peter had excavated in the first chapter of his second treatise. There he had shown that 1 BC belonged to a twelve-year period during which no intercalation was carried out in Rome, in accordance with a reform decree Augustus had passed in the 31st year of his reign. The goal of this decree had been to compensate for the excess intercalation that had occurred during first 36 years of the Julian calendar, which had seen the insertion of 12 rather than 9 bissextile days. When Christ was born on 25 December 1 BC, two of these superfluous bissextile days had already been compensated for, whereas the third was going to be neutralized only as a result of the non-intercalation in AD 3. It followed that 1 BC had in fact been a common year and the correct letter to locate its Sundays was B. Peter's chronology thus turned out to be in harmony with the widely asserted idea that Christ was born on a Sunday. In addition, he was able to maintain the notion that the conception of Christ, on 25 March 1 BC, had originally taken place on a Friday, such that this event mirrored the accepted weekday and calendrical date of his death as well as the weekday of the Fall of Adam (tr. 1, c. 3 [ll. 33–44]).[111]

d. The year of Christ's death

As presented in the *Dyalogus* (tr. 3, c. 2 [ll. 4–128]), the year in which Jesus was killed and rose again from the dead could be derived without much difficulty by treating it as a function of (i) the year of his birth and (ii) the length of his earthly existence. Peter knew from reading Suetonius that Augustus died on 19 August of his 57th regnal year, while the eclipse mentioned by Servius had already convinced him that the first of these years had started in March 41 BC. It followed that the 57th year began in March AD 16 and ended prematurely in the same year on 19 August. If this was accepted as the beginning of Tiberius's reign, the 15th year of this emperor, which

---

[110] Influential examples include Rupert of Deutz, *De divinis officiis* 3.16 (CCCM 7, 86–87); Peter Comestor, *Historia scholastica*, Historia evangelica, c. 5 (PL 198, col. 1540); Vincent of Beauvais, *Speculum historiale*, lib. 4, c. 88 (ed. Douai 1624, 203). See Silvestre, "Le jour et l'heure de la nativité."
[111] See on this point Silvestre, "Le jour et l'heure de la nativité," 621–622.

Peter accepted as the year of Christ's baptism (Luke 3:1), ran from August AD 30 to August AD 31. According to tradition, Christ's baptism took place on 6 January, which was enough to identify the year in question as AD 31. Since the year of the nativity was 1 BC rather than AD 1, one had to concur with John Chrysostom that Jesus had already completed 30 years of his life.[112]

Peter was well aware that some late antique Christian writers, among them Tertullian, had claimed the aforementioned 15th year of Tiberius as the year of the Passion, which implied that only a few months had separated the baptism from the crucifixion. Bede alluded to this opinion in chapter 47 of *De temporum ratione*, warning against attempts to move the Passion to AD 31 for calendrical reasons. According to the conventional 19-year cycle, AD 31 was a year in which 25 March coincided with the 15th day of the paschal lunation, but Peter was once again quick to point out that this cycle did not correspond to the lunar cycle used by the Jews in the first century, which began three years later and would have identified 25 March as the 12th day of the Moon (tr. 3, c. 2 [ll. 50–70]).

At the end of the day, Peter endorsed the standard view according to which Christ's public ministry lasted a full three years and that he had lived for 33 whole years before he was crucified (tr. 3, c. 2 [ll. 12–49]). In squaring the assumption of a three-year long public ministry with the actual Gospel accounts, he assumed that the wedding at Cana took place one year after the baptism. In doing so, he accepted the ecclesiastical tradition of commemorating both the baptism and the wedding as part of Epiphany (6 January).[113] What followed was the Passover mentioned in John 2:13, on which occasion Jesus drove the money lenders out of the temple. The Gospel of John referenced two more Passovers in 6:4 and 11:55, the second of which coincided with Christ's death. Peter was also mindful of an argument made by Eusebius in his *Ecclesiastical History* (1.10), who in turn drew upon Josephus's *Antiquities* (18.34–35). According to the latter, Annas and Caiaphas, the two high priests mentioned in the Gospels, were separated by three other incumbents, each of which seemed to have remained in office for up to a year. If Annas was high priest at the time of Christ's baptism (inferred from Luke 3:2) and Caiaphas at the time of the crucifixion (John 11:49, 51; 18:13, 24), this implied a minimum interval of three years.[114]

---

[112] The same conclusion had been reached in 1443 by Juan de Torquemada, who quoted a greater range of authorities, pointing out that Jesus's age at his baptism had been confirmed by the Council of Neocaesarea (AD 315), which fixed thirty years as the age below which a priest could not be ordained. MS Vatican City, BAV, Vat. lat. 976, fols. 119v–120v.

[113] The one-year interval between the baptism and the wedding at Cana was also upheld by Peter Comestor, *Historia scholastica*, Historia evangelica, c. 33 (ed. PL 198, col. 1554D), and in the anonymous *Questio notabilis de anno, mense, kalendis, luna passionis Christi et de etate eiusdem* (see n. 9 above), MS Oxford, Bodleian Library, Rawlinson G.40, fol. 51v.

[114] In reality, the deposition of Annas and accession of Caiaphas happened long before the start of Christ's ministry, in about AD 15–18. See Finegan, *Handbook of Biblical Chronology*, 352–353.

e. The date and hour of the crucifixion

Peter de Rivo's chronology of the public ministry committed him to the view that Christ died in AD 34, which was the 16th year of the 19-year cycle as well as the 15th year of the solar cycle with C as dominical letter. If one accepted the verdict of these conventional cycles, 25 March AD 34 should have been a Thursday and the 18th day of the lunar month, which was irreconcilable with the common view—supported by authorities such as St Augustine and St Jerome—that this was the historical date of the crucifixion. However, as Peter demonstrated in the final chapters of the *Dyalogus*, the problem disappeared if one was willing to follow his hypotheses concerning the history of the Julian calendar and the *cyclus lunaris* used by the first-century Jews. His hypothesis concerning the Julian calendar amounted to the idea that the intercalation pattern in use during Christ's lifetime was phase-shifted by two years relative to the modern one. According to the historical pattern, AD 34 was in fact a leap year with dominical letters CB, which put 25 March on a Friday. In a similar vein, Peter defended the view that the 19-year cycle known to the Jews of the first century AD was coterminous with the *cyclus lunaris*, which identified AD 34 as the 13th year of the cycle in question. If this was applied to the standard distribution of Golden Numbers across the Julian year, AD 34 turned out to have a calendrical new moon on 11 March, indicating 25 March as the 15th day of the Moon, or 15 Nisan.

Having defended the plausibility of 25 March as the historical date of the Passion, it was left for Peter to explain why some authorities had favoured alternative dates. Traditionally, the most widely cited such alternative was 23 March, which Latin computists could trace back to Bishop Theophilus's words cited in the spurious *Acts of the Council of Caesarea*.[115] Although Peter treated this text as a genuine second-century document, he rejected its crucifixion date as impossible. The ancient Hebrews, he insisted, followed a strict rule according to which the Passover lamb could only be eaten once the vernal equinox had passed. In the year of the Passion, the equinox fell on 22 March or later, so Jesus and his disciple would have violated this rule, had they convened for the Last Supper on the evening of 22 March, as implied in the Caesarean *Acts*. Peter believed that the choice of dates in this text had been motivated not by sound historical information, but by astronomical calculation, more specifically by the fact that the March conjunction in AD 34 fell on 9 March. This made 23 March the 15th day of the lunar month ending in April (tr. 3, c. 3 [ll. 9–85]).

Another alternative with a relatively long history was to put the crucifixion on 26 March, as had been done by Victorius of Aquitaine in the fifth and by Reinher of Paderborn in the twelfth century. Victorius, whose work predated the introduction of the *Anno Domini* era, had been a follower of the "short" chronology of

---

[115] See n. 59 above.

Jesus's life, placing the crucifixion in AD 28. For this year, his 532-year Easter cycle showed a coincidence of Friday and the 14th day of the Moon on 26 March.[116] Peter was unaware of this background and assumed that both Victorius and Reinher had targeted 26 March in AD 34. This date was a Friday according to the conventional solar cycle. It could also be interpreted as the 15th day of the Moon if one assumed that the Jews identified the Golden Numbers with the date of conjunction while preferring to count their lunar months from the following *primatio*. AD 34 was year 13 in the *cyclus lunaris* and the date next to Golden Number 13 was 11 March, making 26 March the 16th day from conjunction, but the 15th day of the actual lunar month (tr. 3, c. 3 [ll. 86–107]).

In using calendrical lunar cycles to investigate the Passion date, Peter partook in a broad consensus among medieval Latin writers that the crucifixion happened on the afternoon of 15 Nisan. Support for this contention came from the way all four evangelists described the Last Supper as a Passover meal, which by implication placed it on the evening that marked the end of 14 Nisan and the beginning of 15 Nisan. A distracting signal came from the Gospel of John, which in 18:28 implied that the Jews on the morning of the crucifixion had not yet assembled for their Passover meal. Seizing on this passage, one could argue that the crucifixion happened on 14 Nisan, in line with the interpretation generally accepted in the Greek Orthodox world.[117] There was also the problem that the remaining three Gospels referred to the day on which the disciples gathered to prepare the meal as *(prima) dies azymorum*, that is, the first day of the festival of unleavened bread (Matthew 26:17; Mark 14:12; Luke 22:7). If this expression was used in accordance with the injunctions found in the Old Testament, it should have referred to 15 Nisan, hence shifting the crucifixion to 16 Nisan.

Peter dealt with the first of these exegetical problems by taking recourse to the Jewish calendar, whose postponement rules (*deḥiyyot*) prevented 15 Nisan from falling on a Monday, Wednesday, or Friday (tr. 3, c. 3 [ll. 175–244]). It appears that Peter knew about these rules from reading the *Additiones* of Paul of Burgos, a converted former rabbi and influential biblical exegete. Paul's detailed commentary on Matthew 26:17 correctly located the reason for the postponement of Passover in Tishri, the seventh month of the Jewish lunar year.[118] If 15 Nisan fell on a Monday or Wednesday, the following 10 Tishri was a Friday or Sunday and hence fell next to a Sabbath. Since 10 Tishri was the Day of Atonement, or Yom Kippur, these scenarios entailed two consecutive days of ceremonial rest, which was best avoided in order to guarantee that fresh food was available and the dead did not remain unburied for more than a day. A different explanation accounted for the prohibited coincidence

---

[116] Nothaft, *Dating the Passion*, 73–74.

[117] Nothaft, *Dating the Passion*, 23–25, 142–146, 189–194; Nothaft, *Medieval Latin Christian Texts*, 190–198, 481.

[118] Paul of Burgos, *Additiones*, Mt 26:17, in *Biblia sacra* (ed. Antwerp 1617), vol. 5, cols. 444–445.

of 15 Nisan and Friday, which would have made 21 Tishri, the feast of Hoshana Rabbah, fall on the Sabbath. This constellation was considered undesirable owing to the ritual beating of willow branches on Hoshana Rabbah, which conflicted with the rules of sabbatical rest.[119]

For reasons that are not fully clear, Peter offered an explanation that deviated from this account to a certain extent. Rather than tying the prohibition of a Friday-Passover to Hoshana Rabbah on 21 Tishri, he claimed that the Jews sought to avoid celebrating the feast days that fell on 1, 15, and 22 Tishri on a Sunday and hence next to a Sabbath, as this made it impossible to care for the sick or bury the dead for a period of 48 hours. Peter followed Paul of Burgos in assuming that the avoidance of Friday-Passovers had already been practiced in the first century, claiming that it was part of a dispensatory law that allowed Jews to make exceptions in order to prevent certain types of hardship from arising. Jesus and his disciples made no use of this dispensation in the year of the crucifixion, but instead observed a rigorous interpretation of the law, one that did not tolerate any deviations from the rule that tied the beginning of Passover to the 15th day of the lunar month. This distinction between the *strict* Passover celebrated by Jesus and the *dispensatory* Passover celebrated by other Jews was enough to explain the aforementioned passage in the Gospel of John (18:28), which could simply be taken to mean that the Jews postponed Passover by moving it from Friday to Saturday.

In solving the second problem, Peter relied on some information he had encountered in Bede's *De temporum ratione*, where it was claimed—incorrectly—that the Hebrews counted their days from sunrise to sunrise, but their feasts from sunset to sunset. Peter believed that this distinction between the "natural" and the "legal" definition of the day held the key to explaining why the synoptic evangelists used the expression "first day of unleavened bread" (which was normally associated with 15 Nisan) when referring to the day that preceded the evening of the Passover meal (which was normally associated with 14 Nisan). On Peter's reading, the "legal" definition of the "first day of unleavened bread" made it begin on the evening that marked the end of 14 Nisan and the start of 15 Nisan. This was the Thursday evening on which Jesus and his disciples gathered for the Last Supper. By contrast, on a "natural" definition the same feast day had already started in the morning, which is why it made sense for the evangelists to write that the disciples prepared for the Passover meal on the "first day of unleavened bread" (tr. 3, c. 3 [ll. 284–285]).

---

[119] On the postponement rules in the Jewish calendar, see Nothaft, *Medieval Latin Christian Texts*, 27–30. On their use in medieval Christian attempts to date the Last Supper and crucifixion, see ibid., 482–484, and Nothaft, *Dating the Passion*, 136–141, 144, 212–222; Nothaft, "Duking it Out," 225–228. The key part of the rule for Passover was also known to the author of the *Questio notabilis de anno, mense, kalendis, luna passionis Christi et de etate eiusdem* (see n. 9 above), which probably dates from the fifteenth century. See MS Oxford, Bodleian Library, Rawlinson G.40, fols. 50v–52r, at fol. 51r: "Nam secundum compotum Hebreorum prima dies azimorum, id est 15ª luna mensis Nisan, numquam concurrit cum feria sexta."

The idea of a "natural" day with a beginning at sunrise also helped explain the significance of the "ninth hour" that was mentioned in the Gospel accounts of Christ's death (Matthew 27:45; Mark 15:33; Luke 23:44). Authorities such as Augustine and Bede identified it with the ninth hour from sunrise and therefore concluded that Jesus had died close to three o'clock in the afternoon. Yet, this interpretation seemed to clash with a custom observed in numerous Churches, which commemorated Christ's death by ringing the bells at noon. A witness in favour of this custom was Albertus Magnus in his commentary on the pseudo-Dionysian epistles, where he claimed that Christ had died on 25 March at noon. In doing so, he may have been guided by the late medieval the habit of observing the divine office known as Nones (from *nona*, the ninth hour of the day) at midday rather than at the border between the third and fourth quarter.[120] Peter argued that the stance taken by Augustine and Bede was correct if applied to the longitude of Jerusalem, where the historical crucifixion took place. For Christians living further West, however, the equivalent moment would have fallen closer to noon, as 15 degrees of geographic longitude corresponded to a time difference of one hour. For Peter's own location in Leuven, the time difference relative to Jerusalem was 42;20° or slightly more than 2 hours 49 minutes, which offered good grounds to conclude that the practice of ringing the bells at noon was chronologically and historically sound (tr. 3, c. 3 [ll. 290–319]).[121]

---

[120] Dohrn-van Rossum, *History of the Hour*, 29–33.

[121] According to Peter (ll. 305–314), the western longitudes of Leuven and Jerusalem are 23;40° (23 2/3°) and 23;40° + 42;20° = 66°, respectively. A table of geographic coordinates in MS Arras, Médiathèque Saint-Vaast, 688 (748), fol. 70v (s. XV^med), places Leuven further east, at 26°.

CHAPTER 3
PETER DE RIVO'S DEBATE WITH PAUL OF MIDDELBURG

Peter de Rivo's investigations into the chronology of Christ's life did not end with the *Dyalogus de temporibus Christi*, a work whose production in 1471 had no measurable impact on contemporary debates. His opinions on the subject became more visible only in 1488, when Peter decided to write a new chronological treatise in response to Paul of Middelburg, a Leuven alumnus who had provoked a storm of indignation on account of his controversial statements concerning the chronology of Christ's crucifixion and resurrection. The backlash was severe enough to prompt Paul into writing an elaborate *Epistola apologetica*, which appeared in print in 1488.[1] Whether Paul intended it or not, the provocative and assertive tone of this publication did little to calm the waves around him. Strong criticism of the *Epistola apologetica* was voiced by Thomas Basin (1412–1490), who then resided as titular bishop of Caesarea at the episcopal court in Utrecht.[2] Basin's death prevented him from making his opinions known to a wider public, as the planned printing of his treatise *Contra errores et blasphemias Pauli de Middelburgo* never came to fruition.[3] Things turned out differently for Peter de Rivo, whose *Opus responsivum ad Epistolam apologeticam M. Pauli de Middelburgo* circulated in a magnificently produced edition issued by the short-lived Leuven press of Ludovicus Ravescot.[4] Paul's fiercely critical response to this work came in the form of a letter written and sent in 1492.[5] It motivated Peter to add to the two treatises that made up the *Opus responsivum* a *Tercius tractatus*, which appeared in print in the same year.[6] Paul responded with another indignant letter critiquing the *Tercius tractatus* as well as with a new chronological treatise composed of 24 books, which has not been found.[7] Its existence is known only from a letter Paul addressed to the University

---

[1]   All subsequent references to this work will be based on the copy in Stuttgart, Württembergische Landesbibliothek, Inc. 4° 11150. Further bibliographical details are provided in Offenberg, "The First Use of Hebrew," 44–47.

[2]   See Quicherat, "Thomas Basin," 374–375; Quicherat, *Histoire des règnes*, 4:105–122; Delisle, "Fragments inédits," 95; Marzi, "Nuovi studii," 641–642; Caroti, "La critica," 653–655; Guenée, *Entre l'église et l'état*, 430–434.

[3]   The original copy of this work is MS Paris, Bibliothèque nationale de France, lat. 3658 (100 fols.), which contains annotations from Thomas Basin's own hand. For Basin's plan to have the work printed, see Peter de Rivo's testimony in the preface to *TerTra*, sig. av.

[4]   All subsequent references to this work will be based on the copy bound into BMaz 300, fols. 325r–369v. On the printer, see Indestege, "New Light"; Renaud, "La circulation des incunables," 1–21. The woodcuts and opening chapters are discussed in Champion, *The Fullness of Time*, 149–158, 164–171.

[5]   BMaz 300, fols. 290v–301r. A revised version appeared in *Paulina*, sigs. G8r–I5r.

[6]   All subsequent references to this work will be based on the copy in London, British Library, IB.49189.

[7]   The letter responding to the *Tercius tractatus* was printed in *Paulina*, sigs. I5v–K8v.

of Leuven in 1494, in which he alleged that Peter de Rivo had schemed to prevent its circulation.[8] Eager to continue the altercation, Paul wrote to his rival again in 1497,[9] but this was apparently not enough to goad Peter into issuing any new response.

The drawn-out polemical exchange between Peter de Rivo and Paul of Middelburg derived additional spark from a slowly burgeoning conflict between two different intellectual cultures. As an ambitious young scholar who had spent the past decade of his life in Italy, Paul had absorbed many of the attitudes, methods, and ideals of quattrocento humanism, which made him look at the chronological problems raised by the Gospels through a philological lens that prioritized the study of ancient languages and classical sources over the dialectic approach championed by scholastic theologians.[10] Some of the results generated by the humanists' approach to the Bible were liable to be viewed as scandalous in a more traditionally minded environment such as Leuven's theological faculty, which was at the time a stronghold of the *via antiqua*.[11] Peter's response to the *Epistola apologetica*, which effectively reiterated the results and overall methodology of his earlier *Dyalogus*, may hence be regarded as part of a wider debate pitting scholastic theology against biblical humanism, which was still in a nascent phase when Peter and Paul locked horns.[12]

Rather than attempting a comprehensive account of their confrontation during the late 1480s and early 1490s, which is characterized by a whole tangle of individual points and counterpoints, the following pages will narrow the focus somewhat to concentrate on those chronological issues that already took centre stage in Peter's *Dyalogus* of 1471. First, however, it will be expedient to take a closer look at Paul of Middelburg and the background that spawned his *Epistola apologetica*.

1.   An Offensive Apology

As the name would suggest, Paul Adriaan of Middelburg was born in Middelburg, a merchant town located in the heart of the island of Walcheren (Zeeland).[13] Paul's epitaph, which is preserved in the Church of Santa Maria dell'Anima in Rome,

---

[8]   BMaz 300, fols. 301r–306r (written on 14 September 1494).

[9]   BMaz 300, fols. 306r–308v (written on Pentecost 1497).

[10]   See, e.g., Monfasani, "Criticism of Biblical Humanists."

[11]   See above, xix. Also de Jongh, *L'ancienne faculté de théologie*; Claes, "Changes in the Educational Context."

[12]   For orientation, see Schwarz, *Principles and Problems*; Bentley, *Humanists and Holy Writ*; Rummel, *The Humanist-Scholastic Debate*, and the articles assembled in Rummel, ed., *Biblical Humanism*.

[13]   The principal source on Paul's life is a biography written by Bernardino Baldi in the late sixteenth century. See Baldi, *Le vite de' matematici* (ed. Nenci, 355–395), as well as Marzi, *La questione della riforma*, 12–16, 39–53, 233–250; de Ceuleneer, "Paulus van Middelburg"; Vernarecci, *Fossombrone*, 2.1:552–573; Struik, "Paolo di Middelburg"; Struik, "Paulus van Middelburg"; Offenberg, "The First Use of Hebrew," 47–48; van Leijenhorst, "Paul of Middelburg"; Guenée, *Entre l'église et l'état*, 430–431; Vanden Broecke, "Paulus van Middelburg"; Welker, "Ottaviano Petrucci"; Hallyn, "Paul de Middelbourg."

gives his date of death as 14 December 1534 and his age as 88, implying a birth in 1446 or late 1445.[14] This would mean that Paul was 20 or 21 years old when he enrolled at the University of Leuven on 6 April 1467.[15] Peter de Rivo, who was at the time still professor of rhetoric, would have been about 25 years his senior. While at Leuven, Paul studied for an Arts degree while also attending lectures in theology and medicine. By 1479, he is found as professor of astronomy-astrology at the University of Padua, where he attained a doctorate in medicine the following year.[16] Not long thereafter, in 1481, he entered the services of Federico da Montefeltro, duke of Urbino. Although employed primarily as personal physician, there are signs that Paul also offered astrological services to Montefeltro and his successors. At any rate, the 1480s saw him publish a series of annual *prognostica* as well as a 20-year astrological forecast covering the years 1484 to 1504.[17] Thanks to his connections to the Urbinese court and the Roman curia, Paul was put on the short track to an illustrious ecclesiastical career, culminating in his appointment to the episcopal see of Fossombrone on 30 July 1494.

As far as can be ascertained from Paul's account in the *Epistola apologetica*, the controversies of 1487/88 and the following years were the outcome of a theological discussion that had taken place at the occasion of one of his visits to his native Low Countries, perhaps in 1484.[18] His interlocutors at the time included a number of high-ranking prelates, among them Jan van Riet (Johannes de Arundine), auxiliary bishop in Utrecht (d. 1497),[19] and Jan van Westkapelle (Johannes de Westcapellis), abbot of the Premonstratensian monastery of St Mary in Paul's hometown Middelburg, to whom he would later dedicate one of his chronological works.[20] The topic of discussion was threefold, covering the date of Easter, the historical date of the

---

[14]   For a photograph and transcription of Paul's epitaph, see Eberhard J. Nikitsch, "DIO 3, Santa Maria dell'Anima, Rom, Nr. 93," http://www.inschriften.net/zeige/suchergebnis/treffer/nr/di0003-0093.html#content (last accessed 12 August 2020). See also Schmidlin, *Geschichte der deutschen Nationalkirche*, 349–350.

[15]   Wils, *Matricule*, 184 (no. 16).

[16]   Sambin, "Il dottorato padovano." See also Favaro, "I lettori di matematiche," 40–41.

[17]   Castelli, "Gli astri e i Montefeltri," 79–83; Castelli, "Magia, astrologia, divinazione e chiromanzia alla corte dei Montefeltro," 39, 45–46, 57–63; de Smet, "Savants humanistes et astrologie," 191–193; Federici Vescovini, "Su un genere letterario astrologico"; Gamba, *Le stelle sopra Urbino*; Heilen, "Paul of Middelburg's Use of the *Mathesis*"; Heilen, "Paul of Middelburg's *Prognosticum*"; Heilen, "Astrology at the Court of Urbino," 336–357.

[18]   Paul is extremely vague as to the date and location of this discussion. His *Epistola apologetica* begins by mentioning that he stopped by in Leuven on his return from Italy in the summer of 1487, only to learn of rumours that had spread about some offensive statements he had made "long ago" (*EpApol*, sig. A2r: "me iampridem aliqua dixisse"). It seems possible that this refers to a previous visit to the Low Countries in summer 1484. This visit is attested in the long preface to Paul's *Prognosticum* for the years 1484–1504, dedicated to the Emperor Maximilian I and printed in Leuven (1484). See Heilen, "Paul of Middelburg's *Prognosticum*," 233–239; Heilen, "Astrology at the Court of Urbino," 347.

[19]   Berbée, "Riet."

[20]   *EpApol*, sig. A3r. The work Paul dedicated to Jan van Westkapelle appears in BMaz 300, fols. 308v–322r. It is described in Chapter 3.5 below.

Passion, and the duration of Christ's stay inside the tomb. When it was Paul's turn to speak, he first railed against the scandalous defects that plagued the ecclesiastical calendar and the existing method of Easter reckoning, which on frequent occasions caused the Church to celebrate Easter Sunday in the wrong week or month.[21] He next turned to the number of days and nights Christ lay dead in his sepulchre. According to Paul, the answer was found in Matthew 12:40, where Jesus tells the Pharisees that "the Son of Man will be three days and three nights in the heart of the earth," in parallel with the three days and nights Jonah remained inside the belly of a fish (Jonah 1:17).[22]

When it came to the actual calendrical dates, Paul claimed that his own calculations had led him to the conclusion that the historical crucifixion had occurred on 22 March, as supposedly supported by some of the earliest Christian writers.[23] Among the authorities Paul adduced in favour of this position was the second-century bishop of Theophilus of Caesarea, whose pronouncements were quoted in the spurious *Acts of the Council of Caesarea*.[24] Paul's citations from this text created the impression that the venerable Theophilus had placed Christ's death on 22 March and his resurrection on 25 March. Theophilus's chronology hence appeared to chime with Paul's contention that the "three days and three nights" of Christ's rest inside the tomb had to be taken literally.[25] His already controversial notion that the crucifixion happened on 22 March (instead of 25 March) was rendered even riskier by his simultaneous acceptance of the mainstream opinion according to which Christ lived in the flesh for 33 years and 3 months and hence died in AD 34. The lunar data for this year seemed to speak in favour of his position, as 22 March would have been the 14th day of the Moon and hence the eve of Passover in the Jewish calendar, making it a suitable date for the crucifixion. At the same time, however, dating the Passion to 22 March in AD 34 made nonsense out of the traditional assumption that Jesus died on a Friday. If true, Paul's hypothesis would have made it necessary to accept that the crucifixion occurred on a Monday.[26]

---

[21]   *EpApol*, sig. A3r–v.

[22]   *EpApol*, sig. A3v.

[23]   *EpApol*, sigs. A3v–4v.

[24]   See n. 59 in the previous chapter.

[25]   For the relevant passage in the Caesarean *Acts*, see *Computus Gerlandi* (ed. Lohr, 244): "Theophilus episcopus dixit: 'Et impium non est, ut passio dominica tantum sacramenti mysterium foras limitem excludatur? Passus namque est Dominus ab IX° Kalendas Aprilis, qua nocte a Iudaeis traditus est, et ab VIII° Kalendas resurrexit. Quomodo ergo tres dies foras terminum excluduntur?'" Paul claimed to have found this passage quoted in Rabanus Maurus's ninth-century *Liber de computo*, but in a version that replaced "impium non" with "impium enim" while omitting the phrase "qua nocte a Iudaeis traditus est". This became a point of contention between Paul and Peter de Rivo. See *OpRes*, sigs. b6v–b7r (tr. 1, c. 2, pt. 8); Paul's letter of response in BMaz 300, fol. 300r; *TerTra*, sigs. a8r–br (tr. 3, c. 1, pt. 5); *Paulina*, sigs. A5v–6v.

[26]   *EpApol*, sig. A4v.

If we can believe Paul's own accounts of the background, a large part of the original impetus for developing these controversial ideas had come from his personal
encounters with Jews in Italy. In a move reminiscent of the prologue to Peter's
Dyalogus, Paul framed his project as a defence of the Christian faith against its
detractors, who criticized not only the methods by which the Church determined
the date of Easter, but outright denied the historicity of the resurrection.[27] Specific objections that had—supposedly—been levelled against him by a certain rabbi
included the brevity of Christ's rest in the tomb, which lasted no more than 30 to
36 hours (from sunset on Friday to midnight or dawn on Sunday) and hence failed
to mirror the three days and three nights mentioned in Jonah 1:17 and Matthew
12:40. According to Paul, the same rabbi also appealed to the opinion of medical
authorities such as Galen, who noted that it was necessary to wait 72 hours before an
individual could be declared dead with full confidence. Since Jesus spent less than
half of this timespan in the grave, there was no guarantee that he had truly died.[28] By
the time Paul finished the *Epistola apologetica*, he had already responded to these
and other Jewish objections in a separate treatise, which he referred to as his *Pentateucus*. Although this work is now lost, it would appear that it defended the bold
conclusion of adding an extra day between the crucifixion and the resurrection in
order to prolong Christ's stay inside the sepulchre. Paul mentions this *Pentateucus*
several times in a letter he sent to Thomas Basin in 1489 or 1490, claiming that
certain unnamed Italian scholars agreed with his arguments after examining the
book.[29] There are no signs that he ever made it available in his native Low Countries,
where his solution to the Passion problem first became known through the speech
he gave at the aforementioned theological discussion.

For all his protestations to have acted in defence of the Christian faith, Paul
must have been aware that this solution had the potential of causing great offence,
considering the way it negated the chronological foundations of commemorating Christ's suffering on Good Friday and his resurrection on Easter Sunday. It
even appeared to contradict an important element of all three ecumenical creeds
(Apostle's Creed, Nicene Creed, Athanasian Creed), which affirmed that Christ
rose again on the third day from his crucifixion. One man in particular, whom

---

[27]   See on this point *EpApol*, sigs. A6v–8v; *Paulina*, sigs. a2v, Ar–B2r, and the letters to Thomas
Basin and Peter de Rivo in BMaz 300, fols. 261r–v, 299r–v. See also Nothaft, "Duking it Out," 229–235.

[28]   BMaz 300, fol. 261r–v: "Inseruit etiam dictus Iudeus medicorum documentum qui pro mortis
contestatione LXXII horas neccessarias asserunt." A more detailed presentation of this argument
appears in *Paulina*, sig. A7r–v.

[29]   See BMaz 300, fols. 262r: "Sicque, pater reverendissime, quamvis magna sis dignitate insigna-
tus, in hac tamen parte qua hereticum me appellas tibi non cedam, quando iam quosdam eorum qui in
Ytalia eruditi habentur ab his studiis meis non abhorere, sed rationibus meis acquiescere animadverti,
qui Pentateucum meum in quo de his disputo diligentius perquirere et sine invidia examinare dignati
sunt." See also ibid., 261r, 263r. Another reference to what appears to be the *Pentateucus* is contained
in *EpApol*, sig. A8r–v: "[U]t in tractatu nostro quem contra iudeos conscipsimus videri licet, ubi errores
etiam consimiles in ipsorum paschatis observatione in eos retorsimus."

Paul kept referring to as his *sycophanta* ("informer"), was so taken aback by Paul's utterances that he embarked on what the *Epistola apologetica* portrayed as a vicious defamatory campaign. Following a visit to Leuven in early 1488, Paul was dismayed to discover that his *sycophanta* had not only been busy spreading rumours at his former university, but had openly denounced him in a letter sent to various of his former benefactors.[30] Only once, at the beginning of his lengthy apology, did Paul allude to the man's name, mentioning that the vernacular form of his family name was *de Hooffsche*.[31] A marginal gloss in one of the printed copies of the *Epistola apologetica* identifies him more fully, giving his first name as Adriaan and his place of origin as Westkapelle, a town on Walcheren in the near vicinity of Middelburg (*Adrianus Hoeffsche Westcapellis*).[32] The first name is confirmed by Thomas Basin, who in his treatise *Contra errores et blasphemias Pauli de Middelburgo* repeatedly chastised Paul for his published insults against a humble priest named *Adrianus*.[33] Rather than acknowledging that Adriaan was a man in holy orders, Paul preferred to draw attention to the fact that he had made his fortune as a merchant in Bruges before turning to the study of theology in his sixties.[34] In one particularly bitter passage of his *Epistola*, Paul questioned his detractor's moral character by writing

> you were neither as scrupulous nor as zealous towards the Lord when you exercised the merchant's craft in Bruges with suppressed conscience, bringing ruin to many. But nowadays you hold disputations about fasting with a full stomach and you hold bacchanals while pretending to be saintly and full of sorrow underneath your grey robe.[35]

What made Adriaan de Hooffsche's accusatory letter particularly galling in Paul's eyes was not so much its content, which he dismissed as hare-brained and inept,

---

[30] *EpApol*, sigs. A2r–3r, A4v–5v. Passages from the letter in question are quoted or referred to ibid., sigs. Dv–2v, D4r–v, D6v, D8v.

[31] *EpApol*, sig. A2r: "Quas quidem mussitationes ortas primum intellexi ex mercatore quondam, nunc studente novello, vulgariter et vernaculo sermone 'de Hooffsche' cognominato, quod quidem faustum agnomen urbanitatem quandam pre se ferre videtur. Sed utinam aliquid in homine isto preter cognomen urbanum esset!" Contrary to what has been written in some of the earlier literature, the main target of the *Epistola apologetica* was not Peter de Rivo. Examples of this mistaken information include de Jongh, *L'ancienne faculté de théologie*, 83–86; Marzi, *La questione della riforma*, 13–14; Marzi, "Nuovi studii," 641; Guenée, *Entre l'église et l'état*, 431; Nothaft, *Dating the Passion*, 232.

[32] Stuttgart, Württembergische Landesbibliothek, Inc. 4° 11150, sig. A2r. It is uncertain if this Adrianus can be identified with "Adrianus Arnoldi de Westcapellis" from the diocese of Utrecht, who enrolled in Leuven as an Arts student on 24 November 1466. See Wils, *Matricule*, 179 (no. 79).

[33] MS Paris, Bibliothèque nationale de France, lat. 3658, fols. 3r, 4r, 27r–v (praef., I.1, I.12).

[34] *EpApol*, sigs. D5v–6v, D7r, D8v. See also ibid., sigs. Dv, Er, where Paul mentions that Adriaan de Hoofsche has become a citizen of Middelburg.

[35] *EpApol*, sig. A4v: "Id saltem scire arbitror quod non tam scrupulosus nec tam zelosus in deum fuisti cum Brugis mercatoriam in perditionem multorum calcata conscientia exercuisti. Sed nunc pleno ventre de ieiuniis disputas et sub veste tua grisea te sanctum ac curium simulas et bacchanalia vivis."

but the fact that Adriaan quoted in it the opinions of some of Leuven's doctors,[36] creating the impression that his attack on Paul came with the university's seal of approval. Although Paul dismissed this idea as pure imposture on Adriaan's part, the very fact that he felt the need to pen an elaborate *Epistola apologetica*—completed in Middelburg on 27 February 1488 and printed in Leuven later that year—suggests that the circle of his critics was both larger and more formidable than just the hapless *sycophanta* he continued to shower with abuse throughout this text.[37] Whatever the truth of the matter, the rhetorical strategy Paul pursued in the bulk of his *Epistola* was liable to increase rather than assuage the outrage his earlier comments had caused. Instead of merely protesting that his arguments had been of a hypothetical nature, the astrologer preferred to showcase his learning and wit by methodically undermining any of the arguments that could be used to demonstrate that Jesus died on a Friday and rose again on the following Sunday. As Paul framed it in the *Epistola apologetica*, both these propositions had to be taken as articles of faith, which one could prove neither on historical nor on rational grounds. Indeed, astronomical calculation showed that not a single year in the relevant range, from the 30th to the 35th year of Christ's life, featured the necessary combination of data, such that a Friday would have been found to fall in March and either on or immediately before the day of Passover.[38]

His plan to refute potential counterarguments naturally forced Paul to make a host of new assertions, some of which were apt to stir up further controversy. With regard to the early history of Easter, for instance, he argued that the custom of celebrating the feast on a Sunday was not in itself proof that Christ had risen from the dead on this particular day of the week. From the writings and actions of early Church fathers such as Polycarp of Smyrna, it was known that Christians in Asia Minor once followed St John the Evangelist in celebrating Easter on the 14th day of the Moon irrespective of the weekday. While the practice of celebrating the feast on a Sunday was later made mandatory at the Council of Nicaea, the status of Sunday as the Lord's Day in the early Church was not necessarily to be explained by its historical role as the weekday of the resurrection. Instead, it was imaginable that Christians began to regard Sunday as the *dies dominica* because it had been the weekday of the Last Supper, as would have been true if the historical date of the crucifixion was Monday, 22 March AD 34.[39]

Paul's argumentation became even more daring when he turned his attention to the pertinent passages in the Gospels, the wording of which had convinced generations of theologians and exegetes that the morning on which Jesus's followers

---

[36]   As indicated by Paul in *EpApol*, sigs. Dv–2r.
[37]   Paul in fact repeatedly alluded to the existence of several accomplices (*complices*), who he believed shared Adriaan's opinion and malicious intent. See *EpApol*, sigs. A5v–6r, D4v–6r, E3r, E4r–v.
[38]   *EpApol*, sigs. E4v–5r.
[39]   *EpApol*, sigs. Br–B6v.

discovered the empty tomb belonged to a Sunday. One of the most obvious counters to Paul's position was drawn directly from the Passion narrative in the four Gospels, which referred to the day of the crucifixion as *parasceve* (Matthew 27:62; Mark 15:42; Luke 23:54; John 19:14, 31, 42), a term commonly understood to mean the day before a Sabbath. Paul rejected this argument, insisting that the Greek παρασκευή denoted no more than a "day of preparation," which could be applied to the eve of any feast day, Sabbath or otherwise. He had a similar rejoinder ready for those who believed that the expressions *prima sabbati* (Matthew 28:1) or *una sabbati* (Luke 24:1; John 20:1) used by the evangelists in connection with the morning of the resurrection referred to the first day after the Sabbath. According to Paul, the word *sabbatum* or σάββατον in the Bible often functioned as a generic term for a "day of rest," regardless of the day of the week on which it fell. Support for this reading seemed to come from Mark's Gospel, which had the plural *una sabbatorum* in place of *una sabbati* (16:2). Paul insisted that *una sabbatorum* was the correct translation also in the case of Matthew (28:1), where the Greek text Ὀψὲ δὲ σαββάτων, τῇ ἐπιφωσκούσῃ εἰς μίαν σαββάτων implied no more than that the resurrection occurred on "one of the feast days," that is, one of the seven days of unleavened bread (15–21 Nisan). The same applied to the parallel passages in Luke (24:1) and John (20:1), where the translator of the Vulgate had rendered the words of the evangelists in a misleading way.[40]

Paul was well aware that his philological musings were apt to raise some disquieting questions about the status of the standard Latin translation, whose wording continued to underpin the theology and liturgy of the Roman Church. In effect, his thesis forced him to engage at some length with the origin and authority of the Vulgate text traditionally attributed to St Jerome, which was directly challenged by his interpretation of the resurrection account.[41] As a counter to those who insisted that the Latin text of the Old and New Testament had to be followed for having been sanctioned by the Roman Church, Paul cast serious doubt on the belief that Jerome was in fact responsible for the translation ascribed to him. Not only had this translation already been in use before Jerome's time, but it was clear from a closer examination that it contained incorrect renderings of the Greek or Hebrew text. Far from being the originator of these mistakes, Jerome could be shown from his own letters to have been a vocal critic of the translation commonly in use. One of several examples Paul brought up in his excursus is the aforementioned opening of Matthew 28:1, where the Vulgate rendered Ὀψὲ δὲ σαββάτων as *Vespere autem sabbati*. Jerome challenged this interpretation in his letter to Hebidia, in which he noted that the correct Latin equivalent of ὀψέ would have been *sero* ("late") rather than *vespere*, which confirmed that the evangelist had meant to indicate that Christ

---

[40]   *EpApol*, sigs. B6v–C2r.
[41]   *EpApol*, sigs. C2r–8r. See on the background Rice, *Saint Jerome in the Renaissance*, 173–189; Dahan, "Critique et défense"; Linde, *How to Correct the Sacra Scriptura*, 57–104.

rose from the dead late at night rather than in the evening.[42] After many further learned disquisitions as well as some cantankerous outbursts directed at Adriaan de Hooffsche, Paul concluded the main part of his letter by asking the doctors of the university for their verdict:

> I desire to learn from you what you recommend should be said about this. For if you say that [Christ's death on a Friday] must be taken on faith, we shall by all means believe it faithfully and add it to our Athanasian Creed and the more arguments we have against it, the more sincere and absolute and more meritorious our faith shall be. For there is no merit in faith where reason provides confirmation. Instead, [faith] is the more meritorious the more it is assailed by reason. This is what Christ taught us when he said to Thomas Didymus "Because thou hast seen me, Thomas, thou hast believed: blessed are they that have not seen and have believed" [John 20:29]. If you should say, however, that this interpretation of the words [of Scripture] is not to be taken on faith, as I also think, but that it can be demonstrated through reasoning and supported by calculation that Christ was crucified on a Friday, then I ask, beseech, and implore you to commit to writing the arguments of your doctors together with their calculation. To them I shall always submit my own utterances and writings for examination and correction. Farewell. From Middelburg, on the fourth day before the Kalends of March [27 February], in the year of the Lord 1488.[43]

2.   Peter's Return to Chronology

Of the various members of Leuven's theological faculty who were in a position to respond to the arguments put forward in the *Epistola apologetica*, few would have been better qualified than Peter de Rivo, who at the time of its publication had been a doctor of theology for close to 11 years. More important, however, than Peter's academic credentials was his authorship of the *Dyalogus de temporibus Christi* of 1471, which had already dealt with several of the questions that had become contentious again as a result of Paul's recent visits to the Low Countries. Provoked by the challenge issued at the end of Paul's *Epistola*, Peter decided to restate his position in a detailed *Opus responsivum* written in 1488 and apparently converted

---

[42] *EpApol*, sig. C2v. For the referenced passage, see Jerome, *Epistulae* 120.4.3 (ed. CSEL 55, 482–483).

[43] *EpApol*, sig. E4r: "His tamen motivis non obstantibus a te doceri cupio quid de hoc dicendum censes. Nam si fide tenendum dixeris credemus utique fideliter et symbolo nostro Athanasii annectemus tantoque sincera magis fides et purior ac magis meritoria in nobis erit quanto plures rationes in contrarium habemus. Fides enim non habet meritum ubi ratio prebet experimentum, sed tanto magis est meritoria quanto magis rationibus impugnatur, quod Christus nos docuit cum Thome Didimo diceret 'tu credidisti quia vidisti, beati que crediderunt et non viderunt' etc. Si vero dixeris fide non esse tenendam hanc vocabulorum interpretationem, ut etiam arbitror, sed rationibus posse probari et calculo confirmari Christum die Veneris fuisse crucifixum, rogo, obsecro et obtestor ut argumenta tuorum doctorum una cum calculo in scriptis redigas, quibus etiam per omnia semper mea dicta et scripta examinanda corrigendaque submitto. Vale. Ex Middelburgo, quarto kalendas Martias, anno domini millesimo quadringentengesimo octuagesimo octavo."

to print during the following year.[44] This handsomely produced book, which came with several full-page woodcuts, easily gave the impression of being the University of Leuven's official response to Paul's controversial claims, although the extent to which Peter acted as part of an organized reaction is difficult to determine.[45]

In the work's prologue, Peter revealed that one of his reasons for taking up the quill against Paul of Middelburg was rooted in his pastoral duties as *plebanus* of the collegiate church of St Peter in Leuven. Personal experience and the testimony of others had taught him that ordinary believers were "troubled to no small extent" when confronted with Paul's claim that Christ suffered on a Monday and rose from the dead on a Thursday "and when they contemplate how a highly skilled calculator adduces what he claims to be a highly reliable calculation against the ancient rite of the Church and the opinions of the old teachers of the Church."[46] The *Opus responsivum* that followed these pronouncements was divided into two treatises of three chapters each. In the first treatise, Peter laid out in careful detail his evidence for accepting that Christ's Passion took place (i) in the 34th year of his life, (ii) on 25 March, and (iii) on a Friday, all while demonstrating why various discrepant opinions, including Paul of Middelburg's, could not be accepted as true. The second treatise played a role analogous to the middle part of the *Dyalogus*, in that its first chapter made the case for assuming that a change in the intercalation-pattern of the Julian calendar had occurred at some point after the crucifixion. The second chapter showed how this hypothesis could help solve a number of apparent contradictions in the chronology of Christ's last days, while the third and final chapter used some of the same insights to explain how most previous authors, including various Church Fathers, had gone wrong in picking the date of the crucifixion.

Although most of the conclusions put forward in the *Opus responsivum* did not deviate dramatically from those in the *Dyalogus*, the new work expanded the evidentiary basis for certain arguments, adding new sources to the mix or presenting

---

[44]   The year of writing (1488) is mentioned in the prologue of *OpRes*, sig. a3r, but this is not necessarily the year in which the book was printed. Paul of Middelburg, in the letter of response he wrote to Peter in 1492, quotes Peter as giving the year of printing as 1489. BMaz 300, fol. 293r: "Nam, ut tu ipse testaris, anno 1489 libellum tuum depresisti." This is not implausible considering Offenberg's argument that the offending *Epistola apologetica* was only printed in the autumn of 1488. See Offenberg, "The First Use of Hebrew," 44–45.

[45]   See *TerTra*, sig. e7v (tr. 3, c. 3, pt. 11), where Peter implies that he acted on his own. The only hint to the contrary comes from his statement that Thomas Basin had been the first to encourage him to write on the topic. *TerTra*, sig. av: "Is me primum adhortatus est, ut calamum suscipiens de tempore scriberem dominice passionis." It is quite possible, however, that this refers not to the *Opus responsivum*, but to the much earlier *Dyalogus*.

[46]   *OpRes*, sig. a3r: "Alterum quod me silere non sinit est caritas qua pusillis compatior. Ex quibus plurimos et ipse scivi et aliorum relatu didici non mediocriter turbari ex epistola M. Pauli dum in ea legunt Christum feria secunda passum et resurrexisse feria quinta, cum hactenus et a cunabilis (ut ita dixero) crediderint dominum passum feria sexta ac die dominica resurrexisse dumque perpendunt contra pristinum ecclesie ritum ac veterum ecclesie doctorum sentencias adduci a peritissimo calculatore certissimum (ut ait) calculum." See also *TerTra*, sig. e7v (tr. 3, c. 3, pt. 11).

those already adduced in the *Dyalogus* at greater length. By far the most important modification that Peter applied to his original set of conclusions concerned the history of the Julian calendar and the concomitant solar cycle. Here the *Opus responsivum* gave him an opportunity to correct a major error in the *Dyalogus*. In the second treatise of the *Dyalogus*, Peter had dated the starting point of the Julian calendar to 1 January 45 BC, but ended up identifying the Julian calendar's 52nd year, which he considered to have been the first "regular" bissextile year in history, with AD 6 rather than AD 7.[47] Although the *Opus responsivum* did not address this error directly, its changes relative to the *Dyalogus* show very clearly that Peter had noticed it and now tried his best to avoid it without compromising his main conclusion. This was easier said than done, since placing the first regular bissextile day in February AD 7 rather than AD 6 was no real step towards the solution he sought for AD 34, the putative year of the Passion. According to the conventional solar cycle, AD 34 was a Julian common year with the dominical letter C, which put 25 March on a Thursday. This situation did not change at all if the bissextile years were placed in AD 7, 11, 15 … 35, as the year AD 34 was still left without a bissextile day that might have shifted the weekday of 25 March from Thursday to Friday.

To maintain his overall strategy, which was to find the key to the Passion problem in the history of the Roman calendar, Peter introduced a number of new assumptions concerning the reform that Julius Caesar had carried out in 46/45 BC with the help of his scribe M. Flavianus (who is mentioned by Macrobius in *Saturnalia* 1.14.2). In particular, he postulated that both the seven-day week and the concomitant system of ferial and dominical letters had already been part and parcel of the Julian calendar when it was first established. Aside from furnishing the newly created calendar with a column showing the ferial letters from A to G, Peter argued that Caesar and Flavianus would have also made sure to begin the first year of this calendar on the first day of the week and hence on a Sunday. For this to be the case, the first year of the Julian calendar (45 BC) required A as the correct dominical letter. Since the same year was *ex hypothesi* also the first year of the Julian leap-year cycle, Peter was committed to arguing that 45 BC corresponded to the 22nd year of the conventional solar cycle.[48] If this new starting point was accepted, it followed that AD 34 originally corresponded to the 16th year of the solar cycle, in which the dominical letter was B and 25 March fell on a Friday.[49]

There remained the challenge of reconciling this hypothetical scenario with the doctrine of the solar cycle currently in use. After all, a retrospective count showed 45 BC to have been the 21st rather than the 22nd year of the cycle, making it a leap year with dominical letters CB. Similarly, AD 34 turned out to be the 15th year of the solar cycle and a common year with dominical letter C. What Peter needed was a

---

[47]   See above, xlii–xliii.

[48]   *OpRes*, sig. d2r–v (tr. 2, c. 1, pt. 2).

[49]   *OpRes*, sig. d3r–v (tr. 2, c. 1, pt. 4).

plausible account as to how and why the solar cycle had been altered subsequent to Christ's crucifixion. In the *Dyalogus*, he had offered the conjecture that the Roman Church once postponed the bissextile day as a means of synchronizing its own celebration of Easter with that in Egypt. Yet this simple sort of postponement was not enough to bring about the displacement of the solar cycle his new hypothesis demanded. Eager to retain the essential outlines of his explanation, he decided to add to it one more assumption. According to the version presented in the *Opus responsivum*, those responsible for this reform decided to take the two dominical letters that jointly served a given bissextile year and split them between two adjacent years. In order to accomplish this, they effectively had to suppress the leap day in one year and then wait another four-year period before finally inserting the next *bissextus*.[50] Table 2 demonstrates how this imagined reform would have sufficed to convert the original cycle devised by Julius Caear into its modern counterpart. By counting eight consecutive common years from some arbitrary point, the reformers would have ensured that one bissextile day was left out of the calendar entirely, while the second ended up being postponed by one year. The end result was a new version of the solar cycle, which was shifted by one year in relation to the old one. In this new cycle 45 BC was no longer the first year after a bissextile year with dominical letter A, but a bissextile year with letters CB.

Original cycle	Reform	Modern cycle
A	A	CB
G	G	A
F	F	G
ED	E	F
C	D	ED
B	C	C
A	B	B
GF	A	A
E	GF	GF

Table 2: Hypothetical reform of the solar cycle according to Peter de Rivo's
Opus responsivum

Peter's argument, although it worked successfully on a purely technical level, left some important questions unaddressed. For one thing, it was far from obvious why this peculiar mode of reform would have been chosen by the party responsible. If the

---

50   *OpRes*, sig. d5v (tr. 2, c. 1, pt. 6), f6r.

reason for the change was rooted in the fact that the Church in Egypt intercalated the bissextile day in a different position than the Church in Rome, it would in principle have been enough to post- or pre-pone a given *bissextus* and then start the leap-year cycle anew. Why, then, was it deemed necessary to drop one of these intercalary days altogether by counting eight common years in a row? Peter's *Opus responsivum* failed to provide a clear answer, even as its author attempted to flesh out his hypothesis by guessing at the approximate time when the solar cycle would have undergone this peculiar shift. In contrast to the *Dyalogus*, where Peter surmised that a reform had been carried out in the second century of the Christian era, he now opted for a later date, claiming that the necessity of synchronizing Roman and Egyptian Easters by omitting the bissextile day was first felt after the Council of Arles (AD 314), which decreed that Easter should be observed by all Christians on the same day.[51]

When writing the *Dyalogus*, Peter had still shunned the use of astronomical tables for calculating conjunctions and oppositions, relying instead as much as possible on calendrical cycles. The *Opus responsivum* took a different approach insofar as Peter now routinely mobilized the calculated times of syzygies (i.e., lunisolar conjunctions and oppositions) to support his historical claims.[52] With regard to the history of the Julian calendar, his reasoning was as follows: from Macrobius's *Saturnalia* it was known that the original Rome calendar introduced by Romulus only numbered ten months or 304 days. Macrobius also claimed that the Romans used to synchronize the beginning of this ten-month long year with the new moon, such that the new year would begin on the evening when the crescent of the new moon appeared. Peter saw in this ancient practice the explanation behind the puzzling phrase *ad lunam dimensionibus constitutum* that Macrobius used to describe the original publication of the Julian calendar (*Saturnalia* 1.14.13). Julius Caesar, he argued, wanted to make sure that his new calendar began with the first new moon after the winter solstice, explaining why the Julian calendar began in 45 BC.[53]

This argument strongly resembled the one already included in the *Dyalogus* (tr. 2, c. 1 [ll. 87–93]), the difference being that Peter now also used it prop up his bold new hypothesis according to which there had been an undocumented suppression of the *bissextus* in late antiquity. He claimed that conventional astronomical tables showed a true conjunction of Sun and Moon to have occurred roughly two hours after midnight on 1 January 45 BC, in which case Julius Caesar would have violated the aforementioned Romulean rule by starting the new calendar before he had a chance to see the new moon crescent. Peter regarded this scenario as unacceptable and treated it as evidence that the number of leap days inserted since the beginning of the Julian calendar was actually lower than assumed by those who cast astro-

---

[51]   *OpRes*, sigs. d5v–d6r (tr. 2, c. 1, pt. 6). For the relevant decree of the Council of Arles, see *Concilium Arelatense*, c. 1 (ed. CCSL 148, 9).

[52]   *OpRes*, sigs. b2r–b3r (tr. 1, c. 2, pt. 3), b5r (tr. 1, c. 2, pt. 5).

[53]   *OpsRes*, sig. d1v (tr. 2, c. 1, pt. 1).

nomical tables. Once the calculations were adjusted accordingly, the date of true conjunction shifted to 31 December, making it possible for the Moon to have made a visible appearance the following evening.[54]

Peter's ability to make this kind of technical argument in the *Opus responsivum* appears to have been the result of his contacts to Oliver Godelof, a Carmelite friar and former theology student who supplied him with computational data as well as with advice on astronomical tables.[55] Godelof's influence on the *Opus responsivum* is especially manifest from the drawn-out sequence of calendrical tables and diagrams that served as an appendix to the work. Included among this material was an annotated calendar limited in range to 8 March–1 May, which was here taken as the range of dates relevant to an analysis of the Passion problem. Among the various annotations pertaining to individual dates, one assigned to 9 March the mean lunisolar conjunction in AD 34, stating that it occurred 10:57h from the previous noon at the geographic longitude of Jerusalem.[56] For the vernal equinox of the year in question, one of the notes gave a date of 22 March (*XXI^a martii completo*) and a time of 22:01h from the previous noon. Another note, placed below the calendar, was a personal statement by Oliver Godelof, who confirmed with his own signature that both calculations were correct according to the Alfonsine Tables.[57]

Neither of these calculated dates took account of the bissextile day that had allegedly been omitted after AD 34, yet this did not keep Peter from utilizing them in the second chapter of the first treatise, where he submitted to critical scrutiny some of the astronomical and calendrical claims contained in Paul of Middelburg's *Epistola apologetica*. Taking some of his cues from the Venerable Bede,[58] Peter here worked on the assumption that the Jews in Jesus's time always began their days at the previous sunset and that the start of a new lunar month had to coincide with the sunset following the last conjunction. This was important, since Godelof's calculation showed that the mean conjunction of March AD 34 occurred during the 11th hour following the noon that preceded 9 March. This was equivalent to the 5th hour of 9 March according to the Jewish reckoning, which in turn implied that the month of Nisan would have only started on 10 March. The afternoon of 14 Nisan was on this count not reached until 23 March, which ran counter to Paul of Middelburg's assertion that 22 March AD 34 had had the lunar age appropriate for being the date of the crucifixion.[59] In addition

---

[54]   *OpRes*, sigs. d5r–v (tr. 2, c. 1, pt. 6).

[55]   *OpRes*, sig. d5v (tr. 2, c. 1, pt. 6). Peter explains the backstory in *TerTra*, sig. bv (tr. 3, c. 1, pt. 6). Godelof was from the diocese of Cambrai and had matriculated in Leuven on 23 February 1455, as seen from Wils, *Matricule*, 17 (no. 109).

[56]   *OpRes*, sig. f6v.

[57]   *OpRes*, sig. f7r: "Quantum ad coniunctionem luminarium mediam supra postiam et quo ad introitum solis in Arietem hic annotatum ego, Oliverius Godelof, manu mea propria necnon et signo meo manuali et consueto calculum affirmo verum et ratum fore secundum tabulas Illustris regis Alfonsii exaratum."

[58]   *OpRes*, sig. b1r. (tr. 1, c. 2, pt. 1); Bede, *De temporum ratione*, c. 43 (ed. CCSL 123B, pp. 412–414).

[59]   *OpRes*, sig. b7r–v (tr. 1, c. 2, pt. 9).

to examining the astronomical age of the Moon, Peter insisted on the ancient Jewish 'rule of the equinox' mentioned in Eusebius's *Ecclesiastical History*.[60] According to this rule, the Jews only celebrated the Passover once the day of the vernal equinox had passed, but never earlier. From Godelof's calculation, which showed that the equinox of AD 34 had occurred on 22 March, it was clear that Christ would not have eaten the Passover lamb on the previous 21 March, as this would have been tantamount to celebrating in the twelfth rather than the first lunar month of the year.[61]

In the third chapter of the first treatise, Peter gathered a plethora of scriptural and patristic arguments in support of the traditional conclusion that the "three days and three nights" Christ spoke of in Matthew 12:40 were just a figure of speech. Against Paul of Middelburg's bold attempt to extend Christ's rest inside the tomb by a full day, Peter insisted on the prevalence of inclusive reckoning in ordinary language. It was reflected, for instance, in the way the days in the Roman calendar were counted backwards from the Kalends, Nones, and Ides, or in the language used by physicians, who labelled the fever that recurred on the third inclusive day of an illness as "tertian fever."[62] In the same vein, it was legitimate to count the Sunday of Christ's resurrection as the "third day" from the Friday on which he died. In reaction to Paul's take on the Greek term *parasceve*, Peter protested that the whole purpose of having a "day of preparation" was to store and prepare food for the following Sabbath, as no work was allowed on that day. He adduced passages in the Book of Exodus to show that the injunction to abstain from work was significantly weaker in the case of feast days such as 15 and 21 Nisan (Exodus 12:16: "you shall do no work in them, except those things that belong to eating") than they were on the Sabbath. The very fact that the evangelists would call the day of the crucifixion *parasceve* hence indicated that the next day was not just 15 Nisan, but also a Sabbath.[63] Another reason for accepting this calendrical coincidence was that it explained away Paul's discovery that the evangelists had originally used the plural form *una sabbatorum* when talking about the morning of Christ's resurrection. As Peter saw it, this was most likely a reference to the fact that the previous Saturday had been occupied by two festive dates at once.[64]

A surprising *volte-face* was on display in Peter's treatment of the postponement rules of the Jewish calendar, which prevented 15 Nisan from falling on a Friday. In the *Dyalogus*, he had still followed Paul of Burgos in treating this rule as an authentic part of the Jewish festive calendar of the first century AD, arguing that there used to be a difference between those Jews who accepted these postponements out of practical convenience and those who zealously observed the regular dates. Jesus and

---

[60] See Eusebius of Caesarea, *Historia ecclesiastica* (trans. Rufinus of Aquileia) 7.32.14–19 (ed. GCS 9.2, 722–726). Peter quotes from this text in *Dyalogus*, tr. 1, c. 3 [ll. 47–56].

[61] *OpRes*, sigs. b7v–b8r (tr. 1, c. 3, pt. 9), e6r (tr. 2, c. 3, pt. 6).

[62] *OpRes*, sig. c1r (tr. 1, c. 3, pt. 3).

[63] *OpRes*, sigs. b8r (tr. 1, c. 3, pt. 1), c2r (tr. 1, c. 3, pt. 5).

[64] *OpRes*, sig. c2v (tr. 1, c. 3, pt. 5).

his disciples belonged to the latter group, explaining why they ended up celebrating the Passover meal one day ahead of the other Jews.[65] In what was a reaction to Paul of Middelburg, who had used the postponement rules to cast doubt on the tradition of placing the crucifixion on a Friday, the *Opus responsivum* offered a very different interpretation, one that used the letter of the synoptic Gospels to argue that the legal 15 Nisan must have coincided with Friday in the year of the crucifixion. Peter now asserted that the Jews had only introduced the rules of postponing Passover in the wake of this event, as a way of exonerating their own leaders. Following an interpretation already voiced by St John Chrysostom, he now took John 18:28 to reveal that these leaders had unlawfully postponed their Passover meal to the evening of the 15th day of the month, because they had been too busy plotting Jesus's death during the previous night.[66] Taking this viewpoint made it necessary to question the authenticity of a Hebrew text Paul had cited in his *Epistola apologetica*, which carried an attribution to Rabbi Gamaliel.[67] In opposition to Paul, who was ready to identify the Gamaliel in question with the one mentioned in Acts 5:34–39 and 22:3, Peter claimed to have detected signs of forgery in the way Paul's Latin translation of Gamaliel's Hebrew referred to the days of the week by their planetary names, in the manner of the pagans, rather than by their ordinal number in relation to the Sabbath.[68] Had Peter known any Hebrew, he would have noticed that these planetary names were absent from the original text printed on the same page of the *Epistola apologetica*.

Peter ended his *Opus responsivum* on a conciliatory note, by stressing the good will he harboured towards his opponent. He even addressed Paul as an old friend, claiming that writing this treatise had often made him feel the wish to discuss these questions face to face, "yet the distance between places has long been separating us from each other."[69] At the same time, he encouraged the target of his criticism to alert him to any errors he might find in the present work,

for if my powers allow for it and the Lord grants it, I shall try to discuss in a third treatise any objections, should it turn out that they are advanced either against

---

65   *Dyalogus*, tr. 3, c. 3 [ll. 183–244].

66   *OpRes*, sig. c5r–v (tr. 1, c. 3, pt. 7). Peter's source is John Chrysostom, *Homiliae in Matthaeum* 84.2 (PG 58, col. 754).

67   *EpApol*, sigs. A7v–8r. Paul later produced a Latin translation of this work, which he dedicated to his friend Jan van Westkapelle, abbot of Middelburg. See the second part of his *Paschalis supputationis ratio triplici lingua*, BMaz 300, fols. 315r–320r. On Paul's use of this text, see Offenberg, "The First Use of Hebrew," 51–52; Nothaft, *Dating the Passion*, 228–233; Grafton and Weinberg, "*I have always loved the Holy Tongue*," 217–219. On medieval appeals to Rabbi Gamaliel as an authority for the Jewish calendar, see Nothaft, *Medieval Latin Christian Texts*, 54, 72, 340, 606–607, and above, x–xi.

68   *OpRes*, sigs. c4v–c5r (tr. 1, c. 3, pt. 7). For the Hebrew quotes in Paul's *Epistola apologetica*, see also Offenberg, "The First Use of Hebrew," 46.

69   *OpRes*, sig. e6v (tr. 2, c. 3, pt. 6): "O quotiens, carissime me, (priusquam opus hoc ederem) tui presentiam optavi, quatinus potuissemus ore ad os in premissis veritatem inquirere. Sed longius nos abinvicem seiunxit locorum distantia." See also *TerTra*, sig. br–v (tr. 3, c. 1, pt. 6), where we learn that Peter and Paul sat down for lunch in the wake of the *Epistola apologetica*.

the truths argued for in the first treatise or against the method of defending them presented in the second treatise.[70]

3.   The Clash of 1492

The continuation of the debate that flared up in 1488 was delayed to a considerable degree by Paul of Middelburg's return to Italy, which meant that he was no longer present in Leuven when Peter's *Opus responsivum* left the press. It would take until early 1492 for a copy of the work to reach the city of Rome, where Paul was moving in the circles of his new patron, Pope Innocent VIII.[71] Paul responded only ten days after the book had first come to his attention, in a lengthy and incensed letter signed on 20 February 1492.[72] The letter reflects Paul's dismay at learning that a man he used to count among his friends in Leuven had joined the camp of his enemies by accusing him of scandalous assertions about the chronology of Christ's Passion. It closes with Paul insisting that he did his best to restrain himself, "because I always knew you as being extremely fond of me and I used to cherish you like a father,"[73] yet there is little moderation detectable in the remainder of the letter, the tone of which fluctuates between bilious sarcasm and unvarnished ire. Both are present in Paul's opening statements, in which he claimed that the arrival of the *Opus responsivum* in Rome had made Peter a laughing stock in the eyes of Rome's learned owing to its computational mishaps and dubious hypotheses.

> [Y]ou perverted all history and based your entire book and all your work on a thing that is as manifestly false, as absurd, and as jarring as it is ridiculous, namely that Julius Caesar established the solar year for the Romans in the first year of his reign. Who is so foolish, so feeble-minded, so mad, that he would not know that this hypothesis of yours is utterly false? Who is so ignorant of letters that he did not read through the history of Julius Caesar and did not recognize that this is completely false? The little boys in Italy certainly know about Caesar's deeds and they are even recited day by day by unmarried girls. It really is shameful for you, whom I have

---

[70]   *OpRes*, sig. e6v: "Nichilominus si visis his libeat caritate tue mecum scriptus fraternaliter conferre, precor obtestorque si tibi videar usquam errasse motiva tua ne me celes. Nam (ut vires dabunt dominusque concedet) obiectus [*sic*] discutere conabor in tercio tractatu, si quos proferri contigerit vel contra veritates in primo tractatu deductas vel contra viam qua defendi possint in tractatu secundo recitatam."

[71]   BMaz 300, fol. 297v: "[E]t summus ipse pontifex Innocentius octavus de sua benigissima humanitate me licet indignum inter suos familiares connumerare dignatus est." In 1491, Innocent VIII had been the recipient of Paul of Middelburg's *Exhortatio pro calendarii emendatione*. See MS Vatican City, BAV, Vat. lat. 3684, fols. 2r–8v; Nothaft, *Scandalous Error*, 286.

[72]   BMaz 300, fol. 300v: "Quod si libellus tuus Romam nuper missus citius ad manus pervenisset, citius tibi respondissem, sed nunc decimus dumtaxat agitur dies quo ad nostram noticiam pervenit."

[73]   BMaz 300, fol. 301r: "Ceterum, ut finem epistole imponam, hortor te ne prima hec disceptionis nostre preludia egro animo feras, quoniam hoc altercationis genus numquam tecum aggressus fuisse, nisi a te provocatus et lacessitus essem. Abstinui etiam et temperam me quantum potui, quia te amicissimum mihi semper cognovi et parentis loco colui."

otherwise always known as a learned man, to have written this thing so incautiously, so rashly, so frivolously and to appear ignorant of things even little boys know, since all historians who ever wrote down the life of Caesar from beginning to end say the complete opposite, asserting that Caesar established the method of the year not, as you assert, in the first year of his reign or dictatorship, but in the final year of his reign and life, after he had subdued Pompey's children in Spain.[74]

As Paul went on to inform his critic with considerable glee, he had made the obvious mistake of basing his reconstruction of Caesar's reign on inadequate sources, ignoring the works of proper historians who wrote close to the events in favour of the poet Lucan and the grammarian Macrobius as well as the medieval chronicler Martin of Opava.[75] In order to get to a reliable understanding of the chronology of Caesar's reign, one had to consult the full range of relevant Roman historiography, from Caesar's own *Commentarii* to the works of Livy, Plutarch, Appian, Florus, and Eutropius. Once this was done and the material was analysed with the proper diligence, it became abundantly clear that the famed calendar reform had taken place not in the first year of his Caesar's reign, but only in the final year of his life, after he had successfully completed the civil war.[76] Peter's mishandling of historical sources was exacerbated by his repeated reliance on unfounded hypotheses, as when he assumed that Julius Caesar or Marcus Flavus inscribed the letters A to G into their calendar to represent the seven days of the week. In reality, there was no evidence at all that Romans in Caesar's time made any use of the seven-day week, or that they called their days by the names of the planets.[77] The same applied to Peter's hypothesis of a late antique reform of the Julian solar cycle, which supposedly involved the counting of eight common years in a row. Peter had tried to pre-empt

---

[74] BMaz 300, fol. 290v: "Quando quidem non solum in calculo aberrasti, verum etiam historiam omnem pervertisti et in re tam manifeste falsa, tam absurda, tam absona quam ridiculo, totum tuum libellum et omnem tuum laborem fundasti, videlicet quod Iulius Cesar primo anno imperii sui Romanis solarem annum instituit. Quis est tam demens, tam mentis inops, tam vecors, qui non noverit hanc tuam hypothesim falsissimam esse? Quis est tam litterarum ignarus, qui Iulii Cesaris historiam non perlegerit et hec falsissima esse non didicerit? Certe pueris in Italia Cesaris gesta sunt nota et ab innuptis etiam puellis in dies decantantur. Pudet profecto cum te virum alioquin doctum semper cognoverim quod hec tam inconsulte, tam temere, tam frivole conscripseris et ignorare videris que pueris sunt nota, cum omnes historiographi qui unquam Cesaris vitam ex ordine scripserunt omnino contrarium dicant, asserentes Cesarem anni rationem instituisse non, ut tu autumas, primo sui imperii sive dictature anno, sed ultimo imperii et vite anno post devictos in Hispania Pompeii liberos."

[75] BMaz 300, fol. 292r.

[76] BMaz 300, fols. 291v–293r.

[77] BMaz 300, fol. 295r–v: "Nunquam certe in ydoneo auctore invenies id quod in secunda tua hypothesi presupponis, videlicet quod Iulius Cesar aut Marcus Flavus distinxit septem dies ebdomadis per septem primas litteras alphabeti Latini, neque usquam invenies Iulium Cesarem inchoasse annum a die solis sive a dominico, nusquam etiam invenies Romanos imposuisse nomina diebus ebdomadis secundum nomina planetarum, immo neque invenies quod unquam his nominibus usi fuerunt, immo neque annum per ebdomades distinxerunt, neque umquam ebdomadibus usi sunt etc. Hec cum idoneo autore invenire non poteris, fatearis oportet has fabellas nuper a te confictos fuisse, ut falso me apud vulgus indoctum criminaveris."

objections against his hypothesis by reminding readers of the murky early history of the city of Rome. "One should not be surprised that it escapes our notice when [this alteration] was made and by whom. For it is clear that Rome was founded, yet there exists among very renowned authors no small disagreement as to who its founder was."[78] Paul was indignant at this weak defence:

> O what splendid analogy, truly worthy of a philosopher! Who is such an insane logician, such a mad sophist that he does not realize that there is no similarity here, since the building of Rome is not only mentioned in writing, but its effect is still apparent to this day. For Rome still exists, yet of the alteration of the calendar after the time of Christ there is no apparent trace whatsoever.[79]

Apart from seeking to demolish the principal arguments Peter de Rivo had deployed in support of a Passion date on Friday, 25 March, Paul used every opportunity to condescend to his opponent for his lack of sophistication in areas such as logic and grammar. Among the smaller mistakes that made Peter an easy target for Paul's ridicule was the way he rendered the name of the main speaker in the calendrical section of Macrobius's *Saturnalia*. The correct spelling of the latter was not *Pretaxatus*, as printed in the *Opus responsivum*, but *Praetextatus*, "for the *praetexta* was the badge of honour of free-born boys, which all those who were honoured with it wore above their tunics, as your Macrobius himself testifies in the fourth chapter of the first [book] of the *Saturnalia*."[80] In a similar vein, Paul felt the need to lampoon Peter for his repeated references to certain *compotistas*

> quite as if you had written your little book over wine and food and wanted to adduce some fellow-drinker as a witness. For in Latin one cannot say *compotista* for someone who is well-versed in the art of calculations. Instead, it refers to a participant in a drinking party, someone who is given to drink.[81]

---

[78]   *OpRes*, sig. d6r (tr. 2, c. 1, pt. 6): "Nec mireris si res quam suffecit semel factam esse posteris per autorem nullum intimata sit. Si queras quo tempore et a quibus facta est dicta annorum variatio, licet indubitanter facta sit, non tamen mirandum est si lateat quando et a quibus facta est. Constat enim Romam factam esse. A quibus tamen condita est non parva est inter autores percelebres dissensio."

[79]   BMaz 300, fol. 296r: "O preclaram similitudinem philosopho profecto dignam! Quis est tam amens logicus, tam vecors sophista qui non animadvertit hanc similitudinem nullam esse, cum edificationis Rome non solum scriptura, verum etiam effectus adhuc ad sursum appareat, adhuc enim est Roma, sed mutationis kalendarii post tempora Christi nullum penitus apparet vestigium."

[80]   BMaz 300, fol. 291r: "Posthabito igitur Macrobio et tuo, ut dicis, Pretaxato, quem rectius Pretaxatum nuncupasses (erat enim pretexta ingenuorum puerorum insigne quod supra tunicas honorati quique sumpserunt, ut ipse tuus Macrobius primo Saturnalium, capitulo quarto, testatur), reliqua que subnectis his scriptis nostris inseremus, sic enim imprimere iussisti." The reference is to Macrobius, *Saturnalia* 1.6.2–18 (ed. Kaster, 52–60).

[81]   BMaz 300, fol. 297r: "Plurimis etiam risum excussit quod totiens compotistas tuos in testimonium vocas, ac si inter vinum et epulas libellum tuum conscripsissess et computatorem aliquem testem afferre velis. Non enim 'compotista' Latine dici potes<t> pro eo qui artem computandi callet, sed potius compotatorem, bibacem significat." Peter de Rivo later defended himself by quoting Giovanni Balbi's thirteenth-century Latin dictionary (the *Catholicon*), which confirmed that the spelling *compotus* reflected the preferred pronounciation of the word. See *TerTra*, sig. a6r (tr. 3, c. 1, pt. 3).

In the conclusion to his letter, Paul patronised his critic one more time by advising him to double-check his future writings before sending any of them to Italy, lest he repeat the embarrassment his previous work had caused. He underscored this point by relating how he had been discussing the *Opus responsivum* with some learned friends in Rome, who, baffled by the absurdity of its contents, began to inquire about the character and circumstances of its author. When Paul responded by talking highly of Peter, praising his qualities as a theologian and teacher of rhetoric, a boy of no more than 15 years interrupted him pertly: "Are you seriously claiming that this man, who has yet to learn how to speak Latin, taught rhetoric to others? Fetch his little book and I can show you a hundred barbarisms, solecisms, and false uses of Latin!" "But I," continued Paul,

> since I have always known you as a man highly learned in all sorts of disciplines, but also out of consideration for the school of Leuven, of which I call myself an alumnus, tried to defend your honour, responding that Holy Scripture is not subject to the laws of grammar. [...] I also blamed some of the defects the boy presented on the carelessness and negligence of the printer, even though the messenger who brought your book to Rome testified that it had been corrected by your own hand. The signs of this were indeed visible in the margins. Yet, since most of the boy's objections consisted in matters of orthography, I thought they should be given little weight.[82]

Not long after Paul dispatched his scathing riposte, Peter was ready to have his answer printed by Johannes de Westfalia, the same printer who had issued Paul's *Epistola apologetica* four years earlier. The tone of this publication, titled the *Tercius tractatus*, differed markedly from the anger and sarcasm that had pervaded Paul's letter. In response to Paul's claim that a teenage boy had publicly disparaged his abilities as a Latinist, Peter depicted himself as cool and unperturbed, but also reminded his former friend of the cruel fate that God held in store for those who mocked his prophets.

> Think not that I am made gloomy by the mockeries of boys (which you fear are a threat to me because of the barbarity of [my] speech) as long as it happens that my

---

[82] BMaz 300, fols. 300v–301r: "Antequam sermoni finem imponerem, quoniam rhetorice mentionem feceram, puer quidam, qui plus visus est sapere quam oportet, patrono suo casu assistens nundum XV annos natus, sciolus tamen gramaticellus, qui etiam ob novum tuum cyclum cunctis admirationi datum libellum tuum perlegerat, ad me conversus in hoc verba prorupit: 'Quid autumas hunc alios docuisse rhetoricam qui nundum ipse Latine loqui didicit? Profer libellum eius et centum barbarismos, soleocismos ac falsas latinitates tibi ostendam'. Ego vero, quoniam te omni litterarum genere doctissimum semper cognovi, tum etiam intuitu Lovaniensis studii, cuius me alumnum profitear, honorem tuum defendere conatus respondi sacram scripturam non subesse legibus grammaticalibus. Causatus etiam fui intui excusationem temporibus brevitatem quamquam turpem innuis libellum tuum secundo anno post nostram apologiam iam satis digestum multis lucubrationibus ruminatum a te in lucem editum fuisse. Nonnulla etiam vicia a puero obiecta impressoris incurie et nigligentie impegi, quamquam nuncius ille qui libellum tuum Romam attulit attestatus est eundem manu tua propria correctum fuisse. Eius etiam indicium in margine extabat. Verum quoniam plurima a puero obiecta in orthographia consistebant parvipendenda putavi."

little work on the date of the Lord's Passion is read by boys in Italy. What kind of harm did Elisha suffer from the words of those boys who in mocking him exclaimed "Go up, thou bald head, go up, thou bald head"? [2 Kings 2:23] None, of course, whereas they themselves [were harmed] in the gravest possible way, as seen from the story recounted in the fourth book of Kings.[83] Nor am I upset by the laughter that (as you write at the beginning) my writings, when they were seen in Rome, elicited from men skilled in the art of calculation. For based on the fifth book of Acts [5:40–41] I know that the apostles, when they had been scourged with whips, went from the presence of the council rejoicing that they were accounted worthy to suffer not just laughter, but reproach for the name of Christ. Truly, I swear by Jesus Christ, who knows the secrets of the hearts, that in putting together the said little work, I intended nothing other than his honour and that of his bride, our holy mother Church. When it comes, however, to the countless insults and ignominies that you assail me with so many times, hear just this: that they do not suffice to extinguish, nor even to diminish, the esteem that once made me fond of you. Instead, it is more after the fashion of aromatic substances, which breathe out much more sweetness when they are rubbed. I shall, therefore, try to do justice to your objections, if I can perhaps manage to do so, and do so with all gentleness, so that you may put aside your satirical habit [...] and at last become more affable and more civil, bit by bit.[84]

In the two chapters that followed this announcement,[85] Peter dissected Paul's lengthy letter almost sentence by sentence, trying his best to show that the objections voiced in it were either ill-conceived or had no true bearing on the validity of his general argument. In practice, this meant that the *Tercius tractatus* was a work rich in subtlety and attention to minute detail, but also one that often did remarkably little to move the debate forward. A fairly typical example concerns Peter's reading of the following passage in Suetonius's biography of Augustus (c. 31.1–2):[86]

---

[83]   The children were mauled by two she-bears. See 2 Kings 2:24.

[84]   *TerTra*, sig. ar: "Letissimus epistolam tuam suscepi, carissime me Paule, michi non secundum faciem, sed animo sincero dilecte. Neque putes quod me contristent puerorum illusiones (quas michi times imminere propter sermonis barbariem) dum opusculum meum de tempore dominice passionis a pueris in Italia legi contigerit. Quid puerorum verba nocuerunt Heliseo prophete que huius illudentes illi acclamabant 'Ascende calve, ascende calve'? Nichil sane, sed sibiipsis gravissime, velut quarti libri Regum pandit historia. Neque me risus ille conturbat quem (ut exordiens scribis) scripta mea Rome visa viris artem supputandi callentibus excusserunt. Novi quidem de apostolis, Actuum quinto, scriptum quod cesi flagellis *ibant gaudentes a conspectu concilii quoniam digni habiti sunt pro nomine* Christi (non modo risum), sed *contumeliam pati*. Testor nempe Ihesum Christum, qui secreta cordium pernovit, quod dictum opusculum conficiens nil aliud intendi quam illius honorem eiusque sponse sacrosancte matris ecclesie. De probris autem et ignominiis innumeris quibus me totiens impetis hoc unum audi quod per ea caritas (qua te pridem dilexi) nec extingui potuit, immo nec minui, magis autem est adinstar aromatum que quo teruntur magis plus suavitatis exalant. Propterea cum omni mansuetudine tuis obiectionibus conabor satisfacere, si forsan sic efficere possim, ut satiricum tuum morem deferens (quo hactenus consuesti singulos invadere, etiam te caritative monentes) tandem affabilior fias et paulatim mansuefias."

[85]   The third chapter of the *Tercius tractatus* was not addressed to Paul of Middelburg but instead dealt with a range of lesser objections that had been raised by Peter's students and friends.

[86]   See Suetonius, [*Lives of the Caesars*:] *Volume 1* (ed. and trans. Rolfe, 196–197).

After he finally had assumed the office of pontifex maximus on the death of Lepidus (for he could not make up his mind to deprive him of the honour while he lived) he collected whatever prophetic writings of Greek or Latin origin were in circulation anonymously or under the names of authors of little repute, and burned more than two thousand of them, retaining only the Sibylline books and making a choice even among those; and he deposited them in two gilded cases under the pedestal of the Palatine Apollo. Inasmuch as the calendar, which had been set in order by the Deified Julius, had later been confused and disordered through negligence, he restored it to its former system.

Postquam vero pontificatum maximum, quem numquam vivo Lepido auferre sustinuerat, mortuo demum suscepit, quidquid fatidicorum librorum Graeci Latinique generis nullis vel parum idoneis auctoribus vulgo ferebatur, supra duo milia contracta undique cremavit ac solos retinuit Sibyllinos, hos quoque dilectu habito; condiditque duobus forulis auratis sub Palatini Apollinis basi. Annum a Divo Iulio ordinatum, sed postea neglegentia conturbatum atque confusum, rursus ad pristinam rationem redegit.

In the *Opus responsivum* Peter had cited no more than a condensed version of the same passage, which merged the second sentence with the end of the previous one, creating a different sense:

After he had assumed the office of pontifex maximus he deposited in two gilded cases under the pedestal of the Palatine Apollo the calendar, which had been set in order by the Deified Julius, but later confused and disordered through negligence; he restored it to its former system.

Postquam pontificatum maximum suscepit condidit duobus forulis auratis sub Palatini Apollinis basi annum a divo Iulio ordinatum, sed postea negligentia turbatum et confusum: rursum ad pristinam ordinationem redegit.[87]

Following the sense of this modified version, Peter treated it as a given that Augustus had rectified the Julian calendar very soon after becoming *pontifex maximus,* which served to corroborate his assigning the original Julian reform to the beginning rather than the end of Caesar's reign. After all, it was known that the error had prevailed for a period of 36 years, whereas Eusebius's *Chronicle* indicated that Augustus already attained the high priesthood in the 31st year of his reign.[88] It is hardly surprising that Paul of Middelburg later accused Peter of misrepresenting Suetonius's account by falsely pretending that the object deposited in two gilded cases was a calendar rather than the Sibylline books.[89] More than that, Peter had committed a logical fallacy when he used

---

[87] *OpRes*, sig. d1r (tr. 2, c. 1, pt. 1).

[88] *OpRes*, sig. d1v (tr. 2, c. 1, pt. 1).

[89] BMaz 300, fol. 291r–v.

the mere fact that Suetonius says that Augustus reformed the calendar after taking up the pontificate to infer he did this in his first year, even though he spent 25 years as *pontifex*. Neither did you cite Suetonius correctly. For Suetonius says "After he finally had assumed the office of pontifex maximus" etc., thereby recording the things he did during his pontificate, that is, he relates his most important deeds not just during the first year of his pontificate, but during the entire duration of the pontificate.[90]

Far from admitting defeat on this score, Peter turned the tables on Paul by pointing out slight discrepancies between Paul's rendering of Suetonius's words and the way they appeared in the 1470 printed edition by Giovanni Andrea Bussi.[91] According to Paul's letter, the relevant two sentences had to be parsed as follows:

> *supra duo milia contracta undique concremavit ac solos retinuit Sybillinos, hos quoque delecto habito **condidit** duobus forulis auratis sub Palatini Appollinis basi. Annum **vero** a divo Iulio ordinatum, sed postea sacerdotum negligentia conturbatum atque confusum, rursus ad pristinam rationem redegit.*[92]

The printed text, Peter objected, had *condiditque* in place of *condidit* and contained no *vero* in *Annum vero a divo Iulio*. Depending on how interpunctuation was used, it was hence still possible to regard *condiditque duobus forulis auratis sub Palatini Appollinis basi annum a divo Iulio ordinatum* as part of one and the same clause.

> Who is so feebleminded that he does not understand that Suetonius used these words to indicate that Augustus, upon having been made *pontifex maximus*, deposited under the pedestal of the Palatine Apollo not the Sibylline books (as you say), but the year Caesar had established?[93]

Peter also denied that he had engaged in any fallacious reasoning, protesting that he had never meant his argument based on Suetonius to be demonstrative or logically stringent. Instead, the argument still worked on a rhetorical level, making it at least plausible that Augustus would have corrected the calendar in the first year of his pontificate. After all, what better reason could there have been for the Roman Sen-

---

90   BMaz 300, fol. 295r: "Non satis fuit semel falaciam consequentis commisisse, denuo reite-
ratanda erat, cum ex hoc solo quod Suetonius dicit Augustum post adeptum pontificatum kalendarium
reformasse infers hoc eum fecisse primo pontificatus sui anno, cum tamen 25 annis in pontificatu
vixerit. Nec recte Suetonium allegasti. Dicit enim Suetonius 'postquam vero pontificatum maximum
suscepit' etc. commemorans ea que in pontificatu gessit, non quidem primo dumtaxat anno pontificatus sui, sed toto tempore pontificatus precipua eius gesta exposuit."

91   C. Suetonius Tranquillus, *Vitae XII Caesarum*, ed. Giovanni Andrea Bussi (Rome: Conradus
Sweynheym and Arnoldus Pannartz, [after 30 Aug.] 1470).

92   BMaz 300, fol. 291v.

93   *TerTra*, sig. b5v (tr. 3, c. 2, pt. 1): "Quis, queso, mentis tam inops est, qui non intelligat Suetonium
his verbis significasse quod Augustus pontifex maximus factus sub basi Apollinis condidit non libros
Sibillinos (ut tu dicis), sed annum quem Iulium instituit?" Peter here conveniently ignored that the
printed edition made *Annum a divo Iulio* the beginning of a new sentence.

ate to appoint him to this high office, if not the fact that he had recently discovered an error in the calendar's intercalation pattern and offered a way to fix it?[94]

One area where Peter, by his own admission,[95] could not compete with his opponent was that of computational astronomy. When writing his *Opus responsivum*, he had tried to make up for his lack of experience by relying on the advice of Oliver Godelof, whom he repeatedly referred to as the man who had taught Paul of Middelburg the art of astronomical calculation.[96] The claim offended Paul, who wrote back insisting that he had received his introduction into astronomy not from Godelof, but from a friend in his hometown Middelburg and to have continued as an autodidact ever since.[97] Eager to assert his dominance in technical matters, he devoted the middle part of his letter to identifying computational mistakes in Peter's work. He managed to score an easy point by noting that the astronomical data Godelof had provided for the year AD 34 failed to take account of Peter's own hypothesis according to which the fourth-century Church had altered the Julian solar cycle by suppressing a bissextile day. If this reform was factored in, the conjunction of Nisan in AD 34 came to fall on 8 March, which meant that it could no longer be used against Paul's claim that 22 March in the year of Christ's death was the eve of Passover.[98]

A more serious charge on Paul's part was that Godelof had managed to bungle the syzygy calculation that was supposed to support his argument according to which the Julian calendar began on 1 January 45 BC. According to the *Opus responsivum*, the standard astronomical tables placed the true conjunction on the first day of the year, yet Paul insisted that the actual date provided by the Alfonsine Tables was 2 January.[99] Peter exploded this objection by pointing out that Paul's calculation was predicated on the conventional solar cycle and hence on the notion that 45 BC had been a bissextile year, whereas his own hypothesis assumed that the Julian calendar had begun in a common year with the dominical letter *A*. Not only could Godelof's conjunction date stand, but it continued to support Peter's idea that the conjunction preceded the beginning of the Julian calendar. After all, the loss of a bissextile day some time after Christ's death meant that the original date of this conjunction shifted to 31 December.[100]

An issue just as fundamental as the original shape of the Julian calendar was the origin and purpose of the Golden Numbers that adorned medieval versions of this calendar. Throughout the *Tercius tractatus*, Peter remained firm in his original

---

94   *TerTra*, sigs. b5v–6r (tr. 3, c. 2, pt. 1).

95   *TerTra*, sig. c2r (tr. 3, c. 2, pt. 3).

96   *OpRes*, sigs. b7r–v (tr. 1, c. 2, pt. 9), d5v (tr. 2, c. 1, pt. 6).

97   BMaz 300, fol. 294r. Peter eventually apologized for his remarks. See *TerTra*, sig. bv (tr. 3, c. 1, pt. 6).

98   BMaz 300, fol. 298r.

99   BMaz 300, fols. 293v–295r.

100   *TerTra*, sigs. c2v–c4r (tr. 3, c. 2, pt. 3), dv (tr. 3, c. 2, pt. 7).

assumption that the Golden Numbers were an Egyptian institution that the Israelites had taken with them when they left the country under Moses's leadership. He also continued to criticize Paul for his stubborn insistence on solving the Passion problem by astronomical means, without regard for the fact that the Jews used a "legal" definition of the age of the Moon that deviated from astronomical reality. Unlike Paul, who had been led astray by a spurious calendrical text transmitted under the name of Gamaliel, Peter believed he had managed to discover the true historical *computus* of the ancient Hebrews, whose rules made it possible to prove that 25 March AD 34 had indeed been the 15th day of the lunar month in the Jewish calendar.[101] Paul naturally begged to differ, although his first letter of response had been too focused on the history of the Julian calendar to allow much room for discussing Peter's hypothesis of a Hebrew *cyclus lunaris* connected to the familiar tableau of Golden Numbers. He accordingly deferred his refutation of this component of Peter's argument until he found the occasion to write a second letter, which only survives thanks to its later inclusion in the *Paulina de recta Paschae celebratione et de die passionis Domini nostri Iesu Christi*, a monumental tome on chronological and calendrical matters Paul published in 1513.[102] Since the relevant chapter of the *Paulina* also features the first letter, but in a heavily redacted form,[103] its rendering of the second letter must be treated with a healthy dose of caution. To judge from the text in its printed form, the letter in question had only been dispatched after Paul had seen the *Tercius tractatus*, which he quotes at several occasions. This suggests a date in late 1492 or even 1493.

Similar to the first letter, Paul's second attack devoted considerable space to small points of calendrical or astronomical detail, which were ultimately there to paint his opponent as a lamentable ignoramus, one who remained unlettered in the art of *computus* despite having invested 30 years in the construction of his chronological system. When it came to the substance of their disagreement, Paul homed in on Peter's idea that the Jews of the first century AD used a lunar cycle that was historically connected to the ancient Egyptian calendar. In the *Opus responsivum*, Peter had used Flavius Josephus's claim that the biblical patriarch Abraham taught arithmetic and astronomy to the Egyptians to support his own conjecture according to which the principles of lunar reckoning first arrived in Egypt when Abraham migrated there.[104] Owing to this knowledge transfer, the Egyptians now disposed of a calendar endowed with Golden Numbers, which identified the dates when Sun and Moon were in conjunction. The first year of the corresponding cycle was the 82nd year of Abraham's life (1933 BC), in which the conjunctions fell on or

---

[101] *TerTra*, sigs. a5v–a7v (tr. 3, c. 1, pt. 3–4), b2r–b3r (tr. 3, c. 1, pt. 6), d2v–d3r (tr. 3, c. 2, pt. 8), e5r–e6v (tr. 3, c. 3, pt. 10).

[102] *Paulina*, sigs. I5v–K8v. This letter has the incipit "Peior est si philosophis creditur..."

[103] *Paulina*, sigs. G8v–I5r.

[104] *OpRes*, sig. b2r (tr. 1, c. 2, pt. 3); Flavius Josephus, *Antiquitates Judaicae* 1.167 (ed. Blatt, 145).

next to the dates marked by the Golden Number 1. When the Israelites left Egypt in the year of the Exodus, it was natural for them to adopt this system for the purpose of calculating Passover, although its accuracy diminished over time. Peter speculated that they continued to use the existing cycle for nine centuries, during which the conjunctions would have shifted by approximately three days relative to the Golden Numbers. The necessary correction was carried out during the reign of King David, who made a decision to re-set the cycle by counting the current year as the first rather than the 17th year of the cycle. As in the *Dyalogus*, Peter supported this hypothesis by reference to the Book of Ecclesiasticus (47:12), which stated that David "added beauty to the festivals and set in order the solemn times even to the end of his life."[105] He linked this passage to 1 Chronicles 23–29, which described in some detail how David reformed the divine services and planned the building of the first temple.

> By doing so, he added beauty to the festivals. And how could he have set in order the solemn times more beautifully than by passing down a lunar cycle by which they could know the new moons of the months and the days of the individual feasts of the Law? I consider this cycle to have been the lunar cycle of the Hebrews.[106]

Paul's response to this revelation was loaded with sneer:

> O what splendid line of argument, made firm by conjectures [...]! O what admirable discourse, truly worthy of the greatest theologian! "David set in order the solemn times, therefore he composed a lunar cycle." Quite as if one were to say: "David set in order the solemn times, therefore an ass can fly."[107]

Paul went on to respond that any theologian worth his salt would have been content with connecting David's act of ordering the solemn times with his documented reforms of the divine cult, in particular the increase of the musicians mentioned in 1 Chronicles 25. The same kind of non-sequitur was detectable in Peter's jump from "Abraham taught the Egyptians astronomy," as attested in Josephus, to the conclusion that, therefore, he must have taught them the lunar cycle. Not only was the basic argument fallacious, but there were serious doubts about the reliability of Josephus's testimony. After all, did not Herodotus (*Histories* 2.4) testify that the Egyptians were the first nation to have used a calendar?[108] That said, the most obvi-

---

[105] *OpRes*, sig. b2v (tr. 1, c. 2, pt. 3).

[106] *OpRes*, sig. b2v (tr. 1, c. 2, pt. 3): "Hec faciens dedit in celebrationibus decus. Et quomodo pulcrius potuisset ornare tempora quam tradendo ciclum lunarem per quem nosci possent neomenie mensium diesque singularum festivitatum legalium? Quem ciclum arbitror fuisse ciclum lunarem Hebreorum."

[107] *Paulina*, sig. I8r–v: "O praeclaram ratiocinationem per coniecturas stabilitam, & per aestimo corroboratam quod rectius latine existimo dixisses, O admirabile dicursum summo theologo profecto dignum. 'David ornavit tempora ergo cyclum lunarem conscripsit', ac si dicatur 'David ornavit tempora ergo asinus volat'."

[108] *Paulina*, sig. I8v.

ous reason why Peter's scenario deserved no credence was hidden in the demonstrable history of the Egyptian calendar, which for most of its course had comprised no more than 365 days per year without intercalation. There had accordingly been no way for Abraham or anyone else to inscribe in this calendar the Golden Numbers of the 19-year cycle, which depended on the Julian year length and, hence, on the inclusion of 4 3/4 bissextile days per average cycle. The old Egyptian version of the lunar cycle, as Paul correctly explained by referring to the tables included in Ptolemy's *Almagest* (6.3), had instead been based on a period of 25 years. Peter's belief that Abraham furnished the Egyptian calendar with the Golden Numbers and the 19-year cycle was clearly false

> because this cycle is not consistent with the old calendar of the Egyptians, who did not restore the day that results from the quarter-day excess, but instead it matches the calendar of the Alexandrians, who intercalated in every fourth year. It is a fact, however, that Alexandria had not yet been founded in Abraham's time. Indeed, there were no Jews yet in Abraham's time, nor had Passover been established.[109]

4.   The Aftermath

Leaving aside for a moment the merits of the individual arguments that went back and forth between Peter de Rivo and Paul of Middelburg in 1488 and 1492, it should have become clear that the debate they engaged in during these years involved a clash not only of personal temperaments, but also of different methodologies. At the heart of the argument Peter made in 1471 and again—in somewhat modified form—in 1488 was the premise that the conventional view, according to which Jesus died on a Friday and rose again on a Sunday, could be true if and only if the solar cycle attached to the Julian calendar had been altered at some stage after the year of the crucifixion. Accepting as authoritative the traditions of his Church, as enshrined in the liturgy of Good Friday, Peter believed it justifiable to affirm the consequent ("Jesus died on a Friday"). Having thus established that the mentioned calendar change had really taken place, Peter was left with the task of constructing a plausible story as to how and why it had come about.[110] Paul of Middelburg made no secret out of the fact that he was appalled by this sort of argument, which put

---

[109]   *Paulina*, sig. Kr: "[F]alsum est igitur quod autumas Abraham primum hunc cyclum lunarem, & aureum numerum inscripsisse calendario Aegyptiorum, quia cyclus iste non est consentaneus prisco illi calendario Aegyptiorum, qui non instaurabant diem ex quadrantibus resultantem, sed congruit calendario Alexandrinorum, qui quarto quoque anno intercalabant. Constat autem Alexandriam tempore Abrahae nondum fuisse conditam, quinimmo tempore Abrahae nondum erant Iudaei, neque pascha fuit institutum."

[110]   In logical terms, Peter's argument went as follows: (1) If Jesus died on a Friday, the Julian calendar must have been changed after his death; (2) Jesus died on a Friday; (3) Therefore, the Julian calendar must have been changed after his death. See *OpRes*, sigs. d4v–d5r (tr. 2, c. 1, pt. 6); *TerTra*, sigs. c7r–dv (tr. 3, c. 2, pt. 7).

logical reasoning in place of solid historical evidence.[111] According to his way of framing things, the idea that Christ died on a Friday was not in dispute as a matter of faith, but in order to assert it as historical fact, the believer had to be able to demonstrate it by properly historical means. This could in principle include the use of astronomical-calendrical reckoning, to ensure that the data found in historical sources agreed with the course of the heavens. That such a demonstration had never been performed successfully was one of the central points made in the *Epistola apologetica* and continued to feature prominently in his later writings.

Beyond this methodological fault line, it is difficult to overlook that Peter and Paul moved to a certain extent in different scholarly cultures. For all his forays into history and astronomy, Peter's writings on chronology remained beholden to the scholasticism practiced at the University of Leuven, both in their verbal style and their use of authorities, which were predominantly patristic or drawn from the standard bookshelf of the medieval university. In this he contrasted markedly with Paul, whose many years of work and leisure in Italy had provided him with the opportunity to immerse himself in the biblical humanism that had already been spreading south of the Alps. This training manifested itself in a more artful register of written Latin, but also in the ambition to exploit rare or previously un-known sources in Greek, Hebrew, and even Aramaic.[112] Paul's superior command of ancient literature put him in a position to undermine the credibility of Peter's theses concerning the history of the Julian calendar, while his familiarity with the intricacies of both the Easter *computus* and mathematical astronomy made it easy for him to debunk the idea of a Hebrew *cyclus lunaris* tied to an ancient Egyptian set of Golden Numbers.

With all this said, Paul was clearly more successful at poking holes in Peter's hypotheses than in defending the numerous contentious claims contained in the *Epistola apologetica*, which had come under fire not just from Peter de Rivo, but also from the eminent Thomas Basin.[113] In the various letters he wrote in his defence, Paul insisted repeatedly and with vehemence that he had never done more than to entertain hypotheses and that it was a calumnious lie for his opponents to claim that he ever asserted with any confidence Christ's death on a Monday or that 22 March was the definitive date of the crucifixion.[114] He also came to realize, however, that, in order to silence his critics and to absolve himself of the charges they had levelled against him, he had to do more than just cast doubt on the consensus view. His best

---

[111] Paul takes Peter to task for his logic both in his first letter of 1492 and the letter he sent to Leuven in 1494. See BMaz 300, fols. 296r, 303v–304r.

[112] See, for instance, Paul's *Paschalis supputationis ratio triplici lingua*, BMaz 300, fol. 320r, where he testifies to having sifted through various libraries owned by Jews, leading him to discover an Aramaic text on the Jewish calendar.

[113] See n. 2 above.

[114] Paul does so in his letter to Thomas Basin, in his first letter to Peter de Rivo, and in his 1494 letter to the University of Leuven. See BMaz 300, fols. 260v, 297r–298v, 300r–v, 304r–v.

line of defence was to provide a constructive solution to the Passion problem, one that—unlike Peter de Rivo's attempt—was supported by sound historical evidence.

As far as the extant sources allow us to conclude, Paul of Middelburg pursued such a solution in a chronological treatise composed of 24 books. Its existence is mentioned in a letter he addressed in 1494 to the doctors of the University of Leuven, which advertised the work in question as one that investigated the date of the crucifixion according to every available type of calendrical calculation (Latin, Greek, Hebrew, Aramaic, Egyptian, and Arabic).[115] Although the original work remains lost, it is very likely that substantial parts of it were later carried over into the second half of the *Paulina*, the magnificent 800-page compendium of calendrical and chronological investigations Paul was to publish two decades later in collaboration with the printer Ottaviano Petrucci.[116] The *Paulina* comprise a total of 33 books, a number that was supposed to mirror the complete years Christ dwelled in the flesh. Of these, the first 14 (corresponding to Christ's years during the reign of Augustus) are devoted to the reckoning of Easter and the reform of the ecclesiastical calendar.[117] The remaining 19 (representing Christ's years during the reign of Tiberius) make up an extremely complex disquisition on the crucifixion date and related issues of New Testament chronology. The overall thesis developed and defended in this part of the *Paulina* was that Christ's crucifixion took place not in AD 34, as Paul had still accepted at the time of writing the *Epistola apologetica*, but in AD 36. This two-year shift paid a decisive dividend insofar as the spring full moon in AD 36 fell on a Friday. Although the date of this full moon, 30 March, was not the same as the orthodox crucifixion date, it at least made it possible to maintain that Christ died on a Friday at the time of Passover, and in the month of March rather than April.[118]

Paul of Middelburg drew no such overt conclusion in his letter of 1494, but merely alluded to it by claiming that a two-year correction of the common *Annus Domini* era carried within it the long-desired solution to the Passion problem. Still, the arguments he presented in favour of this correction were in all essential parts similar to those later deployed in the *Paulina*, which strengthens the impression that the latter work drew much inspiration from his exchange with Peter de Rivo two decades earlier. A clear example of this influence may be discerned in the way Paul seized upon a note in Eusebius's *Chronicle*, which stated that a solar eclipse had taken place in the year of Augustus's death.[119] Long before Paul dealt with this

---

[115] BMaz 300, fols. 301v, 304v.

[116] Boorman, *Ottaviano Petrucci*, 724–740.

[117] For summaries of this section, see Kaltenbrunner, "Die Vorgeschichte," 375–385; Marzi, *La questione della riforma*, 53–72; Steinmetz, *Die Gregorianische Kalenderreform*, 64–66.

[118] *Paulina*, sigs. V2v–X3v. The 30th of March as a suggested crucifixion date is first attested in Peter Diaconus's *Liber de viris illustribus*, who reports that this was the date put forward in a lost work by Pandulphus of Capua. See Cordoliani, "Le comput ecclésiastique," 72–73.

[119] This solar eclipse, which first appears in Cassius Dio, *Roman History* 56.29.3, was probably an erroneous reminiscence of the lunar eclipse on 26 September AD 14. See Demandt, *Verformungstendenzen*, 49.

eclipse in his *Paulina*, its potential had already been noticed by Peter de Rivo, who in his *Tercius tractatus* claimed that an old childhood friend, who also happened to be an astronomer, had pointed out to him that the Alfonsine Tables indicated a total eclipse of the Sun on 15 February AD 17 at the coordinates of Rome. Peter notes that this revelation made him doubt the accuracy of his chronology more so than any of the objections Paul of Middelburg had hurled in his direction. It appears that he was troubled by the fact that a count of Augustus's regnal years that began from 1 January 41 BC would have put this eclipse in the 58th year, which clashed with Suetonius's testimony that the *princeps* died on 19 August in his 57th regnal year. Upon consulting with Oliver Godelof, Peter was offered an attractive alternative in the guise of an annular eclipse on 21 August AD 16. This seemed to match the historically attested date of Augustus's death almost perfectly.[120]

As Paul was to argue in the thirteenth book of the second part of his *Paulina*, the eclipse of AD 16 was an historical mirage, since it would not have been visible from anywhere near the Mediterranean. Rather than using this feeble eclipse to prop up the conventional chronology, it was expedient to go with the one Peter had spurned and therefore conclude that Augustus died some months after the eclipse of 15 February AD 17.[121] Using this eclipse as a chronological linchpin, Paul developed an intricate argument to the effect that the years the Eusebian *Chronicle* put down for Augustus's reign failed to take into account a period of two years immediately after Julius Caesar's assassination, during which Augustus and the other triumvirs established their power over Rome. Once these two years were re-inserted into Roman chronology, it became clear that the 42nd year of Augustus, to which Eusebius and other authorities assigned Christ's nativity, began in AD 3 (rather than AD 1).[122]

Paul's letter of 1494 presented this same argument in a strongly condensed form, noting that a fuller treatment of the matter could be found in the treatise he had written against his critics. In an odd and unexpected turn of events, Paul decided to preface his chronological argument by narrating how its correctness had been confirmed by a vision he had experienced the night before in his sleep, which involved two bedside visits by Mercury and St John Chrysostom. Each of the two visitors addressed Paul in a separate monologue, with Mercury playing the role of a shoulder devil, who tried to dissuade him from sending any more of his chronological writings to Leuven. In doing so, he warned Paul of the machinations of his opponent Peter de Rivo, reminding him that the entire university was under his sway. It was also Mercury who named Peter as the person responsible for having suppressed

[120]   *TerTra*, sig. c3r–v (tr. 3, c. 3, pt. 8).
[121]   *Paulina*, sigs. T2v–3r.
[122]   See BMaz 300, fols. 303r, 304v–305r, and the more extensive discussion in *Paulina*, sigs. T3v–V2r. In Nothaft, *Dating the Passion*, 240, 247, 283, Paul's intended nativity year is mistakenly identified as AD 2.

the 24 books Paul had sent to Leuven the previous year. Even Paul's own friends, who had received copies of the work, were too afraid of Peter's arrogance to dare bring it to light. Worse than that, Peter continued to incite Leuven's doctors against him, using flattery on some and threats on others. Mercury's message was clear: "interrupt, therefore, your work by the lampshade, because you have appointed your false accuser as your judge!"[123] John Chrysostom played the opposing tune, not just by encouraging Paul to share the fruits of his scholarship, but by furnishing him with the proof necessary to demonstrate that the chroniclers had been counting two years too many since Christ's birth.[124]

That Paul would put his own words into the golden mouth of St Chrysostom was certainly no coincidence. More so than the fact that the supposed revelation took place on the night of 13 September, Chrysostom's feast day in the Roman Church, Paul's choice appears to have been dictated by his intention publicly to accuse Peter de Rivo of misquoting Chrysostom's *Homilies in Matthew*. In the first chapter of the *Opus responsivum*, Peter had adduced a passage in these homilies to support the opinion that Jesus had already reached the age of 30 when he was baptized. The quote in question was taken verbatim from Anianus of Celeda's fifth-century Latin translation of Chrysostom's *Homilies in Matthew*, although Peter committed the slight mistake of locating the saint's words in the eleventh rather than the tenth homily.[125] Paul did what he could to use Peter's small mistake to his own advantage and even made the bold claim that the saint who appeared to him last night categorically denied his authorship of any of the words the Leuven professor had attributed to him. More than that, he alleged that Chrysostom had ordered him to write to the university one more time

> so that all may understand that this eminent censor of yours not only attacked you with the false claim that you asserted that the Lord and Saviour was not crucified on a Friday, but that he also ascribed several falsehoods to me and alleged that I wrote things that he will never find in my writings.[126]

---

[123] BMaz 300, fol. 302r: "Disrumpe ergo lucubrationes tuas, quia calumniatorem tuum tibi iudicem constituisti."

[124] BMaz 300, fols. 302r–303r.

[125] Peter de Rivo, *OpRes*, sig a5r (tr. 1, c. 1, pt. 1): "Preterea Crisostomus idem sensit, unde omelia undecima super Matheum ait sic: 'cuius, inquies, rei gratia post triginta annos Christus venit ad baptisma? Quia scilicet post baptisma istud legem erat veterem soluturus. Propterea usque in hanc etatem que omnia capere potest peccata in legis observatione permansit, ne quis eum diceret legem solvisse, quia eam non valuisset implere'." For the source text, see John Chrysostom, *Opera* (Venice: Bernardino Stagnino, 1503), fol. 16r; cf. also John Chrysostom, *Homiliae in Matthaeum* 10.1 (PG 57, cols. 183–184). In the *Dyalogus* (tr. 1, c. 2 [ll. 60–64]), Peter had still cited this passage second-hand, using Peter Comestor's *Historia scholastica*.

[126] BMaz 300, fol. 302r: "Etsi magna ex parte vera sint que Mercurius tibi intimavit, ne desistas tamen cepta perficere, immo denuo scripta tua Lovanium transmitte, ut omnes intelligant quod egregius ille tuus censor non solum tibi falso impegerit te asseruisse dominum salvatorem die Veneris crucifixum non fuisse, verum etiam mihi falsa nonnulla imposuit et a me scripta asseruit que numquam in scriptis meis inveniet."

Whatever Paul may have been thinking when he depicted such nocturnal visions, his letter of 1494 was neither the first nor the last time he resorted to detailed descriptions of dream oracles to bolster or elucidate his claims. Already in 1480 Paul had included in one of his annual prognostications an account of how a visit from Mercury had inspired him to issue a challenge to Italy's astrologers by posting a list of 100 astronomical and mathematical questions.[127] Another intriguing case is the tenth chapter of the second part of his *Paulina*, where it is no longer John Chrysostom, but St Paul the Apostle who presents Paul with a magnificent vision of the crucifixion scene, which happens to encapsulate virtually all of the chronological arguments made in the remainder of the *Paulina*.[128] It is perhaps more than a bit revealing to find that the content and interpretation of this vision differed significantly from yet another dream oracle Paul had reported back in 1497, in what was his third and presumably final letter to Peter de Rivo. For reasons that are unclear, Paul here reneged on the chronological thesis he had defended in 1494 and would again defend in 1513, claiming instead that the solution to the Passion problem was essentially the same as that proposed centuries ago by Marianus Scottus and Sigebert of Gembloux, who had argued that the crucifixion happened in AD 12 and that the Dionysic era of the incarnation was short by 22 years. Paul sought to support this proposition with a fresh chronological argument, which asserted that Eusebius's *Chronicle* had omitted the reigns of several popes, to the extent that 22 years since the birth of Christ remained unaccounted for. As in his previous letter of 1494, Paul alleged that the fundamentals of this argument had been revealed to him in his sleep by a man carrying the insignia of Paul the Apostle, who made him contemplate a vision showing all Roman pontiffs from Peter to Silvester I.[129]

Aside from its technical contribution to the debate, the letter Paul sent to Peter in 1497 could be read as a thinly veiled attempt to provoke the Leuven professor into resuming their argument. In line with this goal, Paul devoted multiple lines to expressing his disappointment at not having received a formal response to his letter of 1494 and the dream oracle it described. He claimed to have learned from trustworthy informants that Peter had denounced the oracle of St Chrysostom as a demonic visitation, "and yet I have not been able to elicit from anyone a [written]

---

[127]   Paul of Middelburg, *Prognosticon anni 1480* (Venice: Adam de Rottweil, 1479/80), sig. b4r–v. See Baldi, *Le vite de' matematici* (ed. Nenci, 359–364); Federici Vescovini, "Su un genere," 77–83; Heilen, "Astrology at the Court of Urbino," 340–342.

[128]   *Paulina*, sigs. Pr–6r. See Gamba, *Le stelle sopra Urbino*, 69–72, 107–109; Grafton, "Mixed Messages," 332–334.

[129]   BMaz 300, fol. 307r–v. The sequence of popes up to Silvester I is also an element of the vision described in the *Paulina*, although Paul eventually rejected the conclusion that 22 years were missing from the chronographic record. See Paul of Middelburg, *Paulina*, sigs. P4v, P6r–7v. The contradiction between the dream oracles of 1494 and 1497 was already remarked upon by the Flemish grammarian Christian Massaeus, who paraphrased their content in the prologue to one of the books of his twenty-book chronicle, published in 1540. See Christian Massaeus, *Chronicorum multiplicis historiae utriusque testamenti ... libri viginti* (Antwerp: Joannes Crinitus, 1540), 91.

copy of your calumny, since everyone asserts unanimously that you merely punched the air and completely failed to take up the quill."[130] Whether these words were fair or not, the impression remains that the *Tercius tractatus* of 1492 had been conceived from the outset as Peter's final word in the tiresome quarrel that had begun in 1488. Rather than indulging his opponent's desire to continue the debate, Peter found it preferable to retreat and let the feisty Zeelander continue to spew his invective into the void.

Paul, for his part, eventually included his first two letters to Peter in his printed *Paulina*, notwithstanding the fact that they contributed rather little to his overall argument. The first 14 books of this famous work would showcase their author as an unrivalled expert on the ecclesiastical calendar, its history, and the means of its correction. In 1514, the year following its publication, Paul was summoned to Rome by Pope Leo X, who wanted him to preside over an effort to reform the calendar in the context of the Fifth Lateran Council (1512–1517). The project ended in disappointment, although it earned Paul a mention in Copernicus's *De revolutionibus orbium coelestium* and generally secured his fame among subsequent generations.[131] In December 1534, the aged bishop of Fossombrone travelled to Rome with the expectation of receiving a cardinal's hat from the newly elected Pope Paul III, but died a week after his arrival.[132]

While the first part of the *Paulina* had a seminal influence on the sixteenth-century debate surrounding the ecclesiastical calendar, the second part was destined to be regarded as a pioneering contribution to the emerging discipline of historical chronology, one that was by no means confined to questions pertaining to the life of Jesus.[133] Those who continued to pursue such questions in the sixteenth and seventeenth centuries were far more likely to consult Paul's *Paulina*, with their numerous jibes at Peter de Rivo,[134] than to examine the arguments contained in Peter's *Dyalogus de temporibus Christi* or even his *Opus responsivum*. As a result, his own role as a chronological trailblazer was quickly forgotten.

---

[130]   BMaz, fol. 306r: "Expectans expectavi iamdiu a tua excellentia responsionem ad epistolam nostram iampridem ad academiam Lovaniensem et ad te datam super divi Crisostomi oraculo et cronographorum errore in annis domini numerandis conscriptam, quam, ut a fide dignis accepi, palam in scolis tuis reprehendisti et criminatus fuisti, nundum tamen ex aliquo copiam calumnie tue elicere potui, cum unanimiter omnes asserant te aerem dumtaxat verberasse et calamum haudquaquam sumpsisse testetur." See also ibid., fol. 306v, where it is mentioned that Peter had dismissed the oracles mentioned in the letter of 1494 as demonic.

[131]   For details, see Marzi, *La questione della riforma*, 72–223; Nothaft, *Scandalous Error*, 286–290.

[132]   Baldi, *Le vite de' matematici* (ed. Nenci, 393).

[133]   On the continuation of the chronological debate in the sixteenth century, see Nothaft, *Dating the Passion*, 241–275. See also the references to Paul of Middelburg in Grafton, *Joseph Scaliger*, 101–102, 105, 181–182, 235, 238–239.

[134]   See *Paulina*, sigs. e7v, k6v–7r, n5v, L8v, T3r, and the two letters printed ibid., sigs. G8r–K8v.

5. Appendix: Texts Relating to Paul of Middelburg in MS Paris, Bibliothèque Mazarine, 300

Our single most important witness to the chronological disputes Paul of Middelburg and Peter de Rivo were engaged in between 1488 and 1497 is a codex of 369 folios now held by the Bibliothèque Mazarine, Paris.[135] It was written in the early sixteenth century at the Rood-Klooster, an Augustinian priory of the Windesheim Congregation located outside Brussels. The first 79 leaves of this neatly written and decorated book are occupied by a heavily revised version of Peter's *Monotesseron*, an intricate harmony of the four Gospels centred on the Gospel of Luke.[136] The Rood-Klooster version of this massive work was the brainchild of the local canon Thierry Bezudens, whose letter justifying the revisions appears in the same codex on fols. 143r–148v. It is preceded and followed by copious supplementary material, some of which was meant to provide a memory aid with respect to the structure and content of Peter's work and the four Gospels themselves (fols. 80r–142v, 149r–160r). A thematically closely related text, St Augustine's *De consensu evangelistarum*, makes up the second part of the manuscript (fols. 162v–242r), while the third part consists of a sequence of texts spawned by Paul of Middelburg's controversies with Thomas Basin and Peter de Rivo (fols. 246v–322r). Bound together with these is a printed copy of the *Opus responsivum* Peter de Rivo published in c.1489 with the assistance of Ludovicus Ravescot (fols. 325r–369v). The full list of relevant texts is as follows:

1. fols. 246v–260r: *Epistola apologetica magistri Pauli de Middelburgo ad Lovaniensem universitatem de paschate observando, de die passionis et mora Christi in sepulchro.* Inc.: "Estate preterita, cum ex Ytalia rediens…" A handwritten copy of the *Epistola apologetica* Paul of Middelburg signed on 27 February 1488 and committed to print in Leuven that same year. This copy omits certain paragraphs, indicating their absence by leaving parts of individual pages blank (fols. 247v, 248r, 249v). Its main purpose was in fact not to present the *Epistola apologetica* itself, but to display Thomas Basin's critical glosses (or *postillae*) on this text, which adorn the margins of most pages.

2. fols. 260r–264v: *Epistola magistri Pauli de Middelburgo ad archiepiscopum Cesariensem in qua malam opinionem quam habuit de scriptis suis partim submovet.* Inc.: "Paulus de Middelburgo Reverendissimo in Christo patri, domino archiepiscopo Cesariensis salutem dicit. Nudiustertius nonnulle tua commenta ad manus meas devenere…" A letter Paul of Middelburg

---

[135] Coll, de Conihout, Grand, and Lanoë, *Reliures médiévales*, no. 9.
[136] For more on the *Monotesseron*, see Champion, *The Fullness of Time*, 137–149; Champion, "'To See Beyond the Moment'," 200–201, 211–219; Masolini, "Petrus de Rivo," 91–109; Masolini, "How to Order Four into One."

wrote to Thomas Basin in order to defend himself against the charges contained in Basin's *postillae* on the *Epistola apologetica*. The letter was signed in Urbino on 25 March (fol. 264v), but the year is not given. Since Basin died on 3 December 1490, the year of the letter was probably 1490 or 1489, but hardly 1488, seeing as the *Epistola apologetica* was only completed on 27 February of that year.

3. fols. 264v–290r: *Epistola responsiva archiepiscopi Cesariensis ad epistolam precedentem*. Inc.: "Cum ad nos, Paule, tuam allatam nobisque scriptam nuper legissemus epistolam..." Thomas Basin's letter of response to the preceding letter by Paul of Middelburg. In the preface Basin indicates that he has nearly reached the 80th year of his life (fol. 264v: "...et gratias Deo usque prope octogesimum etatis annum pervenimus"). Since Basin was born in 1412, this may point to 1490 as the year of writing. Basin still had time to adapt and expand this letter into a lengthy treatise *Contra errores et blasphemias Pauli de Middelburgo* (Inc.: "Cum ad nos, Paule, epistola tua nuper ex Zelandia allata fuisset..."),[137] which suggests a period of several months between the letter's completion and Basin's death on 3 December 1490.

4. fols. 290v–301r: *Epistola magistri Pauli de Middelburgo extemporanea responsionem continens ad libellum quem magister Petrus de Rivo in eum scripsit*. Inc. (1): "Doctissimo viro sacre theologie professori..." Inc. (2): "Risum profecto non mediocrem scripta tua..." Paul of Middelburg's first letter of response to Peter de Rivo's *Opus responsivum*. It is dated 20 February 1492. A redacted version of the same letter was printed in 1513 as part of the *Paulina*.[138]

5. fols. 301r–306r: *Ad prestantissimos Lovaniensis gymnasii doctores almamque studiosorum achademi matrem Pauli de Middelburgo alumni in sancti Iohannis Crisostomi oraculum lucubratio*. Inc.: "Paulus ille Tarsensis vocatus apostolus a perfidis Iudeis apud presidem Iherosolimorum accusatus..." A letter Paul of Middelburg sent to the University of Leuven on 14 September 1494, the day after the feast of St John Chrysostom.[139]

6. fols. 306r–308v: *Epistola magistri Pauli de Middelburgo ad magistrum Petrum de Rivo, in qua petivit responsiones super oraculo pretacto*. Inc. (1): "Paulus de Middelburgo Dei et apostolice sedis gratia episcopus Forosemproniensis venerabili in Christo patri tamquam fratri dilecto magistro Petro de Rivo..." Inc. (2): "Expectans expectavi iamdiu a tua excellentia

---

137   MS Paris, Bibliothèque nationale de France, lat. 3658 (100 fols.).
138   *Paulina*, sigs. G8v–I5r.
139   The opening paragraph of this letter was repeated in the preface to bk. 2, c. 8 of the *Paulina* (sig. L8v).

responsionem ad epistolam nostram..." Paul of Middelburg's final letter to Peter de Rivo, dated Pentecost 1497.

7.   fols. 308v–322r: *Paschalis supputationis ratio triplici lingua, Greca scilicet, Hebraica Chaldaicaque conscripta et in Latinum versa per magistrum Paulum de Middelburgo, missa domino Johanni, abbati Middelburgensi.* Inc.: "Paulus de Middelburgo Zelandie reverendo in Christo patri domino Iohanni abbati Middelburgensi salutem. Nullum esse detestabilius..." This undated work begins with an epistolary preface addressed to Jan van Westkapelle, abbot of Middelburg, in which Paul complains about the attacks he had to sustain on account of his chronological writings. What follows is a treatise in three separate parts, of which the first (fols. 309r–314r) carries a separate dedication to Guidobaldo da Montefeltro, Duke of Urbino. It presents Paul's translation of a Greek text by a certain Nicetas, who dated the birth of Jesus to *Annus Mundi* 5506 (= 25 December 4 BC) and his resurrection to *Annus Mundi* 5539 (= 25 March AD 31). The text itself is prefaced by an introduction and summary, parts of which reappear verbatim in Paul's *Paulina*.[140] Parts II (fols. 314v–320r) and III (fols. 320r–322r) are once again dedicated to Jan van Westkapelle. The first is Paul's translation of a Hebrew work on the Jewish calendar ascribed to Gamaliel, which he had already mentioned in the *Epistola apologetica*.[141] The second is a similar work translated from Aramaic and attributed to a certain Eliezer (*Heleazarus*). Paul later re-used parts of these translations and their respective introductions for the extensive discussion of the Jewish calendar contained in his *Paulina*, printed in 1513.[142]

8.   fols. 325r–369v: *Opus magistri Petri de Rivo, sacre theologie professoris, legentis in universitate Lovaniensi, responsivum ad Epistolam apologeticam M. Pauli de Middelburgo de anno, die et feria dominice passionis.* This is a complete copy of the incunabulum printed by Ludovicus Ravescot in Leuven. All woodcuts and initials were carefully coloured by hand.

---

[140]   *Paulina*, sigs. F8v–G2r.
[141]   Paul first references this text in *EpApol*, sigs. A7v–8r.
[142]   *Paulina*, sigs. Mr–O8v.

Chapter 4
Peter de Rivo on Reforming
the Ecclesiastical Calendar

One of the key insights that Peter de Rivo exploited in his attempts to confirm the canonical date of Christ's crucifixion (25 March AD 34) was that the 19-year lunar cycle of the Roman Church deteriorated over time and required occasional adjustments in order for it to function adequately in the long run. In both the *Dyalogus* and the later *Opus responsivum*, Peter linked the introduction of this cycle and its concomitant scheme of Golden Numbers to the early history of the Hebrew nation, putting forward the novel idea that its first adjustment or 'reform' had taken place during the reign of King David. According to his central hypothesis, this Davidian version of the cycle had still been in use in the year AD 34, when the accumulated error of the 19-year cycle made the Jews celebrate Passover on 25 March, the date of the crucifixion, even though the astronomical full moon had occurred three days or so earlier. The *Opus responsivum* expanded this argument by postulating that the long-overdue second reform of the cycle had been provided for by Eusebius of Caesarea, who shifted forward the beginning of the old lunar cycle by three years, thereby creating the *cyclus decemnovenalis* still in use.[1]

At the time of its supposed introduction by Eusebius, the dates of the Golden Numbers governed by the *cyclus decemnovenalis* were in reasonably close agreement with the beginnings of the respective lunar months, yet this was no longer the case in Peter's own day. The calendrical new moons now trailed behind their proper astronomical locations by three or four days, leading to frequent mistakes in the celebration of Easter Sunday, which was supposed to fall no earlier than the 15th and no later than the 21st day of the first lunar month in spring. Peter and his contemporaries were aware that this discrepancy was the result of an overestimation of the length of the mean lunation, or synodic month, brought about by the way the 19-year cycle equated 235 lunations with 19 Julian years totalling 6939 3/4 days. Based on the Alfonsine Tables, which made a mean synodic month last 29;31,50,7,37,27,8,25d, the length of this period could be computed to exceed the appropriate length by 6,939;45d − 29;31,50,7,37,27,8,25d × 235 = 0;3,40,8,18,42,2,5d, which made for a difference of one complete day every 310.713… years. In place of such precise numbers, late medieval authors such as Peter de Rivo often relied on

---

[1] *Dyalogus*, tr. 2, c. 2–3; *OpRes*, sigs. b2r–b3r (tr. 1, c. 2, pt. 3). Peter's source for the 'Eusebian' reform of the lunar cycle was Bede, *De temporum ratione*, c. 44 (ed. CCSL 123B, 418, ll. 1–12).

a simplified period length of 304 years, which had the virtue of being a complete number of 19-year cycles ($16 \times 19 = 304$).[2]

One superficially obvious way of counteracting this gradual deterioration would have been to re-set the Golden Numbers to align them once again, at least *grosso modo*, with the actual dates of the new moon. This hypothetical approach to reforming the reckoning of Easter was simple enough, but it had the unwelcome consequence of rendering obsolete most of the calendars and computistical tables already in existence, leaving the Church with a gigantic heap of waste paper and parchment. The logistical nightmare of replacing this heap with newly drawn copies every time the calendar was corrected made it seem expedient to seek more conservative solutions. In Peter's opinion, the way towards such a solution had already been pointed by the aforementioned examples of King David and Eusebius of Caesarea, who had supposedly maintained the existing tableau of Golden Numbers and instead shifted the current year of the 19-year cycle in a way that closed the gap between calendrical and astronomical new moons. As Peter wrote in his *Opus reponsivum*, knowledge of these historical precedents made no small contribution

> towards the construction (if it should please our most holy Lord) of a new 19-year cycle, by which it is possible to find the 14th day of the Moon after which Easter must be celebrated with no less precision than [was possible] at the time of the Council of Nicaea with the 19-year cycle currently in use.[3]

An earlier passage in the same work identified another problem with the ecclesiastical calendar by admitting that the Church followed "a certain legal fiction" when it placed the vernal equinox on 21 March, quite as if the date had remained unchanged since the fourth century.[4] From Oliver Godelof, his astronomical adviser, Peter knew that in the present year 1488 the true longitude of the Sun at the meridian of Leuven had already reached 0° on 11 March, at 8 hours and 26 minutes after noon.[5] Since the Alfonsine Tables placed the beginning of the day at the noon preceding the civil date, this was in fact equivalent to 10 March, 20:26h. The stated gap between convention and reality found its explanation in the annually accumulating discrepancy between the Julian year of 365 1/4 days and the actual length of the tropical year, which for calendrical purposes was defined as the interval between two occurrences of the vernal equinox. According to the Alfonsine Tables, the mean

---

[2]   *OpRes*, sig. b1v (tr. 1, c. 2, pt. 2); *TerTra*, sigs. e5v–e6r (tr. 3, c. 3, pt. 10). The 304-year period, which is very common in medieval texts on the calendar problem, can be traced back to Robert Grosseteste, *Compotus*, c. 4 (ed. Lohr and Nothaft, 102–106).

[3]   *OpRes*, sig. b3v (tr. 1, c. 2, pt. 3): "Hiis immorari libuit, tum quia propter eorum ignorantiam opinor plures loquentium de tempore dominice passionis in errorem seductos esse, tum quia eorum noticia non parum conferet ad conficiendum (si sanctissimo domino nostro placuerit) novum ciclum xix, per quem reperiri possit luna xiiii, post quam pascha servandum erit, non minus precise quam tempore Nyceni concilii per ciclum xix nunc currentem." See also *TreTra*, sig. a6v (tr. 3, c. 1, pt. 3).

[4]   See n. 6 below for the full passage.

[5]   *OpRes*, sig. f4r.

value of the latter type of year was 365d 5;49,16h, which was 0;10,44h below the Julian value, causing the date of the vernal equinox to creep upwards in the calendar at an approximate rate of one day every 134 years. The ten-day interval between the "legal" equinox on 21 March and the astronomically correct date created an obvious problem for the reckoning of Easter in all cases where the 14th day of the Moon fell on 11 March or between the two dates. Whenever this happened, Easter Sunday was technically celebrated not just in the wrong week, but in the wrong month, being postponed to the second lunation of spring.[6] Peter made no secret out of the fact that he wanted to see this blemish removed sooner rather than later:

> For if our calendar were reduced to the same state that it had at the time of the Nicene Council (which could be done very easily, as I shall demonstrate elsewhere), it would sew shut the mouths of all those who reproach us as though we observed the feast of Easter against the decrees of the fathers.[7]

He honoured his promise to discuss the restoration of the ecclesiastical calendar at greater length by composing a separate *Reformacio kalendarii Romani*, which dates from 1488 and hence from the same year as the *Opus responsivum*. As a matter of fact, the only manuscript witness to this brief text that is currently known to exist is bound together with a printed copy of the *Opus responsivum* once kept in the library of Bethleem, an Augustinian priory near Leuven.[8] According to its full title, the *Reformacio* was meant to offer a "Reform of the Roman calendar and its reduction to the original state it was in at the time of the fathers who issued decrees and ordinances to ensure that the faithful would only celebrate the feast of Easter on a Sunday" (*Reformacio kalendarii Romani eiusque reductio ad statum pristinum in*

---

[6] *OpRes*, sig. b1v (tr. 1, c. 2, pt. 2): "Insuper comperiunt astronomi in annis fere centum et xxxiiii equinoctium ad unum fere diem anteriorari. Unde fit ut equinoctium vernale quod patres tempore Nycene synodi reppererunt xii kalendas Aprilis nunc temporis reperiatur v ydus Martii, si saltem, ut plures existimant, equinoctium vernale contingat sole secundum verum eius motum signum Arietis ingrediente, quamobrem contingit ut ecclesia celebret aliquando pascha non in mense primo, cuius scilicet luna xv proxime sequitur equinoctium vernale, sed in mense secundo, maxime si sit annus in ciclo decennovenali tertius, xi aut xix. Decretum ergo patrum de pascha celebrando luna xiiii primi mensis intelligendum est non de luna vere xiiii, sed de luna xiiii legali, dicta sic a lege data fidelibus, ut iuxta cursum cicli decennovenalis pascha celebrent donec ad id eis alia lex ab ecclesia statuatur. Nec idem decretum ingelligendum est de mense vere primo, sed de mense primo legali, cuius scilicet luna xv quam ostendit ciclus decennovenalis proxime sequitur diem illum kalendarii in quo fuit equinoctium vernale dum lex data est de pascha celebrando. Tunc enim fuit idem equinoctium xii kalendas Aprilis, ubi quasi quadam iuris fictione servatum est et servabitur donec aliter ordinet ecclesia."

[7] *OpRes*, sigs. b1v–b2r (tr. 1, c. 2, pt. 2): "Tunc enim fuit idem equinoctium xii kalendas Aprilis, ubi quasi quadam iuris fictione hactenus servatum est et servabitur donec aliter ordinet ecclesia. Nec inexpediens esset meo iudicio ordinationem talem ulterius non differri. Siquidem kalendarium nostrum ad eum statum quo fuit tempore Nyceni consilii reductum fuerit (quod facillime fieri posset, velud alias ostendam) omnium illorum consuerentur ora qui nobis improperant quasi festivitatem paschalem contra decreta patrum observemus."

[8] See Champion, *The Fullness of Time*, 134–137, 158–164, for the first published discussion of this work. On Bethleem Priory, see Chapter 5.3 below.

quo fu<i>t temporibus patrum qui decreta et ordinaciones ediderunt ut paschalis
festivitas a fidelibus non nisi die dominico celebretur).

It should be emphasized from the outset that the proposal for a calendar reform
laid out in this text remained without any discernible impact on the discussions that
eventually culminated in the Gregorian reform of 1582. Nevertheless, the *Reforma-*
cio remains valuable for the light it sheds on Peter's personal interest in the matter.
It can in fact be interpreted as an improved and fleshed out version of a reform
proposal Peter had already sketched in far less detail in the second treatise of his
Dyalogus de temporibus Christi (tr. 2, c. 2 [ll. 158–214]). In both cases, his approach
to the problem was clearly indebted to a plan first developed at the Council of Basel,
which had assigned a specially created commission to the task of preparing a reform
of Easter reckoning. In 1437, the commission in question presented to the Council's
general assembly a new reform plan involving two basic components.[9] One of these
components was to subtract three years from any given year in the 19-year cycle,
which was tantamount to counting years in the *cyclus lunaris* rather than in the
cyclus decemnovenalis. In the new calendar, what used to be year 1 became year
17, year 2 became year 18, and so on. The main effect of this measure was to push
the dates of the paschal new moons downwards by three to four days, thereby
increasing the error rather diminishing it. This shift was counteracted, however,
by the omission of one full week from the Julian calendar, which had the combined
effect of narrowing the gap between the vernal equinox and its required position
on 21 March and moving the paschal new moons three to four days in the opposite
direction, bringing them into approximate agreement with the dates of mean conjunction in the mid-fifteenth century. The main advantage of this approach lay in
the fact that it did not interfere with the accepted distribution of Golden Numbers
in the Julian calendar, making it possible to retain in use existing copies of the
ecclesiastical calendar. As a written object, the pre-reform calendar was hence no
different from the post-reform one.

The two steps of the Basel proposal can be studied in more detail from Table 3,
which shows in column I the 19 paschal new moons of the 19-year cycle, as marked
by the conventional Golden Numbers.[10] As seen from column II, subtracting three
years from this cycle will increase these dates by four days in the first three years
of the old cycle and by three days in the remaining years. Column III displays the
effect of omitting a week from the calendar, reducing each date by seven days, while
column IV records the total difference between the conventional and reformed
paschal new moons.

---

[9] See Solan, *La réforme du calendrier*, 39–104; Nothaft, *Scandalous Error*, 247–270.
[10] Note that in the case of years 8 and 19 the date shown in column I is not the new moon of the
paschal lunation, but the new moon of March.

I		II		III	IV
Year		Year		-7d	Diff.
1	23 Mar	17 em.	27 Mar	20 Mar	-3d
2	12 Mar	18	16 Mar	09 Mar	-3d
3 em.	31 Mar	19 em.	04 Apr	28 Mar	-3d
4	20 Mar	1	23 Mar	16 Mar	-4d
5	09 Mar	2	12 Mar	05 Mar	-4d
6 em.	28 Mar	3 em.	31 Mar	24 Mar	-4d
7	17 Mar	4	20 Mar	13 Mar	-4d
8 em.	06 Mar	5	09 Mar	02 Mar	-4d
9	25 Mar	6 em.	28 Mar	21 Mar	-4d
10	14 Mar	7	17 Mar	10 Mar	-4d
11 em.	02 Apr	8 em.	05 Apr	29 Mar	-4d
12	22 Mar	9	25 Mar	18 Mar	-4d
13	11 Mar	10	14 Mar	07 Mar	-4d
14 em.	30 Mar	11 em.	02 Apr	26 Mar	-4d
15	19 Mar	12	22 Mar	15 Mar	-4d
16	08 Mar	13	11 Mar	04 Mar	-4d
17 em.	27 Mar	14 em.	30 Mar	23 Mar	-4d
18	16 Mar	15	19 Mar	12 Mar	-4d
19 em.	05 Mar	16	08 Mar	01 Mar	-4d

Tab. 2: Reform of the lunar cycle proposed at the Council of Basel in 1437

Despite its initially positive reception, which led to the drafting of a formal decree,[11] the project attempted at the Council of Basel soon began to falter. It was officially laid to rest in December 1440, by which time the delegates had come to realize that a reform of this magnitude was simply not feasible under the political circumstances created by the Council's ongoing conflict with Pope Eugene IV. The details of the Basel reform proposal nevertheless continued to attract a good deal of attention in subsequent decades owing to the wide dissemination of some of the relevant literature. Peter de Rivo would have been able to read about the reform plan and its underlying rationale in Hermann Zoest's 1437 treatise *Phaselexis*, which was one of the sources he used for the *Dyalogus* and later mentioned more expressly in his

---

[11]   See Nothaft, "Thomas Strzempiński," 292–303.

Opus responsivum.[12] Another treatise defending the same proposal was Nicholas of Cusa's *De correctione kalendarii* (or *Reparatio kalendarii*), which became more easily available from 1488 onwards owing to the Strasbourg edition of Nicholas's collected works.[13] Peter acknowledges him as a predecessor in both the *Opus responsivum* and the *Reformacio*, placing his name besides that of Pierre d'Ailly.[14] The latter contributed to the calendar question his *Exhortatio ad concilium generale super kalendarii correctione* (1411), which first appeared in print between 1477 and 1483.[15] Peter, for his part, had already seen a copy of the text by the time he penned the *Dyalogus* in 1471.[16]

One of the more significant shortcomings of the plan originally presented at Basel was its omission of no more than seven days, which failed to have the desired effect of moving the date of the vernal equinox back to 21 March. The plan's advocates, Nicholas of Cusa and Hermann Zoest, were aware of this shortcoming and did what they could to downplay its negative consequences.[17] Eager to shield the proposed scheme from criticism on astronomical grounds, they went as far as suggesting that the Alfonsine Tables may be unreliable and that the equinox may occur up to two days later than claimed by those who calculated it in the conventional manner. While this was incorrect as a comment on the true vernal equinox, the proposal of 1437 could be rendered sounder by instead basing the calculation of Easter on the mean equinox, which was the moment when the mean Sun of the Alfonsine Tables reached a longitude of 0°. Since the Alfonsine Tables placed the mean equinox of *c.*1437 on 14 March, the proposed omission of seven days was on this definition sufficient to make the "vernal equinox" fall on 21 March.

An analogous line of thought is pursued in the excursus on calendar reform included in Peter de Rivo's *Dyalogus*, which opens with Gamaliel expressing astonishment at the Church's failure to celebrate Easter in accordance with its own astronomical rules. He brings up the specific example of AD 1470, for which the Alfonsine Tables suggested Thursday, 15 March as the first 14th day of the Moon to come after the vernal equinox. The implied date of Easter Sunday, 18 March, lay more than a month ahead of the date chosen by the Church for its celebration, which in 1470 had taken place on 22 April. Gamaliel's example assumes that the

---

[12]   See above, xxxviii–xxxix.

[13]   Nicholas of Cusa, *Opuscula theologica et mathematica*, vol. 1 (Strasbourg: Martin Flach, [not after 13 Oct.] 1488), sigs. e3r–f4r.

[14]   *OpRes*, sig. b1v (tr. 1, c. 2, pt. 2): "Sicut etiam dicunt dominus Petrus Cameracensis et dominus Nycolaus de Cusa in tractatibus quos ediderunt pro reformatione kalendarii astronomice compertum est in annis ccciiii primationes lune ad unum fere diem anteriorari, quare necesse est in totidem annis anteriorari similiter lunas vere xiiii." See also the mention of "Petrus de Aliaco et dominus Nycholaus de Cuza" in Peter's *Reformacio*, ll. 93–94.

[15]   Pierre d'Ailly, *Imago mundi et tractatus alii* (Leuven: Johannes de Westfalia, 1477/83), sigs. g5r–h2r. For a modern edition and French translation, see Solan, *La réforme du calendrier*, 200–235.

[16]   *Dyalogus*, tr. 2, c. 2 [l. 135].

[17]   This point is explored in more detail in Nothaft, "Strategic Skepticism."

vernal equinox currently resides on 13 March "according to the Sun's mean motion" (*secundum medium motum solis*). This is perfectly in tune with the Alfonsine calculation, provided the hours are counted from midnight or noon of the same day as opposed to noon of the previous day.[18]

Using Gamaliel's interlocutor Paulus as his mouthpiece, Peter goes on to propose a correction that is structurally very similar, but not identical, to the plan proposed in Basel 35 years earlier. An intriguing sign of the changed zeitgeist within the Latin Church is Peter's insistence that the task of reforming the ecclesiastical calendar falls within the sole purview of the pope, whose role as Roman *pontifex* placed him in a historical line of succession with the celebrated calendar reformers of antiquity, Julius Caesar and Augustus.[19] Another deviation from the original proposal concerned the number of days to be omitted from the Julian calendar: rather than suppressing a full week, which had the benefit of leaving the 28-year solar cycle uninterrupted, Peter deemed it necessary to excise eight days, thereby transplanting the mean equinox from 13 March to 21 March.

In the proposal considered at Basel in 1437, a leap backwards in the 19-year lunar cycle by three years was meant to raise the date of the calendrical new moon by three to four days, while the simultaneous suppression of seven days converted this increase into a negative shift of three to four days. Peter's plan of omitting eight days instead of seven hence made it necessary to modify the way the lunar cycle was corrected. In 1476, which was the 14th year of the 19-year cycle and Peter's proposed year of reform, the conventional way of counting would have placed the beginning of the March lunation on the final day of February (29 February, since 1476 is a leap year). Peter assumed that the 19-year cycle had accumulated an error of three full days since its introduction at the time of the Nicene Council, such that the correct date of the new moon in 1476 should have been 26 February. If the March lunation was given 30 days, as was the norm in the ecclesiastical lunar calendar, the new moon of the following lunation was due on 27 March. Yet, the planned omission of all days from 13 March to 20 March would have shifted this date forward by another eight days, to 4 April. This date happened to be marked by the Golden Number 19, hence supporting Peter's conclusion that the calendrical new moons could be made to coincide with the actual new moons by leaping over five years in the 19-year cycle, such that year 1 became year 6.

The success of this correction can be gauged from a look at Table 4, which follows the same principles as Table 3 elucidating the original proposal of 1437. To the four columns found in the latter table, Table 4 adds a fifth column containing the

---

[18] *Dyalogus*, tr. 2, c. 2 [ll. 103–117]. According to the software *Deviations* (http://www.raymondm. co.uk), the Alfonsine mean equinox of AD 1471 fell on 14 March, *c.*09:10h after noon, which is equivalent to a civil date of 13 March, 21:10h.

[19] The same argument was made in 1491 by Paul of Middelburg, who sent a calendar reform proposal to Pope Innocent VIII. See Nothaft, *Scandalous Error*, 286, and n. 71 in Chapter 3.3 above.

mean conjunctions in the 19-year cycle from 1482 to 1500, as calculated according to the Alfonsine Tables. The astronomical comparison shows that the paschal new moon dates in Peter's reformed calendar would have coincided with the calculated dates of the mean conjunction in 10 out of 19 years, provided these dates are all reckoned from noon of the previous day. Two more years, those with Golden Numbers 1 and 16, could be included in this category if the meridian underlying this calculation were shifted further east (e.g., to Leuven, Rome, or Jerusalem). In these years, the mean conjunction at the Toledan standard meridian of the Alfonsine Tables fell within the final hour of the day. In the remaining seven years of the cycle, the calendrical new moon was bound to coincide with the day after the mean conjunction.

I		II		III	IV	V
Year		Year			Diff.	AT 1482–1500
1	23 Mar	6 em.	28 Mar	20 Mar	-3d	20 Mar 04:27h
2	12 Mar	7	17 Mar	09 Mar	-3d	09 Mar 13:16h
3 em.	31 Mar	8 em.	05 Apr	28 Mar	-3d	27 Mar 10:49h
4	20 Mar	9	25 Mar	17 Mar	-3d	16 Mar 19:37h
5	09 Mar	10	14 Mar	06 Mar	-3d	06 Mar 04:26h
6 em.	28 Mar	11 em.	02 Apr	25 Mar	-3d	25 Mar 01:59h
7	17 Mar	12	22 Mar	14 Mar	-3d	13 Mar 10:47h
8 em.	05 Apr	13	09 Apr	01 Apr	-4d	01 Apr 08:20h
9	25 Mar	14 em.	30 Mar	22 Mar	-3d	21 Mar 17:08h
10	14 Mar	15	19 Mar	11 Mar	-3d	11 Mar 01:57h
11 em.	02 Apr	16	06 Apr	29 Mar	-4d	28 Mar 23:30h
12	22 Mar	17 em.	27 Mar	19 Mar	-3d	18 Mar 08:18h
13	11 Mar	18	16 Mar	08 Mar	-3d	07 Mar 17:07h
14 em.	30 Mar	19 em.	04 Apr	27 Mar	-3d	26 Mar 14:40h
15	19 Mar	1	23 Mar	15 Mar	-4d	14 Mar 23:28h
16	08 Mar	2	12 Mar	04 Mar	-4d	04 Mar 08:17h
17 em.	27 Mar	3 em.	31 Mar	23 Mar	-4d	23 Mar 05:49h
18	16 Mar	4	20 Mar	12 Mar	-4d	12 Mar 14:38h
19 em.	04 Apr	5	07 Apr	30 Mar	-5d	30 Mar 12:11h

Table 4: The calendar reform proposal of Peter de Rivo's *Dyalogus*

One objection that contemporary readers were likely to have raised against this reform proposal concerns its reliance on the mean vernal equinox. Medieval computists accepted that the date of Easter was keyed to the vernal equinox because of its symbolic and cosmological significance, being the astronomical beginning of spring and the first day of the year at which the length of night-time no longer exceeded the length of daylight.[20] An 'equinox' of 0° mean solar longitude could easily be seen as a poor substitute for this symbolically rich astronomical event. That Peter himself developed second thoughts on this point is evident from his *Opus responsivum*, where he claims that the vernal equinox currently happens on 11 March, "at least if, as many assume, the vernal equinox occurs when the Sun enters the sign of Aries according to its true motion."[21] He fully accepts this understanding in the *Reformacio kalendarii Romani*, where there is no longer any talk of the mean equinox. Instead, the equinox is defined as the moment when day and night reach the same length, which "only happens when the Sun enters the sign of Aries."[22]

Peter offers this definition in the second part of his brief treatise, while in the third he claims that a retrogression of the vernal equinox in the Julian calendar from 21 March to 18 March had already been noted by Pope Hilarius (461–468), who for this reason asked the computist Victorius (of Aquitaine) to compose a new Easter cycle. This historical note is somewhat mysterious, as the preserved letter in which Hilarius (then still archdeacon rather than pope) commissions this work from Victorius makes no mention whatsoever of the date of the vernal equinox.[23] What Peter may have had in mind here is a passage in Nicholas of Cusa's calendar treatise, which he mentions at the end of the same section of the *Reformacio*. Nicholas alludes to Victorius's letter of response to Hilarius as evidence that in AD 462 certain Latins had found the vernal equinox on 18 March.[24] All this letter says, however, is that the Latin date-ranges for paschal new and full moons begin, respectively, on 5 March and 18 March, which is three days earlier than the lower limits accepted by the Alexandrian Church.[25] That this anticipation of the Easter lunation by three days was due to a change in the date of the equinox was a plausible, if unsupported, conclusion on the part of Nicholas of Cusa and Peter de Rivo.

When Peter presented the first version of his proposal in 1471, it had only been a year since Pope Paul II had issued the bull *Ineffabilis providentia* (19 April 1470),

---

[20]   A *locus classicus* concerning the cosmic significance of the vernal equinox is Bede, *De temporum ratione*, c. 6 (ed. CCSL 123B, 290–295).

[21]   See n. 6 above for the citation.

[22]   *Reformacio*, ll. 44–46: "Precisum autem equinoctium vernale, in quo lumine diurno nocturne coequantur tenebre, non contingit nisi sole signum Arietis ingrediente."

[23]   See the *Epistula Hilari ad Victorium* (ed. Krusch, *Studien* [1938], 16).

[24]   Nicholas of Cusa, *De correctione calendarii*, c. 9 (ed. Stegemann, 78, ll. 13–17). See also ibid., c. 7 (ed. Stegemann, 56, ll. 15–19).

[25]   Victorius of Aquitaine, *Prologus ad Hilarum archidiaconum*, c. 4 (ed. Krusch, *Studien* [1938], 19–20).

decreeing that from 1475 onwards every 25th year of the Christian era should be the occasion of a Jubilee.[26] Inspired by this papal ordinance, Peter suggested that the forthcoming Jubilee in 1475 be used to give the planned reform further leverage. The confluence of pilgrims from all over the Christian world in the city of Rome at the occasion of the Jubilee could be used to advertise the reform in all its details, while its actual implementation was most suitably scheduled for the following year 1476. Peter reiterated this idea in his *Reformacio* of 1488, this time targeting 1500 as the year of the next Jubilee. The fact that this Jubilee was still 12 years in the future meant there was going to be sufficient time for those with the required expertise (l. 107: *qui huius rei periti sunt*) to investigate the calendar problem and choose a suitable mode of correction.

Peter's own plan as to how to conduct this reform assumed that the gap between the legal and astronomical dates of the vernal equinox was going to be 10 days in AD 1501, which was the first year of the following 19-year cycle as well as the hoped-for year of reform. Citing a calculation for the meridian of Rome, he placed the equinoctial date of 1501 on 11 March, 12:51h from the previous noon. For the corresponding time in AD 161 (i.e., 10 × 134 = 1340 years earlier) Peter found 21 March, 14:48h from the previous noon, which justified his conclusion that the vernal equinox could be restored to its legitimate date by removing 10 days from the calendar, namely, the days from 11 March to 20 March (ll. 113–124). One unwelcome consequence of this step was the erasure of certain major saint days, in particular St Gregory's Day on 12 March and the feast of Gertrude of Nivelles on 17 March, which was of particular importance to the city of Leuven. Peter's reaction to this problem was a pragmatic one: make a one-time exception by moving St Gregory's feast to 21 March and Gertrude's to 23 March (ll. 198–202).

Besides swapping the mean for the true equinox, Peter improved upon his earlier proposal by offering a better estimate for the error that had accrued from the overestimation of the length of the synodic month in the 19-year cycle. If the rate of deterioration was one day every 304 years, this error should have grown to four full days between AD 285 and 1501 (as 1501 − 285 = 1216 and 1216 = 4 × 304). Peter confirmed this by noting that the mean lunisolar conjunction of March 1501 was computed astronomically to fall on 19 March, 22:39h from the previous noon, whereas in AD 285 the corresponding conjunction had occurred on 23 March, 20:35h from the previous noon (ll. 125–138). In both cases, his stated result was virtually the same as what could be obtained with the help of the Alfonsine Tables, assuming that Peter or his informant here worked with the meridian of Rome and placed it approximately 25° further east in relation to Toledo.[27]

---

[26]   Paul II, *Bulla anni Jubilaei* (Rome: Sixtus Riessinger, [after 19 Apr.] 1470).
[27]   On the Roman meridian presupposed in these calculations, see the notes on the *Reformacio* below, 113.

As Peter portrayed it in the fifth part of his *Reformacio*, the adequate place-
ment for the Golden Number in 1501 would have been 20 March, since the first
day of the lunar month was not supposed to coincide with the actual date of
conjunction (19 March). Instead, it was meant to begin in the evening that followed the conjunction (ll. 152–154), a rule traceable back to Bede's *De temporum
ratione*.[28] In the case of 1501, which was the first year of the 19-year cycle with
Golden Number 1 on 23 March, this called for a correction that reduced the date
of the paschal new moon by three days (rather than four). Following the principles
that underpinned the Basel proposal of 1437 and Peter's own earlier attempt of
1471, the appropriate correction method skipped enough years in the 19-year cycle
to move the new moon date downward in the calendar by seven days, such that
the simultaneous elimination of 10 days would create a net difference of -3 days.
This could be done by jumping ahead by 13 years, swapping Golden Number 1
for Golden Number 14.

As can be seen from Table 5 below, the net shift was bound to increase to -4
days in no fewer than 12 years of the lunar cycle's 19 years (former years 3, 7–10,
12–18) and to -5 days in two of them (former years 11 and 19). Only five years (former years 1–2, 4–6) retained a three-day gap between the old date of the paschal
new moon and the new one. Column V shows the Alfonsine mean conjunctions
of AD 1501–1519, whose times are here calculated for the aforementioned 'Roman'
meridian located 25° east of Toledo. They have also been shifted by -12h to move
the beginning of the day to midnight. From a comparison of these conjunction
times with the new batch of paschal new moons generated by Peter's proposal,
it can readily be seen that his declared goal of having the lunation start at the
evening following the mean conjunction is fully realized only in years 1, 4, 6,
12, and 17, in which the conjunctions of the first 19-year cycle fulfilled the dual
condition of falling on the previous date in the calendar and before nightfall
(*c.*18:00h). The second of these conditions would have been violated in years 2, 5,
9, 14, 18–19, as here the conjunctions fell too close to midnight. The incongruity
was especially severe in year 11, which would have seen the Alfonsine conjunction
one day after the new moon implied by Peter's scheme. All other years, eight of
them in total, would have put the beginning of the lunation on the day of conjunction itself.

---

[28]   Bede, *De temporum ratione*, c. 43 (ed. CCSL 123B, 412–414). See also above, lxxi.

I		II		III	IV	V
Year	GN	Year	GN	GN new	Diff.	AT 1501–1519
1	23 Mar	14 em.	30 Mar	20 Mar	-3d	19 Mar 10:39h
2	12 Mar	15	19 Mar	09 Mar	-3d	08 Mar 19:28h
3 em.	31 Mar	16	06 Apr	27 Mar	-4d	27 Mar 17:01h
4	20 Mar	17 em.	27 Mar	17 Mar	-3d	16 Mar 01:49h
5	07 Apr	18	14 Apr	04 Apr	-3d	03 Apr 23:22h
6 em.	28 Mar	19 em.	04 Apr	25 Mar	-3d	24 Mar 08:11h
7	17 Mar	1	23 Mar	13 Mar	-4d	13 Mar 16:59h
8 em.	05 Apr	2	12 Mar	02 Mar	-4d	02 Mar 01:48h
9	25 Mar	3 em.	31 Mar	21 Mar	-4d	20 Mar 23:20h
10	14 Mar	4	20 Mar	10 Mar	-4d	10 Mar 08:09h
11 em.	02 Apr	5	07 Apr	28 Mar	-5d	29 Mar 05:42h
12	22 Mar	6	28 Mar	18 Mar	-4d	17 Mar 14:30h
13	09 Apr	7	15 Apr	05 Apr	-4d	05 Apr 12:03h
14 em.	30 Mar	8	05 Apr	26 Mar	-4d	25 Mar 20:52h
15	19 Mar	9	25 Mar	15 Mar	-4d	15 Mar 05:40h
16	06 Apr	10	12 Apr	02 Apr	-4d	02 Apr 03:13h
17 em.	27 Mar	11	02 Apr	23 Mar	-4d	22 Mar 12:01h
18	16 Mar	12	22 Mar	12 Mar	-4d	11 Mar 20:50h
19 em.	04 Apr	13	09 Apr	31 Mar	-5d	30 Mar 18:23h

Table 5: The calendar reform proposal of Peter de Rivo's *Reformacio*

Leaving aside its mixed success in locating the beginnings of the paschal lunation, one deficit that Peter's proposal shared with the plan already pursued at the Council of Basel was rooted in its attempt to correct the solar and lunar components of the ecclesiastical calendar in a single step. Simply put, the problem was that the Julian calendar deteriorated much more swiftly than the 19-year cycle—2.3 times faster, to be precise. Hence, eliminating a day once every 134 years may have been the right measure to keep the vernal equinox from moving away from 21 March, but only at the price of overcompensating for the error in the lunar cycle, whose Golden Numbers slipped away from the new moons at a rate slightly slower than one day in 300 years (ll. 224–233).[29] The Basel reformers had made no attempt to solve this conundrum, but instead simply settled on omitting a bissextile day once every

---

[29]   For a more detailed discussion, see Nothaft, "The Mathematics of Calendar Reform."

three centuries. Nicholas of Cusa and Hermann Zoest, the two main advocates of this proposal, both tried to downplay the problem thus created, even expressing the hope that the actual length of the tropical year might currently be closer to 365 1/4 − 1/300 days than to the approximate Alfonsine value of 365 1/4 − 1/134 days.[30] Peter de Rivo was a good deal more forthright about the limitations of the proposal at hand, as seen from his admission in the *Reformacio* that cancelling a day in 304 years, although enough to keep the Golden Numbers aligned with the new moon, could do no more than slow down the calendrical drift of the vernal equinox (ll. 215–220, 233–235). He nevertheless recommended this measure (ll. 207–214), effectively treating it as inevitable that the calendar would need to be corrected every few centuries (ll. 220–223).

---

[30] Nothaft, "Strategic Skepticism," 91–99; Hermann Zoest, *Phaselexis* (2nd version), c. 10 (ed. Solan, *La réforme du calendrier*, 496–506).

Chapter 5

Peter de Rivo's *Dyalogus de temporibus Christi* and *Reformacio*: Manuscripts, Communities, and Reading

With an understanding of the form and argumentative context of the *Dyalogus de temporibus Christi* and the *Reformacio kalendarii Romani* now to hand, this chapter turns to ask what can be discovered about these texts when they are considered within the cultures of reading, book-production and devotion of the communities where the works were copied and held. The surviving manuscript of the *Dyalogus*, now in the Rare Books and Manuscript Library of Columbia University (Western MS 31), was copied at the house of the Brothers of the Common Life, St Martin's, in Leuven. The *Reformacio* was likewise copied at a reformed religious house, the Augustinian priory of Bethleem at Herent, outside Leuven. The chapter begins with the manuscripts themselves, before turning to short histories of these two houses. It then asks what, if anything, can be learned about these texts from considering them in the light of the manuscript contexts, libraries, book production, and reading practices of these communities, as well as the context of wider Augustinian reform in the southern Low Countries. It concludes with discussion of the possible circulation of the texts, and the question of their role in the intellectual sphere of the late medieval university town of Leuven and beyond. By way of a coda, the chapter asks what the codex from St Martin's, Columbia Western MS 31, might have been doing in seventeenth-century England, where ownership marks show the book to have been connected to the buildings of John Cotton at Landwade, a certain John Gregory, and a James Galloway in the year 1643.

1. Notes on the Codices

At the smallest scale of analysis we might ask whether our readings of the *Dyalogus* and *Reformacio* are illuminated in any way by the particular codices within which they are located.[1] For the *Dyalogus* this is a simpler task, since it exists in a contemporary binding, giving some confidence that the work remains alongside its original book-fellows. The *Dyalogus* is included as the final text in a miscellany, with the majority of texts included written by the famous late medieval reformer, cardinal, and conciliarist Pierre d'Ailly (1350–1420). Immediately preceding the *Dyalogus* is a group of four texts, by Pierre d'Ailly, John of Antioch, and Jean Gerson (1363–1429), all of which relate to the origins of church jurisdiction and the powers of general

---

[1]   For the full description of the manuscripts and their contents, see the section on "The Codices" below.

councils. Sitting in this company, the *Dyalogus* can be seen as being located within a reforming discourse, one urging the church to reform in head and members. This is, of course, the broader historical horizon within which fifteenth-century calendar reform unfolded, as the work of Philipp Nothaft has shown.[2] And reform is certainly one of the purposes of Peter's text. For early readers, then, we could perhaps imagine Peter's proposals accruing authority through proximity to its cover-fellows, like a contact relic at the shrine of the great reformers of recent generations, assuring potential readers of the legitimacy of the reform proposals being offered.[3] In the context of reforming religious houses, where institutional origins were often bound up with the actions and approval of such figures, names like d'Ailly's had added weight. This was certainly the case at Bethleem, whose critical early years overlapped with the Council of Constance (1414–1418), and where d'Ailly was involved in the early processes for approving the foundation.[4]

The case of the *Reformacio* is slightly more complicated, since, as Matthew Champion has shown elsewhere, the original codex that housed the *Reformacio* is now broken into two volumes in two separate locations: MS Brussels, KBR, 11750–11751, and Cambridge, University Library, Inc 3.F.2.9 [3294].[5] The original volume can be reconstructed on the basis of a list at the opening of the Brussels manuscript. Commencing with Augustine's *De Genesi ad litteram*, the volume moves to works by Peter de Rivo, including the *Monotesseron* (his elaborate harmonization of the four Gospels based on Luke's account), his two printed tracts against Paul of Middelburg, and his *Reformacio*. The *Reformacio* is now in the second part of this codex, housed in Cambridge University Library, and wedged between Peter's *Opus responsivum* and *Tercius tractatus*.[6] The original codex had been divided by the time the work was entered in the catalogue of the Flemish bibliophile Jan Frans van de Velde.[7] A seventeenth-century book list from the Bethleem Priory, where the printed works of Peter de Rivo on the calendar appear in a volume with Lorenzo Valla's *Elegantiae*, is further evidence that might suggest that the Brussels volume was already divided before the works entered van de Velde's collection, but unless further evidence is discovered this must remain a conjecture. If, however, we accept that the volume as originally constructed included Augustine's work and the *Monotesseron*, alongside Peter's printed works, we can begin to see this volume as

---

[2]   Nothaft, *Scandalous Error*, 235–270.

[3]   See n. 53 in Chapter 2.1 for the possibility of this method of reading in relation to de Rivo's arguments and Pierre d'Ailly's *Epistola ad novos hebreos*.

[4]   Persoons, "Pieuré de Bethleem." Extracts from the Ympens chronicle relating to d'Ailly and Constance can be found in Kervyn de Lettenhove, *Chroniques relatives à l'histoire de la Belgique*, 3:352–354. For more on Ympens' chronicle, see Chapter 5.3, below.

[5]   For a more complete discussion, see Champion, *The Fullness of Time*, 134–135 and the section on "The Codices," below.

[6]   See Oates, *A Catalogue of the Fifteenth-Century Printed Books*, 633 (no. 3825). Oates's entry is restated in Derolez et al., *Corpus Catalogorum Belgii*, 7:309.

[7]   MS Brussels, KBR, II 1185, Volume 3 (*Sciences et Artes*), entry 183b.

a collection with the effect of granting authority to proposals for reform. Building on Augustine's commentary on Genesis, the work proceeds through Peter's painstaking attempt at a harmonization of the Gospels on the basis of Luke, to assert that the chronologies and reforms proposed in Peter's texts sat firmly within the bounds of pristine orthodoxy.[8] Read in this light, the volume might also be understood as mirroring other fifteenth-century attempts at a synoptic apprehension of time—covering time's flow from its origins (Genesis) to the events of Christ's life at the centre of history, through to the fifteenth-century present.

2.   St Martin's, Leuven

The history of the house of St Martin in Leuven is intimately connected with the history of Leuven's university.[9] Founded in 1425, the new university quickly flourished, drawing teachers and students from across Europe, who would also become involved in the life of St Martin's, as donors and as members. First known as the house of St Gregory, the monastery was founded in 1433.[10] The community itself was founded by Henry Wellens, a university professor and sometime *receptor* (i.e., bursar) of the faculty of arts who donated his house on the Grymstraat to the brothers of the Common Life in his will of 1433.[11] His executors were the priors of Groenendaal, the Rood-Klooster, Sept-Fointaines, and Bethleem Priory.[12] The first two brothers came from Deventer to take possession of Henri's house: Gilles Walrami and Werner de Zutphen.[13] The privileges of the brothers of the Common Life were confirmed by the Bishop of Liège in 1436.[14] St Martin's followed the enclosure movement associated with Bethleem Priory, and was affiliated officially with the Congregation of Windesheim in 1461 and 1465.[15] In the sixteenth century, the house would be intimately involved in text-critical humanist studies, and famously, the work of the humanist and friend of Erasmus, Martin Lipsius.[16]

---

[8]   For work on Peter de Rivo's *Monotesseron*, see Champion, *The Fullness of Time*, 137–149; also Champion, "'To See Beyond the Moment'"; Masolini, "Petrus de Rivo," 91–109; Masolini, "How to Order Four into One."

[9]   For a detailed analysis, see Lourdaux, *Moderne devotie en Christelijk humanisme*, 19–110.

[10]   On the early sources of the house, see Lourdaux, "Prieuré du Val-Saint-Martin." Also D'Hoop, *Inventaire général des Archives ecclésiastiques du Brabant*, 292–301. See also Reusens, ed.,"Testament de Maître Henri Wellens," 223–227; Reusens, ed., *Documents relatifs*, 12:441–471, 13:71–107. Also on the early history of the house, see Sanderus, *Lovaniense coenobium*; Lourdaux, *Moderne devotie en Christelijk humanisme*, 19–25.

[11]   Reusens, "Testament de Maître Henri Wellens." All accounts of this will to date have excised the presence of Henry's natural daughter who is provided for in the will. Her name was Katherine, as was her mother's.

[12]   Lourdaux, "Prieuré du Val-Saint-Martin," 1140.

[13]   Ibid., 1141.

[14]   Ibid.

[15]   Ibid., 1141–1142.

[16]   See Lourdaux, *Moderne devotie en Christelijk humanisme*.

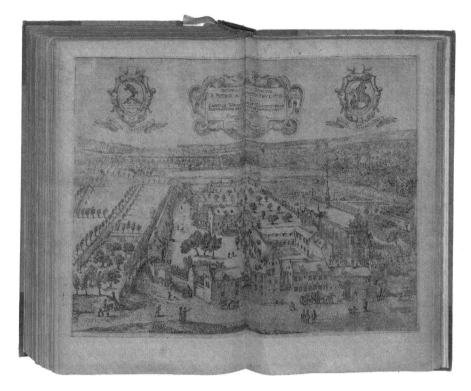

Figure 1: St Martin's, Leuven, from Antonius Sanderus, *Lovaniense coenobium,*
S. Martini brevi historia ex domesticis potissimum ipsius et aliis fide dignis
monumentis contexta (Leuven: Petrus Sassenus, 1663. Image © KBR).

The house and its library have been the subject of extensive research, based on
the rich surviving documentation, particularly an unusual late fifteenth-century attempt to catalogue manuscripts in houses across the region developed at St
Martin's and later taken up by the Rood-Klooster.[17] Surviving reading lists have
also provided scholars with materials for examining the reading practices of the
house and the *devotio moderna* more generally.[18] The first catalogue of the house
was included in a catalogue of works from across the region compiled in *c.* 1487 by
Gerard Roelants.[19] This work is no longer extant, but by good fortune was consulted

---

[17]   For the major work on the library, particularly its manuscript holdings, see Lourdaux and
Haverals, *Bibliotheca Vallis Sancti Martini.* See also Lourdaux, *Moderne devotie en Christelijk humanisme,* 12–16.

[18]   For the most important study, see Kock, *Die Buchkultur der Devotio moderna.*

[19]   Lourdaux and Haverals, *Bibliotheca Vallis Sancti Martini,* 2:48–49; van Mierlo, "Een katalogus
van handschriften." MS Ghent, Universiteitsbibliotheek, 941, a collection of the writings of Hadewijch
from the Bethleem Priory at Herent, includes a note on the inside cover that there was a catalogue of
various manuscripts written in Belgian libraries compiled in around the year 1487 from St Martin's
in Leuven.

in the development of an unusual manuscript now in the National Library in Vienna (series nova 12694). This manuscript is a catalogue of books held in monasteries across the region compiled at the Rood-Klooster between the years 1532 and 1538.[20] This has allowed the extraordinary reconstruction of surviving manuscripts from St Martin's from around the time of Roelant's death in 1490, published as part of a two-volume study of the library of St Martin's by Willem Lourdaux and Marcel Haverals in 1978 and 1982.[21] This study did not, however, include the Columbia codex as a surviving manuscript of the house. This was, in part, a result of limiting its work on the surviving manuscripts to libraries in Europe (including the United Kingdom). Lourdaux and Haveral's study shows how the library of the house grew through donations and through the copying and purchasing of works: in the year 1532 there were works by 151 authors held in the library.[22] These donations show the clear connections of the house to the growing university, and particularly to the faculty of arts with its strong connections to the school of St Martin's.[23] The library of St Martin's was extensive for such a young institution. Alongside its holdings of liturgical, biblical and patristic texts, it held standard works of philosophy, and the works of later theologians and commentators. Its more contemporary holdings show strength in the most famous authors of the *devotio moderna*, including works by Thomas à Kempis, Geert Grote, and Gerard Zerbolt van Zutphen. Among its more unusual items, and a sign of its interest in reform and the present state of the church, was a codex containing up-to-the-minute demonological treatises about a new heretical sect of witches (*Fascinarii*) by the Dominican inquisitor Nicolas Jacquier.[24]

A licensed reading programme survives for novices and professing brothers at St Martin's.[25] Compiled in 1526, it is related to other such lists compiled in *devotio moderna* circles in the fifteenth and early sixteenth centuries. The programme is simple and carefully circumscribed. For novices it includes the obvious candidates—books of the Bible and authorized Church Fathers—alongside a small range of more recent devotional works including Heinrich de Suso's *Horologium divine sapientie*, a crucial text for the development of the *devotio moderna* more gen-

---

[20]   Lourdaux and Haverals, *Bibliotheca Vallis Sancti Martini*, 2:49–50. See also van Mierlo, "Een katalogus van handschriften"; van Mierlo, "De anonymi uit den katalogus van handschriften van Rooklooster"; Lehmann, "Alte Vorläufer des Gesamtkatalogs," 172–183; Obbema, "The Rooklooster Register Evaluated"; Obbema, "The Latin Classics in Monastic Libraries"; Obbema, "Problems in Editing the Rooklooster Register."

[21]   Lourdaux and Haverals, *Bibliotheca Vallis Sancti Martini*.

[22]   Ibid., 2:103–164; also Lourdaux, *Moderne devotie en Christelijk humanisme*, 13.

[23]   Lourdaux, *Moderne devotie en Christelijk humanisme*, 19; Lourdaux, "De Sint-Maartensschool te Leuven."

[24]   MS Brussels, KBR, 733–741. See further Ostorero, *Le diable au sabbat*.

[25]   MS Brussels, KBR, 11915–11919, fols. 67v–70r. See Lourdaux, *Moderne devotie en Christelijk humanisme*, 180–181; Persoons, "Het intellectuele leven," 57; Kock, *Die Buchkultur der Devotio Moderna*, 136–149; Kock, "Lesen nach Vorschrift"; Staubach, "*Memores pristinae perfectionis*," 428–430.

erally.[26] For professing brothers the list of fathers and contemporary theologians expands, but is still tightly controlled. As with earlier accounts of reading practices in the *devotio moderna*, most influentially those of Gerard Zerbolt van Zutphen, the list contrasts texts which are desired to inflame the soul's affects and those which are to enlighten the intellect.[27] The former are more fitting, particularly to the less advanced in their spiritual exercises. The dangers of texts not closely tied to Christ's life is that they might "give information about many things that are doubtful and problematic": readers "should not be admitted to handling books dealing in deep and doubtful matters unless there is reasonable cause because those whose understanding is inadequate are very easily led astray in these matters."[28] The implications for the study of Peter de Rivo's chronological and calendrical texts are clear: they are not the kinds of texts to be read by just anyone since they are not on the surface works designed to inflame the soul. Indeed, given their contested subject matter, they may even have strayed into the realm of doubtful and problematic texts. Nevertheless, "reasonable cause" might have existed for their being read at more advanced levels of the priory on the grounds of their claims about how Christ's life was to be understood historically, and the relationship between Christ's history, the liturgical life of the house, and the wider Christian community.

A final note on St Martin's: there is debate in the historiography on the intellectual history of the Low Countries about the eddying of humanist currents in late fifteenth-century Leuven. The work of Lourdaux makes the strongest case for a Christian humanism in fifteenth-century Leuven, and that work has been supported more recently by a study of the library of the Premonstratensian Abbey of Park and its abbot Thierry van Thulden.[29] On the other hand, the limited nature of northern reception of humanism is stressed in the most famous study of the question, that of IJsewijn, as well as by later book historians.[30] The question is one of intensities of interest and will never be resolved in any ultimate sense. What we do know of the library of St Martin's suggests, however, that fourteenth- and fifteenth-century humanist works were read and copied there, though not widely (the reading programme of St Martin's is clear on this point). As an example of a

[26] Staubach, "*Memores pristinae perfectionis*," 405, 411, 418–419, 425, 426; Künzle, *Heinrich Seuses Horologium Sapientiae*; Kock, *Die Buchkultur der Devotio Moderna*, 127, 218.

[27] On Zerbolt and reading, see Staubach, "*Memores pristinae perfectionis*"; Kock, *Die Buchkultur der Devotio Moderna*; Gerrits, *Inter timorem et spem*.

[28] Staubach, "*Memores pristinae perfectionis*," 429, quoting MS Brussels, KBR, 11915–11919, fols. 69v–70r: "Non enim videntur admittendi ad libros de profundiis materiis et dubiis tractantes nisi causa subsit rationabilis, quia parum intelligentes in his facillime decipiuntur"; Kock, *Die Buchkultur der Devotio Moderna*, 144.

[29] Lourdaux, *Moderne devotie en Christelijk humanisme*; Verweij, "Description and Interpretation of MS 17937."

[30] IJsewijn, "The Coming of Humanism." For an older position, though with some useful detail, see De Vocht, *History of the Foundations*, 1:63–190. See also Obbema, "The Latin Classics in Monastic Libraries," who questions Lourdaux's earlier more positive position.

fifteenth-century St Martin's manuscript with a humanist work, we might take MS London, British Library, Harley 2500, with works by Poggio Bracciolini set alongside Lucius Florus and Orosius and an unattributed synoptic chronicle.[31] Or we could turn to MS London, British Library, Sloane 2509, a copy of Suetonius owned by Adam Jordaens (named in Columbia Western MS 31) that might signal a wider interest in classical Latinity, or might not.[32]

As a further example of these possible ambiguities, we might take the form of the *Dyalogus* itself. Although dialogues were not uncommon in earlier centuries, fifteenth-century interest in the form was undoubtedly strengthened by the tides of humanism—we might take as evidence the copy of Bracciolini's *Dialogus de acerbitate fortunae* in MS Harley 2500, or a later text by Gerard de Marbays, canon of St Mary's in Utrecht and of St Dionysius in Liège, in the library of St Martin's, which takes the form of a dialogue described in its prologue as *Platonico more* (in the Platonic style) dating from 1494.[33] Peter de Rivo used the dialogue form elsewhere in his *Libellus quo modo omnia in meliorem partem sunt interpretanda*, and to introduce the *Monotesseron*, staging a discussion between a student and teacher under the names Symon (for the student) and Peter (the teacher), thereby mapping his programme onto a transformation from the old (Simon) to the new (Peter). It is exactly this intellectual context that underpins the pairing of Paul (the new) and Gamaliel (the old), the interlocutors of the *Dyalogus de temporibus Christi*.[34] Yet there are no strong grounds for seeing this form in itself as evidence of a humanist interest. There is, indeed, one high medieval precedent for a dialogue between Paul and Gamaliel: an anonymous dialogue (*altercatio*) between Synagoga and Ecclesia from the twelfth century takes the form, in part, of a dialogue between Paul and Gamaliel.[35] But does medieval precedent render impossible an interest in the dialogue form shaped by humanism? We know that Peter de Rivo attempted at least one work in a definite humanist mode: a praise of the Emperor Maximilian written later in his career.[36] Perhaps the best way through this situation is simply to stress that the period was one of transition, a moment of "multiple options," to use the useful formulation of John van Engen.[37]

---

[31]   See Lourdaux and Haverals, *Bibliotheca Vallis Sancti Martini*, 1:636–638.

[32]   See ibid., 1:684–686. The dating of the Sloane is manuscript to 1322 in the colophon is misleading. From the hand and decoration, it seems likely that a C has been omitted and that the text was produced in 1422.

[33]   MS London, British Library, Harley 3675. On this manuscript, see Lourdaux and Haverals, *Bibliotheca Vallis Sancti Martini*, 1:671–673.

[34]   For further discussion of the *Libellus*, see above, xix.

[35]   The text is available in a sixteenth-century Cologne print edition: *Altercatio Synagogae et Ecclesiae* (Frankfurt am Main: Melchior Novesianus, 1537). See Blumenkranz and Châtillon, "De la polémique antijuive à la catéchèse chrétienne."

[36]   For further discussion, see above, xx.

[37]   See van Engen, "Multiple Options."

Wherever we leave our understanding of St Martin's, however, we will need to remember Jennifer Summit's important observation that "libraries were dynamic institutions that actively processed, shaped, and imposed meaning on the very materials they contained."[38] Given the growth of the collection at St Martin's and its later status as a site of humanistic studies, we might then ponder how texts like those gathered in Columbia Western MS 31 were treated as part of the dynamic technology of the monastic library in later periods. Here wider humanist interactions with medieval texts elsewhere might provide a prompt: critique was crucial, but older texts did not disappear without trace in the new learning of the sixteenth and seventeenth centuries. Although Peter de Rivo's *Dyalogus* is not cited in later works, perhaps we might imagine a later humanist reader at St Martin's such as Martin Lipsius encountering the text as an object of interest—a text developing a historicist hermeneutic not without its potential for humanist co-option, couched in the style of the fifteenth-century Leuven University master. Equally, of course, we might imagine a reader approaching the text through the polemical lens of Paul of Middelburg's attacks on Peter: here were the old scholastic arguments for authority presented by a figure who had been overtaken and effaced by the new learning. That both possibilities are conceivable points again to the text's position in a period of intellectual and cultural change where allegiances were often proclaimed with force and the nuances and intersections of different approaches sometimes lost in rhetorical furor.

3.   The Priory of Bethleem, Herent

The early history of the Augustinian Bethleem Priory at Herent outside Leuven was traced in an extraordinarily detailed contemporary chronicle by Petrus Ympens (also known as Pierre Ympens and Pieter Impens), at one time a prior of the house. The autograph manuscript is now found as MS Vienna, Österreichische National-bibliothek, ser. nov. 12816. The chronicle consistently stresses the house's reforming zeal in the light of local and wider European conflicts, heresy and schism.[39] The priory itself was founded in 1407, and throughout the later fifteenth century and into the early sixteenth century its membership oscillated between twenty and twenty-five canons living in the house at any one time.[40] It was bound to follow the customs

---

[38]   Summit, *Memory's Library*, 15.

[39]   For a survey of the priory's history and the relevant sources, see Persoons, "Prieuré de Bethleem." Extracts appear in Kervyn de Lettenhove, *Chroniques relatives à l'histoire de la Belgique*, 3:339–468, though unfortunately almost all material on the local life of the Bethleem community is removed. On the chronicle, see Van Engen, "A Brabantine Perspective"; Van Engen, *Sisters and Brothers of the Common Life*, 158–159; as well as Nelis, "Note sur le *Chronicon Bethleemiticum*"; Halkin, "Une œuvre historique belge"; Persoons, *De autograaf van het Chronicon*. See also Champion, *The Fullness of Time*, 135–136.

[40]   Persoons, "Prieuré de Bethleem," 1018. Under the leadership of Petrus Ympens, the membership was fixed at 25 members. For the following, see also Persoons, "Het intellectuele leven."

of the *devotio moderna* community of Windesheim, although it was not yet part of the Windesheim Congregation. Rather, in 1410 it was affiliated with the chapter of the important Brabantine Augustinian house of Groenendaal.[41] In 1412, however, the priory was officially incorporated into the Windesheim Congregation.[42] Pierre d'Ailly approved the earlier provisions of its foundation in 1414, and later also approved its expansion.[43] Book production was an important part of Bethleem's communal life from its origin. In his *Chronicon*, Ympens repeatedly emphasises the role of the community's brothers in book production, including significant space for lists of the brothers and the books they had copied. This emphasis is married with the construction of a clear identity of the house as a leading player in reform within a network of numerous closely connected communities, among them the major houses Groenendaal, the Rood-Klooster in the Zoniënwoud outside Brussels, and more locally, the Brothers of the Common Life at St Martin's in Leuven.[44] The house was, for example, an early and vocal proponent of enclosure, and engaged in a spirited controversy with other local houses over the question.[45] Successive priors would continue to support enclosure over the course of the fifteenth century as part of a wider culture of reform across the region. Bethleem was supported in its zeal for enclosure by the prominent Leuven theologian Heymeric de Campo (1395–1460), who also taught at the Priory, by the universities of Cologne and Paris, and by Philip the Good, Duke of Burgundy (1396–1467), a known supporter of enclosure and monastic reform.[46] The house was visited by prominent figures in the fifteenth century: in 1435, Aeneas Silvius Piccolomini (later Pope Pius II) and Thomas de Zarzan (later Pope Nicholas V) visited in the company of the papal legate Nicholas d'Albergati (1373–1443).[47] Beyond future popes, the Bethleem chronicle also records with evident pride a visit to the house by the cardinal and reformer Nicholas of Cusa in 1452 at the time of the prior Henry van der Heyden.[48] Among the cardinal's

---

[41]   Persoons, "Prieuré de Bethleem."

[42]   Persoons, "Het intellectuele leven," 47.

[43]   Persoons, "Prieuré de Bethleem," 1010.

[44]   Connections between the Rood-Klooster and Peter de Rivo appear in the important collection from the Mazarine Library, BMaz 300, discussed elsewhere in this volume, which gathers materials from the later calendrical debates between Peter de Rivo and Paul of Middelburg. See above, Chapter 3.5. The manuscript also includes materials relating to a reworking of Peter de Rivo's *Monotesseron* that was also copied at the Bethleem Priory. See above, xxiv–xxv, for further discussion of Peter's connection to other religious communities of Brabant. For further discussion of the *Monotesseron* tradition, see Champion, "'To See Beyond the Moment.'"

[45]   For a collection relating to the controversy, see MS Brussels, KBR, 11752–11764. See also Prims, "De Kloosterslot-beweging in Brabant"; van Engen, *Sisters and Brothers*, 158–161.

[46]   Prims, "De Kloosterslot-beweging in Brabant," 32. For Heymeric de Campo's ties to the house, see MS Vienna, Österreichisches Nationalbibliothek, ser. nov. 12816, fols. 82r, 216v, and 224v; also Persoons, "Het intellectuele leven," 58–59, 62.

[47]   Persoons, "Prieuré de Bethleem," 1013.

[48]   Extracts relating to the visit are transcribed in Kervyn de Lettenhove, *Chroniques relatives à l'histoire de la Belgique*, 3:391–392. See also Meuten and Hallauer, eds., *Acta Cusana*, 1.3b:1146–1147 (no. 2258), also 1422 (no. 2206) for the granting of an indulgence to those visiting the Priory church;

copious scholarship was a proposal for reform of the calendar that was known to Peter de Rivo.[49] Henry van der Heyden was a prominent figure in Leuven's religious life: he was offered the role of Abbot of the major Premonstratensian house at Park, but declined, and was placed in charge of the reform of the female Cistercians in Leuven, as well as the convents of Oignies and Rolduc.[50] In 1487, the priors of Bethleem and of St Martin's were given the task of reforming the convent of St Gertrude in 's-Hertogenbosch, a further demonstration of the networks that connected the two houses where these manuscripts were copied.[51]

Bethleem had, like St Martin's, lively connections with the new University of Leuven. As at St Martin's, the priory's brothers were largely drawn from the university's student body.[52] Peter de Rivo's teacher, Johannes Varenacker, a professor in the faculty of theology, donated books to the priory in his will.[53] Bethleem's academic life was intricately bound up with the book production so characteristic of *devotio moderna* houses: elaborate liturgical manuscripts for religious communities were produced at expense alongside swiftly copied and cheaper devotional texts.[54]

4. Reading in the Reformed Religious Houses of the Southern Low Countries

Some years ago, in a rich study of the bookish cultures of the *devotio moderna*, Thomas Kock argued for the crucial function of book production for understanding the development and maintenance of *devotio moderna* religious houses.[55] Kock's work developed a persuasive position against over-emphasizing the *devotio moderna*'s (of course important) lay dimensions at the expense of its monastic forms, as well as identifying crucial problems in modern scholarship on the movement that seeks either to identify its role in the origins of humanism or see it as a last gasp of medieval hyper-religiosity.[56] Kock assesses the different kinds of writing

Persoons, "Prieuré de Bethleem," 1015. For a further account of the visit, see Persoons, "Nikolaas van Cusa te Leuven."

49   See above, xcix.

50   Persoons, "Prieuré de Bethleem," 1015–1017. On Henry and his role in relation to the election of the reform-minded Thierry van Thulden as Abbot of Park, see also Van Waefelghem, "Une élection abbatiale au XVᵉ siècle"; D'Haenens, "Abbaye de Parc, à Heverlee," 805–807.

51   Persoons, "Pieuré de Bethleem, à Herent," 1017.

52   See, particularly, Persoons, "Het intellectuele leven."

53   MS Vienna, Österreichische Nationalbibliothek, ser. nov. 12816, fol. 314v. See also van der Essen, "Testament de Maître Guillaume de Varenacker."

54   Persoons, "Het intellectuele leven," 67–80. For references to Bethleem's library, see Kock, *Die Buchkultur der Devotio Moderna*, 297. For examples of book production, see MS Vienna, Österreichische Nationalbibliothek, ser. nov. 12816, fols. 57r–v, 58v, 66r–v, 118v, 119v, 125v–126r, 148r, and 182r. The priory's reading culture was also clearly shaped by the emergence of print in the first years of the new technology. See Persoons, "De inkunabels van de priorij Bethleem."

55   Kock, *Die Buchkultur der Devotio Moderna*.

56   Ibid., 11, 14. Here Kock draws on the earlier important work of Nikolaus Staubach, especially "Pragmatische Schriftlichkeit."

present in the religious houses of the movement, including the highly valued writing of liturgical books, writing to build the communal library of the house, and the labour associated with writing *pro pretio*—for money—that helped to maintain the convent.[57] Alongside these more public scribal practices, writing was undertaken for personal use, including the famous collections known as the *raparia*.[58] Within Kock's framework, the manuscripts of the *Dyalogus de temporibus* and the *Reformacio* seem to sit most easily within the kind of copying that was done for the house itself, either for the monastery library or for personal interest and use.[59] At St Martin's the importance of the library was signalled in the administrative structure of the house's finances, with the library having its own accounts.[60] With a short text like the *Reformacio* we might speculate that, had Peter's programme gained more traction, efforts in copying the text could have led to income for the house—a possible remunerative investment of time.

Within the world of the *devotio moderna* more generally, Kock clearly stresses writing as a kind of askesis, a labour that was also meant to lead to the meditative internalization of what was written (*die meditative Verinnerlichung des Geschriebenen*).[61] Writing labour could increase with the penitential structure of the liturgical year: the statutes of the house of St Gregory in Emmerich include longer periods of writing during fasting periods.[62] Daily timetables included time set aside for reading and meditation, usually directed by a confessor and overseen, too, by the house's librarian.[63] Within this culture of reading, devotion to books could take on heavily incarnational overtones: the word might become Christ's flesh, to be honoured accordingly. Thomas à Kempis, for example, speaks of reading as a work of piety: the reader of a book was like Simeon embracing the infant Christ.[64] Thus the emphasis on the labour of writing and reading was not clearly separated from an affective cultivation of a devotional habitus. As well as being stirred by what was read in the process of writing, the very act of writing might also be involved in cultivating the writing subject as a lover of truth. Take, for example, a passage from Thomas à Kempis's chronicle of the Augustinian house of Agnietenberg near

---

[57]   On the economics of book production, see Kock, *Die Buchkultur der Devotio Moderna*, 79–121. Also Brandis, "Handschriften- und Buchproduktion"; Staubach, "Der Codex als Ware."

[58]   On *raparia* and for further literature, see Kock, *Die Buchkultur der Devotio Moderna*, 18–19; Staubach, "*Diversa raptim undique collecta*."

[59]   This division is, of course, not absolute, since books for personal use tended to move into communal circulation often within a brother's lifetime or after his death. On writing for the house involving personal use, see Kock, *Die Buchkultur der Devotio Moderna*, 18, citing the Peter Ympens Bethleem Chronicle.

[60]   Ibid., 17; Lourdaux and Haverals, *Bibliotheca Vallis Sancti Martini*, 2:96–97.

[61]   Kock, *Die Buchkultur der Devotio Moderna*, 15–17, quotation at 17.

[62]   Ibid., 43, 90.

[63]   Ibid., 123–124.

[64]   Thomas à Kempis, *Doctrinale sive manuale iuvenum*, c. 5 (*Opera Omnia*, 4:186): "Sic accipe librum in manibus tuis ad legendum, sicut Simeon iustus puerum Jesum in ulnas suas ad portandum et osculandum."

Zwolle, where one figure is described as an *avidus amator scripturarum*, language that blurs the act of writing with the object written.[65]

Although the *Dyalogus* does not immediately fit into this kind of devotional reading culture, its subject matter—intense scrutiny of the timing of Christ's life—might be seen as part of the wider auxiliary disciplines assisting the practice of a historicized devotion to Christ's life. Passion piety again and again surfaces in the writings of the movement, not only in the obvious texts like Heinrich de Suso's *Hundert Betrachtungen*, but more generally.[66] The *Dyalogus* attempts to underpin these high points of devotional activity with chronological specificity, enhancing the "reality effect" of a piety centred around the events of Christ's life. In this regard it may be useful to set the reading and writing of texts like the *Dyalogus* in the context of wider devotions to measurement and time that found their outlet in manuscripts from across the region: devotional images of clocks, for example, or measurements of the length of Christ's side wound.[67]

Indeed, works on the correct chronology of Christ's life such as Peter de Rivo's *Dyalogus de temporibus Christi* lay at the heart of some of the most innovative transformations in the relation between knowledge and devotion effected in *devotio moderna* houses in the late fifteenth century. Peter's own *Monotesseron* has an important place in any list of these works, but we could equally include the appearance of a much more famous work, Werner Rolewinck's *Fasciculus temporum*, which lays claim to being the first horizontal timeline as well as playing a critical role in the innovation of printing techniques across Europe.[68] Such works were often marked by attempts to harmonize their content with wider devotional practices of spiritual ascent and with wider structures of devotion tied to the rhythms of the liturgical year. At St Martin's itself, chronological interest extended beyond the standard medieval chronicle tradition to include an unusual attempt by an unidentified author to construct a synoptic history of the world in 349 chapters, synchronizing the year of salvation (our *anno domini*), the year of the world (*anno mundi*), as well as the reigns of popes and emperors.[69] This attempt stemmed from a similar impulse to the *Fasciculus temporum* to provide a comprehensive and measured account of history—evidence of a culture of monastic reading and text production surrounding questions of historical accuracy. This is, then, one of the wider hermeneutic horizons within which we might situate the *Dyalogus de temporibus Christi*.

---

[65] Kock, *Die Buchkultur der Devotio Moderna*, 30–31, citing Thomas à Kempis, *Opera omnia*, 7:363.

[66] Kock, *Die Buchkultur der Devotio Moderna*, 126; van Aelst, "Het gebruik van beelden."

[67] On such manuscripts, see Rudy, "Kissing Images"; Rudy, *Postcards on Parchment*, 140–155; Lentes, "Counting Piety."

[68] See further Champion, *The Fullness of Time*, 173–196.

[69] MS London, British Library, Harley 2500, fols. 50r–116r. See Lourdaux and Haverals, *Bibliotheca Vallis Sancti Martini*, 1:636–638, for the catalogue of the manuscript's contents.

5.   Circulation of Texts

The *Dyalogus de temporibus Christi* and *Reformacio* do not seem to have circulated widely, and the manuscripts of both works are remarkably clean, leaving us no annotations to offer a sense of readers' responses to, or use of, the texts. We are therefore not in the territory of much of the recent cutting-edge work on the history of reading, which has focused on cases where readers have left clear marks of their own engagement with the text.[70] This means that at a basic level we can only posit three or perhaps four near contemporary readers of one or both of Peter's texts on the calendar.

The first reader is Peter de Rivo himself, who presumably read the work as he was writing it.[71] If we take the colophon to the surviving manuscript to reflect its first transmission, Peter's second reading of the text may have been at the point of its copying at St Martin's. Here we might imagine Peter reading as an editor, making sure that the calculations in the text were correct— these were the site for the most likely confusions in the transmission of these complex texts, as the numerous corrections to print copies of Peter's later calendrical works attest. There are some corrections to the text of the St Martin's *Dyalogus*, but whether these represent Peter's intervention is doubtful—if he did correct the manuscript, several errors remained, as our edition and the notes on it show. More broadly, chapters of this book have offered possible insights into the details of how Peter himself re-wrote (and thereby, perhaps, re-read) passages from his earlier *Dyalogus* in preparing the later *Reformacio* and *Opus responsivum*. His alterations involve shifting details of the wider argument in response to the controversy with Paul of Middelburg. They also include changes made to account for the time that had elapsed between his first calendar reform proposal articulated in a section of the *Dyalogus* in 1471, and the later proposal made in the *Reformacio* for a reform following the year 1500.[72] These include the pragmatic discussions of tying calendar reform to the Roman Jubilee, harmonizing the reform with wider cultural expectations of the Jubilee as a time for correcting past wrongs.[73]

The second reader was the scribe of the *Dyalogus*. The colophon to the Columbia manuscript states that the text was copied in the year 1471 by brother Johannes Jordaens: *Octavo yduum Iuliarum anni 1471 scriptus eram a fratre Johanne Jordani presbitero. Et eodem anno editus in alma universitate studii Lovaniensis per venera-bilem et eruditum virum sacre theologie bacallarium formatum magistrum Petrum de Rivo.* The records of St Martin's allow us to know a little more of this scribe. According to the priory's *Liber fratrum*, Johannes was born in Brussels and went

[70]   To show the fruitfulness of this approach over the last thirty years, see, for example, the famous studies of Jardine and Grafton, "'Studied for Action'," and Calis et al., "Passing the Book."

[71]   For further discussion of writing as reading, see Mertens, "Lezen met de Pen."

[72]   See above, Chapters 3.2 and 4.

[73]   For this argument, see Champion, *The Fullness of Time*, 160.

school shopping before entering St Martin's school on the advice of his parents.[74] His brother Adam also entered the school at the same time.[75] As a long-serving procurator, he was a major figure in the house's administration, eventually retiring to become the rector of the women's house of St-Nikolaasberg at Aarschot, where he died in 1494.[76] The brothers were major donors to the monastery, giving 249 Rhenish guilders, of which a part was to be reserved for the library.[77] In fact, the Columbia manuscript's ties to the Jordaens brothers extends more particularly to Adam Jordaens. On a number of folios from the manuscript the name *Frater Adam de Boghaerden* appears.[78] Adam was extremely active in the life of St Martin's including a period as it seventh prior, and in the development of the house's school and its ties to the university.[79] He was the author, according to a later chronicler, of *multa carmina et epitaphia*, and among his books was a manuscript of Suetonius' *Lives of the Caesars*. His interests in reform and education make him a third possible reader of the work copied by his brother—and a reader possibly interested in the emergence of humanist literary forms.

The fourth reader was the scribe of the *Reformacio*. As with the *Dyalogus* a scribe is named: brother Peter Maes. Peter's name is associated with at least two other manuscripts from Bethleem in the period. The first is in MS Brussels, KBR, 1382–1391, where Maes is recorded as writing a small portion of the manuscript including various ecclesiastical cases.[80] The hand in this manuscript is the same as used for the *Reformacio*. The second manuscript is MS Manchester, John Rylands Library, Latin 476, where Maes copied text to complete an earlier copy of Gregory's *Moralia in Job*. Traces of the same script can be found here too despite the fact that Maes appears to have adapted his hand to match the remainder of the manuscript.[81]

Beyond these immediate readers we can speculate more generally on a limited readership of Peter de Rivo's texts within university circles and the overlapping communities of Brabant's reforming religious houses. Peter was an important figure in Leuven's institutional landscape. It is likely that the manuscript found at least

---

[74]   Leuven, Rijksarchief, Kerkelijk Archief Brabant, 726, no. 20437/2, fol. 1r. See also Reusens, ed., *Documents relatifs*, 13:102. On the school of St Martin's, see Lourdaux, "De Sint-Maartensschool te Leuven," 206 (for the relevant extract from the *Liber fratrum*): "Frater Johannes, in Bruxella natus ac diversis locis scolas perscrutatus, suorum parentum consilio et auxilio ad scolarium domus huius cohabitationem est perductus. Qui liberalium artium cum fere complesset cursum ... (novice in mei 1466, 18 Jaar)". See also Lourdaux, *Moderne devotie en Christelijk humanisme*, 72, 86, 101, 326.

[75]   Leuven, Rijksarchief, Kerkelijk Archief Brabant, 726, no. 20437/2, fol. 1r–v.

[76]   Lourdaux, *Moderne devotie en Christelijk humanisme*, 86.

[77]   Ibid., 101.

[78]   MS New York, Columbia University, Rare Book and Manuscript Library, Western 31, pp. 1, 39, 50.

[79]   Lourdaux, *Moderne devotie en Christelijk humanisme*, 72–74, 93–94, 116–117. Also Lourdaux, "Prieuré du Val-Saint-Martin," 1144.

[80]   Kohl, Persoons, and Weiler, eds., *Monasticon Windeshemense*, 1:24; Van den Gheyn, *Catalogue des manuscrits de la Bibliothèque royale de Belgique*, 3:96–99.

[81]   Ker, *Medieval Manuscripts in British Libraries*, 3:466.

some audience in university circles: St Martin's itself was closely linked to the university, and more particularly to the pedagogy of the Lily.[82] Beyond the university more strictly defined we may speculate, further, on the basis of later fifteenth-century attempts to develop synoptic catalogues of manuscripts held in monasteries across the region— for example the Roelants catalogue, or the later Rood-Klooster manuscript—that the texts may have been known to wider audiences than these houses.[83] If these manuscripts were read beyond the university, the logical networks for their circulation were the Augustinian houses of the reform network: St Martin's, Bethleem, the Rood-Klooster, and Groenendaal among the most important, as well as houses from other religious orders with reforming connections. There is, for example, evidence of Peter de Rivo's printed chronological works being purchased at the Premonstratensian Abbey of Averbode in the period.[84] This kind of wider reception would certainly not be surprising given the *devotio moderna*'s noted penchant for circle building and establishing connections through the circulation of texts.

A final note on manuscript circulation is necessary given the possible existence of a second manuscript of Peter's *Dyalogus de temporibus* at St Martin's. The possibility is introduced by a seventeenth-century catalogue of the manuscripts at St Martin's drawn up before 1639 by Petrus Trudonensis, the house's librarian (d. 1674).[85] The *Index Bibliothecae Martinianae Manuscriptae* is a list by author of the manuscript contents of St Martin's library.[86] The entry for Peter de Rivo lists the *Dyalogus de temporibus Christi*, followed by two different manuscript marks, K.40 and S.19.[87] If traced to their other appearances in the *Index*, these listings allow the reconstruction of the contents of two manuscripts. The first manuscript is the volume that corresponds with the Columbia codex including the works of Pierre d'Ailly.[88] It is this volume that can also be related to the entries for manuscripts of Pierre d'Ailly in the Rood-Klooster register, MS Vienna, Österreichische Nationalbibliothek, ser. nov. 12694, fols. 289v–290r. The second manuscript commences with a work of Matthaeus Palmerius Florentinus, noted as the *Liber de temporibus*.[89] This work is listed on the Rood-Klooster register as the *Cronica temporum* (fol. 243v),

---

[82] On St Martin's and the pedagogy of the Lilly, see Lourdaux, "De Sint-Maartensschool te Leuven," 190–192. Also Bosmans, "De Pedagogie 'De Lelie'."

[83] See above, cx–cxi.

[84] MS Averbode, Archief van de Abdij van Averbode, I, reg. 43, fol. 70v.

[85] On the catalogues of Petrus Trudonensis, see Lourdaux and Haverals, *Bibliotheca Vallis Sancti Martini*, 1:liii–lx.

[86] MS Brussels, KBR, 21874. The *Index* is reproduced in Lourdaux and Haverals, *Bibliotheca Vallis Sancti Martini*, 2:xliv–lxix. See also the *Catalogus alphabeticus auctorum omnium quorum manuscriptae vel typis expressae lucubrationes extant in bibliotheca monasterii Sancti Martini*, found in MS Brussels, KBR, II 1164.

[87] MS Brussels, KBR, 21874, p. 31; Lourdaux and Haverals, *Bibliotheca Vallis Sancti Martini*, 2:lix.

[88] See Lourdaux and Haverals, *Bibliotheca Vallis Sancti Martini*, 2:419, 2:425.

[89] See ibid., 2:404, 2:425.

and corresponds with MS London, British Library, Harley 3675.[90] This manuscript was copied in the year 1494—after Roelants completed his list—although not at St Martin's. The first text, Matteo Palmieri's chronicle, was copied by Johannes Ympens *in valle sancte lucie*, the house of St Lucy in Sint-Truiden.[91] In the light of this location and date, it is unlikely, although not impossible, that another copy of the *Dyalogus de temporibus Christi* was once found at St Martin's. And there is some further ground for skepticism about a second manuscript's existence. The fact that Matteo Palmieri's work is termed *De temporibus* in the Petrus Trudonensis *Index* might suggest a possible confusion of the two works, leading to the stray reference added to the entry for Peter de Rivo. Harley 3675 does not appear incomplete. And comparison with the Rood-Klooster register that might assist in this case does not seem possible, since the entries for Peter de Rivo do not include the *Dyalogus de temporibus Christi*.[92] In all, then, it seems unlikely that this manuscript ever existed—more likely, it is a ghost in the catalogue.

6. A Seventeenth-Century Coda

Columbia Western MS 31 did not stay in the library at St Martin's. At some stage before 1643 it crossed the English Channel. A flyleaf of the manuscript (p. vii) records a Latin text: *propinquus meus Jo: Gregori cum Dno Jacobo Galloway / quod Landwade in aedibus D. Jo. Cotton. 1643*. Beneath this text, a later hand has added: "these two lines were copied from the cover before the manuscript was rebound." This addition is signed J. Lee. Circumstantial evidence that the manuscript had left St Martin's can also be found in Valerius Andreas's *Bibliotheca Belgica* published in 1643, which records works by Peter, including a manuscript of his *Oratio* for Maximillian in the priory's library and a copy of the *Monotesseron* in the library of the Leuven Jesuits, but does not list the *Dyalogus de temporibus Christi*.[93] What are we to make of this absence from Leuven and the seventeenth-century English appearance of the manuscript?

To begin with we have a problem. Are we to read with John Lee and see two separate inscriptions, or are they somehow related? If we see them as separate, then a translation might read: "my neighbour/kinsman John Gregory, together with Lord James Galloway" and then "somehow at Landwade in the buildings of Lord John Cotton, 1643." Might this mean that we are dealing with two different moments of the manuscript's reception? Taking the second half of the inscription first: we can securely locate the place mentioned. Landwade was a small manor on the border of Cambridgeshire and Suffolk, and its owner in 1643 was John Cotton, although

---

90 See ibid., 1:671–673.
91 MS London, British Library, Harley 3675, fol. 48r.
92 See MS Vienna, Österreichische Nationalbibliothek, ser. nov. 12694, fol. 292v.
93 See Andreas, *Bibliotheca belgica*, 758–759.

he was not resident—perhaps an explanation for the attribution *in aedibus*.[94] In the 1640s, Cotton was living at Madingley, just outside Cambridge, following his marriage. A fellow commoner at Caius College, he was the royalist sheriff of Cambridgeshire and Huntingdonshire from 1641–1643.[95] This setting in the midst of the first civil war might suggest some reason for interest in the texts collected in the St Martin's manuscript. The period saw a revival of interest in conciliar theory, as parliamentarians used it as a means to justify the possible deposition of a king.[96] If a pope could be deposed by a general council, a parliament might likewise depose a king. By contrast, royalist responses, often from the episcopacy, stressed the inapplicability of such ideas to a monarch as opposed to a pope. Perhaps the presence of this manuscript in seventeenth-century Cambridgeshire forms part of this wider interest?

A circumstantial case can be built for this kind of context for the manuscript in relation to the first half of the inscription and its reference to John Gregory and James Galloway. Both are not uncommon names in the period, so any case for certain ownership is bound to fail without further evidence.[97] But it is noteworthy that a John Gregory and a Sir James Galloway formed part of royalist resistance to Covenanters in Scotland in the 1630s and early 1640s. John Gregory (1598–1653) was the minister at Drumoak in Aberdeenshire, and refused to sign the Covenant, fleeing to England.[98] In 1639 he returned to Scotland where he was arrested. Although his exact beliefs are unknown, his sermon on a text from Colossians 2 ("I tell you this so that no one may deceive you by fine-sounding arguments") was the subject of further dispute, suggesting that he preached against the arguments of the Covenanters. Sir James Galloway had similar credentials. A royalist, Galloway was the Master of Requests and was appointed by Charles I as a commissioner of the exchequer in Scotland in the early 1640s.[99] During this period he was involved in Scottish parliamentary controversy when he claimed the position of Secretary of State. When the Scottish exchequer resisted paying Galloway, Charles included a command "that this servant of myne be payed" in 1642.[100] Galloway also had royalist form in refusing to take the Covenant, and was summoned by the Scottish

---

[94]   On Landwade and the Cottons, see Palmer, "Landwade and the Cotton Family"; Wareham and Wright, *A History of the County of Cambridge*, 470–472.

[95]   See Venn, *Alumni Catabrigienses*, 1:403.

[96]   For wider discussion, see Oakley, "Constance, Basel and the Two Pisas"; also Oakley, "'Anxieties of Influence'."

[97]   See for example the famous Oxford orientalist John Gregory (1607–1646), whose noted knowledge of chronology might have made the *Dyalogus* an object of interest. This seems, however, less likely than the line pursued in the following. See Hamilton, "Gregory, John."

[98]   For the following, see Spalding, *History of the Troubles*, 1:164, 1:219–220, 1:244–245, 1:295, 2:44–45; Scott, *Fasti ecclesiae scoticanae*, 6:50.

[99]   See Stevenson, "The King's Scottish Revenues," 30–32. Also Paul, *The Scots Peerage*, 3:377–378; Brown, "Courtiers and Cavaliers."

[100]   Stevenson, "The King's Scottish Revenues," 30–32.

parliament.[101] In 1645 he was made Lord Dunkeld by the King. In this context it might be plausible to imagine a conciliarist manuscript making its way from Scotland to England with Scottish supporters of Charles I: certainly a number of key figures from Scotland were present with the King in Oxford in the 1640s.[102] If this circumstantial case for the manuscript's circulation in mid-seventeenth-century royalist networks has any validity, it has the potential to reshape understandings of how conciliarist ideas circulated in the period. Historians of political thought who have addressed this question have largely dealt in the circulation of printed materials—but might manuscripts of conciliarist works yield insights into the processes of knowledge circulation and political developments in the period in unexpected ways? This question must remain unanswered here, but at the very least the presence of this manuscript at Landwade and possibly in Scotland suggests an avenue for further research.

If the history of political thought and the influence of conciliarism seems the most likely context for reading Columbia Western MS 31 in seventeenth-century England and Scotland, we can still ask if perhaps the *Dyalogus* itself might have had some role in prompting consideration of calendar reform at the time. There was certainly interest in calendar reform in royalist Oxford in the period. John Greaves (1602–1652) proposed a reform in 1645 that involved omitting leap days for 40 years rather than dropping 10 days all at once.[103] In the context of a wider crisis of established authority, the assertion of order over disordered time may have offered an escape from the more pressing and immediate questions of spatial hegemony. In the absence of further evidence, however, this remains an unlikely scenario for the reception of our manuscript.

The preceding discussion has outlined a circumstantial case for interest in the contents of Columbia Western MS 31 in seventeenth-century Scotland and England. But how did it make its way from Leuven to Britain? Unless future archival work uncovers direct evidence we are again left to speculation. Here the author of the inscription might be used as the *deus ex machina*. So who might the neighbour or relative of John Gregory have been, and might they have had links to Leuven? Our research thus far has not uncovered such a figure, but that does not mean they did not exist. If they did have links, it is possible that the manuscript was made available to supporters of Charles in the context of continental Catholic interest in the outcome of struggles between Charles, the Covenanters, and the English parliament. The possibility of a seventeenth-century loan from the library is strengthened by the manuscript *Index* of Petrus Trudonensis and the publication of the *Index codicum*

---

[101] NRS, GD220/1/H/4/4/1–2. We are most grateful to Prof. Laura Stewart for her guidance on this point.
[102] On the wider question of royalists in Scotland, though without reference to Galloway or Gregory, see Robertson, *Royalists at War*.
[103] Poole, *Time's Alteration*, 76–77.

mss. adhuc exstantium in bibliotheca can. regul. s. augustini in Valle S. Martini, Lovanii, anno 1639, which was also compiled by Petrus for publication in Antonius Sanderus's *Bibliotheca belgica manuscripta.*[104] In the *Bibliotheca,* Sanderus lists the works of d'Ailly in Columbia Western MS 31 as well as Petrus de Rivo's *Dyalogus de temporibus Christi.*[105] If this list includes manuscripts physically present in the priory in 1639, then there is a small window between that year and 1643 for the manuscript to have left the priory library.

But we also have to admit the possibility that Petrus Trudonensis was working from an older catalogue and did not personally track the presence of each individual manuscript in the house in the seventeenth century. Although the circumstantial evidence does not point in this direction, the path between Scotland and Leuven was well worn in the fifteenth and sixteenth centuries.[106] From the university's foundation in 1426, Scottish students had travelled there, and Flemish clerics had travelled to Scotland. Among the most famous Scottish clerics to study in Leuven were James Kennedy, William Elphinstone, and William Turnbull, founder of the University of Glasgow. William Scheves, future archbishop of St Andrew's had also travelled to Leuven and purchased books there in the 1490s, as did Gilbert Haldane, Rector of Dalry in 1491.[107] The most direct link to St Martin's that we have been able to trace was a brother Otto Palm in the fifteenth century who was noted for his talent as an astronomer, and who, according to the memory preserved at St Martin's, served William Scheves and the Scottish King, James III.[108] It is possible that such a cleric might have carried a manuscript like Columbia Western MS 31 with him at the time—with or without gaining permission from the priory.

[104] Sanderus, *Bibliotheca belgica manuscripta*, 2:206–233.

[105] Ibid., 2:222.

[106] On the wider connections, see McEvoy, "The Historic Irish, Scots and English Colleges"; Lyall, "Scottish Students and Masters." See also the famous student manuscripts now in the University of Aberdeen Library: MSS 195–197 of William Elfinstone, future bishop of Aberdeen and founder of Aberdeen University, student at Leuven in the 1430s, and MSS 109–110 of George Lichton, a student at Leuven in the 1460s, who was later abbot of the Cistercian Abbey of Kinloss. On these manuscripts, see Ker, "'For All That I may Clamp.'" On student culture more generally, see Geudens and Masolini, "Teaching Aristotle at the Louvain Faculty of Arts." See also the project *Magister Dixit* for the digitalization and study of Leuven lecture notes: http://lectio.ghum.kuleuven.be/lectio/magister-dixit (last accessed 12 August 2020).

[107] See Lyall, "Scottish Students and Masters," 65–66. On the library of Scheves and its Leuven sources, see Connolly, "A Manuscript Owned by William Scheves"; Durkhan and Ross, *Early Scottish Libraries*, 47–49. For Haldane's Leuven books, see ibid., 110–111: Edinburgh University Library, Inc.242 and Inc.16.

[108] Lourdaux, "De Sint-Maartensschool te Leuven," 180. Otto Palm was involved in drafting the *calendarium* that is now Leuven, Rijksarchief, Kerkelijk Archief Brabant, 726, no. 15076. For his entry in the *Liber fratrum* of St Martin's, see Leuven, Rijksarchief, Kerkelijk Archief Brabant, 726, no. 20437/2, fol. 2r. See also Lourdaux, *Moderne devotie en Christelijk humanisme*, 73, 88, 95; Lourdaux, "De Sint-Maartensschool te Leuven," 207; Reusens, ed., *Documents relatifs*, 13:76. On Scheves and James III, see Macdougall, *James III*, 263–270.

This coda is yet more evidence for how manuscripts participate in histories far beyond their original context, allowing for new appropriations and roles; reception histories of manuscripts are seldom simple. Indeed, further twists in the manuscript's life are evident after the seventeenth century. In the list of 392 manuscripts compiled in 1785 following the closure of the house, entry 239 may record the manuscript having been returned to St Martin's—certainly a manuscript of d'Ailly's *Epistola ad novos hebreos* is listed there, although there is no record of Peter's *Dyalogus de temporibus Christi*.[109] Sometime after the house was closed, the book entered the antiquarian collection of John Lee (formerly Fiott) (1773–1866), an English antiquarian, collector, treasurer and president of the British Meteorological Society and a member of the Chronological Society.[110] His signature and bookplate appear now in the volume. And, of course, our new edition itself constitutes a new life for these texts. They now find themselves written into revitalized histories of calendar reform and time in medieval and early modern Europe.[111] What the present volume's authors' interests in the manuscript reveal about the early twenty-first century is a question for later students of the manuscript. That next chapter in the manuscript's history is yet to be written.

---

[109]   Brussels, Algemeen Rijksarchief, Comité van de Religiekas, 73/110. This list is reproduced in Lourdaux and Haverals, *Bibliotheca Vallis Sancti Martini*, 2:lxx–lxxxv, with entry 239 on p. lxxix. On this period at St Martin's, see ibid., 2:198–210.

[110]   McConnell, "Lee [*formerly* Fiott], John." See also Filippoupoliti, "Spatializing the Private Collection."

[111]   See Nothaft, *Dating the Passion*; Champion, *The Fullness of Time*.

The Codices

1. New York, Columbia University, Rare Book and Manuscript Library, Western MS 31[1]

Low Countries, 15th century.

Paper, V, 220, IV' fols. Flyleaves in paper (I–III, V, II'–IV') and parchment (IV, I'). Modern pagination in the top outer margin: Arabic numerals, in ink, for the text (pp. 1–441, p. 393 omitted) and Roman numerals, in pencil, for the flyleaves (pp. i–x, i'–ii'). 210 × 140 mm.

Bound in limp vellum with large front lap. On the back cover, in a 15th-century hand: "Epistola d. Petri de Aliaco contra novos hebreos cum apologia eiusdem pro receptis bibliis." On the spine, a modern hand adds in ink: "Epistola de P. Aliate"; in pencil "1451."

According to the colophon on p. 387, the text of the *Dyalogus de temporibus Christi* was copied by brother Johannes Jordaens in 1471. The name of brother Adam Jordaens de Boghaerden also appears in the manuscript, being reported at the end of the initial rubrics of the first three texts. On one of the flyleaves (p. vii), one reads the names of John Gregory, James Galloway, and John Cotton (1643). The manuscript was in possession of John Lee (born Fiott) of Hartwell House (1783–1866), British antiquary and astronomer. It was donated to the Columbia University Library by the antiquarian bookseller John F. Fleming (1910–1987) on 26 December 1972. In particular, we point to the following notes of ownership and use:

> On the inside front cover: a note and early inventory numbers (in the top left corner: "No. 2789", "quest? Hant.? & Stuart" and, on the right: "No. 28/41"); an erased inscription ("G. …tors"); an armorial bookplate with motto "Verum Atque Decens", belonging to John Lee;[2] the ex libris of the Columbia University Library, with the note: "Presented by John F. Fleming"; the current shelf mark in pencil ("Western MS 31 Aliate"); modern notes in pencil ("Butler Ms.," "Aliate Epistolae," "36 MS").

> On p. ii, a modern hand left a list of abbreviations with their resolutions. The same hand adds a partial table of contents (Texts 1–4) on p. iv, and transcribes the beginning of Pierre d'Ailly's *Epistola ad novos hebreos* (Text 1) on p. x.

> In the bottom margin of p. vii one reads: "propinquus meus Jo. Gregori cum Domino Jacobo Galloway quod Landwade in aedibus D. Jo. Cotton. 1643."; "N.B. These two lines were copied from the cover before the manuscript was rebound. J. Lee."

---

[1] The content of the manuscript is listed in Kristeller, *Iter Italicum*, 5:299. One can find a short description and a selection of images on http://www.digital-scriptorium.org (last accessed 12 August 2020).

[2] Cf. Burke, *A Genealogical and Heraldic History*, 2:768–769; Oates, *A Catalogue of the Fifteenth-Century Printed Books*, 820.

On p. ix, table of contents (15th-century hand).

p. 1: "Adam Iordani," p. 39: "Adam," p. 50: "frater Adam de Boghaerden." The names appear at the end of the rubrics.

p. 387: "Octavo yduum Iuliarum anni 1471 scriptus eram a fratre Johanne Jordani presbytero. Et eodem anno editus in alma universitate studii Lovaniensis per venerabilem et eruditum virum sacre theologie bacallarium formatum magistrum Petrum de Rivo."

A modern hand in pencil transcribes the incipit or explicit on pp. 257, 258, and 286.

I

pp. vii–viii, i'–ii'
Low Countries, 15th century.
Parchment. Fragment. 210 × 140 mm.

Document dated 5 May 1419, with notarial mark; used as flyleaves.

II

pp. 1–441.
Leuven, 15th century ¾.
Paper. 1–16¹², 17⁸, 18¹⁰, 19⁸, and two singletons. Catchwords for quires nn. 1–13 (pp. 24, 48, 72, 120, 168, 192, 216, 240, 264, 288); some of the gatherings are numbered alphabetically (nn. 1–4: a–d; n. 8: b; nn. 9–12: d–g); two bookmarks in fabric; margins have been trimmed. 210 × 140 mm. Text on one column. The size of the writing frame and the number of lines per page vary: (A) pp. 1–113: 180 × 115 mm., ll. 36; (B) pp. 113–144: 180 × 115 mm., ll. 39; (C) pp. 145–312: 145 × 100 mm., ll. 28; (D) pp. 313–429: 145 × 110 mm., ll. 28; ruling in lead; pricking at times visible. Blank pp. 74–76, 95, 136–144, 293–312, 388, 398–402, 421, 430–437, 439, 441.
Writing and decoration: several (but quite similar) hands wrote sections A–C; section D was written by Johannes Jordaens. Initials in red; first initials in blue for section A. The first letter of each paragraph is rubricated. Quotations are often underlined in red or black ink. At p. 2, initial M formed of biting grotesques, in pen and ink. A segment of p. 21 was replaced and rewritten (17 lines).

Contents:
1. pp. 1–38: PIERRE D'AILLY, *Epistola ad novos hebreos*
inc.: "Epistola magistri Petri de Alyaco ad dominum Philippum de Maisieres continens prologum in opus sequens scilicet in epistolam ad novos hebreos. *Adam Iordani.* Viro nobili consulari celsitudine et militari fortitudine prepollenti, domino Philippo de Maisieriis"; expl.: "sollerter attendentes quoniam rationum suarum laqueus contritus est et nos liberati sumus. Explicit nova epistola ad novos hebreos

reverendissimi patris et eruditissimi viri magistri Petri de Alyaco cardinalis camaracensi."

2. pp. 39–49: PIERRE D'AILLY, *Apologeticus*
inc.: "Incipit Apologeticus eiusdem postea super eadem materia editus. *Adam*. Adversus novos hebreos epistolam dudum composui quam intitulare ita placuit"; expl.:
"et hec pro defensione translationis eximii doctoris Ieronimi breviter dicta sunt,
cuius doctrina illuminari et precibus adiuvari supplex oro. Finit apologeticus seu
tractatus defensorius translationis Ieronimi a domino Petro de Aliaco Episcopo
cameracensi."

3. pp. 50–73: PIERRE D'AILLY, *Questio utrum indoctus in iure divino possit iuste
preesse in ecclesie regno*
inc.: "Questio notabilis determinata per magistrum Petrum de Aliaco cardinalem
et episcopum camaracensem. *frater Adam de Boghaerden*. Utrum indoctus in iure
divino possit iuste preesse in ecclesie regno. Arguitur primo quod sic, quia iniustus
potest iuste preesse"; expl.: "Ex quibus videtur apparere in quo esset recurrendus
ad consilium generale et sic breviter transeo de predictis duabus viis, quia tercia
magis est ad propositum questionis."

4. pp. 77–86: PIERRE D'AILLY, *Questio utrum tempus ultimi adventus antichristi
possit a nobis determinate presciri*
inc.: "Incipit questio per eudem determinata. Questio est utrum tempus ultimi adventus Christi possit a nobis determinate presciri. Et arguitur quod sic 4^{ci} ratione";
expl. "dictis patet solutio ad omnia superius allegata et ad utramque partem questionis inducta. Et hec de isto dubio sufficiant. Determinatio dubii precedentis facta
est per magistrum Petrum de Aliaco in quodam sermone quem fecit de quadruplici
adventu domini sub themate: Scitote quoniam prope est regnum Dei."

5. pp. 87–94: NICOLE ORESME, *Questio utrum liceat iudici occidere eum quem
certitudinaliter sit innocentem*
inc.: "Determinacio magistri Nicholai de Oresme sacre theologie professoris et
episcopi Lexoviensis super dubio sequenti. Ama deum. Questio est an in aliquo
casu liceat occidere eum quem certitudinaliter sit innocentem. Dicunt hic aliqui
discordare theologos a iuristis"; expl.: "et sic prout sapiens determinabit providere
quantum potest sine peccato. Finit hec determinatio magistro N. Oresme."

6. pp. 97–112: PIERRE D'AILLY, *Sermo de Trinitate*
inc.: "Sermo de sancta trinitate super verbis apostoli 'Communicatio Spiritus Sancti
sit semper cum omnibus vobis'. Magnus christianorum theologus celestis ille secre-

tarius et divinis apostolus Paulus"; expl.: "quod concedere dignetur sancta trinitas unus deus in secula seculorum amen. Explicit sermo de trinitate factus ianue coram domino papa per dominum P. camaracensem episcopum. Anno domini 1405to in festo sancte trinitatis, Occasione cuius edita fuit constitutio Benedicti 13^i kl. Iulii de celebratione eiusdem festi sub equali celebritate et solemnitate qua festa nativitatis et resurrectionis etc. celebrantur."

7. pp. 113–114: BENEDICT XIII, ANTIPOPE, *Constitutio de institutione festi sancte Trinitatis*
inc.: "Benedictus episcopus servus servorum dei ad perpetuam rei memoriam. Rerum omnium creatricem beatissimam trinitatem cuius sapientia conditi sumus"; expl.: "Qui denota de ipsa trinitate commemorationem in ecclesiis fecerint quinquaginta dies indulgentiarum ex liberalitate apostolica in perpetuum misericorditer elargimur. Nulli ergo etc. Ianue kl. Iulii anno xi°."

8. pp. 115–116: <PIERRE D'AILLY?>, *Articuli super ingressu religionis*
(title in the table on p. ix: "Sex errores super materia ingressus ad religionem")
inc: "Quoniam displicet deo infidelis et stulta promissio sicut dicit sapiens, infidelis autem dicitur quando probabiliter presumitur quod non observabitur"; expl.: "non enim esset iste dolus bonus, sed pessimus obvians sacris patrum antiquorum statutis ymmo et regulis christianis."

9. pp. 117–121: PIERRE D'AILLY, *Determinatio de notoriis focaristis*
(title in the table on p. ix: "Determinatio d. Petri de Alyaco de notoriis focaristis utrum eorundem misse vitande seu ne / et an mortaliter peccent qui eas audiunt")
inc.: "Sunt autem quidam in populo predicantes qui dum hec tollere moliuntur in aliud scandalum incidunt, dum hoc crimen acrius improbando"; expl.: "Et non solum mittat sed iam missos nos et vos dignos et ydoneos operarios efficiat. Quod ipse prestare dignetur qui sine fine vivit et regnat in secula seculorum Amen."

10. pp. 122–134: NICOLAS DE CLAMANGES, *De fructu eremi*
inc.: "Tractatus de laude vite solitarie ac de fructu heremi editus a magistro Nycolao de Clamengiis cantore ecclesie Baiocensis. Doceri per me desideras qui ita in solitudinibus atque in heremo"; expl., p. 134: "atque explicat aromata, eorum tamen et virtutis et odorifere expers fragrantie. Explicit."
The text is followed by the dedicatory letter of Nicolas de Clamanges to Pierre d'Ailly:
pp. 134–135: inc.: "Preclarissimo antistiti domino episcopo camaracensi domino et priori prestantissimo, suus orator et discipulus Nycolaus de Clamengiis nuper cum abunde ocia suppeterent quendam de heremi fructum tractatulum rogatus ab ami-

co"; expl.: "Vale pater preclarissime tam mundane prosperitatis quam eternorum gaudiorum assecutione felix. Scriptum apud fontem in bosco xviii Novembris."

11. pp. 145-206: PIERRE D'AILLY, *Tractatus de potestate ecclesiastica*
inc.: "Tractatus de origine et potestate ecclesiastice iurisdictionis per Reverendissimum in christo patrem et dominum dominum Petrum de Aliaco cardinalem tituli sancti Crisogoni Camaracensi vulgariter nuncupatum editus in concilio constanciensi feliciter incipit. Christi nomine invocato cui data est ipso teste"; expl.: "offerens nichilominus ad veritatis elucidacionem me illis qui contra premissa opponere voluerint responsurum. Explicit tractatus de origine et potestate ecclesiastice iurisdictionis, editus a reverendissimo in christo patre et domino domino Petro cardinale camaracensi de Aliaco vulgariter nuncupato, copulatus in sacro generali concilio constanciensi."

12. pp. 207–257: JEAN GERSON, *Tractatus de potestate ecclesiastica*
inc.: "Incipit tractatus de potestate ecclesiastica Editus per venerabilem sacre theologie professorem magistrum Iohannem Gerson Cancellarium parisiensem. Potestas ecclesiastica debet ab ecclesiasticis quid et qualis"; expl.: "Ratus vero dupliciter fit vel de iure vel de facto. De hoc opere laudetur deus benedictus in secula Amen. Explicit tractatus magistri Iohannis Gerson de potestate ecclesiastica et de origine iurium et legum."

13. pp. 258–285: JEAN MAUROUX, *De superioritate inter concilium et papam*
inc.: "Incipit tractatus de potestate concilii Editus per reverendum patrem dominum Iohannem patriarcham Anthiochenum Anno domini 1433 In generali concilio basiliensi Dey°us assit. Sacrosancte generali synodo basiliensi in spiritu sancto legitime congregate universalem ecclesiam representanti vester devotus humilis Iohannes patriarcha Antiochenus [...] Quia nonnulli os suum aperientes"; expl.: "sed ei iuxta decretum concilii constanciensis et alia supradicta tenetur obedire. Explicit laus deo."

14. pp. 286–292: JEAN GERSON, *De modo se habendi tempore schismatis*
inc.: "Conclusiones quidam magistri Iohannis Gersoni cancellarii parisiensis ad tollendam aliquorum pertinaciam quorundam eciam scrupolositatem propter scisma quod incepit per Urbanum sextum et Clementem Anno 1378 et duravit usque ad electionem Martini quinti tempore concilii constancensis Anno domini m°cccc° decimoseptimo. Ad tollendam quorundam in scismate pertinaciam improbitatemque nimiam"; expl.: "ad instar linearum rectarum ad idem centrum ductarum non se mutuo impediunt intersecant vel confundunt. Explicit Deo gratias."

15. pp. 313–429: PETER DE RIVO, *Dyalogus de temporibus Christi*

inc.: "Incipit prologus in dyalogum de temporibus domini nostri Ihesu Christi editum in universitate studii Lovaniensis per venerabilem et eruditum virum sacre theologie bacallarium magistrum Petrum de Rivo. Etsi de rationibus temporum plerique cronicorum subtilissime disseruerint"; expl., p. 387: "Condignas tibi reddere dignetur Ihesus Christus verus noster messias. Et valeto. Octavo yduum Iuliarum anni 1471 scriptus eram a fratre Johanne Jordani presbytero. Et eodem anno editus in alma universitate studii Lovaniensis per venerabilem et eruditum virum sacre theologie bacallarium formatum magistrum Petrum de Rivo."

The text is followed by:

pp. 388–397: *Summarum dialogi de temporibus domini nostri Ihesu christi.*

inc: "Controversie que sunt de anno nativitatis Christi. Secundum Bedam, Orosium, Eusebium et fere omnes historiographos Christus natus est anno imperii Augusti XLII°"; expl.: "in memoriam mortis dominica campana trahitur in meridie, nam occidentalibus fuit meridies Christo pro eis moriente."

pp. 403–429: Diagrams and tables.

pp. 438–441: Flyleaves from a register, in Flemish.

The content of MS 31 coincides almost entirely with that of MS K.40 described in the seventeenth century inventory of the library of the house of St Martin in Louvain by Petrus Trudonensis.[3] Note, however, that Text 8 of MS 31 does not appear in the list of contents of K.40.

2.   A Bethleem Codex, Divided between Brussels and Cambridge

Part 1 = Brussels, KBR, 11750–11751[4]

Leuven; late 15th century.

Paper, II, 181, I fols. Modern foliation in Arabic numbers, in ink, in the top outer corner. 1–6[10], 7[12], 8[2], 9–15[12], 16[12+1]. Catchwords on fols. 31v and 71v; gatherings numbered with alphanumeric sigla in the bottom outer corner. 285 × 205 mm. One can distinguish two main layouts: (A) fols. 2r–83v: writing frame 200 × 150 mm., 41 ll., on two columns; (B) fols. 86r–182v: 210 × 150 mm., lines of text and organization of layout within the writing frame vary; ruling in lead; pricking visible. Blank fols. 83v, 84r–85v.

Half binding, dorse in red leather with titles and royal cypher of Leopold I in gold. Writing and decoration: one hand wrote section (A) (Richardus Hermanni); several hands wrote section (B). Initials decorated in red and blue ink; rubrics.

---

3   Lourdaux and Haverals, *Bibliotheca Vallis Sancti Martini*, 419. See p. cxxi above.

4   Van den Gheyn, ed., *Catalogue des manuscrits de la Bibliothèque royale de Belgique*, 1:164, no. 305.

The manuscript was in the possession of the Augustinian priory of Bethleem, at
Herent, outside Leuven, as witnessed by the ownership notes found on fol. 2r ("be-
thelem"; "Pertinet monasterio beate Marie in Bethleem prope Lovanium").

On fol. 1v, one reads the list of contents of the original volume, accompanied by
comments on who wrote the texts or how they came into possession of the priory:

"In hoc libro continentur

Augustinus super genesim ad litteram – confrater noster Richardus Hermanni
scripsit

Monotesseron evangelicum venerabilis magistri Petri de Rivo – diversi fratres
scripserunt simul

Opera eiusdem contra magistrum Paulum de Middelburgho – data sunt tempori
nostro ab eodem magistro Petro

Idem de reformatione Kalendarii – Frater Petrus Maes scripsit."

Contents:

1. fols. 2ra–83rb: AUGUSTINE, *De Genesi ad litteram*
inc.: "Incipit prefacio beati Augustini episcopi de libro retractacioni. In libro super
genesim ad litteram. Per idem tempus de genesi libros duodecimi scripsi ab exordio
... Omnis divina Scriptura bipartita est, secundum id quod dominus significat";
expl.: "Sed iam universum hoc opus quod duodecim voluminibus continetur isto
tandem fine concludimus."

2. fols. 86r–182v. PETER DE RIVO, *Monotesseron evangelicum de verbo Dei temporaliter incarnato*
inc.: "Presens volumen quod in unum quatuor evangelia complectitur non inepte
dici potest Monotesseron... Prefaciones quas Lucas Matheus et Marcus suis evan-
geliis premittunt. Atribus est opus sacrum prefacio facta."

Peter de Rivo's writings against Paul of Middelburg and the *Reformacio kalendarii*,
which originally belonged to this codex, are now preserved at the University Library
of Cambridge.

Part 2 = Cambridge, University Library, Inc 3.F.2.9 [3294][5]
Leuven, 15th century.
Paper, II, 82, II fols. a–d⁸, e⁶, f⁸, 4 handwritten fols., a–d⁸. 270 × 200 mm. (the volume
has been cut down from his original size). Blank fol. viii.

---

5   Oates, *A Catalogue of the Fifteenth-Century Printed Books*, 633, no. 3825. Cf. Derolez et al.,
Corpus Catalogorum Belgii, 7:309.

Writing frame of the handwritten folios: 200 × 140 mm., ll. 41, on one column; ruling in lead; pricking visible.

Writing and decoration: the text of the *Reformacio* was written by one hand (Petrus Maes, according to the table of contents found in MS Brussels, KBR, 11750–11751, fol. 1v). Rubricated. The woodcuts included in the *Opus Responsivum* are coloured. On the final page of the volume: "Pertinet monasterio beate Marie in Bethleem prope Lovanium."

Contents:

1. PETER DE RIVO, *Opus responsivum ad Epistolam apologeticam M. Pauli de Middelburgo de anno, die et feria dominicae passionis*, Leuven: Ludovicus Ravescot, [1489].

2. PETER DE RIVO, *Reformacio kalendarii Romani* (4 fols., unnumbered:) inc. at fol. [1r]: "Reformacio kalendarii Romani eiusque reductio ad statum pristinum in quo fu<i>t temporibus patrum qui decreta et ordinaciones ediderunt ut paschalis festivitas a fidelibus non nisi die dominico celebretur. Decreta et ordinaciones patrum de paschali festivitate rite servanda. Constat ex cronicis Eusebii Cesariensis"; expl. at fol. [3r]: "ut in solis CCCIIII annis semel cessetur a bissexto. Hec sub omni melius sentientium correctione cum multis lucubrationibus pro reparatione kalendarii Romani elaborata sunt in universitate generalis studii Lovaniensis anno domini millesimo quadringentesimo octogesimo octavo ad laudem Dei et gloriam sacrosancte matris ecclesie sponse eius individue et immaculati. Amen." fols. [3v–4v]: Table and diagrams.

3. PETER DE RIVO. *Tercius tractatus de anno, die et feria dominicae passionis atque resurrectionis*. Leuven: Johannes de Westfalia, 1492.

Principles of Edition

The editions of the *Dyalogus* and *Reformacio* follow the orthography of the respective manuscript, excepting a small handful of instances where it seemed preferable to normalize spelling for the sake of consistency, e.g. *neccesse > necesse, connicere > conicere*. Also, *u/v*-spelling has been normalized throughout. Numbers are transcribed as they appear in the manuscripts, although sometimes expansions were applied to increase readability. Our division of the texts into paragraphs follows that of the manuscripts. Rubricated parts are represented in bold print. Italics in the main text serve to indicate verbatim borrowings from Peter's sources.

Text and apparatus employ the following symbols and abbreviations:

	location of a page break in the manuscript
<...>	editorial or conjectural insertion
a.c.	state of the text before correction (*ante correctionem*)
add.	text added in the manuscript
p.c.	state of the text after correction (*post correctionem*)
s.l.	text added above the line (*supra lineam*)

\<Dyalogus de temporibus Christi\>

\<Prologus\>

Incipit prologus in dyalogum de temporibus domini nostri Ihesu Christi 313
editum in universitate studii Lovaniensis per venerabilem et eruditum
5 **virum sacre theologie bacallarium magistrum Petrum de Rivo.**

Etsi de rationibus temporum plerique cronicorum subtilissime disseruerint,
neminem tamen de temporibus domini nostri Ihesu Christi curam reperio satis
exactam habuisse. Quoto Cesaris Augusti anno natus sit, quotum agens annum,
quo denique mense, quo die, qua hora mortem obierit a diversis non
10 mediocribus viris adeo diverse atque incerte dicitur ut ab emulis Christiane fidei,
si hanc doctorum nostrorum controversiam perpenderint, nobis non modicam
posse putem ignominiam irrogari. Hanc itaque rem viris catholicis mea sentencia
scitu dignissimam tam variis animadvertens intricatam opinionibus multis cepi
lucubrationibus temptare, si forte huiuscemodi controversie causam, et quid in
15 ea verius asserendum sit, pernoscere valerem. Post multos tandem cogitatus non
meis tantum satisfactum sensi conatibus, sed et plurimas alias, velut ex
improviso, michi visus sum veritates repperisse. Ne vero michi soli laboraverim
quicquid in tam arduo perdifficilique negocio scrutatus sum in hoc libello humili
utcumque licuit stilo contexui, quem si huiusmodi rerum periti probaverint,
20 optatissimum pro laboribus premium existimabo aliquid de Christo quod
plurimos latet recte conscripsisse. Sin refutarint, saltem nonnullis data erit
occasio veritatem exquisitius indagandi. Quoniam autem multum habet
suavitatis ac non parum ad doctrinam confert oratio per dyalogum conscripta,
duos colloquentes inducam: Gamalielem et Paulum; Gamalielem quidem
25 Iudeum de dicta stupentem Christianorum varietate, et Paulum Christianum
quascumque difficultatum ambages ille producturus est iuxta
approbatissimorum ecclesie doctorum sentencias dissolventem. Sic velut olim a
Gamaliele Paulus legem didicerat, sic in hoc opusculo que fidei sunt Gamaliel a
Paulo doceri videbitur. Quodsi peritiores, quorum iudicio singula tam dicta mea
30 quam scripta submisi et submitto, hunc meum laborem utilem ecclesie
censuerint, videbitur summus ac sanctissimus noster pontifex dominus Paulus
huius nominis papa secundus, hic illos docere qui de | tempore dubitant 314
dominice nativitatis aut passionis. Ut autem omnia magis sint legentibus
perspicua, opus hoc in tres tractatus divisi, et quemque tractatuum in tria
35 capitula. In primo tractatu Gamaliel singulas quas novit controversias proponet.
Primo de anno nativitatis Christi in primo capitulo, deinde de anno passionis in
2°, et demum de die et hora mortis dominice in capitulo 3°. In 2° tractatu, ad

---

32 dubitant … 33 dominice| dominice dubitant *a.c.*

dissolvendas huiusmodi controversias, dominus Paulus disseret de tribus ciclis, utpote de ciclo solari in primo capitulo, de ciclo decemnovenali in 2°, ac de ciclo lunari in 3°. In 3° tractatu Gamaliel sub brevibus controversias repetet easque   40 dominus Paulus dissolvet. Primo que concernunt annum quo Christus natus est in primo capitulo, dehinc que concernunt annum quo passus est in 2°, et postremo que concernunt diem et horam quibus dignatus est pro mortalibus mortis opprobrium sustinere in tercio. Primum itaque Gamalielem loquentem audiamus.   45

\<Tractatus 1\>

\<Capitulum 1\>

Incipit dyalogus de temporibus domini nostri Ihesu Christi editus anno a nativitate domini 1471. Primus tractatus continet controversias que sunt
5 **circa tempora Christi. Primum capitulum continet eas que sunt de anno sue nativitatis.**

Gamaliel: Cum diutinam generis nostri deiectionem eamque in dies magis magisque invalescere considero, existimare nequeo nos non frustra nostrum Messiam expectare. Nonne Iacob patriarcha de eius prophetans adventu ita
10 exorsus est: *Non auferetur habens potestatem de domo Iuda nec scriba de filiis filiorum eius usque in secula donec veniat Messias?* Nonne et Gabriel archangelus tempus adventus eius Danieli revelans *Septuaginta,* inquit, *ebdomades* decise *sunt super populum tuum et super urbem sanctam tuam ut consummetur prevaricatio et finem accipiat peccatum et deleatur iniquitas et adducatur iusticia sempiterna et impleatur visio et prophetia et ungatur sanctus*
15 *sanctorum?* Cum itaque nusquam supersit habens potestatem de domo Iuda, et citra tempus dicte revelationis effluxerint non sole septuaginta ebdomades, sed circiter duo milia annorum, que faciunt ebdomadas annorum ducentas octogintaquinque, satius creden|dum arbitror non venturum, sed ante multa iam 315 tempora Messiam advenisse. Quamobrem summopere nobis scrutandum est
20 quis ex preclaris viris qui preterierunt conformius ad prophetica de nostro Messia testimonia vixerit quatinus illum verum Messiam confiteamur.

Inspectis autem quamplurimis historiographorum voluminibus nemini pocius congruere video que de Messia prophetata sunt quam Ihesu crucifixo. Hunc ipsum igitur nobis promissum existimarem, nisi de tempore tam nativitatis
25 sue quam mortis eorum qui ipsum colunt adeo differentes essent sentencie ut quasi fabula videatur ipsum preteriisse. Verum si quis me cronicorum de ea quam reperio temporum diversitate certiorem reddiderit, nichil me retrahet quin fidem ipsius amplectar quamprimum. Sed nonne dominum Paulum video, quo presens seculum in rationibus temporum enucleandis peritiorem habet
30 neminem? Solus venit, ut ipsum aggrediar solita eius benignitas michi fiduciam prestat. Salve, mi domine Paule.

---

10 Non…11 Messias] Genesis 49:10, *Translatio Chaldaica* (Targum Onkelos) *ap.* Paul of Burgos, *Scrutinium scripturarum,* pars 1, dist. 3, c. 2 (ed. Strasbourg 1474, fol. 17r).   **12** Septuaginta…15 sanctorum] Daniel 9:24.

---

18 octogintaquinque] 85 *p.c.,* sexagintatres *a.c.*   **21** vixerit] dixerit *p.c.*   **24** promissum existimarem] existimarem promissum *a.c.*

Paulus: Ut item salvus sis, Gamaliel, peropto. Verum in qua fide salventur homines non eque credimus. Absque fide domini nostri Ihesu Christi neminem salvari posse firmiter teneo. Hanc tui vanam et inutilem asseverant.

Gamaliel: Non eadem que reliquis Hebreis michi mens est. Expectant 35 ceteri Messiam, eum iam advenisse reor. Atque eum ipsum Ihesum tuum facile credidero, si nonnullas quas inter Christianos reperio diversitates michi dissolvas.

Paulus: Eas, velim, hic loci in medium proferas, nec mea tibi deerit opera ad veritatem in hiis potissimum rebus indagandam que tue saluti profecture 40 sunt.

Gamaliel: Ut iubes que michi mentem angunt edicam: Ihesum aiunt virum fuisse opere et sermone potentem, sed quando natus sit, quando mortem obierit, tam varie dicitur ut fabula pocius quam historia videatur.

Paulus: Rem, audio, perdifficilem proferes. Ne diffidas tamen ac ordine 45 servato primum singulos illos recita quos nosti circa tempus nativitatis Ihesu Christi dissentire.

Gamaliel: Communis est omni sentencia Ihesum natum esse Augusto 316 regnante, sed quoto eius anno non mediocrem controversiam | invenio, nonnullis dicentibus quod quadragesimosecundo, aliis quod XLI°, aliis quod 50 XXXIX° aut XXXIIII°, aliis quod XXXI° imperii eius anno natus sit.

Beda, qui rationes temporum subtilissime scrutatur, ac historiographi famosiores, ut Orosius, Eusebius, Vincentius, ac plures alii, eum natum dicunt anno imperii Augusti XLII°. Et hec est vulgatior Christianorum opinio.

Tertullianus tamen, maxime olim vir auctoritatis et in doctrina beato 55 Cipriano tam acceptus ut solitus sit numquam absque Tertulliani lectione unam diem preterisse, is, in libro quem Contra Iudeos scripsit, Ihesum natum asserit anno Augusti XLI°. Unde inter cetera eius verba que Iheronimus Super Danielem recitat sic habetur: *Cleopatra cum Augusto regnavit annis tredecim. Post Cleopatram Augustus annis XLIII imperavit. Nam omnes anni imperii Augusti fuerunt* 60 *numero LVI. Videamus autem quoniam in XLI° anno imperii* eius, *qui post mortem Cleopatre imperavit, nascitur Christus.* Hec ille.

---

43 opere…potentem] Luke 24:19.   **53** eum…54 XLII°] Bede, *De temporum ratione*, c. 66 (a. 3952) (ed. CCSL 123B, 495); Orosius, *Historia adversum paganos* 7.2.14 (ed. Arnaud-Lindet, 3:19); Eusebius of Caesarea, *Chronicon* (trans. Jerome of Stridon) (ed. GCS 47, 169); Vincent of Beauvais, *Speculum historiale*, lib. 6, c. 88 (ed. Douai 1624, 203).   **57** Ihesum…58 XLI°] Tertullian, *Adversus Iudaeos* 8.11 (ed. Tränkle, 17–18).   **59** Cleopatra…62 Christus] Jerome of Stridon, *Commentarii in Danielem* 3.9.24 (ed. CCSL 75A, 883, ll. 507–512).

---

39 deerit] deerit

Alphonsus, qui tabulas suas exactissima collegit diligentia, Ihesum natum innuit anno Cesaris XXXIX°. Dicit namque differentiam erarum Cesaris et
65   incarnationis esse quarta 0, tercia tria, secunda quinquagintaunum, prima viginti, que faciunt annos XXXVIII. Si ergo in hac differentia erarum locutus est de Cesare Augusto, constat eum voluisse Ihesum natum esse anno Augusti XXXIX°, quoniam eodem anno Romano incarnatus est et natus. Si locutus est de Iulio Cesare, qui anno sexto ante Augustum regnare cepit, consequens est
70   secundum eum Ihesum natum esse anno Augusti XXXIIII°.

Gerardus Cremonensis, translator Almagesti Ptolomei, Ihesum natum innuit anno Augusti XXXI°. Unde dicit quod annis Arabum quingentis LXXXV, uno mense, XXIIII diebus, XV horis, et XL secundis transactis era Augusti fuit anni MCCXX, dies CXLV, quarte 0, era vero incarnationis anni
75   MCXC, dies LXXXI, quarte due. Iam si a dicta era Augusti subtrahatur era incarnationis remanent anni XXX, dies LXIIII, quare secundum hunc calculum Ihesus incarnatus fuit anno Cesaris Augusti XXXI°. Huic opinionem alludere videtur libellus De vetula, | qui licet dicatur esse Ovidii, tot tamen in eo   317 videntur haberi maxima Christiane fidei misteria ut auctor eius pocius
80   existimandus sit aliquis Christianorum. Unde ibidem sic scribitur: *Una quidem talis*, supple 'coniunctio', *felici tempore nuper / Cesaris Augusti fuit anno bis duodeno / A regni novitate sui, que significavit / Post annum sextum nasci debere prophetam / Absque maris coitu de virgine.* Hunc prophetam aiunt Christiani fuisse Ihesum, qui solus creditur natus de virgine. Natus est ergo post annum bis XII^m ac sextum hoc est
85   tricesimum imperii Augusti, anno scilicet XXXI°.

Si denique anni Ihesu ad annos Dyocleciani comparentur, nativitas eius reperitur tribus annis prius contigisse secundum historiographos quam secundum calculatores astronomos. Beda quidem, Vincentius, et alii historiarum scriptores dicunt imperium Diocleciani cepisse anno incarnationis
90   CCLXXXVII°. Secundum Alphonsum vero cepit anno incarnationis CCLXXXIIII°. Dicit enim differentiam incarnationis et Diocleciani esse quarta 0, tercia XXVIII, secunda XLVI, prima XLVI, que faciunt annos CCLXXXIII, dies CCXL, quare vult imperium Diocleciani cepisse anno incarnationis CCLXXXIIII°. Idem sentit dictus translator Ptolomei. Dicit enim eram

---

64 differentiam…66 XXXVIII] *Tabule astronomice illustrissimi Alfontii regis Castelle* (ed. Poulle, 108).
71 Ihesum…75 due] *Almagestum Ptolomei*, MS Berlin, Staatsbibliothek, lat. fol. 753, fol. 120v.
80 Una…83 virgine] ps.-Ovid *ap.* Roger Bacon, *Opus maius*, lib. IV (ed. Bridges, 1:264); cf. ps.-Ovid, *De vetula* 3.611-615 (ed. Klopsch, 272).   **89** imperium…90 CCLXXXVII°] Bede, *De temporum ratione*, c. 66 (a. 3952, 4263) (ed. CCSL 123B, 495, 507); Vincent of Beauvais, *Speculum historiale*, lib. 12, c. 1 (ed. Douai 1624, 456).   **91** differentiam…94 CCLXXXIIII°] *Tabule astronomice illustrissimi Alfontii regis Castelle* (ed. Poulle, 108).   **94** eram…96 LXXXI] *Almagestum Ptolomei*, MS Berlin, Staatsbibliothek, lat. fol. 753, fol. 120v.

---

81 felici] felicis   **92** CCLXXXIII] CCLXXXIII°

Diocleciani fuisse annos nongentos sex, dies CCVI, quando era Christi fuit anni 95
MCXC, dies LXXXI, a qua era si subtrahatur era Diocleciani remanent anni
CCLXXXIII, dies CCXL, quare ut prius.

Est et alia differentia que michi non mediocrem scrupulum facit, quoniam
Dyonisius abbas Romane urbis primus ab incarnatione Christi annorum
tempora prenotavit cum Greci calculatores cursum temporum ab annis 100
Diocleciani prius observassent. Sigebertus tamen Gemblacensis monachus in
libro suo De viris illustribus, loquens de dicto Dionisio, *Scripsit*, inquit, *post
Cirillum ciclum quinque ciclorum incipiens ab anno nati Ihesu quingentesimo tricesimo
secundo, qui est ultimus magni cicli semel exacti a nativitate Christi.* Et subdit *si nativitas
Christi recte a calculatoribus posita fuisset, debuisset tricesimus tercius vel XXXIIII^{tus} annus* 105
sui magni cicli concordare in ratione compoti evangelice veritati et maiorum auctoritati, que
318   *dicit Christum passum fuisse anno etatis sue XXXII° | vel XXXIII octavo kalendas*
Aprilis in feria sexta et eum resurrexisse VI kalendas Aprilis in prima feria, quod non ita
in ciclo suo reperitur. Et tandem infert quod *nativitas Christi posita est a*
calculatoribus vigintiuno vel XXII annis tardius quam debuit. In quibus omnibus 110
insequi videtur Marianum Scotum, qui, ut idem Sigebertus commemorat,
peregrinans pro Christo in Gallias factus monachus et apud Maguntiam multis annis
inclusus, scripsit cronicam a nativitate Christi usque ad annum domini MLXXXII mira
subtilitate ostendens errorem priorum cronographorum ita ponentium nativitatem Christi ut
annus passionis eius non concordet evangelice veritati. Unde ipse, apponens XXII annos illi 115
anno ubi priores scribunt fuisse natum Christum, ponit in margine pagine alternatim hinc
annos evangelice veritatis, illinc annos false prioris computationis, ut non modo intellectu, sed et
*visu discerni possit veritas a falsita*te.

Gerlandus vero, compotista eximius, videns secundum computacionem
Dionisii ea *salvari non posse* que a patribus dicta sunt de passione Christi, *septem* 120
annos dempsit a *computatione Dionisii et posuit* Ihesum natum fuisse anno nono cicli
decemnovenalis, qui secundum Dyonisium natus fuit anno 2° eiusdem cicli. Ex
dicta differentia intollerabile videtur oriri scandalum apud Christianos, ut scilicet
ignorent quotus sit a nativitate Christi annus presens. Secundum enim
Dyonisium, cuius calculum sequitur ecclesia, est MCCCCLXXI. Secundum 125
Sigebertum et Marianum additis annis XXII est MCCCXCIII. Secundum
Gerlandum vero annis septem demptis est MCCCCLXIIII.

Non videntur eciam compotiste de annis Christi conformem habere
sentenciam. Secundum aliquos natus est anno XXI cicli solaris, secundum alios

---

102 Scripsit…110 debuit] Sigebert of Gembloux, *Catalogus de viris illustribus*, § 27 (ed. Witte, 58–59).
112 peregrinans…118 falsitate] Sigebert of Gembloux, *Catalogus de viris illustribus*, § 160 (ed. Witte,
99).   119 Gerlandus…122 cicli] Roger Bacon, *Opus maius*, lib. IV (ed. Bridges, 1:205); cf. *Computus*
Gerlandi, lib. 1, c. 26 (ed. Lohr, 157–159).

106 ratione] rationem   113 MLXXXII] MLXXXIX

130 anno decimo eiusdem cicli. Insuper, cum ciclus decemnovenalis idem videatur
     esse cum lunari, uterque enim ciclus XIX annos complectens cursum lunaris
     sideris insinuare videtur, admiratione dignum est cur a compotistis Ihesus natus
     dicatur anno secundo cicli decemnovenalis et XVIII cicli lunaris.

     Postremo circa annos Ihesu | non parvum michi stuporem affert quod   319
135 ecclesia Gallicana annos computans ab incarnatione Christi ab ecclesiis Ytalicis
     annos computantibus ab eius nativitate uno anno prevenitur, saltem ab octavo
     kl. Ianuarii usque pascha sequens. Verbi gratia, festum circumcisionis proxime
     preteritum fuit apud Gallos anno ab incarnatione MCCCCLXX° et apud Ytalos
     anno a nativitate Christi MCCCCLXXI°. Unde sequi videtur quod apud hos
140 uno anno prius natus sit quam apud illos, aut quod nativitas Ihesu
     incarnationem precessisset.

     Hee differentie circa annum nativitatis Ihesu michi, domine Paule, nunc
     temporum occurrunt, in quibus nisi me certiorem reddideres credere nequeo
     Ihesum in quem credis precessisse. Qualiter, queso, si precessisset, eius cultores
145 quasi cecutientes de tempore sue nativitatis tam varie sensissent, cum ceteras
     sectas quasque de suo initio adeo concorditer loquentes audiamus?

     Paulus: Dic michi, queso, Gamaliel, an ne urbem Romam conditam putes.
     Id profecto inficiabitur nemo. Est tamen de eius origine non mediocris
     maximorum virorum dissensio. Nonnulli, ut Ysidorus testatur libro
150 Ethimologiarum, eam a Troyanis, alii ab Evandro, alii a Romulo condita
     astruunt. Sic quamquam de temporibus domini nostri Ihesu Christi diverse sint
     Christianorum sentencie, cum tamen tot reliquerit doctrine sue tam sequaces
     quam emulos ambigendum non est ipsum preteriisse. Sed audire libuit egregias
     illas difficultates quas protulisti. Quoniam vero et hee et relique quas proferes
155 eiusdem forsan discussionis egebunt, si quas alias nostrorum differentias noveris
     circa annum passionis dominice, eas, ut simul dissolvantur, denuo velut novum
     sumens exordium in medium adducas.

\<Capitulum 2\>

Secundum capitulum continet controversias de anno passionis Christi.

     Gamaliel: Iussum tuum quoad potero adimplere cupiens, domine mi Paule,
     brevibus annectam quam varie Christianos loquentes reperio de anno quo
5   Ihesum credunt mortem obisse. Astruunt nonnulli id actum anno etatis sue
     tricesimo, alii XXXI°, alii XXXIII°, alii XXXIIII°. Orosius, vir eloquens, ita

---

137 Verbi…139 MCCCCLXXI°] Cf. Pierre d'Ailly, *Elucidarium astronomice concordie cum theologica et hystorica veritate*, c. 38, in idem, *Imago mundi* (ed. Leuven 1477/83, sig. gg5r–v).   **150** eam…151 astruunt] Isidore of Seville, *Etymologiae* 15.1.1 (ed. Guillaumin, 3).

---

146 quasque] quamque

scribit in De ormesta mundi: *Deinde anno eiusdem*, utpote Tiberii XV, *cum Dominus*
320 | *Ihesus Christus voluntarie quidem se tradidit passioni, sed impie a Iudeis apprehensus et*
patibulo affixus, maximo terremotu per orbem facto, saxa a montibus scissa, maximarumque
urbium partes plus solita concussione ceciderunt. Constat autem ex evangelio Luce quod   10
XV *anno Tiberii* Ihesus incepit esse *quasi annorum XXX.* Videtur igitur Orosius
voluisse quod anno etatis sue tricesimo patibulo crucis affixus sit.

Idem sensisse videtur et Affricanus, cuius Eusebius meminit in sexto libro
Ecclesiastice historie. *Per idem*, inquit, *tempus erat Affricanus vir inter ceteros scriptores*
nobilis, et *venerunt ad nos* eiusdem *opuscula et maxime cronica valde diligenter studioseque*   15
composita. Huius opinionem de LXX ebdomadibus Iheronimus, Super Danielem,
de verbo ad verbum recitans inter cetera sic dicit: *Permansit enim regnum Persarum,*
usque ad initium Macedonum, annis ducentis triginta, et ipsi Macedones regnaverunt annis
CCC, *atque exinde usque ad annum XV Tiberii Cesaris, quando passus est Christus,*
numerantur anni LX etc.   20

Tertullianus autem expressius asserit Ihesum passum anno suo XXX°.
Unde Iheronimus eius sentenciam de LXX ebdomadibus pertractans sub eisdem
quibus ipse usus est verbis tandem sic ait: *Post Augustum, qui supervixit post*
nativitatem Christi anni XV efficiuntur. Cui successit Tiberius Cesar, cuius XV anno
Tiberii patitur Christus, annos habens XXX cum pateretur. Quod Iheronimus tam   25
Affricani quam Tertulliani auctoritatem magnifecerit ex hoc liquet quod
priusquam ipsorum ac aliorum sentencias recitat ita premittit: *Quia periculosum est*
de aliquorum *magistrorum ecclesie iudicare sentenciis et alterum preferre alteri, dicam quid*
unusquisque senserit, lectoris arbitrio relinquens cuius expositionem sequi debeat.

Sunt insuper nonnulli compotiste qui Christum passum affirmant anno suo   30
XXXI° innitentes potissimum verbis Bede, qui, de die dominico pasche
disserens, ait inter cetera: *Si sexto kl. Aprilium Dominus resurrexit, XIII^{us} cicli*
decemnovenalis annus extitit lunam habens XIIII^{tam}, ut semper nono kl. Aprilium. Item,
tractans de annis dominice incarnationis, *quod*, inquit, *VIII° kl. Aprilium crucifixus*
sexto earundem kl. die resurrexit, multorum late doctorum ecclesiasticorum constat sentencia   35
vulgatum. Fuit igitur annus quo Ihesus paciebatur XIII^{us} cicli decemnovenalis.
321 Compo | tiste autem concorditer dicunt annum nativitatis Christi fuisse 2um

---

7 Deinde…10 ceciderunt] Orosius, *Historia adversum paganos* 7.4.13 (ed. Arnaud-Lindet, 3:25).
11 quasi…XXX] Luke 3:1, 23.   **14** Per…16 composita] Eusebius of Caesarea, *Historia ecclesiastica*
(trans. Rufinus of Aquileia) 6.31.1–2 (ed. GCS 9.2, 585, 587).   **17** Permansit…20 etc] Jerome of
Stridon, *Commentarii in Danielem* 3.9.24 (ed. CCSL 75A, 867, ll. 190–195).   **23** Post…25 pateretur]
Jerome of Stridon, *Commentarii in Danielem* 3.9.24 (ed. CCSL 75A, 867, ll. 536–541); Tertullian,
Adversus Iudaeos 8.16 (ed. Tränkle, 19).   **27** Quia…29 debeat] Jerome of Stridon, *Commentarii in*
Danielem 3.9.24 (ed. CCSL 75A, 865, ll. 140–143).   **32** Si…33 Aprilium] Bede, *De temporum ratione*, c.
61 (ed. CCSL 123B, 452, ll. 68–71).   **34** quod…36 vulgatum] Bede, *De temporum ratione*, c. 47 (ed.
CCSL 123B, 432, ll. 98–100).

---

10 solita] solito

eiusdem cicli, unde liquet annum eius XVIII fuisse ultimum cicli
decemnovenalis, demum ab anno XIX° Christi, qui fuit primus cicli sequentis,
40   progrediendo invenietur annus XIII incidere in annum a nativitate Christi
XXXI^m, quare eodem anno concludunt Ihesum mortuum esse ac a mortuis
resurrexisse.

Qui rationes temporum ex evangelica scrutantur historia Ihesum aiunt
mortem obisse anno etatis sue vel XXXIII° vel XXXIIII°. Velut enim Luce
45   tercio scribitur, *anno XV Tiberii* Ihesus baptizatus est *incipiens quasi annorum
XXX*, quod factum creditur VIII° ydus Ianuarii. Hinc residuum vite sue
tempus, ut Eusebius in Ecclesiastica testatur historia, reperitur *intra quadriennii
temporis spacium coartari*. Sed quadriennium illud non equaliter ab omnibus
inchoatur. Quidam ipsum inchoant ab anno vite Ihesu XXX°, quidam ab anno
50   eius XXXI°. Primi credunt Ihesum dum baptizaretur complevisse annum
XXIX^m et aliquot dies anni XXX^i. Quoniam igitur dictum quadriennium
incipiunt ab anno Christi XXX°, necesse est ut dicant Ihesum obisse dum ageret
annum etatis sue XXXIII^m. Alii putant Ihesum non prius baptizatum quam
transegisset annum XXX^um cum aliquot diebus anni XXXI^i, quare cum incipiant
55   dictum quadriennium ab anno XXXI° necessario vitam Ihesu protendunt usque
ad annum eius XXXIIII^um. Primorum opinionem amplectitur Magister
Sentenciarum, qui distinctione XLIIII^a 4^ti, loquens de etate resurgentium dicit:
*Etas vero erit ad quam pervenit Christus, scilicet iuvenilis, ut circa triginta annos. Triginta
enim duorum annorum et trium mensium erat etas Christi in qua mortuus est et resurrexit.*
60   Aliorum opinionem amplecti videtur Crisostomus, Omelia decima super
Matheum. *Post XXX*, inquit, *annos Ihesus venit ad baptisma legem veterem soluturus.
Propterea usque in hanc etatem, que omnia capere solet peccata, in legis observatione
permansit, ne quis diceret illum solvisse legem, quia eam non potuisset implere. Et ita per
XXX annos iusticiam legis impleverat et tunc venit ad baptisma evangelium docturus.*
65   Quibus verbis innuit Ihesum quando baptizatus est annum XXX^um implevisse et
sic adiectis quatuor annis quibus supervixit, licet non integre, passus est anno
suo | XXXIIII°.   322

Si denique quis attendat ad ciclum solarem ei forte videbitur Ihesus
crucifixus anno etatis sue vel XXIX vel XXXV, ita ut nullus annorum
70   intermediorum sue videatur passioni congruere. Creditur quidem a Christianis
natus esse VIII° kl. Ianuarii ac VI^to kl. Aprilium resurrexisse, quorum utrumque
contigit prima sabbati seu die dominica, velut testatur eximius ille versificator

---

45 anno…46 XXX] Luke 3:1, 23.   **47** intra…48 coartari] Eusebius of Caesarea, *Historia ecclesiastica*
(trans. Rufinus of Aquileia) 1.10.6 (ed. GCS 9.1, 75).   **58** Etas…59 resurrexit] Peter Lombard,
Sententiae, lib. IV, dist. 44, c. 1.3 (ed. Brady, 2:517).   **61** Post…64 docturus] John Chrysostom *ap.*
Peter Comestor, *Historia scholastica*, Historia evangelica, c. 33 (ed. PL 198, col. 1555A).

---

59 Christi] *add.* etas Christi *a.c.*   **60** Crisostomus] crisostimus

Sedulius, in Libro suo pascali, de quo sic scribitur in Decretis, distinctione XV: *Item venerabilis viri Sedulii paschale opus, quod heroicis descripsit versibus, insigni laude proferimus.* Locuturus enim de resurrectione Ihesu, ita scribit: *Ceperat interea post* 75 *tristia sabbata felix | Irradiare dies, culmen qui nominis alti | A domino dominante trahit primusque videre | Promeruit nasci* dominum *atque resurgere Christum.* Cum itaque VIII° kl. Ianuarii, quando natus est Ihesus, et VI^to kl. Aprilium, quando resurrexit, in kalendario ponatur B, necesse est tam anno nativitatis quam resurrexionis sue B fuisse litteram dominicalem. Primum istorum attendentes 80 compotiste dicunt Ihesum natum fuisse anno XXI° cicli solaris, qui ut semper habet B pro littera dominicali. Cum autem ciclus iste circumvolvatur spacio XXVIII annorum, manifestum est quod pro anno Christi XXIX° iterum B fuit littera dominicalis, pro XXX° A, pro XXXI° G, pro XXXII°, quia bissextilis, FE, pro XXXIII° D, pro XXXIIII° C, et pro XXXV B. Quia ergo annus 85 passionis, qui est idem cum anno resurrectionis, pro littera dominicali habuit B, necesse est, ut videtur, Ihesum passum esse anno suo XXIX° vel XXXV° et non in aliquo annorum intermediorum, quorum nullus habuit B pro littera dominicali.

Non mediocrem eciam michi scrupulum facit Magister in Historiis, 90 loquens enim de anno passionis Ihesu *Si*, inquit, *tabulam compoti diligenter retro percurramus, inveniemus lunam XXII kalendas Aprilis* et *sexta*m *feria*m, unde infert quod *in precedenti feria sexta fuit luna XV.* Sed secundum artem compotisticam retrocurrendo in annis domini, in nullum eorum quibus Christus verisimiliter 323 passus est reperio in kl. Aprilis concurrisse lunam XXII et sex|tam feriam. Ymo 95 pro anno eius XXXI° in eisdem kl. invenitur luna XXII, sed dies dominica, et pro anno XXXV° sexta feria, sed luna sexta. Pro annis vero mediis neutrum predictorum invenitur. Ymo retrocedens in annis domini non reperiet lunam XXII et sextam feriam concurrisse in dictis kl. aliquo annorum intermediorum inter annum Ihesu XII et CCLIX. Non enim contingit dictus concursus nisi in 100 anno XIII° cicli decemnovenalis ac habente B pro littera dominicali, quales fuerunt duo anni predicti et omnium intermediorum nullus. Quamobrem, si verba magistri vera essent, Ihesus obiisset vel anno etatis sue XII° vel ducentesimoquinquagesimonono et non in aliquo annorum intermediorum.

Has differentias circa annum passionis Ihesu adeo repugnantes existimo ut, 105 nisi parte michi reducte fuerint ad aliqualem concordiam, tuam verear amplecti sectam velut plurimis intricatissimis contrarietatibus plenam et figmentis manifestis.

---

74 Item…75 proferimus] *Decretum magistri Gratiani*, pars I, dist. 15, c. 3, §25 (ed. Friedberg, col. 38).
75 Ceperat…77 Christum] Sedulius, *Paschale carmen* 5.315–318 (ed. Springer, 158).   **91** Si…93 XV] Peter Comestor, *Historia scholastica*, Historia evangelica, c. 169 (ed. PL 198, col. 1616B).

Paulus: Nullo credas figmento fidem Ihesu Christi viciatam; sincera est,
110 omni carens ruga et macula. Sed quoniam nullum eciam nostrorum adeo sollicite
ut te tempora Christi indagasse reperio, velut cepisti, si quas circa diem passionis
dominice nostrorum diversitates inveneris, in medium proferas. Spero quidem
divini luminis irradiatione omnes contrarietatum tenebras, que animum tuum a
via veritatis retrahunt, hodierna die repellendas.

\<Capitulum 3\>

Tercium capitulum continet controversias que sunt de die et hora mortis Christi.

Gamaliel: Adeo varie, domine mi Paule, non modo studiosissimos
5 Christianorum, sed et evangelistas tuos invenio de die passionis Ihesu
disseruisse, ut, nisi iuberes, te presente nollem tam pudentem eorum
repugnantiam enarrare. Alii existimant decimo kl. Aprilium ipsum obisse, alii
VIII°, alii VII°, alii VI^{to} earundem kalendarum. Novissime supervenerunt
quidam astruentes quod obierit tercio nonas Aprilis.

10 *Theophilus Cesariensis, antiquus vicinusque apostolicorum temporum doctor*, diem
mortis Ihesu dicit fuisse decimum kl. Aprilium. Unde *in epistola synodica quam
adversus eos qui XIIII luna pascha celebrabant una cum ceteris Palestine episcopi scripsit*
tandem | sic *dicit*: *Passus namque* est *dominus ab XI kl. Aprilis, qua nocte Iudeis est   324
traditus et VIII° kl. Aprilis resurrexit*. Cum ergo Ihesus pridie quam moreretur
15 traditus est Iudeis ac die tercio resurrexit, constat Theophilum voluisse quod
decimo kl. Aprilis mortem perpessus est. Hanc opinionem aliquando secute sunt
ecclesie Gallicane. *Nam, ut Beda commemorat, Galli quacumque die octavus kl.
Aprilium occurrisset, quando Christi resurrextio fuisse tradebatur, pascha semper
celebrabant*. Dictam epistolam Theophili non parum commendat Iheronimus,
20 libro De viris illustribus, ubi tractans de Theophilo dicit ipsum *adversus eos qui
XIIII^{ta} luna cum Iudeis pascha faciebant, cum ceteris episcopis synodicam et valde utilem
epistolam composuisse*. Eam eciam Beda libro De temporibus approbare videtur.
Sexta, inquit, die Deus *animantia terrestria et ipsum hominem formavit, de cuius latere
dormientis matrem omnium vivencium produxit, Evam, que nunc, quantum michi videtur esse
25 credibile, decimus kl. Aprilium dies appellatur*. Unde merito creditur, si non verior vincit
sentencia, quod beatus Theophilus cum ceteris, non solum Palestine, sed et permultis regionum
episcopis de pascha disputans scripsit, eodem decimo kl. Aprilium die dominum fuisse
crucifixum. Decebat enim una eademque die, non solum ebdomadis, sed et mensis secundum

---

10 Theophilus…14 resurrexit] Bede, *De temporum ratione*, c. 47 (ed. CCSL 123B, 432, ll. 102–107).
17 Nam…19 celebrabant] Bede, *De temporum ratione*, c. 47 (ed. CCSL 123B, 433, ll. 111–112).
20 adversus…22 composuisse] Jerome of Stridon, *De viris illustribus*, c. 43 (ed. Ceresa-Gastaldo, 142); cf. Hermann Zoest, *Phaselexis* (2nd version), c. 2 (ed. Solan, *La réforme du calendrier*, 410).
23 Sexta…32 humanum] Bede, *De temporum ratione*, c. 66 (ed. CCSL 123B, 464–465, ll. 57–71).

Adam pro generis humani salute vivifica morte sopitum de productis a *latere suo sacramentis celestibus sponsam sibi sanctificare ecclesiam, qua videlicet die primum Adam, patrem* sci*licet* 30 *humani generis, ipse creaverat eique de latere costam tollens edificavit mulierem, cuius adiutorio genus propagaret humanum.* Hec Beda.

Augustinus Ihesum passum dicit VIII° kl. Aprilium. Unde, XVIII De civitate Dei, *Mortuus est*, inquit, *Christus duobus Geminis consulibus VIII° kl. Aprilium*, et, quarto De trinitate, *Octavo enim kl. Aprilis conceptus creditur quo et* 35 *passus. Concordat cum eo Iheronimus in Martirologio dicens "VIII° kalendas Aprilis Iherosolime crucifixus est dominus."* Hec prius videtur fuisse sentencia Nycene synodi, ut patet ex epistola quam scripsit Cirillus Alexandrinus episcopus synodo 325 Cartaginensi, circa cuius finem de Christo sic scribit: *Eodem die | conceptus in utero est et mortuus in cruce, dum in sexta feria mortuus est Adam in anima pro peccato in* 40 *paradiso et in eodem die Christus obiit in corpore.* Et subditur: *Responsum est, ut opinor, omnibus quibus interrogastis me, et omnia scripta auctentica synodi Nycene protuli.* Cum ergo Ihesus conceptus credatur VIII° kl. Aprilis, conveniens est ut eodem die credatur et mortuus.

Aliis visum est Ihesum pati non potuisse nec X° nec VIII° kl. Aprilium, 45 quoniam nephas erat apud Hebreos equinoctio vernali nundum transacto agnum paschalem immolari. Quod clare conicitur ex verbis Anatolii Laodicie antistitis. Is quidem, de ordinatione temporum tractans, ita scribit: *Et ideo non parum dicimus delinquere eos qui ante hoc initium*, puta equinoctium vernale, *pascha putant celebrandum. Sed nec a nobis primus exordium sum*psit *hec ratio antiquis Iudeis comprobata* 50 *fuisse monstratur et ante adventum Christi observata, sicut evidenter dicit Iosephus, sed et antiquiores Agathobolus et bene eruditus Aristobolus et Paṅitio, qui unus ex illis LXX senioribus fuit qui missi fuerunt a pontificibus ad Ptolomeum regem Hebreorum libros interpreta*turi *in Grecum sermonem, quique multa ex tradicionibus Moysi proponenti regi percontantique respondebant. Ipsi ergo, cum questiones Exodi exponerent, dixerunt pascha* 55 *non prius immolandum quam equinoctium vernale transiret.*

Ypocrates autem in Epistola ad Antigonum regem dicit huiuscemodi equinoctium esse VIII° kl. Aprilis. Ubi eciam Ysidorus Hispalensis, qui floruit circa annum Christi sexcentesimum sexagesimum sextum, ipsum esse opinatus

---

34   Mortuus…35 Aprilium] Augustine, *De civitate dei* 18.54 (ed. CCSL 48, 655, ll. 45–46). **35** Octavo…36 passus] Augustine, *De trinitate* 4.5 (ed. CCSL 50, 172, ll. 11–12).   **36** Concordat… 37 dominus] Jerome of Stridon *ap.* Hermann Zoest, *Phaselexis* (2nd version), c. 2 (ed. Solan, *La réforme du calendrier*, 408); cf. ps.-Jerome, *Martyrologium Hieronymianum* (ed. de Rossi and Duchesne, 36; ed. PL 30, col. 449) .   **39** Eodem…42 protuli] *Epistola Cyrilli*, c. 6–7 (ed. Krusch, *Studien* [1880], 349). **48**   Et…56 transiret] Anatolius of Laodicea *ap.* Eusebius of Caesarea, *Historia ecclesiastica* (trans. Rufinus of Aquileia) 7.32.15–17 (ed. GCS 9.2, 723–725).   **58**   equinoctium…Aprilis] ps.-Hippocrates *ap.* Bede, *De temporum ratione*, c. 30 (ed. CCSL 123B, 372–373).

48 parum dicimus] parviducimus   **55** percontantique] percunctantique | cum] dum

60   est, unde quinto Ethymologiarum, de equinoctiis scribens, dicit *Duo sunt*
     equinoctia, unum vernale, aliud autumpnale. Sunt autem hec equinoctia die VIII° kl.
     Aprilium et VIII° kl. Octobrium. Et licet hiis temporibus equinoctia et solsticia
     reperiantur anteriorata, circa tempora tamen Christi creduntur occurrisse in
     octavis diebus kl. Aprilium, Iuliarum, Octobrium et Ianuariarum. Ihesus ergo,
65   qui legem Moysi solvere noluisset, pascha cum discipulis non manducavit ante
     VIII diem kl. Aprilis, quamobrem nec | eodem die nec prius passus est, cum   326
     constet ipsum pridie quam pateretur agnum paschalem cum discipulis
     manducasse.

     Asserunt itaque nonnulli, ut *Victorius et Reynerus, in libello De correctione*
70   *kalendarii*, Christum passum VII° kl. Aprilium. Alii opinantur eodem die post
     esum agni paschalis Ihesum Iudeis traditum, et postero die, qui est VI^tus
     earundem kalendarum, crucifixum. Quorum opinionem favere videtur
     Augustinus XVIII° De civitate Dei, ubi dicit Spiritum Sanctum missum esse
     ydibus Mayi. Hec etenim missio facta est die penthecostes qui est
75   quinquagesimus a paschali festivitate. Sed a sexto kl. Aprilium computando dies
     quinquagesimus occurrit ydibus Mayi. Apparet ergo solempnitatem paschalem in
     qua Ihesus crucifixus creditur VI^to kl. Aprilium die contigisse.

     Posteriorum quidam artis astronomice periti, ut Iohannes Muris, Rogerius
     Bachon, ac quidam alii, longe aliter senserunt, asserentes Ihesum non in Martio,
80   ut ceteri, sed tercio nonas Aprilis mortem obiisse. Certum est, aiunt, quod
     passus est sexta feria et luna XV, quando scilicet est oppositio luminarium. Sed
     in annis quibus Ihesus verisimiliter mortuus est non reperitur in mense paschali
     oppositio luminarium in sexta feria, nisi in anno Christi XXXIII° tercio nonas
     Aprilis. Tunc enim ex tabulis astronomicis invenitur Iherosolimitanis fuisse
85   oppositio media duobus diebus Aprilis, XVII horis et XV minutis completis,
     hoc est tercia die Aprilis, hora tercia ab ortu solis computando, et in kalendario
     Romano eodem die ponitur B, que tunc signavit feriam sextam. Fuit enim annus
     XXV cicli solaris, qui semper habet D pro littera dominicali. In anno autem
     XXXIIII°, in quo plures Christianorum Ihesum credunt mortem gustasse, fuit

---

60 Duo…62 Octobrium] Isidore of Seville, *Etymologiae* 5.34.3 (ed. Yarza Urquiola and Andrés Santos, 115).   **69** Victorius…70 Aprilium] Hermann Zoest, *Phaselexis* (2nd version), c. 2 (ed. Solan, *La réforme du calendrier*, 410); cf. Victorius of Aquitaine, *Prologus ad Hilarum archidiaconum*, c. 9 (ed. Krusch, *Studien* [1938], 25); Reinher of Paderborn, *Computus emendatus*, lib. 2, c. 15 (ed. CCCM 272, 54).   **73** Spiritum…74 Mayi] Augustine, *De civitate Dei* 18.54 (ed. CCSL 48, 655, l. 62).   **79** Ihesum…81 luminarium] Roger Bacon, *Opus maius*, lib. IV (ed. Bridges, 1:208–210); Jean des Murs, *Sermo de regulis computistarum*, MS Erfurt, Universitäts- und Forschungsbibliothek, Dep. Erf. CA 4° 371, fols. 44vb–45ra; Hermann Zoest, *Phaselexis*, c. 2–3 (ed. Solan, *La réforme du calendrier*, 410, 412–414).   **84** Tunc…85 completis] Roger Bacon, *Opus maius*, lib. IV (ed. Jebb, 131 [facing]).   **88** In…91 completis] Roger Bacon, *Opus maius*, lib. IV (ed. Jebb, 131 [facing]).

---

77 die contigisse] contigisse die *a.c.*

oppositio luminarium XXIII diebus Martii duabus horis et quinque minutis   90
completis, hoc est decimo kl. Aprilium, hora nona ab ortu solis, quo die in
kalendario ponitur E, illo anno significans feriam terciam. Fuit enim annus
XXVI cicli solaris habens C pro littera dominicali. Si igitur Ihesus passus fuisset
anno suo XXXIIII°, concludunt quod die mortis sue vel non fuisset feria sexta,
sed tercia, vel luna non fuisset XV, quorum utrumque dissonare videtur a serie   95
textus evangelici. Similiter probant quod in aliis annis vicinis pati non potuit, |

327   quoniam in nullo ipsorum tempore mensis pascalis coinciderunt eodem die feria
sexta et oppositio luminarium, que non nisi luna XV contingere potest.

   Super omnia michi scrupulum facit dissensio quam in historiis evangelicis
reperio. Ex ipsis quidem mors Ihesu contigisse videtur nunc XIIII^ta, nunc XV,   100
nunc XVI die primi mensis Hebreorum. Dicitur namque Iohannis XVIII° de
Iudeis Ihesum accusantibus *Non introierunt in pretorium* ne *contaminarentur sed ut
manducarent pascha*, quod legitime non manducatur nisi luna XIIII^ta primi mensis,
ut scribitur Exodi XII° et Levitici XXIII. Mors ergo Ihesu secundum Iohannem
contigit die XIIII^ta primi mensis, nec consonum videtur quod per 'pascha', ut   105
quidam volunt, 'panes azimos' intellexerit, quia nusquam legitur a contaminatis
panes azimos manducari non posse, ymo quod per 'pascha' voluerit 'agnum
paschalem' intelligi ex hoc apparet quod capitulo XIX° subdit *Erat autem
parasceve pasche*. Est autem 'parasceve' idem quod 'preparatio'. Voluit ergo quod
eo die fieret preparatio vel agni paschalis, vel festi in quo agnus paschalis   110
immolaretur. Et capitulo XIII premittit: *Ante diem festum Pasche sciens Ihesus quia
venit eius hora ut transiret ex hoc mundo ad patrem*. Et infra: *Surgit a cena et ponit
vestimenta sua* etc. Ubi manifeste vult quod festum Pasche, cuius exordium est a
vespera XIIII^te diei primi mensis, non incepit illo die quo Ihesus cum discipulis
cenavit, sed die sequenti quo crucifixus est. Hanc sentenciam, ut Grecos   115
omittam, Orosius amplecti videtur libro De ormesta mundi. *Eadem*, inquit, *die ab
hora diei sexta sol in totum obscuratus est tetraque nox subdito educta terris, sicut dictum est
'Impiaque eternam timuerunt secula noctem', usque adeo autem neque lunam lumini solis
neque nubes obstitisse manifestum est, ut XIIII die, tota celi regione interiecta, longissime a
conspectu solis abfuisse et stellas tunc diurnis horis vel pocius in illa horrenda nocte toto celo*   120
fulsisse referatur.

   Cum autem Luce XXII° capitulo Ihesus scribitur manducasse pascha cum
discipulis ad vesperam illius diei *in quo necesse erat occidi pascha*; et Marci XIIII°

328   quod Iudei | eodem die pascha immolabant, nonne manifeste dicitur quod
cenam paschalem fecit XIIII^ta die primi mensis? In alio quidem die nec necesse   125

---

102 Non...103 pascha] John 18:28.   **103** legitime...mensis] Exodus 12:6; Leviticus 23:5.
108 Erat...109 pasche] John 19:14.   **111** Ante...112 patrem] John 13:1.   **112** Surgit...113 etc]
John 13:4.   **116** Eadem...121 referatur] Orosius, *Historia adversum paganos* 7.4.14–15 (ed. Arnaud-
Lindet, 3:25).   **123** in...pascha] Luke 22:7.   **124** quod^1...immolabant] Mark 14:12.

erat occidi pascha, nec ab Hebreis immolabatur. Sequens ergo dies, in quo passus est, fuit XV^{tus} primi mensis. Hanc opinionem amplecti videtur ecclesia Romana, eapropter conficiens in azimo quia Ihesus confecit XIIII^{ta} die primi mensis, quando non licuit esse fermentum in domibus Hebreorum.

130 Ex eo autem quod tres evangeliste, Matheus, Marcus et Lucas, discipulos scribunt interrogasse Ihesum primo die azimorum de pascha manducando et Ihesum in crastino, qui necessario fuit 2us dies azimorum, mortem crucis sustinuisse, aperte concludi videtur quod passus est XVI die primi mensis; fuit enim 2us dies azimorum luna existente XVI^a. Unde *Iosephus, litterarum legalium*
135 *doctissimus, in libro Antiquitatum scribit in hunc modum. Decimaquarta luna primi mensis agnus immolatur, XV^a autem succedit festivitas azimorum, que septem diebus celebratur. Secundam vero azimorum die, que est XVI^a, frugum primitias quas metunt offerunt.*

Hec sunt, Paule, in quibus Christiani circa diem mortis Ihesu dissentientes apparent, que meo iudicio adeo repugnant ut ea vix arbitrer ad concordiam
140 reduci posse. Quod si preter spem efficere poteris, nichil ex fide tua quantumcumque stupendum proponas quod existimabo non credendum.

Paulus: Si quicquam aliud tibi fuerit ambiguum circa tempus passionis dominice, proferas, velim, quatinus omnium dubietatum caligines in simul discutiantur.

145 **Gamaliel**: Ut nichil subticeam, vacillare michi videntur Christiani de hora mortis Ihesu. Hora nona secundum evangelium expiravit, sed nonnulli per hanc horam eam intelligunt qua completa sol attingit meridianum. Alii horam terciam post meridiem, cuius initium est postquam sol a meridiano duabus horis declinavit ad vesperam. Huius 2^e opinionis fuit Beda, qui in Omelia vigilie
150 pascalis ait sic: *Circa horam quippe nonam cum inclinata iam esset ad vesperam dies et tepefactus a meridiano fervore radius solis misterium victoriosissime passionis consummavit.* Sic sensit et Augustinus, 4to De trinitate. *Ab hora*, inquit, *mortis usque | ad* 329 *diluculum resurrectionis hore sunt quadraginta ut ipsa hora nona connumeretur.* Et post pauca: *A vespere autem sepulture usque ad diluculum resurrectionis XXXVI sunt hore.*
155 Supersunt ergo quatuor ultime hore illius diei in qua crucifixus est, quarum prima secundum Augustinum fuit hora nona in qua exspiravit. Fuit autem hora nona ab ortu solis, ita ut hora proxime sequens solis ortum dicatur prima et occasum immediate precedens XII^a. Hunc modum horas computandi evangeliste secuti sunt. Unde Mathei XX, *qui circa XI^{am} horam* diei ad vineam

---

130 discipulos…131 manducando] Matthew 26:17; Mark 14:12; Luke 22:7. **134** Iosephus…137 offerunt] Flavius Josephus *ap.* Bede, *De temporum ratione,* c. 63 (ed. CCSL 123B, 454–455, ll. 25–31). **150** Circa…151 consummavit] Bede, *Homeliae evangelii* 2.7 (ed. CCSL 122, 225, ll. 9–11). **152** Ab… 153 connumeretur] Augustine, *De trinitate* 4.6 (ed. CCSL 50, 174, ll. 23–24). **154** A…hore] Augustine, *De trinitate* 4.6 (ed. CCSL 50, 174, ll. 30–31). **159** qui…160 venerant] Matthew 20:9.

---

159 secuti sunt] sunt secuti *a.c.*

venerant una tantum hora dicuntur laborasse, quia scilicet de die sola restabat   160
hora XII^a. Ritus vero quarundam ecclesiarum approbare videtur primam
opinionem. In eis quidem campana trahitur circa meridiem in memoriam mortis
Ihesu, quod non fieret nisi crederetur circa meridiem expirasse. Idem testatur
non tantum fama popularis, sed et Albertus Magnus, qui, exponens Epistolam
Dyonisii ad Policarpum, inter cetera dicit *Secundum kalendarium autem XXV^a die*   165
Martii passus est *dominus in meridie.*

Ut iussisti, domine Paule, quicquid controversie repperi circa tempora tam
nativitatis quam mortis Ihesu in medium attuli. Iam tui erit officii vel tantam
Christianorum diversitatem ad concordiam reducere vel saltem ostendere
quorum sentenciis pocius adherendum est.   170

Paulus: Quoniam Christus natus asseritur anno XXI° cicli solaris ac 2°
cicli decemnovenalis et decimo octavo lunaris, votis tuis, ut reor, satisfacere
nequibo, nisi de hiis tribus ciclis pauca prius disseram. Horum forsan ignorantia
una fuit ex precipuis causis tante diversitatis.

Gamaliel: Nichil nisi quod pro tantis enucleandis difficultatibus   175
accuratissimum erit te dicturum scio. Incipias igitur ut libet nec desidem me
invenies auditorem.

---

165 Secundum…166 meridie] Albertus Magnus, *Super Dionysii Epistulas*, ep. 7 (ed. Simon, 509, ll. 26–28).

---

172 satisfacere] fatisfacere

<Tractatus 2>

<Capitulum 1>

Secundus tractatus est de ciclis. Primum capitulum est de ciclo solari.

Paulus: Priusquam naturam cicli solaris explanem, in primis expediet aliquorum
5 meminisse que in Saturnalibus Macrobii Pretexatus cum Choro, disputans de
annis Romanorum, commemorat. *Romulus,* | inquit, *annum decem mensium, dierum*   330
vero quatuor et tricentorum, esse constituit mensesque ita disposuit ut quatuor ex eis triginta,
sex vero dies haberent unum et triginta. *Sed cum is numerus nec solis nec lune cursui*
conveniret, nonnunquam evenit ut frigus anni mensibus estivis et calor hyemalibus proveniret,
10 *quod ubi contigisset tantum dierum* spacium *sine ullo mensis nomine patiebatur assumi,*
quantum sufficere videbatur ut *celi habitus instanti mensi aptus inveniretur.* Post
Romulum, Numa Pompilius *quinquaginta dies addidit* annumque fecit XII
mensium ac dierum trecentorum quinquaginta quatuor, Grecos forsitan
imitatus. *Paulo post in honorem numeri imparis unum adiecit diem, ut tam in anno quam in*
15 *mensibus numerus impar servaretur. Ianuarius* itaque, *Aprilis, Iunius, Sextilis, September,*
November et *December* XXIX dies habebant. *Martius vero, Mayus, Quintilis* et *October*
dies unum et triginta. *Solus* autem *Februarius viginti octo dies retinuit. Cum* igitur
Romani ex hac distributione Pompilii annum proprium computarent, necessario more
Grecorum mensem interkalarem constituerunt. *Nam Greci* solis cursum *animadvert*entes
20 suo perpenderunt *anno deesse dies XI* cum *quadrante,* quamobrem *octavo quoque anno*
nonaginta dies, utpote *tres menses XXX dierum, interkalar*unt. Dies quidem XI cum
quadrante, si multiplicentur octies, proveniunt nonaginta. *Hunc ergo ordinem*
Romanis imitari placuit atque per *octo annos nonaginta* dies superaddebant, non simul,
ut Greci, sed alternis annis vigintiduos, alternis vero vigintitres. Tandem tamen
25 propter unum diem in honorem numeri imparis superadditum *non nonaginta in*
octennio, sed uni diebus demptis LXXXII dies interkalarunt, *omni autem*
*interkalationi Februarium deputa*bant. Hac deinde interkalandi ratione sublata
nonnunquam per gratiam sacerdotum quam *publicanis* fecerant, dies anni minui aut
proferri contigerat, qua ex re *maior emer*sit *confusionis occasio.* Quam demum Iulius
30 Cesar considerans *nove ordinationis exordium initurus* dies omnes qui adhuc confusionem
facere | *poterant as*sumpsit, *eaque re factum est ut annus confusionis ultimus in*   331
quadringentosquadragintatres dies protenderetur. Post hoc imitatus Egiptios ad numerum
solis, qui trecentissexagintaquinque diebus et quadrante cursum conficit, annum dirigere

---

6 Romulus…11 inveniretur] Macrobius, *Saturnalia* 1.12.38–39 (ed. Kaster, 1:154).   **11** Post…14
imitatus] Macrobius, *Saturnalia* 1.13.1 (ed. Kaster, 1:154–156).   **14** Paulo…22 nonaginta]
Macrobius, *Saturnalia* 1.13.5–9 (ed. Kaster, 1:156–158).   **22** Hunc…27 deputabant] Macrobius,
Saturnalia 1.13.11–14 (ed. Kaster, 1:160).   **27** Hac…29 occasio] Macrobius, *Saturnalia* 1.14.1 (ed.
Kaster, 1:166).   **29** Quam…34 contendit] Macrobius, *Saturnalia* 1.14.3 (ed. Kaster, 1:166).

---

contendit, decem dies observationi veteri superaddens, *et, ne quadrans deesset, statuit* 35
ut quarto quoque anno sacerdotes qui curabant mensibus et diebus unum diem interkalarent. 35
Hac ordinatione: Ianuarius, Martius, Mayus, Iulius, Augustus, October et
December unum et XXX dies continebant. Aprilis, Iunius, September et
November triginta. Februarius vero, ut prius, XXVIII. *Annum* hunc *civilem Cesar*
habitis ad lunam dimensionibus constitutum edicto palam posito publicavit, stare quoque
potuisset in posterum, *ni*si *sacerdotes errorem sibi novum ex ipsa emendatione fecissent.* 40
Nam cum oporteret diem qui ex quadrantibus conficitur quarto anno completo *antequam*
quintus inciperet interkalare, illi quarto non peracto, sed incipiente interkalabant. Hic error
annis 36 perstitit, in *quibus interkalati sunt dies XII cum* tantum *novem debuerunt*
interkalari. Errorem istum *sero deprehensum correxit Augustus, qui annos XII sine*
interkalari die transigi iussit, ut illi tres dies qui per XXXVI annos vicio sacerdotum 45
excreverant, annis XII nullo die interkalato devocarentur. Post hoc unum diem secundum
ordinationem Iulii quarto *quoque anno interkalari iussit.* Hec fere eadem sunt verba
quibus in Saturnalibus Pretexatus usus est.

Suetonius quoque Libro de XII Cesaribus eandem innuens sentenciam, in
Vita Iulii Cesaris ita scribit: Iulius Cesar *ad ordinandum rei publice statum* dies *fastos* 50
correxit iam pro sacerdotum licencia *adeo turbatos, ut neque messium ferie estati, neque*
vindemiarum autumpno dies *competerent; annumque ad cursum solis commodavit, ut*
trecentorum sexaginta quinque dierum esset et interkalario mense sublato unus dies quarto
332 *quoque anno interkalaretur.* Ut *autem magis | in posterum nobis ratio temporum congrueret,*
inter Novembrem et Decembrem duos alios menses interiecit; fuitque is annus quo hec 55
constituebantur XV mensium cum interkalario, qui ex consuetudine in eum annum inciderat.
Deinde, describens vitam Augusti, dicit: *Condiditque duobus forulis auratis sub*
Palatini Apolinis basi. Annum a divo Iulio ordinatum, sed postea negligentia sacerdotum
conturbatum atque confusum, rursus ad pristinam rationem redegit.

Gamaliel: Res novas atque michi prius inauditas profers, quas cum audiam 60
celeberrimorum virorum auctoritatibus communitas, de eis nequeo sinistre
suspicari. Ut tamen omnia lucidius intelligam, dic, queso, quotus fuerit annorum
imperii Cesaris annus ille confusionis ultimus ac quoto sui imperii anno
Augustus errorem sacerdotum qui emerserat deprehendit.

Paulus: Inquiris que et scitu iocunda sunt et cause nostre conferentia non 65
parum. In quibus etsi nichil certi scriptum invenerim, variis tamen ex coniecturis
existimo annum confusionis ultimum fuisse primum quo Cesar regnare cepit
atque Augustum errorem sacerdotum deprehendisse anno imperii sui XXXI°.
Velut quidem historiographi scribunt, Iulius Cesar Pompeio devicto occupavit

---

34 et…35 interkalarent] Macrobius, *Saturnalia* 1.14.6 (ed. Kaster, 1:168).   **38** Annum…47 iussit]
Macrobius, *Saturnalia* 1.14.13–15 (ed. Kaster, 1:172–174).   **50** Iulius…56 inciderat] Suetonius, *De*
vita Caesarum, I, *Divus Iulius*, c. 40 (ed. Ihm, 20, ll. 11–21).   **57** Condiditque…59 redegit] Suetonius,
De vita Caesarum, II, *Divus Augustus*, c. 31 (ed. Ihm, 64, ll. 21–25).

70 Alexandriam Egipti, ubi Lucanus scribit eum usque in profundam noctem
    disputasse ac ab Aquoreo sacerdote plurima de annis Egiptiorum sciscitatum.
    Hinc Romam regressus singulare primus obtinuit imperium atque inter honores
    sibi a senatu decretos dictator perpetuus factus est. Qua dignitate fretus, ut in
    Saturnalibus legitur, Marco Flacco scriba sibi annuente, Egiptios imitatus
75 annorum inconstanciam apud Romanos reformavit. Tandem, Beda teste, *post
    annos quatuor et menses sex quam regnare ceperat* in Capitolio *confossus interiit*, ydibus
    Martii, ut Suetonius scribit. Apparet ex hiis Iulium Cesarem anno imperii sui
    primo, de annis usualibus Romanorum loquendo, solis quatuor mensibus non
    integris regnasse, dehinc quatuor annis completis et sexto anno ydibus mensis
80 tercii ab emulis interemptum. Quia ergo Romani omni interkalationi Februarium
    deputarunt, suspicor Iulium, | qui inter Novembrem et Decembrem in anno   333
    confusionis ultimo duos menses interkalavit, mox ut regnare cepit annorum
    reformationi vacasse ac eam noluisse usque ad Februarium deferre. Unde eum
    arbitror in Novembri, cum ex Egipto redisset, regnare cepisse atque omnes dies
85 superfluos in duos menses redactos inter Novembrem et Decembrem
    interiecisse. Sic quippe in anno primo quatuor mensibus non integris regnavit,
    utpote Novembri et Decembri ac duobus interiectis. Quam michi coniecturam
    augere videntur verba Macrobii, qui Iulium dicit *annum civilem habitis ad lunam
    dimensionibus constitutum publica*sse. Quibus verbis michi significari videtur quod,
90 velut Romani prius annum ad lune cursum mensurarunt, X aut XII menses
    lunares pro anno computantes, sic Iulius annum regularem, qui proxime annum
    confusionis ultimum sequebatur, ad lune dimensionem instituit ea, ut reor, lege
    quod a prima incensione lune proxima post hyemale solsticium inchoaretur.
    Inter annos autem imperii Cesaris circa initium solius secundi contigit lunaris
95 incensio, quod si per tabulas astronomicas experiri pigeat, constare poterit ex
    aureo numero, ut servit ciclo decemnovenali. Ille quidem, ut inferius audies, eo
    tempore precise vel quasi lunares incensiones demonstrabat. Annum quippe
    quadragesimumsecundum omnes fatentur fuisse 2^m cicli decemnovenalis. Unde
    retrogredienti in eodem ciclo facile constare potest annum 2^m imperii Cesaris
100 fuisse decimumquartum eiusdem cicli. Cum itaque numerus ille prenotetur
    XXX° diei Ianuarii, liquet circa kalendas Ianuarias eiusdem anni fuisse lunarem
    incensionem. Mediant enim inter duas proximas coniunctiones luminarium dies

---

70 ubi…71 sciscitatum] Lucanus, *De bello civili* 10.172–218 (ed. Shackleton Bailey, 272–273).
74 Marco…75 reformavit] Macrobius, *Saturnalia* 1.14.2–3 (ed. Kaster, 1:166).   **75** post…76 interiit]
Bede, *De temporum ratione*, c. 66 (a. 3910) (ed. CCSL 123B, 494, ll. 938–939).   **76** ydibus…77 scribit]
Suetonius, *De vita Caesarum*, I, *Divus Iulius*, c. 80 (ed. Ihm, 40, l. 17).   **88** annum…89 publicasse]
Macrobius, *Saturnalia* 1.14.13 (ed. Kaster, 1:172).

XXIX, hore XII, minuta XLIIII. Hinc eciam conicio apud Romanos novum
cepisse cursum annorum anno primo Cesaris quod Anthioceni, cum paulo ante
Romanis subiugati essent, ab eodem tempore, ut Eusebius in Cronicis annotat, 105
sua ceperunt tempora computare.

Gamaliel: Primum illorum duorum que postulaveram rationabiliter
334 suasisse videris. Nunc cur Augustum existi|mes anno suo XXXI° sacerdotum
errorem deprehendisse audire desidero.

Paulus: Ut id existimem eiusdem Eusebii me monent verba, quibus in 110
Cronicis scribit Augustum anno suo XXXI° pontificem maximum a senatu
appellatum. Cuius rei nullam aliam reor fuisse causam quam quod errorem
pontificum qui diebus interkalandis preerant Augustus anno illo deprehendens
legem eis tradidit qua in perpetuum possent errorem talem devitare. Patuit
insuper ex Saturnalibus Macrobii errorem sacerdotum annis perstitisse XXXVI. 115
Fuit autem annus XXXI^us ab exordio imperii Cesaris tricesimus sextus,
quamobrem probabile videtur eodem anno sacerdotum errorem ab Augusto
fuisse deprehensum.

Gamaliel: Non parvi videntur momenti hee coniecture. Quoniam autem
de annis eciam tam Egiptiorum quam Grecorum meministi, dicas, velim, an 120
similis in eis inconstantia fuerit.

Paulus: De annis Grecorum audisti quod olim quisque ex diebus trecentis
et quinquaginta quatuor constabat. Et quoniam deerant dies XI cum quadrante,
quos cursus solis postulabat, octavo quoque anno nonaginta dies interkalarunt.
Dehinc Greci tantam in annis suis inequalitatem perpendentes (superabat enim 125
quisque octavus reliquos in nonaginta diebus) Romanos imitari maluerunt. Non
tamen a kalendis Ianuarii, ut Romani, sed a kalendis Decembris, quemadmodum
Beda scribit, annum suum inchoarunt, ob id forte, quod in reformatione per
Iulium facta is mensis fuit primus regularis. Continet autem annus Grecorum
XII menses in numero dierum (ut Beda demonstrat) mensibus Romanorum 130
penitus equales. Idem Alphonsus innuit, in uno tamen a Beda discrepat quod
primum mensem Grecorum non Decembrem existimat, sed Octobrem. De
annis Egiptiorum vult Alphonsus quod initium sumunt ab Octobri quodque
singuli sunt dierum XXX quibus completis superadduntur dies quinque. In
Saturnalibus Macrobii Chorus, postquam dixit mensibus Egiptiorum quorum 135

---

103 Hinc…106 computare] Eusebius of Caesarea, *Chronicon* (trans. Jerome of Stridon) (ed. GCS 47,
156).   **111** Augustum…112 appellatum] Eusebius of Caesarea, *Chronicon* (trans. Jerome of Stridon)
(ed. GCS 47, 167).   **126** Non…131 equales] Bede, *De temporum ratione*, c. 14 (ed. CCSL 123B,
327–328).   **131** Idem…132 Octobrem] *Tabule astronomice illustrissimi Alfontii regis Castelle* (ed. Poulle,
Les Tables Alphonsines, 110).   **132** De…134 quinque] *Tabule astronomice illustrissimi Alfontii regis Castelle*
(ed. Poulle, *Les Tables Alphonsines*, 110–111).   **134** In…139 inchoari] Macrobius, *Saturnalia* 1.15.1
(ed. Kaster, 1:174).

---

103 XII] XIIII *a.c.*

quisque constat ex XXX diebus quinque dies adici, subdit quod *quarto quoque*
anno | *exact*o inter Augustum et Septembrem servant *diem interkalarem, qui ex*   335
quadrantibus confit. Unde innuere videtur annum Egiptium kalendis Septembris
inchoari. Beda vero, de huiusmodi annis loquens, a predictis in uno discrepat
140   quod eos inchoari dicit quarto kl. Septembrium. Nec annos Egiptiorum varios
repperi, hoc solo dempto quod diversi alia et alia ipsorum initia statuerunt.
      Gamaliel: Hec audisse libuit, sed naturam cicli solaris, uti pollicitus es,
declares, queso.
      Paulus: Qui annis solaribus CCCLXV dierum ac unius quadrantis atque
145   ebdomadibus per litteras distinctis utuntur duplices habent annos, aliquos
CCCLXV dierum, ac aliquos uno die, qui ex quadrantibus constat, excrescentes,
quos Romani bissextos appellant, quia in eis bis occurrit dies sextus kl.
Martiarum. Uterque dictorum annorum ultra LII ebdomadas continet, annus
communis unum diem et bissextus duos. Que dierum ultra ebdomadas
150   excrescentia id efficit ut annis singulis littera dominicalis varietur, duo autem
dies in anno bissextili superexcrescentes duas in eo efficiunt litteras dominicales,
quarum una currit usque sextum kl. Martii, ubi fit interkalatio, alia hinc ad finem
anni. Quoniam autem septem diebus ebdomade totidem respondent littere,
quarum singulas contingit quadriphariam representare diem, quam nos
155   'dominicam', Gentiles 'solis' appellant, utpote vel in anno bissextili vel in aliquo
trium annorum communium, necesse est ut annis quater septem, id est XXVIII,
revolutis eedem que prius et sub eodem ordine redeant littere dominicales. Ex
tot itaque annis ciclus solaris conficitur, in quo licet ubilibet, velut in omni ciclo,
initium assignari contingat, Gerlandus tamen ac cum eo plurimi compotistarum
160   ipsum incipiunt ab anno communi proximo post bissextilem ac habente F pro
littera dominicali. Dyonisius vero ipsum incipit ab anno bissextili pro litteris
dominicalibus habente GF.
      Gamaliel: Ex hiis michi videor cursum cicli solaris intellexisse. Sed doceri
peto an ne cum ceteris compotistis Ihesum natum existimes anno primo post
165   bissextum ac habente B pro littera dominicali.
      Paulus: Certum reor Iulium voluisse quem | libet quartum annum imperii   336
sui esse bissextilem, licet sacerdotes, ut audisti, usque ad annum Augusti XXXI
tercium quemque annum bissextum facientes tres dies ultra quam debuerant
interkalarint. Ad quos devocandos ab omni interkalatione Augusto iubente XII
170   annis cessatum est, utpote ad annum eius XLIII. Dehinc annis plene reformatis

---

139   Beda…140 Septembrium] Bede, *De temporum ratione*, c. 11 (ed. CCSL 123B, 318–319).
159 Gerlandus…161 dominicali] *Computus Gerlandi*, lib. 1, c. 3, 9 (ed. Lohr, 99–100, 113–114); *Tabula*
Gerlandi (ed. Pedersen, 1:400).   **161** Dyonisius…162 GF] *Tabula Gerlandi* (ed. Pedersen, 1:400).

---

144 Paulus] Paululum   **146** aliquos] alios   **147** quia] quod

cepit apud Romanos cursus cicli solaris, qui quia quartum quemque annum
bissextilem postulat pro primo suo bissexto habuit annum Augusti XLVII. Cum
ergo nemo misterium incarnationis post annum Augusti XLII dicat impletum,
liquide constat Christum ex virgine natum priusquam anni Romanorum plene
reformati essent et ita ante omnem ipsorum ciclum solarem.   175

Gamaliel: Hiis assentirem facile, nisi suppositionem unam enervari
viderem, qua tam astronomi quam compotiste supponunt quemlibet annum
Christi quartum fuisse bissextilem, quam suppositionem, si admiserimus, cum
Ihesus anno Augusti XLII natus credatur, dicere cogimur annum eiusdem
Augusti tam XLV quam XLIX, qui fuerunt quartus et octavus Christi,   180
indubitanter fuisse bissextilem, ac annum XLVII, qui fuit sextus Christi, inter
annos communes secundum, quem tamen dixisti fuisse bissextum.

Paulus: Hunc annum XLVII Augusti fuisse bissextilem apud Romanos eo
liquere videtur quod anni post reformationem ab Augusto factam eundem
habuerunt cursum quem habituri fuissent ex ordinatione Iulii, si nullus error 185
intervenisset. Si autem sacerdotes non errassent et Iulius, uti probabile est,
quemque annum quartum a reformatione quam fecit anno imperii sui primo
voluit esse bisextilem, constat annum predictum Augusti, puta XLVII, fuisse
bisextum. Fuit enim ab initio imperii Cesaris quinquagesimussecundus, quo
numero per quaternarium diviso nil superest. Stantibus ergo dictis ypothesibus 190
idem annus fuit bissextilis. Quod a plerisque creditur fuisse 2ᵘˢ communis eo
contingit quod cursum cicli solaris (postquam cepit apud Romanos) nullatenus
putant immutatum, quem tamen immutari oportuit. Ad cuius dilucidationem
conferunt verba Bede, qui libro De temporibus dicit diem quem interkalamus
337 VI° kl. Martii ab Egiptiis prius interkalari ante quartum kl. | Septembrium anni 195
precedentis. Hinc dicit annis bissextilibus oriri *dissonantia*m *in lune compoto* et
dierum festivitate quam a tempore ab eis interkalati quadrantis usque *nostre interkalationis*
tempus non contingit *recipere concordiam*. Verbi gratia, idem dies festus et eadem
luna, que apud nos est 2ᵃ sabbati, ab illis 3ᵃ sabbati computatur. Est autem
egregie perspectum ne dicta dissonantia mensem paschalem contingat. Si   200
quidem eum contingeret, non semper eodem die paschalis festivitas ab Egiptiis
et Romanis servaretur. Nam si luna XIIIIᵃ paschalis apud hos in sabbato et apud
illos die dominica occurreret, primi eadem die dominica suum pascha servarent,
alii vero ad proximam sequentem dominicam transferrent. Iuxta namque decreta
patrum luna XIIIIᵃ paschali in die dominica incidente pascha ad dominicam   205
proximam transferendum est. Proveniret autem dicta dissonantia in mense
paschali, si diem ab Egiptiis in fine sui anni interkalatum ecclesia Romana
interkalaret in Februario alterius anni quam proxime sequentis, ut perpendenti

---

194 diem…196 precedentis] Bede, *De temporum ratione*, c. 38 (ed. CCSL 123B, 400, ll. 30–32).
196 Hinc…198 concordiam] Bede, *De temporum ratione*, c. 11 (ed. CCSL 123B, 319, ll. 103–108).

manifestum est. Dum autem Romani Cesaris instituta sequebantur, eundem
210 diem interkalarunt in Februario non anni sequentis sed precedentis. Verbi gratia,
annus Augusti XLIX (si cursus nostri cicli solaris ad illa tempora retrotrahatur)
reperietur bissextilis, quamobrem anno eius XLVIII° interkalatum erat ab
Egiptiis. Apud Romanos autem ordinationem Iulii sequentes annus XLVII
fuerat bissextilis, ita ut in eo interkalarent diem ab Egiptiis anno sequenti
215 interkalandum, quamobrem dicta dissonantia permansit a VI° kl. Martii anni
XLVII usque ad quartum kl. Septembris anni XLVIII, quo tempore medio
necesse erat bis mensem paschalem intervenisse. Postquam igitur in ecclesia
statutum est ut pascha celebretur dominica proxima post lunam XIIII mensis
paschalis, necesse fuit Romanos (quatinus se Egiptiis conformarent, quibus
220 tamquam astronomie peritioribus primo commissa fuit cura scrutandi lunas
XIIII[as]) instituta imperatorum gentilium pretermittere ac cursum cicli solaris
pristinum immutare, ita ut velut olim Romani per annum ante | Egiptios   338
interkalare consueverant, sic ecclesia Romana deinceps post Egiptios anno
proxime sequenti interkalaret. In qua immutatione non post solos tres, sed
225 quinque annos communes ecclesia bissextum servasse creditur ordinans deinde
annum quemque quartum fore bissextilem.

Gamaliel: Scire velim quo tempore hec immutatio facta sit.

Paulus: Tunc eam factam suspicor cum apud Romanos statutum est
paschalem festivitatem non nisi dominica proxima post lunam XIIII[am] primi
230 mensis celebrari, quod contigit tempore Victoris pape. Is quidem, ut in Cronica
Martiniana legitur, *ad sacerdotum interrogationem de termino paschali celebravit concilium
in Cesarea* Palestine, *cui inter*erat *Narcissus patriarcha Iherosolimorum, Theophilus
Cesar*iensis, *Hireneus Lugdunensis. Ubi statutum est pascha die dominico celebrar*i *a XIIII[a]
luna* primi *mensis usque* in *XXI*, quod Beda actum innuit sub Helio imperatore,
235 utpote circa annum domini centesimum nonagesimum.

Hec, etsi non omnia demonstrata sint (nec enim *in omnibus acribologia
mathematica expetenda est*), ob id tamen credibilioria existimo, quoniam post
plurimas lucubrationes commodiorem invenire nequivi viam ea salvandi que a
maioribus nostris accepimus.

240   **Gamaliel**: De ciclo solari iam michi satis abunde disseruisse videris.
Progredere, queso, et vim naturamque cicli decemnovenalis explanes.

---

219 quatinus…221 XIIIIas] Cf. Bede, *De temporum ratione*, c. 44 (ed. CCSL 123B, 418–419).
231 ad…234 XXI] Martin of Opava, *Chronicon pontificum et imperatorum* (ed. Weiland, 412).
234 quod…235 nonagesimum] Bede, *De temporum ratione*, c. 66 (a. 3952, a. 4146) (ed. CCSL 123B,
495, 502).   **236** nec…237 est] Cf. Aristotle, *Metaphysica*, trans. William of Moerbeke, 2.3 (995a15)
(ed. Vuillemin-Diem, 2:47, ll. 116–117).

<Capitulum 2>

Secundum capitulum est de ciclo decemnovenali.

Paulus: Ad declarandum cicli decemnovenalis naturam non incongruum erit novisse quod transactis a nativitate domini annis circiter centumquinquaginta, Anthonio pio regnante, sub Pio papa, Hermes scripsit librum in quo continetur 5 angeli preceptum ut pascalis festivitas non nisi dominico die celebretur. Paulopost adhuc Anthonio regnante, dum Anizetus Romanam regeret ecclesiam, Policarpus *Iohannis apostoli discipulus et ab eo Smirne ecclesie episcopus ordinatus*, teste Iheronimo, libro De viris illustribus, *Romam venit super quasdam* de *die pasche questiones.* Qui enim ecclesiis Azie preerant, crediderunt a Christianis 10
339 *obser|vandum pascha quando Iudeis agnus paschalis immolari precipitur,* in *quacumque* ebdomadis die luna XIIII^a contingat. Sed de hac questione Anizetus et Policarpus convenerant ut neuter obstinata contentione suam sentenciam defenderet. Neque enim Anizetus Policarpo persuadere poterat ut non observaret ea que noverat Iohannem et ceteros apostolos, cum quibus semper 15 fuerat, observasse. Neque rursus Policarpus Anizeto persuasit ea deserere que ille dicebat maiorum more servari, et ita ab invicem integra caritate discesserunt. Dehinc dicta differentia magis ac magis invalescente illorum tandem prevaluit sentencia qui non nisi die dominico pascha servandum astruebant. Velut ergo Iudeis decimaquarta luna primi mensis agnus pascalis immolari precipitur, sic 20 apud Christianos decretum est ut non eodem die, sed dominico proxime sequenti pascha celebretur. Ut autem Christifideles omniquaque dispersi concorditer absque errore uno die paschalem servarent festivitatem sancti patres primitus Alexandrino commiserunt antistiti ut singulis annis quo die foret XIIII^a luna paschalis (cuius peritiam maxime habebant Egiptii) indagaret. Idque 25 congruo tempore apostolice sedi intimaret, quatinus per eius scripta longinquiores ecclesie de pascha servando possent certiorari. Verum, ut tantus labor tandem quiesceret, nonnulli compendiosam ceperunt inquirere regulam qua rite inveniri possent XIIII^{te} lune pascales. Cum multi frustra conarentur nec ad veram pasche rationem pervenirent, Eusebius Cesariensis ciclum confecit 30 decemnovenalem per quem tam XIIII^{te} lune primi mensis quam paschalis

---

3 Ad... 6 celebretur] ps.-Pius I, *Epistola ecclesiis omnibus missa ut die dominica pascha celebretur,* in *Decretales pseudo-Isidorianae* (ed. Hinschius, 116). **7** Paulopost...10 questiones] Jerome of Stridon, *De viris illustribus,* c. 17.1–2 (ed. Ceresa-Gastaldo, 108–110). **11** observandum...12 contingat] Eusebius of Caesarea, *Historia ecclesiastica* (trans. Rufinus of Aquileia) 5.23.1 (ed. GCS 9.1, 489). **22** Ut...32 inveniretur] Bede, *De temporum ratione,* c. 44 (ed. CCSL 123B, 418–419); cf. Hermann Zoest, *Phaselexis,* c. 7 (ed. Solan, *La réforme du calendrier,* 448–452).

---

29 inveniri] invenieri

festivitas inveniretur. Concorditer ad inventum Eusebii *Pachomius monachus cenobiorum Egipti fundator*, ut in Epistola Cirilli legitur, *litteras edidit quas angelo dictante perceperat* pro solempnitate paschali invenienda. Huius itaque cicli
35 circuitum patres qui Nycene synodo intererant numquam vacillare posse sperantes ipsum decreverunt perpetuis temporibus observandum. Unde in epistola quam ad Leonem papam scripsit Pro | therius Alexandrine urbis antistes 340 in hunc modum legitur: *Beatissimi patres ciclum decemnovenalem certius affigentes, quem violari impossibile est velut crepidinem, fundamentum, et regulam, statuerunt non iuxta*
40 *Iudeorum indoctas ineptas*que *actiones, neque secundum* ceterorum *putativam fictamque prudentiam, sed secundum gratiam sancti spiritus instituti in revolutione memorati decemnovenalis cicli XIIII^{tas} lunas pascales annotarunt.* Et Beda, libro De temporibus, cum luna biduo priusquam prima caneretur ab aliquibus visa fuisset ita dicit: *Si quis a nobis rationem huius cause exegerit, hic nostra pusillitas, ne sui fragilitate deficiat, ad*
45 *paterne, ymo divine auctoritatis auxilium concurrat. Paterne etenim auctoritatis subsidio fulcimur, dum Nycene synodi scita sectamur, que XIIII^{tas} lunas pascales tam firma stabilitate prefixit, ut decemnovenalis earum circuitus nusquam vacillare, nusquam fallere possit.* Et paucis interpositis subdit: *Sed speciali*bus *divine auctoritatis indiciis observantiam lunarem quam tenemus defendimus*, ubi consequenter subdit verba beati Cirilli de
50 Pachomio monacho preallegata.

   Gamaliel: Huius cicli quem adeo commendare videris naturam et cursum aperias, queso. Si tante eius, ut astruis, sint laudes, non modo Christianis, sed et nobis Hebreis utilis videretur.

   Paulus: Annos cicli decemnovenalis, qui ad XIIII^{tas} lunas paschales
55 inveniendas institutus est, non reor, ut plerique, per aureum numerum qui lune primationes ostendit putari, sed per alium numerum, aureo tamen numero proportionalem. Cum quidem servari non debeat paschalis festivitas nisi equinoctio transacto, quod dum id ciclus institueretur occurrit XII kl. Aprilium, eapropter ab eodem die usque XIIII kl. Mayarum XIX numeri prenotati sunt, ea
60 lege ut primo illorum dierum prenotentur XVI, secundo V, quarto XIII, quinto II, et sic deinceps adinstar aurei numeri. Ex cuius numeri prenotacione mox de quolibet anno cognoscitur quo die luna eius XIIII^{a} paschalis occurrat. Constito namque quotus est annus in ciclo decemnovenali numerus anni ostendit lunam XIIII^{tam} | eo die provenire cui prenotatus est. Neque hic silentio pretereundum 341
65 est unum quod plurimos latere reor, ubi scilicet anni cicli prescripti et initium

---

32 Pachomius...34 invenienda] *Epistola Cyrilli*, c. 5 (ed. Krusch, *Studien* [1880], 346); cf. Bede, *De temporum ratione*, c. 43 (ed. CCSL 123B, 416, ll. 81–84). **38** Beatissimi...42 annotarunt] Proterius of Alexandria, *Epistola ad Leonem papam*, c. 7 (ed. Krusch, *Studien* [1880], 276). **43** Si...47 possit] Bede, *De temporum ratione*, c. 43 (ed. CCSL 123B, 414–415, ll. 53–66). **48** Sed...49 defendimus] Bede, *De temporum ratione*, c. 43 (ed. CCSL 123B, 416, ll. 79–80).

---

44 pusillitas] possibilitas

sortiantur et finem. Non profecto (licet id plerique putent) kalendis Ianuarii, ubi aureus numerus innovatur, incipiunt, qui error facile convincitur. Nam sic unus huiusmodi annorum alium non nisi uno die excederet, si forsan esset bissextus, cum tamen constet aliquos ipsorum esse communes trecentorum quinquagintaquatuor dierum et aliquos embolismales dierum CCCLXXXIIII. 70 Volebant autem huius cicli institutores annos eius finiri XIIIIª luna paschali et in crastino annum novum inchoari, eo pacto ut quilibet eo die finiatur cui ex XIX numeris predictis ille qui eidem anno respondet prenotatur. Verbi gratia, annus primus cicli decemnovenalis finitur nonis Aprilis, ubi prenotatur unitas. In crastino illius diei incipit annus secundus, qui trecentis quinquaginta quatuor 75 diebus transactis finitur VIIIº kl. Aprilis, cui diei prenotatur binarius. In cuius crastino incipit annus tercius qui, quia est embolismalis, finitur transactis diebus CCCLXXXIIII ydibus Aprilis, quoniam ibidem ternarius prenotatur, et sic deinceps. Si quis hac in re michi non assenserit, formulam legat quam ad sciendum quo die annus quisque decemnovenalis terminetur Dyonisius 80 descriptam reliquit et me conformiter ad illam dixisse mox intelliget. Invenietque annum tercium, sextum, octavum, undecimum, XIIII, XVII et XIX embolismales, reliquos vero communes.

Hinc liquet illos errare qui, cum Christum natum audiunt anno 2º cicli decemnovenalis, putant pro anno illo Romano circa cuius finem Christus natus 85 est binarium lune primationes demonstrasse, cum illas eodem anno unitas demonstrarit. Annus quidem 2ᵘˢ cicli decemnovenalis in quo Christus natus est finiebatur VIIIº kl. Aprilis post ipsius nativitatem. Huic enim diei inter numeros decimasquartas lunas representantes prenotatur binarius. Cum ergo per eundem numerum representetur in mense paschali lune XIIIIᵗᵉ et in toto anno lunares 90 primationes, consequens est anno nativitatem Christi sequente, in cuius scilicet exor|dio circumcisus est, binarium lune primationes ostendisse ac unitatem anno illo quo misterium tam incarnationis quam nativitatis est adimpletum. Ex hiis eciam perspicuum videtur radices incarnationis Christi quibus astronomi communiter utuntur monstrare qualiter situati fuerunt planete pridie kl. Ianuarii 95 in meridie, non ante nativitatem Christi, sicut plures opinati sunt, sed post eam. Facta enim additione dierum XI ad radices luminarium reperietur eorum media coniunctio pridie ydus Ianuarii, aut eo circa, quo die prenotatur binarius per quem, ut dixi, lunares primationes aut pocius incensiones pro anno nativitatem Christi sequente monstrabantur. Constat igitur easdem radices situs luminarium 100

342 exor|dio (margin note at line 91–92)

---

79 formulam…83 communes] Dionysius Exiguus, *Epistola ad Bonifacium et Bonum* (ed. Krusch, *Studien* [1938], 85).

---

79 hac in] in hac *a.c.*   **93** est adimpletum] adimpletum est *a.c.*

monstrasse precise ante initium illius anni in cuius kalendis Ianuariis circumcisus
est Christus.

Gamaliel: Hunc numerum de quo locutus es aliquibus kalendariis
prenotatum vidi. Et quid velis teneo. Sed quo pacto credere potero ciclum illum
105 XIX^{lem} nullum errorem continere, cum ecclesiam Romanam eundem, ut reor,
ciclum sequentem ad oculum viderim anno MCCCCLXX^o palam contra patrum
ecclesie primitive decreta pascha suum servasse? Decreverunt quidem ut a
XIIII^{ta} luna primi mensis usque XXI^{am} ipso die dominico pascha celebretur,
sicut liquet ex decreto synodi Cesariensis cui Theophilus prefuit, ac ex verbis
110 Victoris pape que Gratianus allegat, De consecratione, distinctione tercia,
'Celebritatem'. Primus autem mensis est cuius plenilunium cadit in equinoctio
vernali vel statim post. Cum igitur hoc equinoctium secundum medium motum
solis reperiatur tercio ydus Martii ac anno domini predicto secundum calculum
astronomicum luna fuit decimaquarta eisdem ydibus, aut eo circa, celebritas
115 paschalis iuxta patrum canones servanda venit sequenti die dominica, que fuit
XV kl. Aprilis, quam tamen ecclesia Romana dictum ciclum secuta de primo
mense in 2um declinans decimo kl. Mayarum noscitur observasse.

Paulus: Potuit profecto ciclus XIX^{lis} non vacillare, sed error quem contra
nos evidenter concludis ex nimia fortasse provenit reverentia que paternis
120 tradicionibus est habita. Postquam enim in Nycena synodo, | que fuisse creditur 343
circa annum domini CCCXXII, approbatus fuit ciclus XIX^{lis} omnes fere
crediderunt quocumque die semel luna XIIII^{ta} paschalis contigisset eam eodem
die kalendarii XIX annis quotienscumque revolutis in perpetuum inveniri. De
equinoctio eciam vernali, quod tunc XII° kl. Aprilium occurrit, a maximis viris
125 creditum est quod ibi semper fixum et immobile permaneret. Quorum
utrumque ex longo temporis tractu et ad oculum et ex astronomica calculatione
minus verum reperitur. Aureus namque numerus ciclo XIX^{li} correspondens ad
longa iam tempora non recte nec novilunia nec XIIII^{tas} lunas demonstravit.
Equinoctium quoque ad multos iam dies anterioratum est. Unde Iohannes de
130 Lineriis, in Epistola ad Clementem papam sextum, se dicit per calculum
invenisse in annis CCCX cum CCLX diebus novilunium ad unum diem
anteriorari. Hinc hodiernis diebus evenit ut lune primationes aureum numerum
pluribus diebus antecedant. Annus quoque solaris non constat precise ex
CCCLXV diebus et quadrante, ymo vera eius quantitas est minor in sexta parte

---

107 Decreverunt…109 prefuit] Hermann Zoest, *Phaselexis* (2nd version), c. 4 (ed. Solan, *La réforme du calendrier*, 420); cf. ps.-Theophilus of Caesarea, *Acta Synodi*, c. 4 (ed. Krusch, *Studien* [1880], 310).
109 ac…111 Celebritatem] *Decretum magistri Gratiani*, pars 3, dist. 3, c. 22 (ed. Friedberg, col. 1358).
129 Iohannes…132 anteriorari] Jean des Murs and Firmin de Beauval, *Epistola super reformatione antiqui kalendarii*, c. 2.2 (ed. Schabel, 202).

unius hore et amplius, ita ut secundum dominum Petrum Cameracensem et   135
Iohannem de Lineriis tam equinoctia quam solsticia in CXXXIIII annis per
unum diem anteriorentur. Quam anteriorationem patres primitive ecclesie non
attenderunt, ymo Beda de primo die seculi loquens voluit eodem die kalendarii
quo in origine mundi contigit equinoctium in eternum absque omni variatione et
immobiliter permanere. Sed eius sentencie nos non sinit adherere certissima   140
quam ad oculum habemus experientia. Equinoctium enim vernale quod ex
tabulis astronomicis secundum medium motum solis fuit circa tempora Christi
decimo kl. Aprilium iam ad decem dies, utpote ad tercium diem yduum Martii,
videtur anterioratum. Probabile est eciam anno nativitatis Christi citra tempus
date legis similem factam equinoctii anteriorationem. Nam secundum   145
Vincentium, in Speculo, Christus natus est anno a datione legis MVᶜIX, quare
post datam legem usque Christum equinoctium non minus anterioratum est
344   quam modo citra ipsius | nativitatem. Dum itaque lex dabatur occurrit
equinoctium vernale (si kalendarium Romanum ad illa tempora retrotrahatur)
circa initium Aprilis. Unde et primus mensis Hebreorum, quem Nysan appellant,   150
olim frequentius cum Aprili concurrebat, quamobrem LXXVI distinctione,
'Primum vero', dicitur quod primus mensis est Aprilis. Nunc vero Martium
primum mensem appellare debemus propter scilicet anteriorationem predictam.

Gamaliel: Lucide declarasti cur Christiani ciclum XIX^lem sequentes hiis
diebus non iuxta patrum decreta paschalem servant festivitatem. A te nunc   155
audire cupio si ne dictus ciclus reformari posset, ut sicut olim sic et nunc absque
errore demonstret lunas XIIII^tas primi mensis.

Paulus: Posset dominus apostolicus, si sue sanctitati placeret, ciclum
XIX^lem ad morem pristinum reformare. Inter omnes autem reformationis
modos, qui plures sunt, eum qui meo iuditio et brevior et facilior est edicam.   160
Patres, quando hoc ciclo uti ceperant, reppererunt equinoctium vernale XII kl.
Aprilium. In primis itaque conandum ut idem equinoctium, quod secundum
medium motum occurrit tercio ydus Martii, ad XII kl. Aprilium retrotrahatur,
quod fiet in uno anno octo dies kalendarii pretereundo. Poterunt autem hii dies
commode subtrahi in Martio a tercio ydus Martii ad XII kl. Aprilium diebus   165
omnibus intermediis omissis transiliendo, eo pacto ut in crastino Gregorii
festum Benedicti in ecclesia teneatur. Nec merito pigeret Romanum pontificem
taliter annum abbreviare, cum Iulius Cesar olim annum Romanum ad XV

---

135 secundum…137 anteriorentur] Jean des Murs and Firmin de Beauval, *Epistola super reformatione antiqui kalendarii*, c. 1.3 (ed. Schabel, 198–199); Pierre d'Ailly, *Tractatus de legibus et sectis contra superstitiosos astronomos*, c. 10, in idem, *Imago mundi* (ed. Leuven 1477/83, sig. g3r); d'Ailly, *Exhortatio ad concilium generale super kalendarii correctione*, c. 2 (ed. Solan, *La réforme du calendrier*, 206).   **138** Beda…
140 permanere] Bede, *De temporum ratione*, c. 6 (ed. CCSL 123B, 290–295).   **146** Christus…MVcIX]
Vincent of Beauvais, *Speculum historiale*, lib. 6, c. 88 (ed. Douai 1624, 203).   **151** LXXVI…152
Aprilis] *Decretum magistri Gratiani*, pars I, dist. 76, c. 6 (ed. Friedberg, col. 269).

menses auxerit et post eum Octavianus in XII annis tres dempserit bissextos, ut
170   gentiles rite suos dies fastos observarent. Quoniam autem sacrosancto sedi
apostolice placuit in antea annum quemlibet XXV^{tum} iubileum efficere, congrue
fieri poterit abbreviatio predicta anno domini MCCCCLXXVI qui proxime
sequetur iubileum. Christianis enim ex quacumque terre plaga in iubileo Romam
confluentibus facile posset dicta temporum reformatio publicari. Nec sufficeret
175   octo dictorum dierum preteritio, quinymo necesse foret cursum cicli tam solaris
quam XIX^{lis} immutari. Erit quidem annus predictus in ciclo solari XII habens
GF pro litteris domini|calibus, sed dictis octo diebus subtractis pro littera   345
dominicali haberet G. Eodem quippe anno dies sextus yduum Martii erit
dominicus, a quo si octo diebus pretermissis transiliatur ad XII kl. Aprilium
180   occurret dies dominicus VIII° earundem kl. ubi collocatur G. Oporteret insuper
lune primationes, que citra Nycenam synodum ad quartum diem anteriorate
sunt, rectificari. Luna enim que secundum cursum aurei numeri ciclo XIX^{li}
correspondentis indicatur prima hiis temporibus diceretur quarta. Anno igitur
predicto, qui erit XIIII^{tus} cicli XIX^{lis}, luna caneretur prima pridie kl. Martii, cui
185   diei idem numerus XIIII prenotatur, sed vere dicenda esset prima quinto
earundem kl. Hinc computando, si dies octo pretereantur, dies tricesimus
occurreret tercio nonas Aprilis. Et in crastino, cui prenotatur aureus numerus
XIX, inciperet novus mensis lunaris. Ex tunc ergo lunares primationes eiusdem
anni per XIX presentarentur. Et quoniam idem numerus inter numeros XIIII^{tas}
190   lunas paschales representantes prescribitur XV° kl. Mayi, eodem die luna esset
decimaquarta et in proxima sequenti dominica, que erit decimus earundem kl.,
servaretur paschalis solemnitas. Annus vero proxime sequens, qui erit
MCCCCLXXVII ac primus reformatus, esset in utroque ciclo primus habens
pascha iuxta patrum instituta. Tandem tamen error qui nunc est emergeret nisi
195   eum qui huius rei periti sunt studuerint precavere.

Gamaliel: Dic, queso, si in hanc reformationem summus tuus consentiret
pontifex, qua lege Christiani in antea noscerent quotus esset quisque annus in
ciclo tam solari quam XIX^{li}, quoniam, quantum conicere possum, legem
oporteret immutari?
200   **Paulus**: Recte sentis. Atque ad id noscendum acciperemus annum Christi
quasi fuisset nonus cicli solaris et septimus cicli XIX^{lis}. Ad inveniendum ergo de
quolibet anno quotus sit in ciclo solari annis domini adderentur octo totumque
divideretur per XXVIII et quod queritur ex supercrescenti cognosceretur. Ad
inveniendum vero quotus sit quilibet annus in ciclo XIX^{li} annis domini
205   adderentur sex et toto diviso | per XIX ex eo quod post divisionem remanserit   346
statim sciretur quod querebatur. Nec mirum si in hac re falsis utamur
suppositionibus cum ceteri compotiste de quolibet anno domini scrutantes
quotus sit in ciclo solari supponant annum nativitatis Christi fuisse aut decimum

aut XXI eiusdem cicli et tamen, ut audisti, nativitas Christi precessit cursum cicli
solaris Romanorum. Et ne huic temporum reordinationi adversentur astronomi,   210
quibus in suis calculationibus impedimentum prestari videretur, hanc
brevissimam legem dari expediet ut semper postea meminerint octo dies
subtractos sicque, dum ex tabulis confectis calculare voluerint, sciant octo dies
adiciendos aut octo diebus adiectis radices antiquas immutent.

Gamaliel: Eo tuam reformationem tendere sentio ut post XIIII^tam lunam   215
primi mensis quando a nobis agnus paschalis immolandus est non tunc, sed
proxima sequenti dominica pascha servetur a Christianis. Sed quod dixisti
Christianos deinceps iubileum servaturos quolibet anno XXV° minus congruum
apparet, tum quia plurimum discrepat a nostre legis observantia que annum
quinquagesimum iubileum constituit, tum quia remissioni peccatorum, que a   220
Christianis in iubileo copiosius speratur, nullus numerus magis congruere
videtur quam quinquagenarius. Resultat enim ex partibus aliquotis quadragenarii,
que sunt unum, duo, quatuor, quinque, octo, decem et viginti. Sicut ergo
numerus quadragenarius penitencie maxime deputatus est, sic remissioni
peccatorum, quam per penitenciam consequi speramus, precipue   225
quinquagenarius congruere videtur.

Paulus: Non putes numerum XXV a multiplici vacare misterio. Est
quidem numerus circularis. Nam finalis eius denominatio eadem est sue radici,
que est quinque; quinquies enim quinque XXV reddunt. Sed numerus circularis
non inepte statui illorum tribuitur quibus peccata remittuntur, tales namque ad   230
suum principium redeunt a quo prius cum impiis in circuitu ambulantes
deviarunt. In circulo quidem ad idem principium reditur a quo prius recessum
est. Est preterea numerus XXV quadratus ex ductu quinarii in seipsum
347 resultans. Qualis numerus illis videtur aptari quamoptime qui per ple|nariam
peccatorum remissionem iustificati sunt quo modo Aristotiles felicem   235
tetragonismo comperat. Nam iustificatus per gratiam spiritus sancti quam
suscepit omniquaque adinstar quadrati firmam habet basim cui quicquid adversi
contigerit securus possit incumbere. Insuper ex partibus aliquotis numeri
memorati, que sunt unitas et quinarius, resultat primus numerus perfectus, puta
senarius, quo non incongrue signatur perfecta peccatorum remissio in anno   240
iubileo concedenda. Nec silentio pretereundum videtur quod numerus XXV
precise constat ex unitate et omnibus numeris imparibus sub limite numerorum
contentis. Unitas enim, ternarius, quinarius, septenarius et novenarius efficiunt
XXV. Qua ex re nobis significari videtur credentes in Deum, qui unus est in
essencia et trinus in personis, virtute passionis Christi, qui per quinarium   245
vulnerum ipsius exprimitur, anno iubileo septiformem gratiam sancti spiritus

---

236 spiritus sancti] sancti spiritus *a.c.*

consecuturos, per quam si decesserint mox angelorum consortio sociabuntur,
qui novem ordinibus distinguuntur. In legem itaque veteri quamquam remissioni
peccatorum annus quinquagesimus congruerit, ei tamen in nova lege, que est lex
250 perfecte libertatis, optime videtur aptari posse annus XXV^{tus}. Hinc forte viri
faciem habentes ad orientem et ad ortum solis adorantes, quomodo nove legis
observatores adorant, in Ezechiele describuntur fuisse vigintiquinque.

Gamaliel: Hanc digressionem audisse placet, sed ad inceptum redeundo
doceri cupio de tercio ciclo, quem lunarem appellant.

<Capitulum 3>

Tercium capitulum de ciclo lunari est.

Paulus: Velut circuitus XIX numerorum, quos mensi paschali ad
representandas lunas XIIII prenotandos dixi, ciclum decemnovenalem conficit,
5   sic omnibus mensibus kalendarii prenotatur aureus numerus ad insinuandum
lunares primationes, in cuius numeri circuitu consistit ciclus lunaris. Qui duo
cicli, etsi equali circumvolvantur tempore, eos tamen ex hoc constat manifestam
habere differentiam quod simul nec incipiunt nec finiuntur. Primus quidem
annus cicli XIX^{lis} est XVII cicli lunaris et primus lunaris | quartus XIX^{lis}. Hinc 348
10 evenit ut misterium nativitatis Christi 2° anno XIX^{li} et lunari XVIII° dicatur
adimpletum. De cicli XIX^{li} audisti a quibus et ad quid inventus sit. De lunari
vero que gens eo usa sit a plerisque dubitatur.

Gamaliel: Cur in dubium vertis quod a Beda tamquam certum asseritur?
Is de ciclo lunari tractans dicit quod *proprie est Romanorum ad mensem Ianuarium*
15 *pertinens. Nam sicut annus quisque XIX^{lis} propter legalem observationem a mense paschali*
*incho*atur *ibique finitur, ita et hic Romanorum institutione a luna mensis Ianuarii incho*atur
et finitur.

Paulus: Propter hec verba Bede autumant nonnulli aureum numerum qui
ciclo lunari subservit a Iulio Cesare kalendario Romano prenotatum. Alii id
20 actum putant ab Octaviano, cui inter cetera munera per que Herodes regnum
Iudeorum obtinuit aureum numerum suspicantur oblatum. Sed quomodo
credam aureum numerum vel a Iulio vel Augusto kalendario prenotatum cum
huius prenotationis nec Suetonius meminit in libro De XII Cesaribus, nec
Macrobius in Saturnalibus, nec Ovidius in De fastis, quos tamen omnes
25 diligenter tractasse videmus de annis per dictos duos imperatores institutis?
Quomodo verisimile est scriptores adeo celebres id silentio preterisse quod
memoratu pulcherrimum est? Quid enim in kalendario pulchrius quam numeras
singulas lune primationes representans? Solet insuper libro De fastis annotari

---

250 viri … 252 vigintiquinque] Ezekiel 8:16.   **14** proprie … 17 finitur] Bede, *De temporum ratione*, c. 56
(ed. CCSL 123B, 445, ll. 4–8).

kalendarium continens iuxta dictorum imperatorum reformationem sex primos menses per kalendas, nonas et ydus distinctos, cui tamen nullus reperitur numerus prenotatus. Quod si ab altero dictorum imperatorum prepositus fuisset kalendario aureus numerus, ille temporibus eorum ostendisset incensiones lune pocius ut servit ciclo XIX^{li} quam lunari. Quod, ut planum fiat, scies plurimam esse differentiam inter incensionem lune et eius primationem. Contingit quidem singulis horis diei lunam incendi, cum scilicet soli coniungitur, sed non incipit dici prima nisi in vespera | proxime sequente suam incensionem, quamobrem incensio lune eius primationem antecedit, aliquando pluribus, aliquando paucioribus horis. Verbi gratia, si statim post occasum solis contingat luminarium coniunctio eodem momento luna dicitur incendi et precedit talis coniunctio, et per consequens incensio lune, primationem horis fere XXIIII. Quoniam Beda teste luna non computatur prima priusquam occurrerit sequens vespera, a qua usque aliam vesperam patres eam primam nominari voluerunt. Unde liquet quod inchoando diem a vespera dies incensionis lunaris semper est prior die quo luna prima computatur. Idem itaque numerus qui ostendit tempore Nycene synodi lunam primam temporibus Christi et dictorum imperatorum eque precise representavit lunarem incensionem. Fuit enim Nycena synodus circa annum Christi trecentesimum vicesimumsecundum, quanto tempore, ut famatissimi volunt astronomi, lune primationes ad unum diem anteriorantur. Tempore autem dicte synodi, ante quam non longe inventus est ciclus XIX^{lis}, aureus numerus, ut servit eidem ciclo, representabat lune primationes; ergo, ut eidem servit ciclo non minus precise representavit sub dictis imperatoribus lunares incensiones. Hoc idem deducitur ex eclipsi cuius super Georgica Virgilii Servius commeminit: *Constat*, inquit, *occiso Cesare in senatu pridie yduum Mayarum solis fuisse defectum ab hora sexta usque noctem; quod quia multis pro*tractum est horis dicit Virgilius '*Impiaque eternam timuerunt secula noctem*'. Sed non contingit solis defectus nisi tempore lunaris incensionis, quare pridie yduum Mayarum anno primo Augusti fuit lunaris incensio. Prenotatur autem eidem diei numerus XVIII. Videatur iam in quo ciclo annus ille fuerit decimusoctavus et invenietur quod in ciclo XIX^{li}, quoniam in annis Augusti progrediens (si primus ponatur XVIII^{us}) reperiet XLII^{um} esse secundum eiusdem cicli. Omnes autem fatentur eundem annum Augusti fuisse 2um cicli XIX^{lis}, sic quod eius lunares incensiones per binarium presentabantur, quod non tantum ex arte compotistica, sed et ex astronomica calculatione manifestum est.

30

35

40

45

50

55

60

---

41 luna … 42 voluerunt] Bede, *De temporum ratione*, c. 43 (ed. CCSL. 123B, 412–414). **53** Constat … 55 noctem] Servius, *In Vergilii Georgica commentarii* 1.466 (ed. Thilo, 212).

---

54 pridie] pridrie

Liquet ex hiis Romanos (si illis temporibus | aliquo usi fuissent ciclo) illum   350
65   pocius fuisse XIX^{lem} quam lunarem. Fuit quidem annus primus Augusti
quintusdecimus cicli lunaris, qui numerus non pridie yduum predictarum sed
quarto diei sequenti prenotatur.

Gamaliel: Si ciclum lunarem existimes non fuisse proprium Romanorum,
que igitur gens eo usa sit dicas, queso.

70   **Paulus**: Inter omnes hac in re michi rectius sensisse videtur Rogerius
Bachon, in Epistola ad Clementem papam quintum. *Sicut*, inquit, *nos utimur ciclo
XIX^{li} sic* Hebrei *lunari, cuius annus primus incipit quarto anno nostro*. Unde ait *falsum*
illos dixisse *qui posuerunt Hebreos non uti ciclo. Habent enim embolismos in suo ciclo sicut
nos in nostro, ymo nos habuimus ab eis*. Innuit ergo ciclum lunarem proprium esse
75   Hebreorum, sicut decemnovenalis est proprius Christianorum. Postquam enim
ecclesia decrevit sacrosanctum pascha celebrari die dominica post XIIII^{tam}
lunam primi mensis, ut ab omnibus uno die servetur, inventus est ciclus XIX^{lis}.
Sic postquam Iudeis data est lex de pascha singulis annis servando luna XIIII^{ta}
primi mensis opus habebant regula per quam solempnitatem paschalem
80   invenirent. Nec ea tantum egebant pro inveniendo pascha, sed et pro ceteris
eorum festivitatibus, nam in singulis lune primationibus servabant festum
neomenie atque secundum eas servabant reliquas festivitates. Egerunt ergo ciclo
qui lunares eis monstraret primationes. Et ille secundum Rogerium fuit ciclus
lunaris. Quod autem soliti sunt uti huiusmodi ciclo ex aliquibus videtur ostendi
85   posse. Quidam enim doctores Hebreorum, ut dicit dominus Petrus
Cameracensis, ponunt *annum primum revolutionis prime solum fuisse in ymaginatione
exceptis sex diebus ultimis*, quorum postremum dicunt fuisse feriam sextam, in qua
formatus est Adam. Insuper dicunt eodem die fuisse primam coniunctionem
mediam et Adam ad vesperam illius diei vidisse lunam primam. In crastino vero,
90   qui fuit dies sabbati quo Deus ab omni opere quievit, ponunt incepisse annum
2um prime revolutionis. Intelligunt autem per 'revolutionem' tempus XIX
annorum in quo contingit lunam revolvi. Dicit preterea | Beda, libro De   351
temporibus, quod *Anno XV° Tiberii dominus post baptism*a *quod Iohannes predicavit
regnum celorum annunciat peractis a principio mundi secundum Hebreos* (*ut Eusebius in
95   cronicis* notat) *annis quatuor milibus, annotando quod XVI° anno Tiberii principium fuit
LXXXI iubilei*. A dicto numero annorum subtractis **XXX**, quoniam secundum
evangelium Luce Christus baptizatus est *incipiens annorum quasi XXX*, remanent
tria milia annorum nongenti et septuaginta. Et toto anno a creatione mundi
Christus secundum Hebreos predictos natus est. Dividamus hos annos per XIX

---

71 Sicut…74 eis] Roger Bacon, *Opus maius*, lib. IV (ed. Bridges, 1:197–198).   **85** Quidam…91
revolutionis] Pierre d'Ailly, *Elucidarium astronomice concordie cum theologica et hystorica veritate*, c. 14, in
idem, *Imago mundi* (ed. Leuven 1477/83, sig. ee8r–v).   **93** Anno…96 iubilei] Bede, *De temporum
ratione*, c. 66 (a. 3981) (ed. CCSL 123B, 496, ll. 997–1102).   **97** incipiens…XXX] Luke 3:23.

et inveniemus in numero quotiens ducentas et octo revolutiones ac in residuo 100
annos XVIII. Secundum Hebreos ergo Christus natus est anno XVIIIº
revolutionis lunaris. Omnes autem compotiste Christum fatentur natum anno
XVIIIº cicli lunaris. Quare liquet illorum lunarem revolutionem penitus eandem
esse cum ciclo quem lunarem appellamus. Solent eciam nonnulli Hebreorum ad
primationem lune inveniendam annis Christi addere tria milia annorum 105
septingentos et sexaginta quasi tot anni ipsius nativitatem precessissent, quem
numerum annorum anno dominice incarnationis addito, si dividamus per XIX,
in numero quotiens inveniemus centum nonagintaseptem revolutiones et in
residuo annos XVIII. Sicut igitur secundum compotistas Christus natus est anno
cicli lunaris XVIIIº, sic secundum Hebreos anno revolutionis ipsorum XVIIIº. 110
Unde iterum liquet Hebreorum lunarem revolutionem in nullo distinctam esse a
ciclo lunari.

Gamaliel: Quoniam efficaciter probasse videris hunc ciclum aliquando
fuisse proprium Hebreorum, eius cursum et a quo inventus est summopere scire
desidero. 115

Paulus: Ex voluminibus doctorum tuorum quod a me postulas planius, ut
reor, scrutari posses. Ut tamen tibi morem geram tuis (utcumque potero) votis
satisfacere conabor. Sed in primis opus erit pauca disserere de numero quem
aureum appellant, quem sane primo prenotatum existimo non nostro, sed
Egiptiorum kalendario, quod a nostro in numero dierum non discrepat. Et 120
352 quoniam quarto kl. Septembrium secundum | Bedam Egiptii annum suum
inchoant, eos ibidem reor hunc numerum innovare atque ex eo die usque kl.
Ianuarii non eundem numerum quem nos, sed alium habere, qui nostrum in
unitate superat. Verbi gratia, cum tercio kl. Septembris habeamus octenarium,
ipsi habent novenarium et sic deinceps usque kl. Ianuarii, quibus kl. ordo numeri 125
postulat ternarium prenotari. Hinc usque ad exordium anni ipsorum in cursu
dicti numeri cum eis convenimus. Et ne me divinare putes, cur sic existimem
adverte. Exigit aureus numerus ut in qualibet XIX annorum revolutione saltus
lune semel servetur, quod fit anno illo cuius primationes per XIX designantur.
Huiusmodi saltus sic servatur: Tres menses quisque XXIX dierum sibi continue 130
succedunt cum tamen pro ordine solito medius eorum dies XXX
complecteretur. In quo mense medio luna saltare fingitur, quoniam cum esset
pronuncianda trecesima eiusdem mensis pronunciatur prima mensis sequentis,
quasi unum diem transiliisset. Dicti tres menses inchoantur quarto nonas Iunii et
terminantur ad quartum kl. Septembrium, ut aureum numerum (si recte 135
prenotatus sit) aspicienti perspicuum est. Quod ibidem lune saltus servetur nulla
alia videtur assignabilis ratio nisi quod dum aureus numerus institutus est illi tres
menses erant ultimi illius anni cuius primationes per XIX monstrabantur
quodque eis finitis inchoabatur annus cuius primationes per unitatem

140 ostendebantur. Preterea numerus aureus sic collocatus est ut in quolibet anno
   embolismali continui sint duo menses quisque XXX dierum. Continet enim talis
   annus XIII menses lunares, sex XXIX dierum et septem dierum XXX. Quorum
   duorum mensium qui continue XXX dies continent secundus non inepte potest
   nuncupari embolismus, id est 'supercrescens'. Nam reliqui menses, nisi bissextus
145 aut saltus lune impediat, alternatim continent unus XXIX dies et alius XXX.
   Dicti menses embolismi reperiuntur ex aurei numeri situatione sparsim incipere
   in kalendario. Nam primo die Ianuarii | incipit talis embolismus pro tercio anno   353
   cicli primationes lune presentantis. Et tercia die eiusdem mensis pro anno XI.
   Similiter quinta Martii pro anno XIX° et sexta ipsius pro VIII°. Item prima
150 Septembris pro anno XVII et 2ª ipsius pro VI°. Ac demum 2ª Novembris pro
   anno XIIII°. Sunt enim dicti anni embolismales utpote tercius, sextus, octavus,
   XI, XIIII, XVII et XIX. Primis diebus mensium embolismorum idem
   prenotatur numerus qui primationes anni representat, nisi quod in nostro
   kalendario pro anno XVII, VI° et XIIII eis presignatur numerus in unitate
155 minor. Verbi gratia, primo die Septembris incipit embolismus anni XVII, cui
   diei in nostro kalendario prenotatur numerus XVI, et sic de aliis duobus
   embolismis quorum unus incipit tercia Septembris et alius 2ª Novembris. Qua
   ex re coniciendum videtur quod illi a quibus aureus numerus primo inventus est
   prenotarunt in Septembri et tribus mensibus sequentibus numerum qui nostrum
160 superat in unitate.

   Gamaliel: Quid velis sentio. Sed dic, precor, quem huius numeri putes
   inventorem?

   Paulus: Quoniam, *ut Iosephus testatur, Abraham patriarcha* in *astro*nomi*a doctus*
   *a Calde*is hanc *disciplinam veracius intellectam Egiptiorum genti, cum apud eos exularet,*
165 *advexit,* non incongruum apparet si tam annus Egiptiorum quam aureus numerus
   sibi prescriptus ab Abraham putetur institutus aut a *familiarissimo Dei amico*
   Moyse, in hac re ad summum erudito, dum post exitum ex Egiptiaca servitute
   Israelitis *precepit festa legis veteris secundum dies lunationum celebrari.*

   Gamaliel: Animum michi magis inflammas ad perquirendum qualiter ex
170 aureo numero lunares primationes inveniantur.

   Paulus: Scies igitur quod licet per hunc numerum non ita precise sicut per
   calculum astronomicum lunares primationes aut incensiones scieri possint, tum
   quia bissexti in diversis ciclis differenter se habent, tum quia pluribus diebus in
   quibus luna vere vel inceditur vel primatur nullus numerus | prescribitur, ipse   354

---

163 ut…165 advexit] Flavius Josephus *ap.* Bede, *De temporum ratione,* c. 6 (ed. CCSL 123B, 294, ll.
86–90).   **166** familiarissimo…168 celebrari] Hermann Zoest, *Phaselexis* (2ⁿᵈ version), prol. (ed.
Solan, *La réforme du calendrier,* 396).

---

148 tercia…mensis] die eiusdem mensis tercia *a.c.*

tamen (si modicus adhibeatur labor) poterit absque errore, saltem vulgo   175
perceptibili, in perpetuum huiusmodi primationes aut incensiones insinuare.
Quamquam enim dictus numerus ciclo XIX^{li} correspondens hiis temporibus
non recte nobis representet lunares primationes, nichilominus duo sunt modi et
facillimi quibus posset rectificari. Unus quod eo die in quo luna veraciter est
prima ipsa prima computetur atque annus currens ab eo numero denominetur   180
qui eidem diei reperitur prenotatus. Verbi gratia, hoc anno MCCCCLXXI
aureus numerus a quo nos Christiani lunam primam computamus est novem,
cum tamen in veritate pronuncianda esset prima quarto die precedenti, cui
numerus XII presignatur. Quamobrem, si aurem numerum rectificare velimus,
eodem die poterimus lunam computare primam et annum qui denominatus est   185
nonus in ciclo reformato denominare duodecimum.

Alius modus est ut occurrente die vere primationis lunaris illo et diebus
mediis pretermissis mox transeatur ad diem cui prenotatus est numerus a quo
annus currens denominatur. Verbi gratia, anno presenti luna vere dicenda esset
prima eo die cui numerus XII prenotatur, quod si illo die et duobus sequentibus   190
pretermissis mox in kalendario transeatur ad quartum, cui preponitur novenarius
(est enim annus iste nonus cicli XIX^{lis}), ex tunc incipient per aureum numerum
sic presentari lune primationes sicut circa tempora consilii Nyceni, in quo
approbatus fuerat ciclus XIX^{lis}.

Si altero dictorum modorum numerus aureus rectificatus fuerit,   195
representabit precise vel quasi ad annos circiter tricentos lunares primationes,
que, ut astronomi notarunt, annis tricentis et decem anteriorantur. Facta autem
anterioratione notabili, quam vulgus percipere posset, denuo poterit aureus
numerus altero dictorum modorum rectificari.

Gamaliel: Hactenus me latuit tantam esse vim illius numeri quem   200
kalendariis prenotatum vidi. Credidi quidem, si denuo per ipsum vere insinuari
355   deberent primationes lune, quod abradendus esset et quis|que quarto die
precedenti collocandus. Plurimum autem gaudeo quod numerum tam utilem
(quem non incongrue ab auro, quod metalla cetera precellit, 'aureum' appellant)
a patre nostro Abraham vel a Moyse nostro legislatore adinventum suades. Sed   205
nondum novi cicli lunaris cursum aut a quibus adinventus sit.

Paulus: Quoniam de David scribitur Ecclesiastici XLVII° *dedit in*
celebrationibus decus et ornavit tempora usque ad consummationem vite, coniciendum reor
aliquid circa temporum reformationem a David ordinatum. Eum quippe constat
ad decorandum cerimonias templi ac dies celebres Iudeorum solicitum fuisse,   210
quare de eo scribitur quod *dedit in celebrationibus decus*. Cum igitur huiusmodi dies

---

207 dedit … 208 vite] Ecclesiasticus 47:12.

---

179 facillimi] facilimi *p.c.*

celebrabantur vel in initiis vel certis diebus mensium lunarium, opus erat Iudeis aliqua regula qua scierent qua die quisque mensis lunaris inchoaretur. Quam regulam, quia a David inventa existimo, recte michi videtur de eo dictum quod
215   *ornavit tempora usque ad consummationem vite.*

Hanc autem regulam suspicor fuisse ciclum lunarem. Cui suspicioni non parvam michi fidem adicit quod calculus astronomicus ostendit incensiones post quas in proxima vespera mensis lunaris incipit circa tempora David eisdem fere contigisse diebus quibus aureus numerus ciclo lunari serviens prenotatur. Hinc
220   evenisse puto ut temporibus Christi luna non incenderetur eo die cui aureus numerus ciclo lunari serviens prenotatur, sed quarto die precedenti. Incensiones enim lunares, sicut de primationibus dictum est, ad annos circiter trecentos ad unum diem anteriorantur. Christus autem ab initio regni David secundum Eusebium natus est anno millesimo centesimo quarto. Quare, sicut citra
225   tempora Nycene synodi, in qua ciclus XIX^{lis} approbatus est, lune primationes iam ad diem quartum precedentem aberrarunt, sic citra tempus David, a quo ciclum lunarem inventum existimo, necesse est lunares incensiones eciam ad quartum diem temporibus Christi aberrasse. Et velut ad nostrum pascha servandum non sequimur calculum | astronomicum, sed cursum cicli XIX^{lis}, sic   356
230   citra tempus David usque post Christi nativitatem Iudei tam pascha suum quam ceteras festivitates servarunt non rationem astronomicam secuti, sed cursum cicli lunaris. Ac tunc demum eundem ciclum dereliquerunt cum non a solis astronomie peritis, sed et a popularibus eius error deprehenderetur.

Hec sunt que de tribus ciclis dicere statui.
235   **Gamaliel**: Ea et audisse collibuit et firma memoria teneo. Iam in difficultatibus discutiendis, ne quid indiscussum pretereas, pedetentim quas proposui controversias aggredi digneris. In primis autem dicas, velim, quoto Cesaris Augusti anno Ihesum natum opineris.

---

223 Christus…224 quarto] Eusebius of Caesarea, *Chronicon* (trans. Jerome of Stridon) (ed. GCS 47, 67a, 169).

---

234 que de] de que *a.c.*

\<Tractatus 3\>

\<Capitulum 1\>

Tercius tractatus continet solutiones dictarum controversiarum. Primum capitulum earum que concernunt annum nativitatis Christi.

Paulus: Ihesum Christum Augusto regnante natum esse Lucas in evangelio suo 5
testatur, ubi scribit Mariam pregnantem una cum Ioseph in Bethleem ascendisse
ibique peperisse Christum cum exisset *edictum a Cesare Augusto ut universus orbis*
describeretur.

Ad scrutandum quoto eius anno misterium nativitatis Christi adimpletum
sit animadvertendum quod annus solaris est duplex, emergens et usualis. 10
Emergens est spacium temporis ubilibet incipiens currensque donec sol motu
suo circulum compleverit. Usualis est spacium quo sol unam revolutionem
complet inchoando a certo die kalendarii, utpote apud Romanos a kalendis
Ianuarii, apud Egiptios a quarto kl. Septembris et apud Grecos a kl. Decembris.
Annus proprius Hebreorum, cum ex revolutionibus lune constet, non est solaris. 15
Incipit autem secundum nonnullos a coniunctione luminarium equinoctio
vernali propinquiori, secundum alios a luna XV^{ta} mensis paschalis.

Si loqui placeat de annis emergentibus quibus Augustus regnavit, eos ab
ydibus Martii in quibus Iulius Cesarem predecessorem suum occisum constat
inchoando, Christum natum opinor anno Augusti XLI°. Similiter, si loquimur de 20
annis usualibus Romanorum. Sin de annis Hebreorum, Grecorum et Egiptiorum
357 loqui malimus, eum natum puto | anno Augusti XLII. Rationem diversitatis
facile est considerare. Nam inter ydus Martias in quibus imperium Augusti
exordiendum dixi et octavum diem kl. Ianuarii, quando Christus natus creditur,
annum suum renovant Hebrei, Greci et Egiptii, non autem Romani nec eciam 25
medio tempore renovantur anni ab imperio Cesaris Augusti emergentes.
Quoniam autem nichil eorum que proposuisti indiscussum preteriri desideras,
tuum erit paulatim in medium proferre sentencias iis que dicturus sum
contrarias. Ego utcumque potero vel ad veritatem eas reducam, vel probabilem
causam erroris assignabo. 30

Gamaliel: Modum iam video quo dissolvi possit differentia que videtur
esse inter Tertullianum dicentem Christum natum anno Augusti XLI° et alios
historiographos id actum asserentes anno ipsius XLII°. De Alphonso autem,
quid dicendum censebis, qui ex differentia erarum Cesaris et incarnationis
innuere videtur nativitatem Christi contigisse anno Augusti vel XXXIX° vel 35
XXXIIII°?

---

7 edictum…8 describeretur] Luke 2:1.   **12** Usualis…14 Ianuarii] Pierre d'Ailly, *Elucidarium*
astronomice concordie cum theologica et hystorica veritate, c. 38, in idem, *Imago mundi* (ed. Leuven 1477/83,
sig. gg5v).

Paulus: In hac re ne Alphonso fidem habeas, nec mirum si in dicta differentia erarum defecerit, quia Romani non leguntur certas eras suorum imperatorum notasse. Et Dyonisius abbas, qui fuit circiter annum domini
40 quingentesimum, primum cepit, ut Beda testatur, ab incarnatione domini annorum tempora prenotare, cum prius ab annis Dyocletiani principis observarentur. Patres eciam primitive ecclesie non leguntur precisam eram Christi posteris reliquisse. Ne tamen omnino irrationabiliter Alphonsus errasse putetur, adverte quomodo ad sic errandum induci potuit ex duabus eclipsibus,
45 quarum una secundum Servium contigit anno primo Augusti pridie yduum Mayarum, cui diei preponitur numerus XVIII. Aliam eclipsim credimus contigisse die Passionis Christi, quam propterea miraculosam putamus, quia sol cum eclipsari non soleat nisi tempore coniunctionis, illa contigit tempore dyametralis oppositionis, utpote luna decima quinta. Et cum tempus medium
50 inter oppositionem et coniunctio|nem sit XIIII dies, hore XVIII, cum certis   358 minutis, Christus autem passus putatur VIII° kl. Aprilis, apparet quod XV^{to} die precedenti, videlicet quinto ydus Martii fuit coniunctio luminarium, cui diei numerus XIII prenotatur. Progrediendo iam in aureo numero a primo anno Augusti, in quo fuit eclipsis solis et ita coniunctio luminarium eo die cui
55 prescribitur numerus XVIII, inquirantur anni sequentes in quibus occurrit numerus XIII easdem coniunctiones representans, quoniam in uno talium annorum Christus creditur mortem obisse. Fuerunt autem huiuscemodi anni annus XV^{tus} Augusti, XXXIIII^{us}, LIII et LXXII. Nec progredi oportet ad annum nonagesimum primum ante quem Christus indubitanter mortuus est.
60 Cum ergo constet ipsum non esse passum aliquo trium primorum annorum, consequens videtur annum LXXII ab initio Augusti fuisse illum in quo Christus mortis sustinuit obprobrium. A quo numero annorum si XXXIII subtrahantur (nam Christus toto anno crucifixus creditur) remanent anni XXXIX, quare anno Augusti XXXIX° natus creditur. Quod Alphonsus credidit. Que deductio, etsi
65 plurimam habeat apparentiam, innititur tamen uni suppositioni, licet famose, minus tamen vere, nisi recte intellectam sit. Supponitur quidem quod VIII° kl. Aprilis dum Christus pateretur luna fuit decimaquinta, quasi tunc fuisset oppositio luminarium.

Sed hic est advertendum quod duplex est luna XV, vera et legalis. Vera
70 non contingit nisi die dyametralis oppositionis. Legalis autem, que scilicet sumitur secundum legem aliquam datam ad inveniendum quota est luna, aliis diebus contingere potest. Verbi gratia, in mense paschali anni presentis vera luna

---

39 Et...42 observarentur] Bede, *De temporum ratione*, c. 47 (ed. CCSL 123B, 427).   **45** una...46 XVIII] See tr. 2, c. 3, ll. 52–58.

---

52 Martii] Aprilis   **54** luminarium] lunarium   **72** presentis] 1471 *s.l.*

XV fuit nonis Aprilis, tunc enim fuit oppositio luminarium, sed luna XV legalis, que sumitur secundum legem cicli decemnovenalis, fuit sexto ydus Aprilis. Sic in die passionis Christi fuit luna XV legalis sumpta secundum legem cicli lunaris 75 quo populus Israheliticus illis temporibus utebatur, ut supra declaravi. Fuit enim 359 annus quo passus est XIII^{us} cicli lunaris, qui numerus prenotatur | diei precedenti diem passionis, sed vera luna XV fuit decimo kl. Aprilis, ut patet ex calculo Rogerii Bachon in Epistola sua ad Clementem papam. Sicut igitur Christiani ad inveniendum pascha non attendunt ad veram lunam XIIII^{tam}, sed 80 ad eam que ostenditur eis ex ciclo XIX^{li}, sic olim Hebrei ad inveniendum suas festivitates non attenderunt ad lunam quota esset secundum veritatem, sed tantummodo ad cursum cicli lunaris. Christus itaque passus est luna decimaquinta legali, non tamen tempore dyametralis oppositionis sicut in dicta deductione supponebatur. 85

Gamaliel: Non facile possum hiis assentire, tum quia calculantes ex tabulis Alphonsi certissime inveniunt tempora coniunctionum, oppositionum et eclipsium, fundamentum tamen ipsorum est radix solis et lune sumpta pro anno incarnationis Christi, quare circa eram Christi non videtur Alphonsus errasse, tum quia, sicut dicit Orosius, die passionis Ihesu luna *a conspectu solis longissime* 90 abfuit, sed non abest longissime nisi dum dyametraliter opponitur, quare eodem die fuit oppositio ac vera luna XV, tum quia Albertus exponens epistolam Dyonisii ad Policarpum dicit se ex revolutionibus annorum secundum ordinem Ptolomei pro anno Christi XXXIIII invenisse tempus oppositionis fuisse in Martio *XXIII dies, XV horas, LV minuta et XIIII secunda*, subdens: *et cum dies* 95 *secundum astronomos incipiat a meridie, oppositio solis et lune fuit in nocte que sequitur XXIIII diem Martii, novem horis a crepusculo, scilicet tribus horis post mediam noctem, ergo novem horis ante meridiem XXV^{te} diei Martii*. Invenit igitur per calculationem astronomicam VIII° kl. Aprilis, quando Ihesus passus creditur, luminaria opposita et ita veram lunam XV^{tam}. 100

Paulus: Licet Alphonsus precisius dicatur calculasse motus planetarum quantum scilicet spacium peragrant in anno, mense, die, hora etc., non tamen mirandum est si in differentiis erarum defecerit, quoniam eas scire non poterat 360 nisi ex cronicorum aut historiographorum libris, qui | frequenter mendosi reperiuntur. Et licet non recte differentiam erarum Cesaris et incarnationis 105 notaverit, radices tamen que tabulis eius pro annis incarnationis annotantur satis precisas puto. Sed si ex eis elicerentur radices pro annis Augusti iuxta differentiam erarum ab Alphonso positam, ille ostenderent situm planetarum non pro primo anno Cesaris Augusti set quarto.

---

78 vera…79 papam] Roger Bacon, *Opus maius*, lib. IV (ed. Jebb, 131 [facing]).   **90** die…91 abfuit] Orosius, *Historia adversum paganos* 7.4.15 (ed. Arnaud-Lindet, 3:25).   **93** se…98 Martii] Albertus Magnus, *Super Dionysii Epistulas*, ep. 7 (ed. Simon, 509, ll. 19–26) .

110   Cum Orosius dicit Christo paciente lunam a conspectu solis longissime
abfuisse, non intelliges quasi longius abfuisse non potuerit, sed quia abfuit valde
longe. Quod sic intellexerit patet quia diem illum dicit fuisse XIIII^tum lune, sed
die XV^to constat lunam a sole longius abesse.

        De calculo Alberti scies quod licet precisus videatur aut quasi ex eo tamen
115   inferri non potest oppositionem luminarium eo die contigisse quo Christus
crucifixus est, puta VIII° kl. Aprilis. Ad hoc tamen inferendum Albertus assumit
pro medio quod dies secundum astronomos incipit a meridie quasi diem quem
Romani a media nocte ad mediam computant astronomi inciperent a meridie
eiusdem diei, cum tamen ipsum incipiant a meridie diei precedentis. Primum
120   enim diem anni incipiunt non a meridie kalendarum Ianuarii, sed pridie
earundem kalendarum. Sic XXIII^us dies Martii secundum compotum
astronomicum incipit undecimo kl. Aprilium in meridie et X° earundem kl. in
meridie finitur, quem tamen Albertus finiri putat nono huiusmodi kl. Unde
admisso quod anno passionis dominice tempus oppositionis fuit in Martio
125   XXIII dies, XV hore etc. non tamen sequitur hanc oppositionem fuisse VIII°,
sed IX° kl. Aprilium per novem horas ante meridiem.

        Secundum Rogerium autem fuit decimo earundem kl. per duas horas post
meridiem. Nichil itaque eorum que produxisti te cogere videtur ut ab hiis que
dixi dissentias.

130   **Gamaliel**: Ad illorum progrediamur opinionem qui Ihesum natum
asserunt anno Augusti XXXI°. An eciam eos existimandum est errasse?

        Paulus: Eorum opinio facile cum veritate concordari potest. Quamvis
enim universi anni quibus imperavit Augustus fuerint LVI cum aliquot | 361
mensibus, ut tamen Suetonius dicit, *per XII fere annos cum Anthonio, novissime per*
135   *XLIIII annos solus rem publicam tenuit.* A tempore igitur monarchie sue nonnulli
annos ipsius computant et secundum hos Christus natus est anno Augusti
XXXI°, nam a duodecimo eius anno quando solus regnare cepit computando
reperitur annus XXXI^us coincidere cum XLII° tocius temporis quo regnavit.
Liquet igitur hos premisse veritati in nullo contravenisse.

140   **Gamaliel**: Perspicuum satis michi videris fecisse quoto Cesaris Augusti
anno Ihesus natus est. Dehinc aperias, queso, quot annis eius nativitas imperium
Diocleciani principis antecessit. An cum astronomis opinandum sit eius
imperium cepisse anno Ihesu CCLXXXIIII°, an pocius cum historiographis
quod cepit anno CCLXXXVII°?

145   **Paulus**: Quod cum astronomis senciendum sit videtur convinci posse ex
epistola Protherii ad Leonem papam sic inter cetera scribentis: *In LXXXIX°*

---

127 Secundum…128 meridiem| See tr. 1, c. 3, ll. 88–91.   **134** per^1…135 tenuit| Suetonius, *De vita Caesarum*, II, *Divus Augustus*, c. 8 (ed. Ihm, 50, ll. 13–15).   **146** In…150 dominicum| Proterius of Alexandria, *Epistola ad Leonem papam*, c. 4 (ed. Krusch, *Studien* [1880], 273).

anno ab imperio Dyocletiani superstite beate memorie patre nostro et episcopo Athanasio cum
XIIII luna paschalis XXVIII° die mensis Phaminoth, id est nono kl. Aprilium, provenisset
die dominico, in sequentem translatus est dominicam, ita quod quinto die mensis Parmuthi, id
est pridie kl. Aprilium, celebraretur pascha dominicum. Quoniam igitur ea tempestate   150
XIIII^te lune paschales secundum cursum cicli XIX^lis servabantur, ut ex eadem
epistola constat, idem annus necessario fuit XIII^us cicli XIX^lis, alias non fuisset
luna XIIII^a nono kl. Aprilium. Oportuit eciam eundem annum esse totum in
ciclo solari ut haberet F pro littera dominicali, quoniam tam nono quam pridie
kl. Aprilium prenotatur F. Videamus iam secundum quorum calculum annus   155
LXXXIX predictus fuit XIII^us cicli XIX^lis ac habens F pro littera dominicali.
Fuit autem annus ille secundum astronomos CCCLXXIII, nam numerus iste
resultat ex CCLXXXIIII ac LXXXIX. Cui numero, si addatur unum totumque
dividatur per XIX post divisionem supererunt XIII, quare secundum artem
compotisticam annus predictus fuit XIII^us cicli XIX^lis. Iterum a CCCLXXIII   160
subtrahantur octo, numero remanente diviso per XXVIII superest unum. Idem
362 igitur annus | secundum Gerlandum fuit primus cicli solaris habens, ut semper,
F pro littera dominicali. Ex quibus liquet astronomos sensisse concorditer ad
epistolam Protherii.

Historiographi vero discrepant ab ea in utroque ciclo. Nam secundum eos   165
annus LXXXIX Diocleciani fuit a nativitate Christi CCCLXXVI, qui secundum
calculum compotisticum reperitur fuisse XVI^us cicli XIX^lis, habens lunam
XIIII^am non nono, sed duodecimo kl. Aprilium. Reperitur insuper fuisse quartus
cicli solaris et bissextus pro litteris dominicalibus habens CB, quo anno occurrit
nono et pridie kl. Aprilium non dies dominica, sed feria quinta. Est igitur in hac   170
re astronomorum opinioni pocius standum quam historiographorum, quos, si
errarint, ob id errasse reor quod numerum suum ex annis imperatorum
collegerant, fractiones annorum aliquando pro annis integris computantes.

Gamaliel: Iam dicas si Dyonisium abbatem putes, sicut Sigebertus et
Marianus asserunt, in annis XXI vel XXII defecisse.   175

Paulus: Quomodo putare possim virum adeo divinarum scripturarum
scientia fulcitum in eo precipue negocio in quo sentenciam eius ecclesia sequitur
delinquere potuisse? Sigebertum et Marianum pocius existimo defecisse, quia
crediderunt ciclum XIX^lem temporibus Christi fuisse regulam ad inveniendum
lunam XIIII^tam paschalem, cum tamen huiusmodi ciclus longe post inventus sit.   180
Unde volentes salvare quod Christus cum discipulis pascha manducavit IX kl.
Aprilium luna XIIII^a et feria quinta opinati sunt annum sue passionis fuisse
XIII^um cicli XIX^lis ac habuisse B pro littera dominicali. Sed ante annum Christi
quadragesimum secundum calculum Dyonisii, ante quem indubitanter mortem

---

157 CCCLXXIII] CCCLXIII *a.c.*   **158** CCLXXXIIII] CCLXXXIII   **168** duodecimo] decimo *a.c.*

185 obiit, solus annus eius XII^{mus} fuit XIII^{us} cicli XIX^{lis} ac habens CB pro litteris
dominicalibus. Fuit enim quartus cicli solaris. Et licet annus Christi XXXI eciam
fuerit XIII^{us} cicli XIX^{lis}, fuit tamen secundum calculum compotisticum XXIII^{us}
cicli solaris, pro littera | dominicali habens non B, sed G. Opinabantur igitur   363
annum qui secundum Dyonisium fuit XII^{us} a nativitate Christi in veritate fuisse
190 annum sue passionis. Cum autem passus credatur anno etatis sue XXXIII° vel
XXXIIII asseruerunt eundem annum XII^{um} in veritate fuisse XXXIII^{um} aut
XXXIIII^{um} a nativitate Christi. Propterea cogebantur dicere Christum natum
annis XXI aut XXII prius quam Dyonisius opinatus est.

Gamaliel: Gerlandum forte, qui ab annis domini octo demendos dixerat,
195 eciam errasse dices, sed causam erroris sui scire peropto.

Paulus: Hunc propterea in errorem devenisse suspicor, quoniam cum non
videret modum defendendi opinionem Iheronimi et Augustini dicentium
Christum passum VIII° kl. Aprilis adhesit Theophilo, qui dixit ipsum passum
decimo earundem kl., luna XV^a et sexta feria. Quare, cum putaret paschalem
200 festivitatem illius temporis servatam fuisse correspondenter ad ciclum tam
XIX^{lem} quam solarem quibus iam utimur, necessario credere debuit annum
dominice passionis fuisse quintum cicli XIX^{lis} ac habentem G pro littera
dominicali, ut manifestum est kalendarium inspicienti. Talis autem fuit annus qui
fuit secundum calculum Dyonisii XLII^{us} a nativitate Christi et omnium
205 precedentium nullus. Illum igitur putavit vere esse annum in quo Christus
passus est, utpote XXXIIII^{tum} ab eius nativitate. Differentia autem XXXIIII
annorum et XLII est anni octo, quare tot Gerlandus credidit demendos esse ab
annis Dyonisii. Sed deceptus est, quia Iudeos putavit temporibus Christi suum
pascha servasse secundum cursum cicli XIX^{lis}, quod tamen, ut supra deduxi,
210 secundum cursum cicli lunaris servare consueverant.

Gamaliel: Recte michi suadere videris atque ex hiis que pridem dixisti
nonnullas apparentes controversias facile ad concordiam duci posse perpendo.
Quod quidem ab aliis Christus natus dicitur anno cicli solaris decimo et ab aliis
anno XXI° ex hoc provenire video quod ciclus solaris a diversis differenter
215 inchoatur, a Dyonisio quidem ab anno bissextili habente GF pro litteris
dominicalibus | et a Gerlando ab anno communi proximo post bissextum ac   364
habente F pro littera dominicali. Quod eciam Christus natus dicitur anno cicli
lunaris XVIII° et cicli XIX^{lis} secundo nichil iam video controversie continere.
Nam hii duo cicli, licet equalis temporis spacio circumvolvantur, simul tamen
220 nec incipiunt nec finiuntur. Quare hoc unum quod circa annum nativitatis
Christi me facit ambiguum discutiendum restat: Cur scribentes a nativitate usque
sequens pascha uno anno prevenire videntur illos qui scribunt ab incarnatione,

---

186 solaris] lunaris *a.c.*   **194** octo] septem *a.c.*   **207** octo] septem *a.c.*

cum tamen constet nativitatem Christi novem mensibus eius incarnatione fuisse posteriorem?

Paulus: Ad id concordandum dominus Petrus Cameracensis distinguit   225
duplicem annum, usualem et emergentem, dicens Ytalos a nativitate Christi computantes uti annis usualibus Romanorum, qui kl. Ianuariis annum suum incipiunt, Gallos vero qui ab incarnatione computant uti annis emergentibus, quos a die quo Christus incarnatus est inchoant, aut pocius a pascha proximo. Sic quidem circumcisio Christi et purificatio virginis contigerunt anno 2º a   230
nativitate, quia kl. Ianuarii, quo die Christus circumcisus est, completus fuerat annus unus Romanorum circa cuius finem de virgine natus est. Vixit quidem solis septem diebus in anno primo usuali et die octavo cum circumcideretur incepit annus secundus. Sed circumcisio Christi et purificatio virginis contigerunt anno primo ab incarnatione, nondum enim completus fuerat annus   235
eo die emergens quo fuit incarnatus. Si hanc sequimur opinionem dicere cogimur quod computantes annos domini ab eius nativitate renovare debent huiusmodi annos non nisi in kl. Ianuarii. Quod quia contrariari videmus practice notariorum, qui annum a nativitate Christi innovant VIIIº earundem kl., quoniam eo die natus creditur, opus esse videtur ut alius modus concordandi   240
dictam differentiam inveniatur. Aliis itaque visum est quod utrique, tam prenotantes annos domini ab incarnatione quam a nativitate, loquantur de annis
365   emergentibus, sed dicunt eos qui scribunt ab incarnatio|ne loqui de annis completis et qui scribunt a nativitate de annis currentibus. Et hac distinctione putant omnem differentiam dissolvisse, quoniam annus primus a nativitate   245
tribus mensibus prius currere ceperat quam primus annus ab incarnatione compleretur. Sed modus iste concordandi non videtur omnem evacuare difficultatem, quoniam si scribentes a nativitate Christi loquantur de annis currentibus annus presens secundum eos erit MCCCCLXXI currens non completus. Et sicut annus presens est septimus cicli solaris habens pro littera   250
dominicali F, sic primus annus Christi fuit XXI eiusdem cicli habens B pro littera dominicali. Quare sicut hoc anno post kl. Ianuarii dies dominicus representatur per F et ante eas representatus est per G, sic anno primo Christi currente dies dominicus representatus fuisset per B post kl. Ianuarii et ante eas per C. Quo admisso consequens videretur nativitatem Christi, quam omnes   255
confitentur adimpletam VIIIº kl. Ianuarii, non die dominico, sed sabbato contigisse. Ponitur enim ibidem B, non C, que diem dominicum significasset. Que deductio plane videtur predictos convincere, si saltem cursum cicli solaris

---

225 Ad…236 incarnatus] Pierre d'Ailly, *Elucidarium astronomice concordie cum theologica et hystorica veritate*, c. 38, in idem, *Imago mundi* (ed. Leuven 1477/83, sig. gg5v).   **237** computantes…238 Ianuarii] Pierre d'Ailly, *Elucidarium astronomice concordie cum theologica et hystorica veritate*, c. 38, in idem, *Imago mundi* (ed. Leuven 1477/83, sig. gg5v).

citra tempus Christi putent immutatum perstitisse. Si vero assentiant hiis que
260 supra de ciclo solari dicta sunt, utpote quod priusquam huiusmodi ciclus apud
Romanos cursum haberet Christus natus est quodque in anno nativitatis sue de
illis tribus diebus ad quos propter errorem sacerdotum in kalendario Romano
anterioratio facta fuit unus restabat devocandus, perspicuum erit eandem
deductionem nullis viribus subsistere. Licet enim ex cursu nostri cicli solaris ad
265 illa tempora retrotracti reperiatur pro primo anno a nativitate Christi C fuisse
littera dominicalis ante kl. Ianuarii, error tamen sacerdotum gentilium effecit ut
apud Romanos per litteram priori diei prenotatam, puta per B, dies dominicus
presentaretur. Adhuc enim fuit anterioratio unius diei in eorum kalendario, qui
per omissionem unius bissexti post Christi nativitatem restabat devocandus. Qui
270 mecum in hiis sentiunt dicere | possunt presentem annum MCCCCLXXI a   366
nativitate Christi currere cepisse VIII kl. Ianuarii novissime preteriti ac in pascha
subsequenti totum annum ab incarnatione fuisse completum. Pariformiter in
paschali festivitate anni XLII Cesaris Augusti completum reor annum primum
ab incarnatione et octavo kl. Ianuarii precedente currere cepisse annum primum
275 ab eius nativitate. Contigisset tamen eadem nativitas VII° earundem kl. si
sacerdotes Romani non errassent.

   Gamaliel: Nichil michi superest scrupuli de anno nativitatis Ihesu. Iam
progredere, precor, ac tuam profer sentenciam quoto etatis sue anno crucifixus
est.

\<Capitulum 2\>

Secundum capitulum continet solutiones controversiarum de anno passionis Christi.

   Paulus: Si, ut mox cepimus, loquamur de annis emergentibus, a nativitate
5   quidem Christi currentibus, ab incarnatione vero completis, sic evangelicam
scrutans veritatem reperire michi videor Christum anno suo ab incarnatione
XXXIII° et a nativitate XXXIIII° mortis obprobrium sustinuisse, ita quod VIII°
kl. Ianuarii proximo ante passionem Christi currere cepit annus ab eius nativitate
XXXIIII quodque totus annus ab incarnatione non prius fuit completus quam
10 in crastino dominice passionis, cui diei respondet profestum paschalis
festivitatis, in quo iuxta ritum ecclesie dum cereus paschalis benedicitur anni
incarnationis innovantur. Quam rem ut tibi planiorem efficiam, scias, velim,
quod anno Tiberii XV°, dum Iohannes predicare cepit baptismum penitencie,
Christus ab eodem baptisatus est factus *annorum quasi triginta*, ut Lucas meminit.
15 Et illud actum creditur octavo idus Ianuarii, quo die anno revoluto in Cana
Galilee aquam in vinum convertit. Cuius rei testis est Maximus episcopus in

---

14 annorum … triginta] Luke 3:23.

sermone quodam diei Epiphanie. *Sicut*, inquit, *posteritati sue fidelis mandavit antiquitas, hodie salvator a Caldeis adoratus est, hodie fluenta Iordanis benedictione proprii baptismatis consecravit, hodie invitatus ad nuptias aquas in vinum vertit.* Hinc in proximo
367 pascha, Iohanne nondum in carcere misso, ementes et vendentes | eiecit de   20
templo. Imminente pascha anni sequentis audiens Iohannis mortem secessit in desertum, ubi quinque panibus et duobus piscibus quinque milia hominum saciavit. Demum ante sex dies pasche anni sequentis in Bethaniam venit et in crastino, qui fuit decimus dies primi mensis, super azinam sedens intravit Iherosolimam. Eiusdem mensis die XIIII^ta ad vesperam cum discipulis agnum   25
paschalem tipicum manducavit ac eis seipsum, qui verus est agnus, invisibiliter sub specie panis et vini tradidit et postridie visibiliter Deo patri in ara crucis immolavit. Huius historie seriem clare nobis insinuat Iohannes evangelista.

Liquet ex hiis tempus predicationis Christi tempore predicationis sui precursoris connumerato fuisse trium annorum et medii, quod congruit tempori   30
tam per Iohannem in Apocalipsi quam per Danielem designato. Predicavit enim per tempus, et per tempora, et per dimidium temporis, id est per unum annum, per duos annos, et per annum medium, quoniam postquam Iohannes predicare ceperat baptismum penitencie, quod probabile est accidisse in Septembri, qui pro magna sui parte apud Iudeos penitencie deputatus fuit, Christus in quarto   35
pascha sequenti, ut ex premissis apparet, mortem passus est. Quod verbis Iosephi consonat, qui *refert quatuor per ordinem post Annam*, cuius tempore Christus baptizatus est, usque ad Caypham, sub quo mortem pertulit pontificatus officio *perfunctos. Valerius*, inquit, *Graccus, Anna sacerdotio deturbato, Ysmaelem pontificem designavit filium Bassi. Sed et hunc non multo post abiciens Eleazarum Anne pontificis filium*   40
pontificatui surrogavit. Post annum eciam hunc arcet officio et Simoni cuidam Canuphi filio pontificatus tradidit ministerium. Qui non amplius et ipse quam unius anni spacio perfunctus Iosephum, cui et Cayphas nomen fuit, accepit successorem. Quia ergo sub Caypha Christus passus est, et sub Anna baptizatus, colligitur quod non quatuor annis
368 integris duravit predicatio Christi, quoniam *quatuor iste* | *quas Iosephus* commemorat   45
successiones pontificum describuntur vix per singulos annos ministrate, ut dicit Eusebius in Ecclesiastica historia. Ex hiis liquet Christum, qui factus quasi annorum XXX baptizatus est et dehinc quatuor annis non integris predicavit, anno suo XXXIIII° a nativitate crucis improperium sustulisse.

---

17 Sicut…19 vertit] ps.-Maximus of Turin, *Homilia de baptismo Christi* (ed. PL 57, col. 289).
19 Hinc…21 templo] John 2:13–15.   **21** Imminente…23 saciavit] Matthew 14:1–21; Mark 6:16–44; Luke 9:7–17; John 6:4–13.   **23** Demum…25 Iherosolimam] John 11:55, 12:1–15.
31 per[1]…33 medium] Revelations 12:14; Daniel 7:25, 12:7.   **37** refert…43 successorem] Flavius Josephus *ap.* Eusebius of Caesarea, *Historia ecclesiastica* (trans. Rufinus of Aquileia) 1.10.4–5 (ed. GCS 9.1, 75).   **45** quatuor…47 historia] Eusebius of Caesarea, *Historia ecclesiastica* (trans. Rufinus of Aquileia) 1.10.6 (ed. GCS 9.1, 75).

---

21 Iohannis] Ihesus *a.c.* | Iohannis mortem] mortem Iohannis *a.c.*

50   **Gamaliel**: Quid igitur movere poterat Affricanum, Tertullianum, et Orosium, ut Christum anno XV^{to} Tiberii, quando secundum evangelium Luce fuit incipiens quasi annorum XXX, patibulo crucis affixum astruerent?

    Paulus: Ut horum sentenciam devitemus Beda nos monet libro De temporibus. *Tantum*, inquit, *diligentissime cave ne cronicorum scripta defensando*
55 *intemerabile legis vel evangelii testimonium videaris impugnare, dicendo dominum salvatorem XV°* anno *imperii Tiberii Cesaris, vel XXIX* vel *XXX etatis sue anno sacrum crucis subisse misterium, cum evangelia manifeste significent XV anno Tiberii precursorem domini predicare cepisse ipsumque inter alios baptizasse Ihesum incipientem iam* esse *annorum quasi triginta.* Dictos tres doctores hac existimo ratione deceptos: Christum quidem
60 passum crediderunt VIII° kl. Aprilis, luna XV^{ta}, et non potuit luna eo die esse XV nisi fuisset annus XIII^{us} cicli currentis, velut eciam Beda testatur. Cum igitur inter omnes annos Tiberii, cuius tempore Christum constat esse passum, solus XV^{tus} fuerit XIII^{us} cicli XIX^{lis}, ut patet retrogrediendo usque primum annum Augusti, qui fuit XVIII eiusdem cicli, velut apparet ex illa eclipsi cuius Servius
65 meminit, consequens videtur Christum passum esse anno Tiberii XV. Hec ratio duobus innititur fundamentis non sane intellectis. Unum est quod Christus passus est luna XV^a, quod intelligendum est de luna XV^a non vera, sed legali, sequendo scilicet ciclum lunarem; aliud est quod annus passionis Christi fuit XIII^{us} cicli currentis, quod intelligendum de ciclo non XIX^{li}, sed lunari, quo
70 ciclo olim Hebrei, sicut audisti, uti consueverant.

    Gamaliel: Eadem ratione deceptos sentio compotistas illos | qui Christum 369 mortuum asserunt anno suo XXXI, quoniam, si loquamur de annis usualibus Romanorum, annus Christi XXXI fuit in ciclo XIX^{li} XIII^{us}, secundum cuius cicli cursum opinantur Iudeos dudum suam servasse paschalem festivitatem, cum
75 tamen, ut michi rationabiliter suasisse videris, eam circa tempora Christi secundum cursum cicli lunaris observarint. Nunc, velim, dicas cur illorum pocius approbes sentenciam qui Ihesum baptizatum aiunt anno suo XXX° completo, quam qui id actum dicunt anno eodem adhuc currente.

    Paulus: Horum opinio propterea mihi verior apparet quod Christum
80 natum reor anno Augusti XLI°. Cum enim secundum Suetonium Augustus obierit anno imperii sui LVII, XIIII° kl. Septembris, constat Christum a nativitate sua vixisse sub imperio Augusti XV annis integris ac tot diebus quot sunt ab VIII° kl. Ianuarii usque XIIII diem kl. Septembrium, qui sunt dies CCXXXVIII. Est autem baptizatus, velut evangelica testatur historia, anno XV

---

54 Tantum…59 triginta] Bede, *De temporum ratione*, c. 47 (ed. CCSL 123B, 433, ll. 115–123). **64** illa…65 meminit] See tr. 2, c. 3, ll. 52–58.   **80** Augustus…81 Septembris] Suetonius, *De vita Caesarum*, II, *Divus Augustus*, c. 100 (ed. Ihm, 108, ll. 3–6).

---

56 imperii Tiberii] Tiberii imperii *a.c.*

Tiberii, VIII° ut creditur ydus Ianuarii, hoc est XIIII annis a morte Augusti, cui 85
Tiberius successerat, completis ac tanto temporis spacio quantum interiacet a
XIIII° kl. Septembrium usque VIII diem yduum Ianuariarum, quod est dies
CXL. Colligendo XV annos predictos cum CCXXXVIII diebus ac annos XIIII
cum CXL diebus reperientur anni integri XXX cum XIII diebus. Toto ergo die
anni XXXI a sua nativitate Christus baptisma suscepit. Eadem deductione 90
liqueret Christum anno suo XXX° currente fuisse baptizatum, si, ut plerique
putant, natus fuisset anno imperii Augusti XLII.

    Gamaliel: Sed cur pocius eum natum putes anno Augusti XLI° quam
XLII° dicas, precor.

    Paulus: Ad id putandum me stringit auctoritas venerabilis illius Dyonisii, 95
qui primus annotare cepit annorum tempora ab incarnatione domini nostri
Ihesu Christi. Is quidem in formula quam descripsit ad sciendum quo die
quisque annus cicli XIX^{lis} incipit et finitur, dicit quod anno XIX^{li} *2° ab octavo ydus*
370   *Aprilis | usque VIII diem kl. Aprilium, quia communis est dies sunt CCCLIIII.* Quem
annum VIII kl. Aprilium finiri dicit ob id, ut reor, quod illi diei inter numeros 100
XIIII^{tas} lunas paschales representantes binarius qui eidem anno respondet
prenotatur. Cum ergo omnes fateantur annum quo Christus natus est fuisse
secundum cicli XIX^{lis}, consequens est lunam XIIII^{tam} paschalem proximam post
nativitatem Christi occurrisse VIII° kl. Aprilis, que tunc per binarium illi diei
prenotatum monstrabatur. Idem autem numerus monstrat in mense paschali 105
lunas XIIII^{tas} et per totum annum in aureo numero lunas primas, quare in anno
illo Romano cuius primo die Christus circumcisus est binarius representabat
lunares primationes aut, ut verius dicatur, lunares incensiones, que in anno
precedenti, circa cuius finem Christus natus est, representabantur per unitatem.
Opinor itaque Christum natum esse anno Augusti XLI°, quoniam lunares 110
incensiones eiusdem anni per unitatem representabantur. Quod videtur convinci
posse ex eclipsi quam Servius contigisse dicit anno primo Augusti pridie yduum
Mayarum. Ex ea quidem (quoniam illi diei numerus XVIII preponitur) liquet
anno illo quo Augustus regnare cepit lunares incensiones precise monstratas
esse per XVIII, quare in annis Augusti progrediendo invenietur anno eius XLI° 115
easdem incensiones monstratas esse per unitatem. Et cum idem evenerit anno
quo Christus natus est, ut deduxi ex verbis Dyonisii, constare videtur eodem
anno adimpletum esse misterium dominice nativitatis. Insuper ad id credendum
moveor ex verbis Bede, qui libro De temporibus agens de annis dominice
incarnationis inter cetera sic dicit: *Habet, ni fallor, ecclesie fides dominum in carne* 120
pauloplus quam XXXIII annos usque ad sue tempora passionis vixisse. In cuius

---

98 anno…99 CCCLIIII] Dionysius Exiguus, *Epistola ad Bonifacium et Bonum* (ed. Krusch, *Studien*
[1938], 85).   **112** eclipsi…113 Mayarum] See tr. 2, c. 3, ll. 52–58.   **120** Habet…121 vixisse] Bede,
De temporum ratione, c. 47 (ed. CCSL 123B, 430–431, ll. 60–62).

confirmationem non longe post subdit: *Sancta siquidem Romana et apostolica ecclesia*
hanc se habere *fidem et ipsis testatur indiculis que suis in cereis annuatim scribere solet, ubi*
tempus dominice passionis in memoriam | populo recovans numerum annorum XXX semper   371
125   *et tribus annis minorem quam ab eius incarnatione Dyonisius ponit annotat.* Quibus in
verbis innuit Beda eam esse fidem ecclesie quod Christus passus est anno suo
XXXIIII°, quod, sicut patet ex precedentibus, non videtur posse salvari nisi
misterium nativitatis dominice contigerit anno Augusti XLI°.

     Gamaliel: Si Christus passus sit anno etatis sue XXXIIII°, cur, quaeso,
130   Magister Sentenciarum etatem in qua mortuus est dicit fuisse XXXII annorum
et trium mensum?

     Paulus: Id eum sensisse reor propter alteram duarum causarum: aut quia
historiographos dicentes Christum natum esse anno Augusti XLII° (cum
loquantur de annis Hebreorum, Grecorum, aut Egiptiorum) locutos credidit de
135   annis Romanorum – quicumque enim Christum natum putant anno Romano
Cesaris Augusti XLII° coguntur dicere, ut patuit, Christum mortuum esse anno
etatis sue XXXIII; aut quia, cum compotiste dicant Christum natum esse anno
2° cicli XIX^lis, propterea credidit primationes lunares illius anni circa cuius finem
natus est representatas esse per binarium, quas tamen eodem anno, sicut ex
140   verbis Dyonisii ostensum est, unitas representabat. Cum itaque nativitatem
Christi opinatus est uno anno tardius contigisse quam debuit, quid mirum si
tempus vite Christi uno anno minus quam debuit computarit? Quare, si magister
tempus etatis Christi in qua mortuus est non recte posuerit, id tamen ipsum
fecisse absque probabili ratione nequaquam credendum est.

145   **Gamaliel**: Satis michi suasum videtur Ihesum anno etatis sue XXXIIII°
mortem obisse. Sed qualiter tam eidem anno quam anno nativitatis sue B
congruerit pro littera dominicali cupio ut planius declares.

     Paulus: Quoniam Christus natus est VIII kalendarum Ianuarii ac VI^to kl.
Aprilium resurrexit, quorum utrumque actum est die dominico, necesse est
150   utique, tam anno nativitatis Christi, quam anno sue gloriose resurrextionis, B
fuisse litteram dominicalem, in utroque enim dictorum dierum signatur B. Sed
quod istud plerique comprehendere nequeunt eis ex hoc pervenire reor, quia | 372
ciclum solarem quo nunc utimur semper putant suum cursum habuisse, cum
tamen, velut audisti, Christus natus sit priusquam ciclus solaris currere cepisset
155   apud Romanos, neque ciclus noster, si ad tempora Christi retrotrahatur, cum
ciclo quo Romani primo usi sunt concordabit. Ciclo quidem nostro ad illa
tempora retrotracto reperietur pro anno Augusti XLI°, quo Christum natum
credo, C fuisse litteram dominicalem, cum tamen propter errorem sacerdotum
tunc apud Romanis B fuerit littera dominicalis. Quoniam enim ex illis tribus

---

122   Sancta…125 annotat] Bede, *De temporum ratione*, c. 47 (ed. CCSL 123B, 431, ll. 68–72).
130 Magister…131 mensum] See tr. 1, c. 2, ll. 56–59.

diebus per quos anterioratio facta fuit propter tres bissextos plus debito servatos   160
unus adhuc dies dum Christus nasceretur devocandus restabat, id quod ex
nostro ciclo reperitur contigisse VII kl. Ianuarii apud Romanos contigit pridie
eiusdem diei, puta VIII° earundem kalendarum, ubi notatur littera B. Insuper ex
nostro ciclo reperietur annus XXXIIII^tus ab incarnatione Christi fuisse 2us
communis, utpote VI^tus, cum tamen ex institutione Iulii fuerit apud Romanos   165
bissextilis. Fuit enim ab exordio imperii Iulii Cesaris LXXX, quo numero per
quaternarium diviso nichil restat, quare fuit bissextilis iuxta ordinationem Iulii,
qui quemlibet quartum annum imperii sui voluit esse bissextum. Licet igitur ex
cursu nostri cicli pro anno XXXIIII° Christi C fuisset littera dominicalis, in eo
tamen post locum interkalationis Romani pro littera dominicali habebant B. Si   170
enim duobus similiter annum incipientibus unus interkalet et alius non,
manifestum est eum qui interkalat post suam interkalationem alium semper uno
die prevenire donec ille eciam interkalet. Quoniam igitur XXXIIII^tus annus
Christi fuit apud Romanos interkalaris, utpote bissextilis, quem tamen in nostro
ciclo retrogredientes bissextilem non inveniunt, eundem diem dominicum quem   175
noster ciclus ostendit evenisse quinto kl. Aprilium Romani servabant die
precedenti, qui fuit VI earundem kl., quo die Christum credimus resurrexisse.

Gamaliel: Si res sic se habeant, quomodo Magister in Historiis dicit quod
tabulam compoti retropercurrens inveniet pro anno passionis Christi kalendis
373   Aprilis lunam XXII et sextam feriam? Et cum eodem die po|natur G, videtur   180
quod secundum compotistas qui cursum nostri cicli solaris sequuntur G
representaverit pro anno passionis Christi sextam feriam, quare et B diem
dominicam et non C, quemadmodum dixisti.

Paulus: Hoc firmiter teneas quod retrogrediens secundum artem
compotisticam in ciclo XIX^li non inveniet pro anno passionis Christi in kl.   185
Aprilis lunam XXII sed vel lunam XXV^tam, si passus sit anno etatis sue
XXXIIII°, vel lunam XIIII^tam, si anno suo XXXIII° passus sit. Insuper
retrogrediens in ciclo solari quo compotiste nunc utuntur pro neutro dictorum
annorum inveniet in kl. Aprilis feriam sextam, ymo illo die pro anno Christi
XXXIIII° occurrit feria quinta, nam fuit XVIII^us cicli solaris habens C pro littera   190
dominicali, et pro anno XXXIII° feria quarta, quoniam fuit XVII^us eiusdem cicli
pro littera dominicali habens D. Non apparet igitur qualiter verba Magistri
verficari possint nisi forte loquatur de retrogressu qui fieret tam in ciclo lunari
quam in ciclo solari per Iulium Cesarem instituto. Retrogrediens enim in ciclo
lunari ad annum Christi XXXIIII, inveniet illum fuisse XIII euisdem cicli. Et   195
quia idem numerus prenotatur quinto ydus Martii, hinc progrediendo reperietur

---

178 Magister…180 feriam] See tr. 1, c. 3, ll. 90–93.

---

165 VItus] XXVI^tus   **166** LXXX] LII

in kl. Aprilis luna XXII^a. Retrogrediens eciam in ciclo solari ad intencionem Iulii, inveniet in eisdem kl. feriam sextam. Si enim ciclus ille usque in hec tempora cucurrisset, annus presens qui secundum compotum Gerlandi est septimus

200 nostri cicli solaris fuisset XIII^{us} illius cicli ac proximus post bissextum habens E pro littera dominicali. In hoc ergo ciclo retrorsum currendo annus Christi XXXIIII^{tus} reperietur quartus huius cicli, utpote bissextilis pro litteris dominicalibus habens CB, quare post locum interkalationis dies dominica representabatur pro B ac feria sexta pro G, que notatur kl. Aprilis.

205   **Gamaliel**: Satis me certioratum sentio de anno mortis Ihesu. Te iam novissime disserentem audire cupio de die et hora quibus crucifixus est.

Paulus: Quoniam te curiosissimum de temporibus Christi scrutatorem considero, aliqua sunt scitu digna de annis vite domini nostri Ihesu Christi que te celare nolo. Omne tempus vite eius ab instanti conceptionis usque horam

210 mortis fuit anni XXXIIII, | qui numerus a misterio non vacat. Sunt enim sub   374 centenario soli duo numeri perfecti, sex et XXVIII, qui pariter collecti faciunt XXXIIII. Congruebat itaque Christum mori mox ut habuit annos XXXIIII, quoniam sua benedictissima morte ad duplicem nos provexit perfectionem, beatificationem scilicet tam anime quam corporis. Continet eciam tempus vite

215 Ihesu extra uterum maternum annos XXXIII ac menses tres, qui faciunt dies duodecies mille centum trigintaseptem. Ex quibus integrantur anni Romulei fere quadraginta. Romulus enim, sicut in Saturnalibus Macrobii legitur, annum voluit esse dierum CCC et quatuor, per quem numerum si dividatur dictus numerus dierum quibus Christus vixit extra uterum matris, numerus quotiens erit XXXIX

220 supercrescentibus diebus ducentis octogintaunus, qui ab anno Romuli in solis vigintitres diebus deficiunt. Quamobrem non inepte Christo potest adaptari verbum illud Daviticum: *Quadraginta annis proximus fui generationi huic* et cetera. Quoniam per annos Romuleos quadraginta fere completos nobis mortalibus assimilari dignatus est ac deinde morte gustata factus est immortalis.

225   **Gamaliel**: Hanc digressionem audisse delectat. Nunc tercium quod superest, qua die, qua hora, Ihesus mortem gustavit, tam planum ut precedentia facias, queso.

---

217 annum…218 quatuor] See tr. 2, c. 1, ll. 6–8.   **222** Quadraginta… cetera] Psalm 94:10.

199 presens] 1471 *s.l.*   **219** uterum] *u* rubricated   **220** octogintaunus] nonagintanovem *a.c.*
221 vigintitres] quinqe *a.c.*

\<Capitulum 3\>

Tercium capitulum continet solutiones controversiarum que sunt de die et hora mortis Christi.

Paulus: Quamvis ex textu evangelico declarare nequeam quo die kalendarii misterium dominice passionis adimpletum sit, tam patentia tamen sunt 5 Iheronimi et Augustini et, quod maius videtur, Nycene synodi testimonia ut omnino credendum existimem dominum Ihesum VIII° kl. Aprilium passum et VI° earundem kl. resurrexisse.

Gamaliel: Sed nonne eque aut pocius assentiendum esset testimonio Theophili, qui eum passum asserit X° kl. Aprilium? Ipse quidem fuit vicinior 10 temporibus apostolorum et eius sentenciam approbasse videntur Iheronimus et Beda, viri apud Christianos non mediocris auctoritatis.

Paulus: Eius tamen sentencie non video qualiter assentire possim, 375 quoniam, | velut constat ex verbis Anatholii, nephas erat apud Hebreos equinoctio vernali non transacto agnum paschalem immolari. Reperitur autem 15 ex tabulis astronomicis anno mortis Christi huiusmodi equinoctium fuisse post XI diem kl. Aprilis, quare Christus eo die agnum paschalem non manducavit nec in crastino, qui fuit decimus earundem kl., crucifixus est. Ad id tamen dicendum Theophilus tali forsan motus est ratione: Eius quidem tempore nondum inventus fuit ciclus XIX^{lis}, sed lune XIIII^{te} paschales ex arte astronomica per 20 antistitem Alexandrinum invente servabantur. Quoniam ergo per tabulas astronomicas anno Christi XXXIIII° reperitur Iherosolimitanis fuisse media coniunctio luminarium VII° ydus Martii, non longe post meridiem, propterea forte credidit eo die incepisse primum mensem Hebreorum, quare XIIII^{to} die sequenti, qui est XI^{us} kl. Aprilium, Christus visus est ei pascha cum discipulis 25 manducasse et postridie mortem obiisse. Que ratio, licet non modicam habeat apparentiam, deficit tamen, quia supponit Hebreos temporibus Christi secundum calculum astronomicum suas servasse festivitates, ad quas tamen inveniendas usi sunt ciclo lunari, qui ab astronomica veritate tunc per dies aliquot aberravit. Neque Iheronimus, dicens Theophilum utilem epistolam 30 composuisse adversus eos qui pascha cum Iudeis faciebant, aliud videtur approbasse quam quod dixit nos debere nostrum pascha non cum Iudeis qualibet die servare, sed die tantum dominica. Similiter Beda dicens merito credendum esse Theophilo dicenti Christum decimo kl. Aprilium crucifixum noluit simpliciter eius adherendum esse sentencie, ymo notanter interiecit *nisi* 35 *verior sentencia vincit*, quibus verbis innuit se aliquantulum de die mortis dominice dubitasse. Congruentia illa per quam videtur favisse sentencie Theophili, utpote

---

14 ex…Anatholii] See tr. 1, c. 3, ll. 48–56.   **35** nisi…36 vincit] See tr. 1, c. 3, ll. 25–26.

quod secundum eam eodem die mensis Eva ex latere Ade dormientis et ecclesia
ex latere Christi in cruce soporati formata esset, innititur fundamento quod ad
40   oculum constat a veritate deficere. Credidit quidem equinoctium vernale semper
fixum stetisse XII° kl. Aprilis, et quoniam in hoc equinoctio putavit luminaria
cre|ata quarto die seculi, consequens fuit ut opinaretur hominem productum   376
decimo kl. Aprilium, quo die secundum Theophilum Christus crucifixus est. Sed
ad oculum videmus equinoctia ad dies plures anteriorata, ymo astronomice
45   compertum est ea quibuslibet CXXXIIII annis ad unum diem anteriorari. Unde
si anni quinquies mille centum nonagintanovem, qui teste Beda ab initio mundi
usque Cristum fluxerant, ac anni de post secuti, qui sunt MCCCCLXX, qui
pariter faciunt VI^m VI^cLXIX, dividantur per CXXXIIII, numerus quotiens erit
XLIX supercrescentibus annis CIII. Unde liquet post creationem mundi (si
50   kalendarium Romanum semper fuisset) equinoctia anteriorata esse ad dies fere
quinquaginta. Cum ergo equinoctium vernale iam reperiatur secundum medium
motum tercio ydus Martii, idem equinoctium (si nulla intervenisset mutacio)
occurrisset quinquagesimo die sequenti, videlicet ipsis kalendis Mayi, quod si in
hoc equinoctio creata sint luminaria, ut Beda voluit, Adam productus fuisset
55   tercio die Mayi, quando inventio sancte crucis in ecclesia festivatur.

Gamaliel: Sed si non licebat nisi preterisset equinoctium vernale agnum
paschalem immolari, non apparet Christum pascha manducasse IX° kl.
Aprilium, nondum enim preterierat equinoctium, sicut convincitur ex Epistola
Ypocratis.

60   **Paulus**: Equinoctia, ut dixi, in singulis CXXXIIII annis ad unum diem
anteriorantur. Quare licet Ypocrates, qui floruit dum Xerxes regnaret, ante
Christum annis circiter CCCC, equinoctium vernale reppererit VIII° kl.
Aprilium, ibi tamen non permansit usque tempora Christi, ymo anno nativitatis
sue fuit ad diem tercium anterioratum. Unde secundum precisionem loquendo
65   Christus nec passus est in equinoctio vernali, nec natus in solsticio hyemali, licet
id plures asserant. Natus est enim octavo kl. Ianuarii solsticio existente decimo
earundem kl. Nam Ptolomeus anno Christi CXL° dictum solsticium invenit XI
huiusmodi kl., in quo temporis spacio non multoplus potuit quam per unum
diem anteriorari. Hoc eciam te meminisse velim quod diu post dictum
70   Ypocratem | adinventum est kalendarium Romanum quo nunc utimur, dum   377
scilicet Iulius Romanis annum instituit trecentorum sexagintaquinque dierum.
Videtur itaque dictus Ypocrates locutus de diebus cuiusdam alterius quam nostri

---

46 anni…47 fluxerant] Bede, *De temporibus*, c. 22 (ed. CCSL 123C, 607, l. 4).   **58** Epistola…59
Ypocratis] See tr. 1, c. 3, ll. 57–58.   **67** Nam…68 kl] Roger Bacon, *Opus maius*, lib. IV (ed.
Bridges, 1:273); cf. Ptolemy, *Almagestum* (trans. Gerard of Cremona), lib. 3, c. 1, 4 (ed. Venice 1515,
fols. 28r, 31r).

---

44 dies plures] plures dies *a.c.*   **49** CIII] CXIII *a.c.*

kalendarii. Scies eciam quod licet plerique dicant equinoctium vernale causari ex
introitu solis in Arietem, sunt tamen qui putant ipsum non contingere nisi
postquam sol plures gradus Arietis transierit. Nam Plinius secundus, qui floruit 75
regnante Trayano annis circiter centum post Christi nativitatem, sic dicit in libro
Naturalis historie: *Sol ipse quatuor differentias habet, bis equata nocte diei, verno et
autumpno, in centrum incidens terre octavis in partibus Arietis et Libre* etc. Quibus verbis
innuit equinoctia contingere non quando sol Arietem aut Libram ingreditur, sed
quando est in octavis eorum partibus. Cum autem signum XXX gradus 80
contineat octava eius pars est tres gradus cum XLV minutis. Secundum Plinium
ergo equinoctium vernale contingit sole existente in quarto gradu Arietis. Et licet
huiusmodi equinoctium temporibus Christi provenerit VIII kl. Aprilis,
equinoctium tamen quod causatur ex introitu solis in Arietem fuit 3º die
precedenti. 85

Gamaliel: Dic iam, quaeso, quid Victorium et Reynerum movere potuit ut
Christum obisse dicerent VIIº kl. Aprilium.

Paulus: Quoniam pro viribus anniti soleo ad concordandum doctorum
sentencias, audi qualiter istorum opinionem putem a veritate predicta non
discrepare. Annum etatis Christi XXXIIIIᵃᵐ apud Romanos dixi fuisse 90
bissextilem. Et cum in eorum kalendario Christus mortuus sit VIIIº kl.
Aprilium, consequens est apud alios quibus idem annus fuit communis mortem
Christi die sequenti contigisse, utpote VIIº earundem kl. Nam quicumque diem
interkalant post huiusmodi interkalationem uno die precedunt non interkalantes,
si prius in diebus convenerant. Qui autem in ciclo solari quo iam utimur 95
retrocedunt, inveniunt anni Christi XXXIIIIᵃᵐ fuisse communem. Quid igitur
378 mirum si tales Christum obisse putent VIIº kl. | Aprilium, precipue si eos lateat
ciclus per Iulium Cesarem institutus? Si denique ciclus lunaris institutus sit a
David ad representandum per aureum numerum lunares incensiones, post quas
in proxima vespera luna dicitur prima, apparet Christum apud Hebreos passum 100
esse VIIº kl. Aprilium. Sic enim incensiones lune monstrabantur per XIII, qui
numerus Vᵗᵒ ydus Martii prenotatur. A vespera ergo illius diei usque vesperam
sequentem luna dicebatur prima. Hinc computando luna XVᵃ, quando Christus
mortem obiit, occurrit VIIº kl. Aprilis. Licet igitur VIIIº kl. Aprilium Christus
passus sit apud Romanos, apud Hebreos tamen et apud illos quibus annus 105
passionis Christi fuit communis passus videtur die in kalendario sequenti, licet a
parte rei fuerit unus et idem dies.

Gamaliel: Ex hiis plane video salvari posse quod Victorius et Reynerus
non realiter adversentur Iheronimo et Augustino. Sed declarare ne pigeat

---

77 Sol … 78 etc] Pliny, *Naturalis historia* 2.81 (ed. Beaujeu, 35).

---

78 incidens] incedens

110   qualiter Augustinus asserens Christum VIII° kl. Aprilium crucifixum potuerit
dicere, XVIII° De civitate, spiritum sanctum missum fuisse ydibus Mayi,
quoniam sic non ipso die penthecostes, qui est, ut aiunt, quinquagesimus ab esu
agni paschalis, spiritus sanctus super apostolos descendisset. A nono enim kl.
Aprilium, quando secundum Augustinum Christus pascha manducavit, usque
115   ydus Mayi, quando missum dicit spiritum sanctum, reperiuntur dies
quinquagintatres.

     Paulus: Non recte videntur opinari qui diem penthecosten
quinquagesimum dicunt ab esu agni paschalis, ymo secundum legem fuit
quinquagesimus ab altera sabbati paschalis. Unde Levitici XXIII° sic scribitur:
120   *Numerabitis ergo ab altero die sabbati in quo obtulistis manipulos septem ebdomadas usque*
alteram diem expletionis ebdomade septime, id est quinquaginta dies, et sic offeretis sacrificium
novum domino ex omnibus habitaculis vestris etc. Quis sit ille dies in quo manipuli
primiciarum iubentur offerri Iosephus, in libro Antiquitatum, hiis verbis
exprimit: *XIIII^a luna primi mensis agnus immolatur, XV^a succedit festivitas azimorum que*
125   *VII diebus celebratur. Secunda vero azimorum die fru | gum primitias quas metunt offerunt.* 379
Idem innuit Moyses in dicto capitulo loquens de festis paschalibus. *Cum*, inquit,
ingressi fueritis in terram quam ego dabo vobis, feretis manipulos spicarum primicias messis
vestre ad sacerdotem, qui levabit fasciculum coram domino ut acceptabile sit pro vobis altero die
sabbati, id est paschalis festivitatis, qui est secundus dies azimorum. Ab hoc ergo
130   die numerantur dies quinquaginta et quinquagesimus est dies penthecostes.
Verbi gratia, anno passionis Christi dies penthecostes fuit quinquagesimus, non
a cena agni paschalis, sed a die dominice resurrectionis, que, ut infra audies, fuit
altera sabbati, in qua primicie frugum offerebantur. Congruebat quippe
Christum, qui est *primitie dormientium*, eo die resurgere quo primitie frugum
135   secundum legem offerebantur.

     Gamaliel: Quod dicis diem penthecosten non esse quinquagesimum ab
esu agni paschalis ab illis que scribuntur in Exodo dissonare videtur. Unde
ibidem sic scribitur: *Mense tercio egressionis de terra Egipti in hac die venerunt in*
solitudinem Egipti. Et infra: *Sanctifica illos hodie et cras laventque vestimenta sua et sint*
140   *parati in diem tercium, die enim tercio descendet dominus coram omni plebe super montem*
Syna. Que verba exponens Augustinus in Epistola ad Ianuarium *tercia*, inquit, *die*
descendet dominus in monte Syna coram omni populo. Tunc data est lex, tercia scilicet die
tercii mensis. *Numera itaque a XIIII^a primi mensis, qua factum est pascha, usque diem*
tercium tercii mensis, et invenies XVII dies primi mensis, XXX secundi mensis et tres tercii,

---

111 spiritum…Mayi] See tr. 1, c. 3, ll. 73–74.   **120** Numerabitis…122 etc] Leviticus 23:15–17.
124 XIIIIa…125 offerunt] Flavius Josephus *ap.* Bede, *De temporum ratione*, c. 63 (ed. CCSL 123B,
454–455, ll. 27–31). See tr. 1, c. 3, ll. 134–137. **126** Cum…129 azimorum] Leviticus 23:10–11.
134 primitie dormientium] 1 Corinthians 15:20.   **138** Mense…139 Egipti] Exodus 19:1.
139 Sanctifica…141 Syna] Exodus 19:10–11.   **141** tercia…145 quinquaginta] Augustine, *Epistula*
55.30 (ed. CCSL 31, 259–260, ll. 648–653).

qui fiunt quinquaginta. Ex quibus habetur clare quod dies in qua lex data est, et 145
que in legis date memoriam apud Hebreos celebris est sub nomine penthecostes,
fuit quinquagesimus a luna XIIII^a primi mensis, cum agnus paschalis
immolabatur.

Paulus: De hac calculatione quinquaginta dierum Beda libro De
temporibus se scrupulo moveri dicit, nec irrationabiliter, quoniam secundum 150
380 eam duo primi menses Hebreorum constarent uterque ex XXX | diebus, cum
tamen duo proximi menses eorum regulariter non LX sed LIX diebus
terminentur. Nam tempus medians inter duas coniunctiones luminarium est dies
XXIX, hore XII, cum certis minutis, quare Iudei has coniunctiones attendentes
menses suos faciunt unum ex XXIX diebus et alium ex XXX. Neque in Exodo 155
expresse dicitur quod lex tercio die tercii mensis data est, neque ibidem legitur
quod prima die eiusdem mensis dominus Moysi dixerit *sanctifica illos hodie et cras et
sint parati in diem tercium*. Ymo textu salvo dici potest quod hoc dixerit quarta die
mensis tercii, ut lex data credatur sexta die eiusdem mensis. Sic namque
haberentur de primo mense XIIII dies residui, inchoando a XVI^a die primi 160
mensis, que est altera sabbati, et de secundo dies XXX, et de tercio sex, qui
pariter faciunt dies quinquaginta. Si diligenter advertas dictum textum ab
Hebreis sic expositum invenies. Augustinus autem in dicta epistola forte secutus
est illorum opinionem quos venerabilis Beda, harum rerum scrutator
sagacissimus, summa cum modestia reprehendit. 165

Gamaliel: Quid de Rogerio Bachon et Iohanne Muris, qui Christum
passum autumant tercio nonas Aprilis michi dicturus esse ex precedentibus
perpendo. Eos quidem propterea deceptos dices quod putabant Hebreos suum
pascha servasse secundum veritatem astronomicam, cum tamen illud secundum
cursum cicli lunaris observarint. Satis itaque, domine mi Paule, iam michi 170
instructus videor quoto mense Romano quotoque eius die Ihesus crucifixus est.
Sed quo die primi mensis Hebraici id actum sit non mediocris apparet inter
evangelistas controversia, quoniam ex eorum scriptis obisse videtur nunc XIIII^a
die, nunc XV^a, nunc XVI^a primi mensis Hebreorum.

Paulus: Ad hanc apparentem controversiam concordandam opus est, 175
scias, quod apud Hebreos neomenia primi mensis limes fuit et regula tocius
anni, quoniam XXIX dies ab eo computati primum mensem efficiunt, XXX
381 sequentes secundum. Et sic | deinceps XXIX et XXX dies alternatim regulariter
complent menses Hebreorum. Inchoabatur autem dicta neomenia a vespera
proxima post lunarem incensionem equinoctio vernali propinquiorem, non 180

---

149 De^1...153 terminentur] Bede, *De temporum ratione*, c. 11 (ed. CCSL 123B, 314–315).
157 sanctifica...158 tercium] Exodus 19:10–11.

---

160 primi...161 mensis] mensis primi *a.c.*

quidem post illam que per calculationem astronomicam, sed per ciclum lunarem inveniebatur. Hinc computant usque XIIII[tam] lunam qua advesperascente agnum paschalem manducabant. Hec fuit lex Israelitis data. Sed quia nimis onerosum videbatur eam a populo quibuslibet annis observari, precipue cum neomenia
185 primi mensis occurreret 2[a], 4[ta], aut sexta feria, superiores Hebreorum, quasi per epikeiam rigorem legis moderantes, ordinarunt ut dicta neomenia quandocumque in aliquam predicarum feriarum incideret ad crastinum differretur. Nichilominus viris religiosis licuit sequi legis rigorem. In proposito sufficiet eas difficultates et onera declarare que contigerunt neomenia primi
190 mensis occurrente in sexta feria. Nam ita contigit anno quo Christus mortem pertulit. In hoc quippe casu neomenia septimi mensis in diem dominicum incidit. Nam sex primi menses continent ter XXX et ter XXIX dies, id est dies CLXXVII, qui faciunt ebdomadas XXV ac duos dies, quorum duorum dierum primus iterum est sexta feria et secundus sabbatum. Primus ergo dies sequens,
195 qui est neomenia septimi mensis, cadit in diem dominicam et similiter dies XV[tus] ac XXII[us] eiusdem mensis, in quorum nullo licuit facere opus servile. Unde Levitici XXII[o]: *Mense septimo prima die mensis erit vobis sabbatum memoriale clangentibus tubis et vocabitur sanctum. Omne opus servile non facietis in eo.* Et infra: *A XV[a] die mensis huius septem erunt ferie tabernaculorum VII diebus domino. Primus vocabitur celeberrimus*
200 *atque sanctissimus. Omne opus servile non facietis in eo.* Et infra: *Dies quoque octavus,* utpote XXII[us] eiusdem mensis, *erit celeberrimus atque sanctissimus et offeretis holocaustum domino. Est enim cetus atque collecte. Omne opus servile non facietis.* Et quoniam die sabbati Iudeis omne opus servile fuit inhibitum, necessario qui rigorem dicte | legis servabant ter in septimo mense duobus diebus continuis ab   382
205 omni opere servili cessare debebant. Quod valde onerosum fuit quo ad illud saltem opus quod est egros curare vel mortuos sepelire, in eo potissimum mense quo solent homines plures egritudines incurrere. Hec fortassis et similia incommoda superiores Iudeorum attendentes statuerunt ut neomenia primi mensis in sextam feriam incidens ad diem sequentem transferretur, idem eciam
210 propter incommoda similia de 2[a] et 4[ta] feriis ordinantes. Unde, Rabbi Paulo teste, apud Hebreos est *regula in kalendariis eorum divulgata et inviolabiliter usque in hodiernum diem observata* quod prim*us dies solempnitatis paschalis numquam est feria secunda, quarta,* vel *sexta,* quare nec neomenia primi mensis, quoniam in eadem feria contingunt primus dies primi mensis et XV[us] in quo servabant paschalem
215 festivitatem. Ex hiis liquet duplicem fuisse neomeniam primi mensis, unam

---

197 Mense…198 eo] Leviticus 23:24–25.   **198** A…200 eo] Leviticus 23:34–35.   **200** Dies…202 facietis] Leviticus 23:36.   **211** apud…213 sexta] Paul of Burgos, *Additiones*, Mt 26:17, in *Biblia sacra cum glossa ordinaria* (ed. Douai/Antwerp 1617, 5:445).

---

190 sexta feria] feria sexta *a.c.*

rigorosam, que secundum verba legis servabatur, alteram dispensatoriam, que ex superiorum dispensatione in crastinum neomenie rigorose transfferebatur. Si primus mensis inchoetur a neomenia rigorosa, Christus passus est luna XV^a; si a dispensatoria, luna XIIII^a. In anno quidem XXXIIII Christi, quo passus est, neomenia primi mensis incidit in sextam feriam, et ab ea Christus et alii legis 220 rigorem servare cupientes computabant lunam XIIII^{tam}, ad cuius vesperam agnum paschalem manducarunt. Principes vero sacerdotum ac ceteri Iudei, qui uti malebant dispensatione, ad vesperam sequentis diei, in quo luna fuit XIIII^a a neomenia dispensatoria, pascha suum immolabant. Unde Christus passus est eo die ad cuius vesperam scribe et principes Iudeorum manducaturi erant suum 225 pascha. Et pridie illius diei Christus legis rigorem observans agnum paschalem cum discipulis manducavit. Sic facile videbis evangelistarum verba ad claram deduci posse concordiam. Iudei quidem, | ut Iohannes scribit, *non introierunt pretorium* ne *contaminarentur sed manducarent pascha*, id est agnum paschalem, quoniam eo die quo Christus crucifixus est omnes incipientes mensem a 230 neomenia dispensatoria facto vespere agnum manducabant. Erat eciam tunc parasceve pasche, id est preparatio agni paschalis ab eisdem ad vesperam manducandi. Christus eciam cum discipulis cenavit ac eorum pedes lavit ante diem festum pasche, quia ad vesperam diei sequentis totus fere populus legis moderationem suscipiens paschalem festivitatem incepit. Sic secundum 235 Orosium Christus passus est luna XIIII^a, computando scilicet ab eo die ad quem dispensative dicta neomenia fuit translata. Et licet hanc computationem sequendo dominus agnum paschalem manducaverit luna XIII^a, nequaquam tamen credendum videtur quod aliis panibus quam azimis vescebatur. Qui enim rigorem legis secutus est in pascha manducando eundem in aliis legalibus non 240 omisit. Insuper, sicut Lucas dicit, eo die quo Christus cum discipulis cenavit atque eorum lavit pedes *necesse erat occidi pascha*, ab illis saltem qui rigorem legis sequendum putabant. Eo eciam die, ut Marcus scribit, *immolabant pascha*, qui scilicet verba legis pocius quam superiorum dispensationem sequi maluerunt.

Gamaliel: Multa que nobis eciam Hebreis cognitu necessaria sunt 245 declarasti, sed quoto die primi mensis nostri Ihesus mortuus sit plene nondum intellexi.

Paulus: Ad id intelligendum non parum confert scire quod dies ex XXIIII horis constans a diversis nationibus differenter iniciatur: a nonnullis ab initio lucis, ab aliis ab initio tenebrarum, ab aliis a medio lucis, ab aliis a medio 250

---

228 non…229 pascha] John 18:28. **235** Sic…237 translata] See tr. 1, c. 3, ll. 116–121. **242** necesse …pascha] Luke 22:7. **243** immolabant pascha] Mark 14:12.

---

219 dispensatoria] dispensatoriam   **242** lavit pedes] pedes lavit *a.c.*

tenebrarum. Unde Beda, libro De temporibus, loquens de die *Hebrei*, inquit, *Caldei et Perse iuxta prime conditionis ordinem diei cursum a mane ad mane deducunt, umbrarum videlicet tempus luci supponentes. At contra Egiptii ab occasu ad occasum. Porro Romani | a medio noctis in medium. Umbri et Athenienses a meridie ad meridiem dies suos* 384

255 *computare maluerunt.* Et paucis interpositis questionem subiungit. *Merito,* inquit, *queritur quare populus Israel, qui diei ordinem iuxta Moysi tradicionem a mane usque mane servabat, festa tamen omnia, sicut et nos hodie facimus, vespere incipiens, vespere consummarit, dicente legislatore 'a vespera usque in vesperam celebrabitis sabbata vestra'.* Quam questionem ibidem insolutam relinquit. Quam tamen pro mei ingenii tenuitate

260 sic reor dissolvi posse quod Deus voluit filios Israel illius maximi beneficii iugiter memorari quod eis cum educerentur de Egiptiaca servitute collatum est. Ut igitur in festis potissime hoc eis beneficium in memoriam reduceretur, mandavit singulos eorum dies festos non iuxta suorum dierum cursum, sed more Egiptiorum, a quorum potestate erepti fuerant, inchoari. Utebantur ergo

265 Iudei duplici die, uno naturali, qui ab ortu solis incipit, deinde tenebras complectens; altero legali, qui ab occasu solis incipit, primo tenebras continens, deinde lucem. Hoc premisso facile perpendes quod apud eos qui pascha suum manducarunt legis rigorem sequentes anno passionis Christi primus dies azimorum naturalis incepit in diluculo ferie quinte et legalis in eius vespera. Sed

270 apud acceptans dictam moderationem legis primus dies azimorum naturalis incepit in diluculo ferie sexte et legalis in eius vespera. Ex hiis apparet anno passionis Christi quadruplicem fuisse primum diem azimorum. De primo qui incepit in diluculo ferie quinte et qui propterea dictus est primus dies azimorum, quia ad eius vesperam azimis uti ceperunt servantes rigorem legis, tres

275 evangeliste locuti sunt cum scribunt disciplulos domini interogasse primo die azimorum ubi vellet pascha parari. Iosephus vero, qui vult primum diem azimorum esse lunam XV^ta | et secundum luna XVI^a locutus est de primo die 385 azimorum legali, qui secundum rigorem legis anno passionis dominice incepit in vespera ferie quinte, sed secundum superiorum dispensationem in vespera ferie

280 sexte et terminabatur ad vesperam sabbati. In crastino ergo sabbati, quando Christus resurrexit a mortuis, apud utentes eadem dispensatione fuit 2us dies azimorum, in quo primitie frugum offerebantur et a quo dies penthecostes fuit quinquagesimus. Si secus dicatur, spiritus sanctus, qui secundum Augustinum ydibus Mayi missus est, non reperietur die penthecostes super apostolos

285 descendisse.

    Gamaliel: Ob id michi gratior est tua doctrina quod in multis nostros doctores Hebreos imitaris et tamen que tue fidei sunt perpulchre michi salvare videris. Iam ad ultimum perge ac tuam profer sentenciam de hora qua Christum

---

251 Hebrei…255 maluerunt] Bede, *De temporum ratione*, c. 5 (ed. CCSL 123B, 288, ll. 107–112).
255 Merito…258 vestra] Bede, *De temporum ratione*, c. 5 (ed. CCSL 123B, 290, ll. 134–139).

credis expirasse.

Paulus: Christum expirasse credas non quando sol tetigit aut fuit prope   290
meridianum Iherosolimitanorum, sed hora tercia post recessum solis ab eorum
meridiano. Hec etenim hora nona est ab ortu solis, a quo suas horas Hebrei
computare consueverant, nec mirum, quoniam ab ortu solis suum diem
naturalem inchoarunt. Rationabiliter tamen sustineri potest ritus illarum
ecclesiarum in quibus circa meridiem campana trahitur in memoriam mortis   295
dominice. Quod ut intelligas, opus est scire quod sicut non omnibus unus est
meridianus, ita nec idem meridies. Ymo inter quos est differentia XV graduum
in longitudine meridies eorum qui magis accedunt ad orientem una hora prior
est meridie aliorum. Revolutio namque circuli equinoctialis, qui continet gradus
trecentos sexaginta, facit diem XXIIII horarum aut quasi, quare differentia XV   300
graduum, qui sunt vicesimaquarta pars trecentorumsexaginta graduum, causat
differentiam unius hore. Est autem inter civitatem Iherosolimitanorum, extra
cuius portas Christus passus est, et urbem Romanam logitudo fere XXX
386   graduum secundum | dominum Petrum Cameracensis in sua Cosmographia.
Dicit enim quod longitudo Iherosolime est LXVI graduum et longitudo urbis   305
Rome XXXVI graduum ac duarum terciarum. Est igitur in Iherusalem fere
duabus horis prius meridies quam in urbe Romana. Quare, si Christus obierit
circa initium hore tercie post meridiem Iherosolimitanorum, consequens est
mortem suam contigisse non longe post meridiem Romanorum. Quod si magis
ad occidentem procedatur, verbi gratia, usque ad opidum ipsum Lovaniensem,   310
cuius longitudo est XXIII graduum ac duarum terciarum, reperietur differentia
fere trium horarum. Nam longitudo media inter Iherusalem et Lovanium est
gradus XLII cum una tercia, que causat differentiam duarum horarum et parum
amplius quam XLIX minutorum. Si ergo Christus mortem perpessus sit
quinquagesimo minuto hore tercie post meridiem, necesse est eo moriente   315
solem tetigisse meridianum Lovaniensem aut saltem ei fuisse propinquissimum.
Quamobrem non est mirandum si in ecclesiis occidentalibus fiat pulsus campane
circa meridiem quatinus Christifideles mortem domini sui memorentur. Fuit
enim eis meridies quando Christus pro ipsis mortem gustare dignatus est.

Gamaliel: Omnes iam ambages controversiarum que michi causa fuerunt,   320
ne Ihesum verum messiam crederem, lucida tua doctrina dissolutas video. Nichil
prorsus impedimenti michi est, quoniam eius fidem libens amplectar. Ostendas,
precor, quibus opus est ut unus Christianorum efficiar. Pro veribus adimplere
studebo quicquid iubebis.

---

305 longitudo[1]...306 terciarum] Pierre d'Ailly, *Compendium cosmographie*, c. 5, 7, in idem, *Imago mundi* (ed. Leuven 1477/83, sigs. i2r, i3v).

---

298 longitudine] latitudine   **305** LXVI] LXV

325   **Paulus**: Advesperascit. In hac tamen opinione constans perseveres. Quod
ex me audisti hac nocte tecum repetas. Si scrupuli quicquam tibi succreverit, in
crastino redeas et id utcumque potero dissolvam. Interea quibus opus erit pro
tua conversione solicitus curabo.

        Gamaliel: Ut iubes faciam. Sed de tam suavi colloquio doctrinaque
330 dilucida | grates, fateor, longe viribus meis impares debeo. Condignas tibi   387
reddere dignetur Ihesus Christus verus noster messias. Et valeto.

Octavo yduum Iuliarum anni 1471 scriptus eram a fratre Johanne Jordani
presbytero et eodem anno editus in alma universitate studii Lovaniensis per
335 venerabilem et eruditum virum sacre theologie bacallarium formatum magistrum
Petrum de Rivo.

389

Summarium dyalogi de temporibus domini nostri Ihesu Christi

Controversie que sunt de anno nativitatis Christi

Secundum Bedam, Orosium, Eusebium et fere omnes historiographos Christus natus est anno imperii Augusti XLII°. Secundum Tertullianum anno eius XLI°. Secundum Alphonsum anno eius XXXIX° vel XXXIIII°. Secundum Gerardum 5 Cremonensem et Ovidium in De vetula natus est anno Augusti XXXI°. Secundum eundem Gerardum et Alphonsum ex differentia erarum Christi et Dyocleciani Christus reperitur tribus annis prius natus secundum historiographos quam secundum astronomos, quoniam secundum hos imperium Dyocleciani cepit anno Christi CCLXXXIIII°, secundum illos anno 10 Christi CCLXXXVII°.

Dyonisius abbas, cuius calculum sequitur ecclesia Romana, primus cepit scribere annos ab incarnatione Christi. Ad annos tamen ipsius Marianus et Sigebertus apposuerunt annos XXII. Et Gerlandus ab eis dempsit septem.

Preterea secundum Dyonisium Christus natus est anno decimo cicli solaris. 15 Et secundum Gerlandum anno eiusdem cicli XXI°. Dicitur eciam a compotistis Christus natus anno 2° cicli XIX^{lis} et XVIII° cicli lunaris, cum tamen ciclus XIX^{lis} idem videatur esse cum lunari.

Scribentes a nativitate Christi ab VIII° kl. Ianuarii usque sequens pascha uno anno preveniunt scribentes ab incarnatione. Unde videtur Christus 20 secundum illos uno anno prius natus quam secundum hos, aut quod prius natus fuerit quam incarnatus.

Controversie de anno passionis Christi

Secundum Orosium, Affricanum, et Tertullianum Christus passus est anno etatis sue XXX°. Secundum nonnullos compotistas qui cursum cicli XIX^{lis} attendunt 25 passus est anno suo XXXI°. Secundum Magistrum Sentenciarum anno XXXIII°. Sed secundum Crisostomum et Ysidorum passus est anno suo XXXIIII°.

390 Attendentes ad cursum cicli solaris et opinantes Christum die | dominico tam natum VIII° kl. Ianuarii quam resurrexisse VI° kl. Aprilis dicunt Christum 30 passum anno suo XXIX° vel XXXV°, ita ut nullo annorum intermediorum possibile fuerit ipsum esse passum.

Magister in Historiis dicit quod tabulam compoti diligenter retrocurrendo pro anno passionis Christi invenietur kl. Aprilis luna XXII et sexta feria. Et si quis in annis domini secundum artem compotisticam 35 retrocurrat reperiet lunam XXII et sextam feriam concurrisse anno Christi XII et anno eius CCLIX° et non in aliquo annorum intermediorum. Quare secundum eius doctrinam Christus videtur obisse in altero dictorum annorum et non in aliquo intermediorum.

40 **Controversie de die et hora mortis Christi**

Secundum Theophilum Christus passus est decimo kl. Aprilium. Secundum Iheronimum et Augustinum VIII° earundem kl. Secundum aliquos ad equinoctium attendentes passus est post eundem diem kl. Aprilium, utpote VII° earundem kl. secundum Victorium et Reynerum, aut VI° huiusmodi kl.
45 secundum eos qui attendunt ad missionem spiritus sancti, que secundum Augustinum contigit ydibus Mayi. Et secundum Iohannem Muris et Rogerium Bachon passus est 3° nonas Aprilis.

Ex evangelio Iohannis videtur Christus crucifixus luna XIIII^ta. Ex verbis Luce et Marci luna XV. Et ex eo quod evangeliste scribunt discipulos Christum
50 interrogasse de pascha manducando primo die azimorum videtur crucifixus 2° die azimorum, qui secundum Iosephum occurrit luna decimasexta.

Secundum Augustinum et Bedam Christus expiravit hora tercia post meridiem. Nichilominus Albertus dicit ipsum expirasse in meridie. Cui opinioni favet et fama popularis et ritus aliquarum ecclesiarum in quibus campana
55 trahitur in meridie in memoriam mortis dominice.

De ciclo solari

Annus Romanorum a Romulo institutus fuit dierum trecentorum et | quatuor. 391 Institutus a Numa Pompilio fuit dierum CCC et LIIII. Sed Iulius Cesar eum constituit ex CCC et LXV diebus cum quadrante, ordinans quod quartus
60 quisque annus esset bissextilis. Sacerdotes autem quolibet quarto anno incipiente servabant bissextum quem servare debuissent anno quarto completo. Quem errorem, cum XXXVI annis perstitisset, Augustus deprehendens ordinavit XII annis abstinendum esse a bissexto, statuens dehinc secundum ordinationem Iulii annos servari debere. Dictam ordinationem fecit Iulius anno imperii sui primo.
65 Et Augustus anno imperii sui XXXI° errorem sacerdotum deprehendit.

Greci olim habuerunt annos CCC et LIIII dierum, et quoniam dies XI cum quadrante deerant quolibet anno VIII° interkalabant dies XC. Postea anni eorum facti sunt tam in mensibus quam diebus penitus conformes annis Romanorum. Et secundum Bedam inchoantur a kl. Decembris, secundum
70 Alphonsum vero a kl. Octobris. Anni Egiptiorum et Romanorum in numero dierum sunt equales. Incipiunt autem Egiptii annos suos secundum Bedam quarto kl. Septembris et secundum Alphonsum kl. Octobris.

Ciclus solaris qui XXVIII annis circumvolvitur apud Romanos cursum suum habere cepit post annum Augusti XLIII. Cuius cicli cursus tunc in ecclesia
75 mutatus conicitur quando per Victorem papam ordinatum est non nisi die dominica post lunam XIIII^am primi mensis Hebreorum pascha celebrandum. Opus autem erat hac mutacione quatenus Romani cum Egiptiis, quibus primo commissa fuit cura scrutandi lunam XIIII^am, uno die suum pascha celebrarent.

De ciclo XIX^{li}

Postquam ordinatum est ut post lunam XIIII^{am} primi mensis die dominica   80
proxima paschalis servaretur celebritas multi scrutati sunt regulam qua sciretur
392   quo die quolibet anno occurreret huiusmodi luna XIIII^{ta}. Tan|dem pro tali
regula Eusebius Cesariensis invenit ciclum XIX^{lem} quem eciam Pachomius
monachus sub certis litteris quas angelo dictante perceperat cenobiis que
fundaverit in Egipto publicavit.   85

Ciclus XIX^{lis} consistit in circumvolutione XIX numerorum, qui preter
aureum numerum prenotatur kalendariis a XII kl. Aprilium usque XIIII^{um} kl.
Mayarum. Ostendit autem dictus ciclus lunas XIIII^{tas} paschales. Hoc pacto:
constito de quolibet anno quotus est in ciclo XIX^{li} numerus anni demonstrat
lunam XIIII^{am} eo die provenire cui prenotatus est. Finitur autem quilibet annus   90
XIX^{lis} eo die cui ex XIX numeris prescriptis ille prenotatur qui eidem anno
correspondet. Unde liquet binarium (si ciclus XIX^{lis} ad tempora Christi
retrotrahatur) representasse lunam XIIII^{am} paschalem proximam post Christi
nativitatem, quare in aureo numero ut eidem ciclo correspondet binarius eciam
representavit lunares primationes pro anno Romano in cuius initio Christi est   95
circumcisus.

Licet ciclus XIX^{lis} hiis temporibus non recte representet lunas XIIII^{tas}
paschales, posset tamen per dominum apostolicum facile et ad maximam forte
suam gloriam reformari si anno proximo post sequentem iubileum octo dies
kalendarii preterirentur ac annus sequens, qui erit MCCCCLXXVII, a   100
Christifidelibus in ciclo tam solari quam XIX^{li} diceretur primus. Neque vacat a
multiplici misterio quod apud Christianos annus iubileus est a XXV^{to} anno in
XXV^{tum} institutus.

De ciclo lunari

Licet ciclus lunaris tanto tempore circumvolvatur quanto ciclus XIX^{lis} non   105
tamen simul cum eo incipit, ymo primus annus lunaris est quartus XIX^{lis} et
primus XIX^{lis} XVII^{us} lunaris. Nec huiusmodi ciclus fuit proprius Romanorum,
licet id plerique putent, ymo videtur fuisse proprius Hebreorum cum simul
394   incipiat et finiatur cum lunaribus revolutionibus qui|bus utantur Hebrei.

Aureus numerus primo videtur fuisse prenotatus kalendario Egiptiorum,   110
qui, quia secundum Bedam annum inchoant quarto kl. Septembris, ibidem
aureum numerum innovant ac inde usque kl. Ianuarii aureus numerus ipsorum
nostrum superat in unitate cum in reliqua parte anni apud nos et illos sit penitus
idem. Prenotavit autem illorum kalendario dictum numerum vel Abraham
patriarcha, cum apud eos exularet, vel Moyses legislator, cum post exitum ab   115

---

109 quibus] the page numbering skips p. 393

Egiptiaca servitutute Israelitis precepit festa legalia iuxta lune primationes celebrari.

Si semel aureus numerus lunares primationes aut incensiones debite representet, easdem ad multa tempora absque errore vulgi perceptibili
120 representabit. Ubi vero notabiliter aberraverit, duo sunt modi ipsum rectificandi. Et quia ut servit ciclo lunari precise vel quasi representabat lunares incensiones pro temporibus David, ab eodem coniicitur ciclus lunaris institutus, attento quod de David in Ecclesiastico legitur quod *ornavit tempora usque ad consummationem vite.*

125 ## Quo anno Christus natus est

Christus natus est anno imperii Augusti XLI° si loquitur de annis eius emergentibus aut de annis usualibus Romanorum. Si vero loquamur de annis usualibus Hebreorum, Egiptiorum aut Grecorum, natus est anno imperii eius XLII°.
130 Alphonsus credidit Christum natum esse anno Augusti XXXIX ob hoc forte, quia eum passum putavit vera luna XV^{ta}, cum passus sit luna XV^a legali, que sumitur secundum legem cicli lunaris.

Astronomi dicentes Christum natum anno Augusti XXXI° non errant cum loquantur de annis sue monarchie. Recte eciam dicunt astronomi imperium
135 Dyocleciani cepisse anno Christi CCLXXXIIII, licet secundum historiographos inceperit anno Christi | CCLXXXVII°.   395

Dyonisius abbas recte calculavit annos domini. Marianus, Sigebertus et Gerlandus ipsum reprehendentes decepti videntur, quia putabant ciclum XIX^{lem} Iudeis fuisse regulam ad inveniendam XIIII^{tam} lunam paschalem, quam
140 temporibus Christi servabant secundum cursum cicli lunaris. Cum Dyonisius Christum natum dicit anno solari decimo et Gerlandus anno solari XXI° nulla est inter eos realis dissensio, cum ciclum solarem differenter inchoent. Similiter nulla est dissensio cum Christus dicitur natus anno XIX^{li} 2° et lunari XVIII°. Nam licet hii duo cicli equali tempore circumvolvantur, non tamen simul
145 incipiunt nec finiuntur.

Licet scribentes a nativitate aliquando videantur uno anno prevenire eos qui scribunt ab incarnatione, inter eos tamen (quoniam non similiter loquuntur de annis) non est realis dissensio. Scribentes enim a nativitate secundum dominum Petrum Cameracensem loquuntur de annis usualibus Romanorum et
150 alii de annis emergentibus. Aut pocius scribentes a nativitate loquuntur de annis currentibus et scribentes ab incarnatione de annis completis.

---

123 ornavit … 124 vite] Ecclesiasticus 47:12.

---

125 natus est] est natus *a.c.*

Quo anno Christus passus est

Christus passus est anno suo XXXIIII currente a nativitate et XXXIII completo
ab incarnatione.   155

Affricanus, Tertullianus, Orosius, et compotiste eum passum dicunt anno
suo XXX° aut XXXI°, forte quia crediderunt pascha temporibus Christi
observatum esse secundum cursum cicli XIX^lis, cum observaretur secundum
cursum cicli lunaris.

Ad declarandum autem Christum passum esse anno suo XXXIIII°   160
confert scire quod anno Augusti XLI° natus est ac baptizatus anno suo XXX°
transacto.

Magister Sentenciarum dixit etatem Christi in qua mortuus est fuisse
396   XXXII annorum et trium mensium, aut quia Christum natum | credidit anno
Augusti XLII° de annis usualibus Romanorum loquendo, aut quia credidit anno   165
quo natus est binarium lune primationes representasse.

Si ciclus solaris ecclesie ad tempora Christi retrotrahatur annus tam
nativitatis quam passionis dominice reperietur habere C pro littera dominicali.
Error tamen sacerdotum effecit ut apud Romanos pro anno nativitatis Christi B
esset littera dominicalis. Et ex ordinatione Iulii annus passionis Christi fuit   170
bissextus pro litteris dominicalibus habens CB. Quamobrem in tabula compoti
retrocurrendo non reperitur pro anno passionis Christi kl. Aprilis feria sexta nisi
in ciclo solari Iulii retrocurratur. Non reperitur eciam eiusdem kl. luna XXII^a nisi
retrocurratur in ciclo lunari.

Non vacat a misterio tempus a conceptione Christi usque eius mortem   175
fuisse XXXIIII annorum cum numerus iste constet ex duobus numeris
perfectis. Et cum tempus a nativitate Christi usque eius mortem contineat annos
XXXIII ac tres menses, qui faciunt annos Romuleos fere XL, non inepte
Christo potest applicari illud Psalmi *Quadraginta annis proximus fui* etc.

Qua die et hora Christus mortuus est   180

Christus crucifixus est VIII° kl. Aprilium. Theophilus eum dicit passum X°
earundem kl., forte quia credidit Hebreos sua festa servasse secundum calculum
astronomicum. Congruentia quam pro eius opinione adducit Beda innititur
suppositioni minus vere, quod scilicet equinoctium vernale semper fixum stetit
XII° kl. Aprilium. Neque eciam verum est dictum quorundam quod huiusmodi   185
equinoctium temporibus Christi fuit VIII° kl. Aprilium. Et licet apud Romanos
eodem VIII° die kalendarum Christus passus sit, apud alias tamen nationes,

---

179 Quadraginta…etc] Psalm 94:10.

quibus annus dominice passionis non erat bissextus, passus videtur VII° kl.
Aprilis, ut dicunt Victorius et Reynerus.

397

190   Dicentes Christum passum VI° kl. Aprilis errarunt, forte quia putabant
diem penthecostes fuisse quinquagesimum ab esu agni paschalis, cum fuerit
quinquagesimus ab altera sabbati paschalis.

Iohannes Muris et Rogerius Bachon asseruerunt Christum mortem obisse
tercio nonas Aprilis, quia Iudeos putabant pascha suum secundum
195 astronomicam calculationem observasse.

Hebrei utebantur duplici neomenia primi mensis, una rigorosa et altera
dispensatoria, que servabatur in crastino rigorose quandocumque illa incidit in
feriam 2ᵃᵐ, quartam aut sextam. Christus passus est luna XV a neomenia
rigorosa et luna XIIII a neomenia dispensatoria. Item Hebrei utebantur duplici
200 die, uno naturali, qui incipit ab ortu solis, altero legali, qui incipit ab occasu.
Apud inchoantes primum mensem a neomenia rigorosa Christus passus est
primo die azimorum legali et 2° naturali. Sed apud inchoantes ipsum a neomenia
dispensatoria passus est primo die azimorum naturali et ante primum legalem.

Christus expiravit hora tercia post meridiem, licet Albertus ipsum dixerit
205 in meridie expirasse. Nichilominus sustineri potest ritus quarundam ecclesiarum
occidentalium in quibus in memoriam mortis dominice campana trahitur in
meridie, nam occidentalibus fuit meridies Christo pro eis moriente.

403

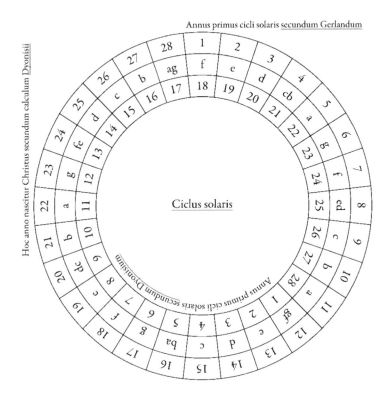

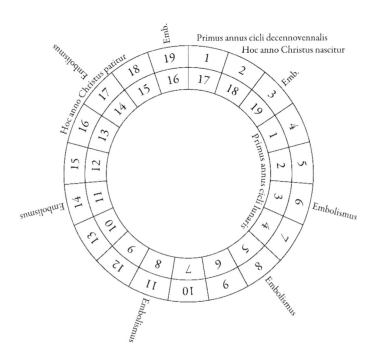

Ianuarius			
3	A	Kl	Embolismus pro anno tercio
	b	4	
11	c	3	Embolismus pro anno XI°
	d	2	
19	e	Non	
8	f	8	Christus baptizatur
	g	7	
16	A	6	
5	b	5	
	c	4	
13	d	3	
2	e	2	
	f	Yd	
10	g	19	
	A	18	
18	b	17	
7	c	16	
	d	15	
15	e	14	
4	f	13	
	g	12	
12	A	11	
1	b	10	
	c	9	
9	d	8	
	e	7	Mechir sextus mensis Egiptiorum
17	f	6	
6	g	5	
	A	4	
14	b	3	
3	c	2	

		Februarius	
	d	Kl	
11	e	4	
19	f	3	
8	g	2	
	A	Non	
16	b	8	
5	c	7	
	d	6	
13	e	5	
2	f	4	
	g	3	
10	A	2	
	b	Yd	
18	c	16	
7	d	15	
	e	14	
15	f	13	
4	g	12	
	A	11	
12	b	10	
1	c	9	
	d	8	
9	e	7	
	f	6	
17	g	5	Phamenoth mensis septimus
6	A	4	
	b	3	
14	c	2	

405

	Martius				406
	3	d	Kl		
		e	6		
	11	f	5		
		g	4		
	19	A	3	Embolismus pro anno XIX°	
	8	b	2	Embolismus pro anno VIII°	
		c	Non		
	16	d	8		
	5	e	7		
		f	6		
Iune XIIII^{te} paschales	13	g	5		
	2	A	4		
		b	3		
	10	c	2		
		d	Yd	Iulius moritur	
	18	e	17		
	7	f	16		
		g	15		
	15	A	14		
	4	b	13		
16		c	12		
5	12	d	11		
	1	e	10	Christus patitur secundum Theophilum	
13		f	9		
2	9	g	8	Christus patitur secundum Iheronimum	
		A	7	Christus patitur secundum Victorium	
10	17	b	6	Permuthi mensis octavus. Christus patitur secundum aliquos	
	6	c	5		
18		d	4		
7	14	e	3		
	3	f	2		

407

Aprilies				
14		g	**Kl**	
5	11	**A**	4	
		b	3	Christus patitur <u>secundum</u> Rogerium
12	19	c	2	
1	8	d	**Non**	
	16	e	8	
9	5	f	7	
		g	6	
17	13	**A**	5	
6	2	b	4	
		c	3	
14	10	d	2	
3		e	**Yd**	
	18	f	18	
11	7	g	17	
		A	16	
19	15	b	15	
8	4	c	14	
		d	13	
	12	e	12	
	1	f	11	
		g	10	
	9	**A**	9	
		b	8	
	17	c	7	
	6	d	6	Pathoni <u>mensis nonus</u>
		e	5	
	14	f	4	
	3	g	3	
		A	2	

	Maius			408
11	b	Kl		
	c	6		
19	d	5		
8	e	4		
	f	3		
16	g	2		
5	A	Non		
	b	8		
13	c	7		
2	d	6		
	e	5		
10	f	4		
	g	3	Spiritus sanctus mittitur	
18	A	2		
7	b	Yd		
	c	17		
15	d	16		
4	e	15		
	f	14		
12	g	13		
1	A	12		
	b	11		
9	c	10		
	d	9		
17	e	8		
6	f	7	Pauni mensis decimus	
	g	6		
14	A	5		
3	b	4		
	c	3		
11	d	2		

409		Iunius		
		e	Kl	
	19	f	4	Pro anno XIX° sequuntur tres menses continue quisque XXIX dierum
	8	g	3	
	16	A	2	
	5	b	Non	
		c	8	
	13	d	7	
	2	e	6	
		f	5	
	10	g	4	
		A	3	
	18	b	2	
	7	c	Yd	
		d	18	
	15	e	17	
	4	f	16	
		g	15	
	12	A	14	
	1	b	13	
		c	12	
	9	d	11	
		e	10	
	17	f	9	
	6	g	8	Iohannes nascitur
		A	7	Epiphi mensis undecimus
	14	b	6	
	3	c	5	
		d	4	
	11	e	3	
		f	2	

410

	Iulius		
19	g	Kl	
8	A	6	
	b	5	
16	c	4	
5	d	3	
	e	2	
13	f	Non	
2	g	8	
	A	7	
10	b	6	
	c	5	
18	d	4	
7	e	3	
	f	2	
15	g	Yd	
<4>	A	17	
	b	16	
12	c	15	
1	d	14	
	e	13	
9	f	12	
	g	11	
17	A	10	
6	b	9	
	c	8	Messor mensis XII
14	d	7	
3	e	6	
	f	5	
11	g	4	
19	A	3	Saltus lune
	b	2	

411

		Augustus	Aureus numerus Egiptiorum	
8	c	Kl		
16	d	4		
5	e	3		
	f	2		
13	g	Non		
2	A	8		
	b	7		
10	c	6		
	d	5		
18	e	4		
7	f	3		
	g	2		
15	A	Yd		
4	b	19		
	c	18		
12	d	17		
1	e	16		
	f	15		
9	g	14		Augustus moritur
	A	13		
17	b	12		
6	c	11		
	d	10		
14	e	9		
3	f	8		
	g	7		
11	A	6		
19	b	5	1	
	c	4		Toth primus mensis Egiptiorum secundum Bedam
8	d	3	9	
	e	2		

	September				412
16	f	\<Kl\>	17	Embolismus pro anno XVII	
5	g	4	6	Embolismus pro anno VI	
	A	3			
13	b	2	14		
2	c	\<Non\>	3		
	d	8			
10	e	7	11		
	f	6			
18	g	5	19		
7	A	4	8		
	b	3			
15	c	2	16		
4	d	\<Yd\>	5		
	e	18			
12	f	17	13		
1	g	16	2		
	A	15			
9	b	14	10		
	c	13			
17	d	12	18		
6	e	11	7		
	f	10			
14	g	9	15		
3	A	8	4		
	b	7			
11	c	6	12		
19	d	5	1		
	e	4		Faosi mensis secundus	
8	f	3	9		
	g	2			

413

		October		
16	A	Kl	17	Hic incipit annus tam Grecorum quam Egiptiorum secundum Alphonsum
5	b	6	6	
13	c	5	14	
2	d	4	3	
	e	3		
10	f	2	11	
	g	Non		
18	A	8	19	
7	b	7	8	
	c	6		
15	d	5	16	
4	e	4	5	
	f	3		
12	g	2	13	
1	A	Yd	2	
	b	17		
9	c	16	10	
	d	15		
17	e	14	18	
6	f	13	7	
	g	12		
14	A	11	15	
3	b	10	4	
	c	9		
11	d	8	12	
19	e	7	1	
	f	6		
8	g	5	9	Athir mensis tercius
	A	4		
16	b	3	17	
5	c	2	6	

		November		
	d	Kl		
13	e	4	14	Embolismus pro anni XIIII
2	f	3	3	
	g	2		
10	A	Non	11	
	b	8		
18	c	7	19	
7	d	6	8	
	e	5		
15	f	4	16	
4	g	3	5	
	A	2		
12	b	Yd	13	
1	c	18	2	
	d	17		
9	e	16	10	
	f	15		
17	g	14	18	
6	A	13	7	
	b	12		
14	c	11	15	
3	d	10	4	
	e	9		
11	f	8	12	
19	g	7	1	
	A	6		
8	b	5	9	Choar mensis quartus
	c	4		
16	d	3	17	
5	e	2	6	

		December		
415				
	f	**Kl**		Hic incipit annus Grecorum secundum Bedam
13, 2	g	4	14. 3	
	A	3		
10	b	2	11	
	c	**Non**		
18	d	8	19	
7	e	7	8	
	f	6		
15	g	5	16	
4	**A**	4	5	
	b	3		
12	c	2	13	
1	d	**Yd**	2	
	e	19		
9	f	18	10	
	g	17		
17	**A**	16	18	
6	b	15	7	
	c	14		
14	d	13	15	
3	e	12	4	
	f	11		
11	g	10	12	
19	**A**	9	1	
	b	8		Christus nascitur
8	c	7	9	
	d	6		Tibi mensis quintus
16	e	5	17	
5	f	4	6	
	g	3		
13	**A**	2	14	

Formula ad sciendum quo die mensis quisque annus 19^{lis} incipiat et finiatur 416

Anno 19^{li} primo	a 15 kl. Mayi	usque ad nonas Aprilis	quia communis est fiunt dies 354
Anno 19^{li} 2°	ab 8 ydus Aprilis	usque ad 8 kl. Aprilis	quia communis est fiunt dies 354
Anno 19^{li} 3°	a 7 kl. Aprilis	usque ad ydus Aprilis	quia embolismus fiunt dies 384
Anno 19^{li} 4to	a 18 kl. Mayi	usque ad 4^{tum} nonas Aprilis	quia communis est fiunt dies 354
Anno 19^{li} 5^{too}	a 3° nonas Aprilis	usque ad 11 kl. Aprilis	quia communis est fiunt dies 354
Anno 19^{li} 6to	a 10 kl. Aprilis	usque in 4^{tum} ydus Aprilis	quia embolismus fiunt dies 384
Anno 19^{li} 7to	a 3° ydus Aprilis	usque in 3^{m} kl. Aprilis	quia communis est fiunt dies 354
Anno 19^{li} 8vo	a pridie idus Aprilis	usque in 14^{tum} kl. Mayi	quia embolismus fiunt dies 384
Anno 19^{li} nono	a 13° kl. Mayi	usque in 7^{mum} ydus Aprilis	quia communis est fiunt dies 354
Anno 19^{li} 10mo	a 6to ydus Aprilis	usque ad 6^{tum} kl. Aprilis	quia communis est fiunt dies 354
Anno 19^{li} 11mo	a 5to kl. Aprilis	usque ad 17 kl. Mayi	quia embolismus fiunt dies 384
Anno 19^{li} 12mo	a 16to kl. Mayi	usque ad pridie nonas Aprilis	quia communis est fiunt dies 354
Anno 19^{li} 13°	a nonis Aprilis	usque in 9 kl. Aprilis	quia communis est fiunt dies 354
Anno 19^{li} 14°	ad 8vo kl. Aprilis	usque in pridie idus Aprilis	quia embolismus fiunt dies 384
Anno 19^{li} 15to	ab ydibus Aprilis	usque in kl. Aprilis	quia communis est fiunt dies 354
Anno 19^{li} 16to	a 4to nonas Aprilis	usque ad 12 kl. Aprilis	quia communis est fiunt dies 354
Anno 19^{li} 17mo	ab 11 kl. Aprilis	usque in 5^{tum} ydus Aprilis	quia embolismus fiunt dies 384
Anno 19^{li} 18vo	a 4to ydus Aprilis	usque in 4^{tum} kl. Aprilis	quia communis est fiunt dies 354
Anno 19^{li} 19no	a 3° kl. Aprilis	usque in 15 kl. Mayi	quia embolismus fiunt dies 384

Idcirco Dyonisius ab eodem die quo ultimi anni decemnovenalis conclusit metas primi inchoavit principium, et non a die sequenti, ut in ceteris, ne propter saltum lune eidem anno dies unus deesse videtur.

417 Ciclus decemnovenalis primo representat lunas decimasquartas paschales. Deinde cognita littera dominicali paschalem festivitatem, que semper servatur dominica proxima post huiusmodi lunas decimasquartas. Ac demum representat omnia festa mobilia, sicut ad oculum patet de Septuagesima, die cinerum, Penthecoste, Adventu domini et de dominicis intermediis inter Penthecostem et Adventum. Advertentdum tamen quod in anno bissextili nec Septuagesima nec dies cinerum ante sextum kl. Martiarum eodem die servatur qui hic notatur, sed sequenti.

LXXᵃ	Dies cinerum		littere dominicales	Pascha	Pentecoste	Adventus	Dominice medie
Ianuar.	**Februar.**	16	c	**Martius**	**Mayius**	**November**	
15	2	5	d	11	6	3	28
14	None		e	10	5	2	28
13	8	13	f	9	4	**Kl Decemb.**	28
12	7	2	g	8	3	4	28
11	6		A	7	2	3 Non	28
10	5	10	b	6	Yd	5	27
9	4		c	5	17	4	27
8	3	18	d	4	16	3	27
7	2	7	e	3	15	2	27
6	Yd		f	2	14	**Kl Decemb.**	27
5	16	15	g	**Kl Aprilis**	13	4	27
4	15	4	A	4	12	3 Non	27
3	14		b	3	11	5	26
2	13	12	c	2	10	4	26
Kl Febr.	12	1	d	None	9	3	26
4	11		e	8	8	2	26
3	10	9	f	7	7	**Kl Decemb.**	26
2	9		g	6	6	4	26
None	8	17	A	5	5	3 Non	26
8	7	6	b	4	4	5	25
7	6		c	3	3	4	25
6	5	14	d	2	2	3	25
5	4	3	e	**Yd**	**Kl. Iunii**	2	25
4	3		f	18	4	**Kl Decemb.**	25
3	2	11	g	17	3	4	25
2	**Kl Martii**		A	16	2	3 Non	25
Yd	6	19	b	15	None	5	24
16	5	8	c	14	8	4	24
15	4		d	13	7	3	24
14	3		e	12	6	2	24
13	2		f	11	5	**Kl Decemb.**	24
12	None		g	10	4	4	24
11	8		A	9	3	3 Non	24
10	7		b	8	2	5	23
9	6		c	7	Yd	4	23
Kl Martii	Yd		**Kl Mayi**			**Kl Decembris**	

Ciclus 19lis ostendens lunas XIIIItas paschales post quas in proxima dominica occurrens pascha tenetur

Ciclus magnus 532 annorum resultans ex ductu cicli XIX^{lis} continens annos XIX														
I	DC	A	E	B	GF	D	A	E	CB	G	D	A	FE	C
II	B	GF	D	A	E	CB	G	D	A	FE	C	G	D	BA
III	A	E	CB	G	D	A	FE	C	G	D	BA	F	C	G
IIII	G	D	A	FE	C	G	D	BA	F	C	G	ED	B	D
V	FE	C	G	D	BA	F	C	G	ED	B	F	C	AG	E
VI	D	BA	F	C	G	ED	B	F	C	AG	E	B	F	DC
VII	C	G	ED	B	F	C	AG	E	B	F	DC	A	E	B
VIII	B	F	C	AG	C	B	F	DC	A	E	B	GF	D	A
IX	AG	E	B	F	DC	A	E	B	GF	D	A	E	CB	G
X	F	DC	A	E	B	GF	D	A	E	CB	G	D	A	FE
XI	E	B	GF	D	A	E	CB	G	D	A	FE	C	G	D
XII	D	A	E	CB	G	D	A	FE	C	G	D	BA	F	C
XIII	CB	G	D	A	FE	C	G	D	BA	F	C	G	ED	B
XIIII	A	FE	C	G	D	BA	F	C	G	ED	B	F	C	AG
XV	G	D	BA	F	C	G	ED	B	F	C	AG	E	B	F
XVI	F	C	G	ED	B	F	C	AG	E	B	F	DC	A	E
XVII	ED	B	F	C	AG	E	B	F	DC	A	E	B	GF	D
XVIII	C	AG	E	B	F	DC	A	E	B	GF	D	A	E	CB
XIX	B	F	DC	A	E	B	GF	D	A	E	CB	G	D	A
Ciclus XIX^{lis}														

in ciclum solarem continentem annos XXVIII, quo revoluto redit idem cursus temporis															420
G	D	BA	F	C	G	ED	B	F	C	AG	E	B	F	1	
F	C	G	ED	B	F	C	AG	C	B	F	DC	A	E	2	
ED	B	F	C	AG	E	B	F	DC	A	E	B	GF	D	3	
C	AG	E	B	F	DC	A	E	B	GF	D	A	E	CB	4	
B	F	DC	A	E	B	GF	D	A	E	CB	G	D	A	5	
A	E	B	GF	D	A	E	CB	G	D	A	FE	C	G	6	
GF	D	A	E	CB	G	D	A	FE	C	G	D	BA	F	7	
E	CB	G	D	A	FE	C	G	D	BA	F	C	G	ED	8	
D	A	FE	C	G	D	BA	F	C	G	ED	B	F	C	9	
C	G	D	BA	F	C	G	ED	B	F	C	AG	E	B	10	
BA	F	C	G	ED	B	F	C	AG	E	B	F	DC	A	11	
G	ED	B	F	C	AG	E	B	F	DC	A	E	B	GF	12	
F	C	AG	E	B	F	DC	A	E	B	GF	D	A	E	13	
E	B	F	DC	A	E	B	GF	D	A	E	CB	G	D	14	
DC	A	E	B	GF	D	A	E	CB	G	D	A	FE	C	15	
B	GF	D	A	E	CB	G	D	A	FE	C	G	D	BA	16	
A	E	CB	G	D	A	FE	C	G	D	BA	F	C	G	17	
G	D	A	FE	C	G	D	BA	F	C	G	ED	B	F	18	
FE	C	G	D	BA	F	C	G	ED	B	F	C	AG	E	19	

Ciclus XIXⁱⁱˢ

422

Ciclus lunaris	Ciclus XIX^{lis}	Ciclus solis ecclesie	Anni Romani	Anni imperatorum	
10	13	D	C		Iulius regnavit
11	14	CB	B	2	
12	15	A	AG	3	
13	16	G	F	4	Cleopatra urbem ingressa est
14	17	F	E	5	
15	18	ED	DC		Octavianus regnavit
16	19	C	B	2	
17	1	B	A	3	
18	2	A	GF	4	
19	3	GF	E	5	
1	4	E	D	6	Herodes Iudee perficitur
2	5	D	CB	7	
3	6	C	A	8	Salustius moritur
4	7	BA	G	9	
5	8	G	FE	10	
6	9	F	D	11	Cleopatra et Anthonius se perimunt
7	10	E	C	12	
8	11	DC	BA	13	
9	12	B	G	14	
10	13	A	F	15	
11	14	G	ED	16	
12	15	FE	C	17	
13	16	D	B	18	
14	17	C	AG	19	
15	18	B	F	20	Christus secundum Marianum natus est
16	19	AG	E	21	
17	1	F	DC	22	
18	2	E	B	23	
19	3	D	A	24	
1	4	CB	GF	25	

423

Ciclus lunaris	Ciclus XIX^lis	Ciclus solis ecclesie	Anni Romani	Anni imperatorum		
2	5	A	E	26	Virgilius Brundisii moritur	
3	6	G	D	27		
4	7	F	CB	28		
5	8	ED	A	29		
6	9	C	G	30		
7	10	B	FE	31	Augustus pontifex maximus appellatur	
8	11	A	D	32		
9	12	GF	C	33		
10	13	E	B	34		
11	14	D	A	35	Horatius 58 etatis sue anno Rome moritur	Anni XII absque bissexto
12	15	C	G	36		
13	16	BA	F	37		
14	17	G	E	38		
15	18	F	D	39		
16	19	E	C	40		
17	1	DC	B	41	**Christus nascitur**	
18	2	B	A	42	Christus circumciditur	
19	3	A	G	43	Hic incipit ciclus solaris Romanorum	
1	4	G	F	44	ad intentionem Iulii	
2	5	FE	E	45		
3	6	D	D	46	Herodes miserabiliter moritur	
4	7	C	CB	47		
5	8	B	A	48	Archelaus in locum Herodis substituitur	
6	9	AG	G	49	Christus secundum Gerlandum natus est	
7	10	F	F	50		
8	11	E	ED	51		
9	12	D	C	52		
10	13	CB	B	53		
11	14	A	A	54		
12	15	G	GF	55		

Ciclus lunaris	Ciclus XIX^{lis}	Ciclus solis ecclesie	Anni Romani	Anni imperatorum	
13	16	F	E	56	Archelaus in Viennam religatur
14	17	**ED**	D		Tiberius regnavit
15	18	C	C	2	
16	19	B	**BA**	3	
17	1	A	G	4	Livius et Ovidius moriuntur
18	2	**GF**	F	5	
19	3	E	E	6	
1	4	D	**DC**	7	
2	5	C	B	8	
3	6	**BA**	A	9	Tiberius Drusum consortem regni facit
4	7	G	G	10	
5	8	F	**FE**	11	
6	9	E	D	12	
7	10	**DC**	C	13	Pilatus procurator Iudee mittitur
8	11	B	B	14	
9	12	A	**AG**	15	
10	13	G	F	16	Christus baptizatur
11	14	**FE**	E	17	Aquam in vinum vertit
12	15	D	D	18	Saciat quinque milia hominum
13	16	C	**CB**	19	**Christus crucifigitur**
14	17	B	A	20	
15	18	**AG**	G	21	
16	19	F	F	22	Persius poeta nascitur
17	1	E	**ED**	23	
18	2	D	C		Gayus Caligula regnavit
19	3	**CB**	B	2	
1	4	A	A	3	Pilatus propria se manu interimit
2	5	G	**GF**	4	
3	6	F	E		Claudius regnavit
4	7	**ED**	D	2	Petrus Romam mittitur

Christus secundum evangelium Luce baptizatus est anno Tiberii XV. Nec illi obstat quod pro anno sui baptismatis hic notatur annus XVI Tiberii. Quod enim hic scribitur intelligendum est de annis usualibus Romanorum, Evangelium vero loquitur de annis emergentibus a coronatione Tiberii Cesaris etc.

Ciclus lunaris	Ciclus XIX^{lis}	Ciclus solis ecclesie	Anni Romani	Anni imperatorum	
5	8	C	C	3	
6	9	B	BA	4	Agabus prophetat famem futuram
7	10	A	G	5	
8	11	GF	F	6	
9	12	E	E	7	
10	13	D	DC	8	
11	14	C	B	9	
12	15	BA	A	10	Felix mittitur procurator Iudee
13	16	G	G	11	
14	17	F	FE	12	
15	18	E	D	13	
16	19	DC	C	14	
17	1	B	B		Nero regnavit
18	2	A	AG	2	Festus succedit Felici et Paulus Romam mittitur
19	3	G	F	3	
1	4	FE	E	4	
2	5	D	D	5	
3	6	C	CB	6	
4	7	B	A	7	Iacobus frater domini occiditur
5	8	AG	G	8	
6	9	F	F	9	
7	10	E	ED	10	
8	11	D	C	11	
9	12	CB	B	12	Seneca incisione venarum periit
10	13	A	A	13	
11	14	G	GF	14	Petrus et Paulus occubuerunt
12	15	F	E		Vespasianus regnavit
13	16	ED	D	2	Titus Iherosolimam subvertit
14	17	C	C	3	
15	18	B	BA	4	

426

Ciclus lunaris	Ciclus XIX^lis	Ciclus solis ecclesie	Anni Romani	Anni imperatorum	
16	19	A	G	5	
17	1	GF	F	6	
18	2	E	E	7	Colosus altus 107 pedibus erectus est
19	3	D	DC	8	
1	4	C	B	9	
2	5	BA	A	10	
3	6	G	G		Titus regnavit
4	7	F	FE	2	Anacletus Rome episcopus ordinatur
5	8	E	D		Domicianus regnavit
6	9	DC	C	2	
7	10	B	B	3	
8	11	A	AG	4	Abilius secundus Alexandrie episcopus
9	12	G	F	5	
10	13	FE	E	6	
11	14	D	D	7	
12	15	C	CB	8	Domicianus mathematicos et philosophos urbe pepulit
13	16	B	A	9	Capitolium factum est
14	17	AG	G	10	
15	18	F	F	11	
16	19	E	ED	12	Clemens Romane ecclesie prefuit
17	1	D	C	13	Iosephus librum antiquitatum scribit
18	2	CB	B	14	Iohannes in Pathmos religatur
19	3	A	A	15	
1	4	G	GF	16	
2	5	F	E		Nerva regnavit
3	6	ED	D		Trayanus regnavit
4	7	C	C	2	Iohannes usque ad hec tempora vixit
5	8	B	BA	3	Evaristus ecclesie Romane prefuit
6	8	A	G	4	
7	10	GF	F	5	

Ciclus lunaris	Ciclus XIX^{lis}	Ciclus solis ecclesie	Anni Romani	Anni imperatorum	
8	11	E	E	6	
9	12	D	DC	7	
10	13	C	B	8	
11	14	BA	A	9	Primus Alexandrine ecclesie prefuit
12	15	G	G	10	
13	16	F	FE	11	Ignatius Anthiochenus episcopus Rome bestiis traditur
14	17	E	D	12	Alexander ecclesie Romane prefuit
15	18	DC	C	13	Plinius secundus insignis habetur
16	19	B	B	14	
17	1	A	AG	15	
18	2	G	F	16	
19	3	FE	E	17	
1	4	D	D	18	
2	5	C	CB	19	
3	6	B	A		Adrianus regnavit
4	7	AG	G	2	
5	8	F	F	3	Plutarchus philosophus insignis habetur
6	9	E	ED	4	Sixtus preest ecclesie Romane, Iustus autem ecclesie Alexandrine
7	10	D	C	5	
8	11	CB	B	6	
9	12	A	A	7	
10	13	G	GF	8	
11	14	F	E	9	Quadratus apostolorum discipulus
12	15	ED	D	10	
13	16	C	C	11	
14	17	B	BA	12	Telesforus episcopatum Rome tenet
15	18	A	G	13	
16	19	GF	F	14	Hermes Alexandrine ecclesie preest
17	1	E	E	15	
18	2	D	DC	16	

428

Ciclus lunaris	Ciclus XIX^{lis}	Ciclus solis ecclesie	Anni Romani	Anni imperatorum	
19	3	C	B	17	
1	4	**BA**	A	18	
2	5	G	G	19	
3	6	F	**FE**	20	
4	7	E	D		Anthonius Pius regnavit
5	8	**DC**	C	2	
6	9	B	B	3	
7	10	A	**AG**	4	Iustinus philosophus
8	11	G	F	5	Pius Rome episcopus ordinatur et Marcus Alexandrie
9	12	**FE**	E	6	
10	13	D	D	7	
11	14	C	**CB**	8	
12	15	B	A	9	
13	16	**AG**	G	10	
14	17	F	F	11	
15	18	E	**ED**	12	
16	19	D	C	13	Apollonius philosophus illustris
17	1	**CB**	B	14	
18	2	A	A	15	
19	3	G	**GF**	16	Celandion Alexandrie ecclesie preest
1	4	F	E	17	
2	5	**ED**	D	18	
3	6	C	C	19	
4	7	B	**BA**	20	Anicetus Rome episcopatum tenet
5	8	A	G	21	
6	9	**GF**	F	22	
7	10	E	E	23	
8	11	D	**DC**		Marcus Anthonius regnavit
9	12	C	B	2	
10	13	**BA**	A	3	
11	14	G	G	4	

Ciclus lunaris	Ciclus XIX^lis	Ciclus solis ecclesie	Anni Romani	Anni imperatorum	
12	15	F	**FE**	5	
13	16	E	D	6	Agripinus ecclesie Alexandrine preest
14	17	**DC**	C	7	
15	18	B	B	8	
16	19	A	**AG**	9	Soter Rome episcopatum tenet
17	1	G	F	10	Theophilus Anthiocie episcopus
18	2	**FE**	E	11	
19	3	D	D	12	
1	4	C	**CB**	13	
2	5	B	A	14	
3	6	**AG**	G	15	
4	7	F	F	16	
5	8	E	**ED**	17	Eleutherius ecclesise Romane preest
6	9	D	C	18	
7	10	**CB**	B	19	Iulianus Alexandrine ecclesie preest
8	11	A	A		Commodus regnavit
9	12	G	**GF**	2	
10	13	F	E	3	Hireneus episcopus Lugdunensis
11	14	**ED**	D	4	
12	15	C	C	5	
13	16	B	**BA**	6	
14	17	A	G	7	
15	18	**GF**	F	8	
16	19	E	E	9	
17	1	D	**DC**	10	Demetrius Alexandrine ecclesie preest
18	2	C	B	11	
19	3	**BA**	A	12	
1	4	G	G	13	
2	5	F	F		Helius pertinax regnavit
3	6	E	E		Victor XIII Rome episcopus datus late libellis constituit pascha die dominica celebrari 14ta luna primi mensis usque in XXI^am,
4	7	**DC**	**DC**		quamobrem coniciendum videtur ab eo immutatum esse ciclum solarem Romanorum a gentilibus imperatoribus institutum quatenus ab omnibus Christifidelibus uno die pascha celebretur, que immutatio facta est post quinque annos communes semel unum servando bissextilem.

Reformacio kalendarii Romani eiusque reductio ad statum pristinum in quo fu<i>t temporibus patrum qui decreta et ordinaciones ediderunt ut paschalis festivitas a fidelibus non nisi die dominico celebretur

Decreta et ordinaciones patrum de paschali festivitate rite servanda

5 Constat ex cronicis Eusebii Cesariensis, que a beato Iheronimo translata sunt, quod anno quarto Victoris pape, *orta questione an secundum legem Moysi XIIII^a die primi mensis servandum esset pascha, Victor* ipse *plurimique ecclesiarum pastores quid eis probabile visum fuerat <litteris> ediderunt.* Decretum quidem Victoris habetur De consecracione, distinctione tercia, sub hac forma: *Celebritatem sancti pasche die*
10 *dominica agi debere et predecessores nostri iam statuerunt.* Et infra: *A XIIII^a luna primi mensis usque XXI^a eiusdem mensis eadem festivitas celebretur.* Predecessores eius hoc idem statuentes erant Pius et Eleutherius. Unde eadem distinctione premittitur hoc decretum Pii: *Nosse vos volumus quod pascha domini die dominico annuis temporibus sit celebrandum.* Et Beda, libro De temporibus, *Victor,* inquit, *constituit pascha*
15 *celebrari, sicut et predecessor eius Eleutherius.*

Cirillus *primus scripsit ciclum paschalem,* ut dicit Ysidorus, VI° Ethimologiarum, de hinc *Ypolitus,* ut Beda dicit, ubi supra, *sedecennalem pasche circulum reperiens Eusebio, qui decemnovenalem ciclum composuit, occasionem dedit.* Idem ciclus decemnovenalis anno Silvestri pape XIII° in Nycena synodo canonizatus
20 est presidentibus in ea CCCXVIII episcopis. Hunc ciclum representant numeri XIX quibusdam kalendariis a XII° kal. Aprilis usque XIIII^a kl. May prenotati, denotantes quisque eo die cui preponitur reperiendam esse lunam XIIII^am paschalem illius anni qui ab eodem numero in ciclo XIX^li denominatur. Numerus autem lunam XIIII^am paschalem representans diei XIIII° precedenti
25 prescriptus denotat eo die esse inicium eiusdem anni ac neomeniam primi mensis ipsius.

Scribit Eusebius in Cronicis Christum natum esse Olimpiadis centesimenonagesimequarte anno tercio ac pontifices prescriptos, qui statuerunt de pascha servando, suscepisse papatum, Pium quidem Olimpiadis CCXXX^e
30 anno II°, Eleutherium Olimpiadis CCXXXIX^e anno I°, Victorem Olimpiadis

---

6 anno…8 ediderunt] Eusebius of Caesarea, *Chronicon,* trans. Jerome of Stridon (ed. GCS 47, 174). **9** Celebritatem…11 celebretur] *Decretum magistri Gratiani,* pars III, dist. 3, cap. 22 (ed. Friedberg, col. 1358). **13** Nosse…14 celebrandum] *Decretum magistri Gratiani,* pars III, dist. 3, c. 21 (ed. Friedberg, col. 1358). **14** Victor…15 Eleutherius] Bede, *De temporum ratione,* c. 66 (a. 4146) (ed. CCSL 123B, 502, ll. 1180–1181). **16** Cirillus…17 Ethimologiarum] Isidore of Seville, *Etymologiae* 6.17.1 (ed. Chaparro Gómez, 87). **17** Ypolitus…18 dedit] Bede, *De temporum ratione,* c. 66 (a. 4175) (ed. CCSL 123B, 503, ll. 1224–1228). **18** Idem…20 episcopis] Cf. Eusebius of Caesarea, *Chronicon* (trans. Jerome of Stridon) (ed. GCS 47, 230). **27** Christum…31 II°] Eusebius of Caesarea, *Chronicon* (trans. Jerome of Stridon) (ed. GCS 47, 169, 202, 207, 210, 229).

---

17 sedecennalem] se decennalem

CCXLIIIᵉ anno Iᵒ, et Silvestrum Olimpiadis CCLXXIIᵉ anno IIᵒ. Ex quibus facile colliget expeditus calculator quoto anno domini quilibet eorum ad papatum assumptus sit. Si namque dictum tempus Christi nativitatem concernens, preter annum in quo natus est, a tempore quod elevationem cuiuslibet illorum concernit subtrahatur computeturque quadriennium pro 35 qualibet Olimpiade, constabit Pium in papam assumptum fuisse anno Domini CXLIIIᵒ, Eleutherium CLXXIXᵒ, Victorem CXCVᵒ, et Silvestrum CCCXIIᵒ ac Nycenam synodum sub eo celebratam esse anno domini CCCXXIIIIᵒ.

De equinoctio vernali et lunis decimis quartis paschalibus

Qui conati sunt invenire ciclum quo sciri possit singulis annis quo die occurreret 40 luna XIIIIᵃ paschalis reppererunt suo tempore equinoctium vernale XII kl. Aprilis, quamobrem eo die signarunt numerum primam XIIIIᵃᵐ lunam paschalem representantem. Pascha enim non prius immolandum erat nisi hoc equinoctio transvadato, ut scribit Anatholius. Precisum autem equinoctium vernale, in quo lumine diurno nocturne coequantur tenebre, non contingit nisi 45 1v sole signum Arietis ingrediente. Qualis ingressus, | si in anno bissextili contigerit aliqua hora diei naturalis, in singulis trium annorum sequentium retardatur ad horas fere sex. In anno de hinc sequenti (cum sit bissextilis) sol eodem die, ymmo eodem fere momento diei, intrat Arietem quibus intravit in priori bissexto. Inde fit quod equinoctium annis pluribus in eodem permanet die 50 kalendarii.

Ut precise sciatur quota in veritate sit luna nosse oportet tempus coniunctionis luminarium secundum medium motum. Nam, ut docet Beda, libro quo dicta, a proxima vespera sequenti usque ad vesperam crastinam luna vere dicenda est prima. Similiter die XIIIIᵃ sequenti dicenda est XIIIIᵃ. Quoniam 55 autem annis XIX revolutis coniunctio eisdem redit diebus, ymmo fere momentis eisdem, consequens est similiter redire tam primationes lune quam XIIIIᵃˢ lunas paschales. Et in huiusmodi reditu fundatur cursus tam aurei numeri quam cicli XIXˡⁱˢ.

Pontifices qui tradiderunt decreta pro pascha servando non curarunt 60 tantam precisionem, vel in equinoctio, vel in XIIIIⁱˢ lunis paschalibus inveniendis, quanta posset haberi per calculum astronomicum. Sed eis suffecit ut error notabilis precaveretur, qui scilicet non nisi cum gravi scandalo posset a populo deprehendi. Intenderunt quidem tradere regulam per quam singulis prelatis ecclesiarum, et per illos eorum subditis, innotesceret dies quo paschalis 65

---

43 Pascha…44 Anatholius] Anatolius of Laodicea *ap.* Eusebius of Caesarea, *Historia ecclesiastica* (trans. Rufinus of Aquileia), 7.32.15–19 (ed. GCS 9.2, 723–725). **54** a…55 prima] Bede, *De temporum ratione*, c. 43 (ed. CCSL 123B, 412–414).

festivitas annis singulis ab omnibus fidelibus per universum orbem terrarum celebretur.

De anteriorationibus tam equinoctii vernalis quam lunarum XIIII paschalium

70 Hilarius in papam assumptus, ut constat ex Cronicis Mathei Palmerii, anno domini CCCCLXV°, perpendens equinoctium vernale suis temporibus in kalendario ad XV^am diem kl. Aprilis retrocessisse, suasit Victorio ut ciclum novum conficeret. Prevaluit tamen aliorum sentencia qui Nycene synodi decretis adherentes (dicto retrocessu non obstante) dictarunt ciclum XIX^lem sectandum
75 esse, sicut Beda scribit libro De temporibus. Orta est etiam ex dicto retrocessu equinoctii dissensio illa inter Grecos et Latinos cuius meminit Ysidorus VI Ethimologiarum. Greci namque non ante VIII^um ydus Marcii primum anni mensem inchoantes servarunt lunam XIIII^am paschalem iuxta ordinacionem Nycene synodi non ante XII^am kl. Aprilis, quibusdam Latinorum propter dictum
80 equinoctii retrocessum inchoantibus mensem primum anni ultimi XIX^lis tercio nonas Marcii servantibusque lunam XIIII^am pachalem eiusdem anni XV° kl. Aprilis. Sed prevaluit Grecorum sententia.

Temporibus Bede (qui secundum Cronica dicti Mathei floruit anno domini DCXCIIII°) quidam (dum curreret annus ultimus XIX^lis) asseruerunt se
85 vidisse lunam novam quarto nonas Aprilis existimantes propterea lunam XIIII^am paschalem servandam esse XVII° kl. May, quam tamen ecclesia cursum cicli XIX^lis sequens servatura erat XV° earundem kl. Et ut ita servaretur Beda suasit illorum assertione non obstante, sicut patet libro suo De temporibus. Nec mirandum est si in dictis duobus casibus ecclesia secuta sit ciclum XIX^lem,
90 quoniam ex anteriorationibus tunc factis, vel in equinoctio vernali, vel in luna XIIII^a paschali, populus non offendebatur.

Reverendissimi in Christo patres, dudum ecclesie Romane cardinales dignissimi memorieque percelebris, dominus Petrus de Aliaco et dominus Nycholaus de Cuza, in tractatibus quos ediderunt pro reparacione kalendarii,
95 asserunt equinoctium vernale singulis CXXXIIII annis anteriorari ad unum diem

---

70 Hilarius…71 CCCCLXV°] Matteo Palmieri, *Liber de temporibus* (a. 465) (ed. Scaramella, 50). Hilarius … 82 Aprilis] Cf. Victorius of Aquitaine, *Prologus ad Hilarum archidiaconum*, c. 4 (ed. Krusch, *Studien* [1938], 19–20). **72** suasit…75 esse] Bede, *De temporum ratione*, c. 43 (ed. CCSL 123B, 417, ll. 112–118). **75** Orta…77 Ethimologiarum] Isidore of Seville, *Etymologiae* 6.17.19–20 (ed. Chaparro Gómez, 103–105). **83** Temporibus…88 temporibus] Bede, *De temporum ratione*, c. 43 (ed. CCSL 123B, 414–418, ll. 53–126). | floruit…84 DCXCIIII°] Matteo Palmieri, *Liber de temporibus* (a. 693) (ed. Scaramella, 67). **93** dominus¹…98 esse] Pierre d'Ailly, *Exhortatio ad concilium generale super kalendarii correctione*, c. 2 (ed. Solan, *La réforme du calendrier*, 206, 208); Nicholas of Cusa, *De correctione kalendarii*, c. 2, 10 (ed. Stegemann, 20, 82–84).

---

86 May] Aprilis *a.c.*

kalendarii ac primationes lune et lunas XIIII^{as} paschales similiter ad unum diem anteriorari singulis annis CCCIIII affirmantes utrumque per calculum astronomicum compertum esse.

De anno quo kalendarium aptissime poterit reformari

2r Cum tam equinoctium vernale quam lune XIIIIe paschale hiis temporibus reperiantur ad plures dies kalendarii retrocessisse idque ad oculum pateat non fidelibus tantum, sed et emulis fidei, qui plane intelligunt nos contra decreta patrum paschalem servare festivitatem, in non parvam ignominiam matris ecclesie, ad quam tollendam, que non nisi ex deformatione kalendarii provenit, expediens videretur iam tandem ipsum kalendarium reformari. Ad quam rem vix tempus aliud aptius posset offerri quam annus proximus post instantem iubileum. Interea quidem ab hiis qui huius rei periti sunt indagari poterit modus reformandi convenientissimus, quatinus inventus una cum iubileo per orbem terrarum fidelibus publicetur. Sique quid dubietatis in eo suboriri contigerit, id declaretur illis qui ad urbem confluent pro indulgenciis iubilei, quatinus illis ad propria redeuntibus paschalis festivitas ab omnibus eodem die ritissime celebretur.

Annus proximus post instantem iubileum erit millesimus quingentesimus primus, a quo numero annorum si subtrahantur anni MCCCXL supererunt CLXI. Cum igitur in annis subtrahendis decies contineantur anni CXXXIIII, in quibus, ut dictum est, equinoctium ad unum diem anterioratur, consequens est quod anno predicto citra annum domini CLXI^{um}, qui fuit XIX^{us} a coronacione Pii ac similiter XIX^{us} ante coronacionem Eleutherii, anterioratum erit equinoctium vernale ad X dies kalendarii. Intrabit quidem dicto anno sol Arietem X die Marcii completa, horis XII post meridiem et minutis LI secundum longitudinem urbis Rome, hoc est more Romanorum diem a medio noctis inchoando V^o ydus Martii, hora prima currente. Sed anno domini CLXI^o sol intravit Arietem die XX^a Martii completa, horis XIIII post meridiem et minutis XLVIII, hoc est more Romano XII kl. Aprilis, hora tercia currente.

Insuper, si quis ab annis domini MDI, quorum ultimus erit primus post instantem iubileum, subtraxerit MCCXVI, supererunt anni CCLXXXV. Cum igitur in annis illis subtrahendis quater contineantur anni CCCIIII in quibus, ut dictum est, lune XIIIIe paschales anteriorantur ad unum diem, consequens est quod anno predicto citra annum domini CCLXXXV^{um}, qui fuit a coronatione Victoris XC^{us} et ante coronationem Silvestri XXVII^{us}, anteriorata erit luna XIIII^a paschalis ad quatuor dies et similiter lune primatio. Erit enim dicto anno coniunctio luminarium secundum medium motum ad longitudinem urbis Rome

100

105

110

115

120

125

130

---

111 eodem] eodiem   124 currente] currenti   128 paschales] *add.* ad quatuor dies et similiter lune primacio *a.c.*   129 predicto] predictio

XVIII^a die Marcii completa, horis XXII post meridiem et minutis XXXIX, hoc est more Romano XIIII^a die kl. Aprilis, currente hora XI^a, quare in vespera
135 eiusdem diei luna incipiet dici vere prima. Sed anno domini CCLXXXV° media coniunctio luminarium fuit XXII Marcii completa, horis XX^ti post meridiem et minutis XXXV, hoc est more Romano X kl. Aprilis, currente hora IX, et in vespera proxima sequenti luna cepit dici vere prima.

Modus reducendi kalendarium ad statum pristinum in quo fuit
140 **temporibus patrum pascha instituentium**

Erit igitur unus modus reparandi kalendarium qui meo iudicio et facilior est et magis accommodus ad servandum pascha iuxta prima patrum instituta, utpote si anno primo post proximum iubileum VI° ydus Marcii completo omissis X diebus sequentibus transiliatur ad XII^am diem kl. Aprilis. Hoc etenim facto
145 equinoctium vernale eo die kalendarii reperietur quo primo patres qui ceperunt ordinare de pascha ipsum reppererunt. Tunc enim sol (qui si non fieret saltus intraturus esset Arietem V° ydus Martii) facto huiusmodi saltu intrabit Arietem XII kl. Aprilis.

Quoniam annus proxime sequens instantem iubileum erit primus in ciclo
150 XIX^li | luna secundum cursum eiusdem cicli eodem anno in ecclesia   2v pronunciabitur prima X kl. Aprilis. Illi enim diei in aureo numero prenotatur unitas. In veritate tamen erit prima XIII° die earundem kalendarum, quoniam ex quo die precedenti continget coniunctio luminarium ad vesperam eius luna incipiet dici vere prima. Attamen, si (ut dictum est) X dies pretereantur, luna
155 vere erit prima tercio kl. Aprilis et consequenter erit vere XIIII^a pridie ydus Aprilis. Cui diei quoniam inter numeros qui lunas XIIII^as paschales representant preponitur numerus XIIII, idem annus qui ante predictum saltum dicebatur primus cicli XIX^lis eo facto dicendus erit XIIII^us cicli XIX^lis innovati.

Et quoniam idem annus secundum compotum Dyonisii abbatis urbis
160 Rome erit XXVI^us in ciclo solari primusque communis post bissextum habens C pro littera dominicali, indubitanter nonis Martii erit dies dominica. Ibi enim ponitur littera C. Inde progrediendo pretereundoque dies X predictos occurret dies octava, et per consequens dominica, IX° kl. Aprilis, ubi ponitur littera F, quare idem annus post pretericionem X dierum (ut maneat, sicut prius, primus
165 post bissextum) dicendus erit XVIII^us cicli solaris innovati. Secundum autem compotum Gerlandi erit primus eiusdem cicli.

---

158 cicli¹] cicili *a.c.*

Provisio ne contingant inconvenientia propter dictam kalendarii reformationem   170

Annus predictus proximus post iubileum, ut dictum est, ante preteritionem X dierum erit primus in ciclo XIX^{li} et post XIIII^{us} eiusdem cicli, quare primo erit communis et postea embolismalis. Cum tamen Paschasius in Epistola ad Leonem papam proximum predecessorem Hilarii prohibuerit ne de embolismo annum communem faciamus, huic igitur prohibicioni adversari videtur dictus 175 modus reformandi kalendarium. Hinc turbari non oportet. Paschasius enim scripsit epistolam illam contra Latinos illos qui propter anteriorationem equinoctii ad XV^{am} kl. Aprilis existimabant lunam XIIII^{am} paschalem eo tempore servandam esse non XII°, sed XV° kl. Aprilis, quo admisso annus VIII^{us} et XIX^{us} quandocumque occurrerent essent communes et annus primus 180 et IX^{us} essent embolismales contra intentionem patrum qui ciclum XIX^{lem} canonizarunt. Sed dicta reformacio (si sanctissimo domino nostro placuerit) fieret ut cursus cicli XIX^{lis}, aut perpetuo, aut quam longissime, perseveret. Hoc tamen semel contingeret ut unus annus, qui non facta reformacione esset communis, ea facta efficeretur embolismalis.   185

Ne ex dicta kalendarii reformacione prestetur impedimentum vel astronomis, vel compotistis, expediet ut astronomi preter radices quibus hactenus usi sunt pro tempore futuro novas conficiant X dies addiciendo. Opus eciam erit compotistis ut in antea novis utantur regulis. Verbi gratia, si postea scire velint de anno aliquo quotus sit in ciclo XIX^{li} annis domini, addent XIIII 190 dividentque totum per XIX et ex superexcrescenti scient quotus sit in ciclo XIX^{li} innovato. Consimiliter, si de aliquo anno scire desiderent quotus sit in ciclo solari annis domini, addent unum et totum divident per XXVIII. Scient autem ex superexcrescenti quotus sit in ciclo solari innovato. Nec de hiis regulis novis mirandum est. Nam si cicli isti innovandi retrotrahantur ad tempus 195 nativitatis Christi ipse reperietur natus anno secundo cicli solaris et XV° cicli XIX^{lis}, ut patet in ciclis infra descriptis.

Ne eciam propter dictam decem dierum pretericionem festivitatibus sanctorum preiudicetur, ordinari poterit ut festum Gregorii, quod signatur secundo dierum pretereundorum, celebretur XII° kl. Aprilis et festum Benedicti, 200 quod eodem die signatur, transferatur ad crastinum. Festum vero Gertrudis virginis, quod apud nos celebre est, servetur X^{o} kl. Aprilis. De die autem pasche,

---

173 Cum…175 faciamus] Paschasinus of Lilybaeum, *Epistola ad Leonem papam*, c. 1 (ed. Krusch, *Studien* [1880], 248).

---

181 IXus] XI^{us} **201** signatur] signatum

dominica in LXX^a, et diebus dominicis intermediis, quando servandi erunt ad oculum apparet ex hiis que hic lateraliter annotantur.

3r

205 Provisio ne kalendarium dicto modo reformatum non oporteat denuo reformari

Ne kalendarium (si dicto modo reformatum fuerit) necesse sit propter anteriorationem que fieri solet in lunis XIIII^{is} paschalibus denuo reformari, cessabitur deinceps singulis CCCIIII annis ab uno bissexto, ita ut cum occurrerit
210 annus MDCCCIIII^{us}, bis millesimus CVIII^{us}, bis millesimus CCCCXII, et sic consequenter, serventur absque omni intercalatione tamquam communes, quamquam alias essent bissextiles. Detinebuntur enim hoc pacto tam primaciones lune quam lune XIIIIe paschales, ne dies kalendarii solitos, vel numquam, vel non nisi post annos plurimos, egrediantur.

215 Si, velut dictum est, singulis CCCIIII annis cessetur a bissexto, multo tardius equinoctium vernale retrocedet quam prius. Si enim in annis DCLXX numquam cessetur a bissexto, equinoctium retrocedet ad V dies, cum in annis illis contineantur quinquies anni CXXXIIII. Sed si in eis cessetur a bissexto, ut dictum est, propter duplicem huiusmodi cessationem retrocedet ad tres tantum
220 dies et aliquot horas. Si autem sic cessando reperiatur pluribus elapsis seculis equinoctium vernale exorbitanter retrocedere, ita ut scandalum aliquod timeatur, illi occurrendum erit certos dies kalendarii (prout casus exigit) iuxta modum reformationis prenarratum pretereundo.

Posset eciam equinoctium vernale detineri ne ad annos plurimos ultra
225 diem unum retrocederet, utpote si singulis CXXXIIII annis semel abstineretur a bissexto. Aliud tamen ex hoc inconveniens emergeret. Nam sic abstinendo aliquanto tractu temporis tam primationes lune quam XIIIIe lune paschales ad dies qui sunt in kalendario posteriores protraherentur. Verbi gratia, si in annis DCLXX singulis CXXXIIII annis cessaretur semel a bissexto, in hoc toto
230 tempore fiet huiusmodi cessatio quinquies, tociens enim in eo continentur CXXXIIII anni. Cum igitur in tot annis ad retinendum XIIII^{as} lunas paschales in diebus suis sufficeret bina cessatio, alia trina cessatio hoc efficeret quod eedem lune XIIIIe protraherentur ad tres dies in kalendario subsequentes. Sufficet igitur ad retardandum anteriorationem equinoctii ut in solis CCCIIII annis semel
235 cessetur a bissexto.

Hec sub omni melius sentientium correctione cum multis lucubrationibus pro reparatione kalendarii Romani elaborata sunt in universitate generalis studii Lovaniensis anno domini millesimo quadringentesimo octogesimo octavo.

---

220 Si] Sic

Ad laudem Dei et gloriam sacrosancte matris ecclesie sponse eius individue   240
et immaculate.

Amen.

---

241 immaculate] immaculati

Cursus temporis in Anno domini Millesimoquingentesimoprimo a dominica in septuagesima usque octavas pasche si tamen placuerit presens reformatio

Anni communes CCCLIIII dierum. Et omnes terminantur eo die cui prenotatur numerus anno correspondens

Ciclus decemnovenalis

Aureus	Litt.	(Romana)	Dies	Festum	Ciclus decemnov.	(Aureus)	Litt.	(Romana)	Dies
III	C	KL	Februarii	Dominica in LXXa	XVI	X	B	III	XIII
XI	D	IIII	II	Purificacio Marie	V	XVIII	C	II	XIIII
XIX	E	III	III			VII	D	Ydus	XV
VIII	F	II	IIII		XIII	XV	E	XVII	XVI
	G	Nonas	V			IIII	F	XVI	XVII
XVI	A	VIII	VI		II	XII	G	XV	XVIII
V	B	VII	VII	Dominica in LXa			A	XIIII	XIX[b]
	C	VI	VIII		X		B	XIII	XX
XIII	D	V	IX			XVII	C	XII	XXI[c]
II	E	IIII	X		XVIII	VI	D	XI	XXII
	F	III	XI				E	X	XXIII
X	G	II	XII		VII	IX	F	IX	XXIIII
XVIII	A	Ydus	XIII				G	VIII	XXV
VII	B	XVI	XIIII		XV	XVII	A	VII	XXVI
	C	XV	XV	Dominica in La		VI	B	VI	XXVII
XV	D	XIIII	XVI		IIII		C	V	XXVIII
IIII	E	XIII	XVII			XIIII	D	IIII	XXIX[d]
	F	XII	XVIII		XII	III	E	III	XXX
XII	G	XI	XIX				F	II	XXXI
I	A	X	XX		I	XV	G	KL	Aprilis
	B	IX	XXI			IIII	A	IIII	II
IX	C	VIII	XXII	Dominica in XLa	XII		B	III	III
	D	VII	XXIII	Cathedra Petri		XIX	C	II	IIII
	E	VI	XXIIII	Mathie		VIII	D	Nonas	V
						XVI	E	VIII	VI

dies pretereundi

- Gregorii
- Benedicti
- Gertrudis
- Dominica Letare
- Annunciacio
- Dominica Iudica

					Lune XIIIIe paschales					
XVII	G	V	XXV		IX	V	F	VII	VII	Dominica Palmarum
VI	A	IIII	XXVI			XIII	G	VI	VIII	
	B	III	XXVII	Dominica Reminiscere	XVII	II	A	V	IX	
XIIII	C	II	XXVIII		VI	X	B	IIII	X	
III	D	KL	Marcii				C	III	XI	
	E	VI	II		XIIII	XVIII	D	II	XII	
XI	F	V	III		III	VII	E	Ydus	XIII	
	G	IIII	IIII				F	XVIII	XIIII	Dominica Pasche
XIX	A	III	V		XI	XV	G	XVII	XV	
VIII	B	II	VI			IIII	A	XVI	XVI	
	C	Nonas	VII	Dominica Oculi / Decem	XIX		B	XV	XVII	
XVI	D	VIII	VIII		VIII	XII	C	XIIII	XVIII	
V	E	VII	IX			I	D	XIII	XIX	
	F	VI	X		XVI		E	XII	XX[1]	
XIII	G	V	XI(a)		V		F	XI	XXI	Octava pasche
II	A	IIII	XII				G	X KL	May	

Anni embolismales CCCLXXXIIII dierum

a) equinoctium in anno reformacionis
b) coniunctio luminarium in anno reformacionis hora XI
c) equinoctium tempore Pii et Eleutherii
d) hic erit predicta coniunctio et ad vesperam luna incipiet vere prima si fieret dicta reformatio

---

[1] XX] XXI

4r

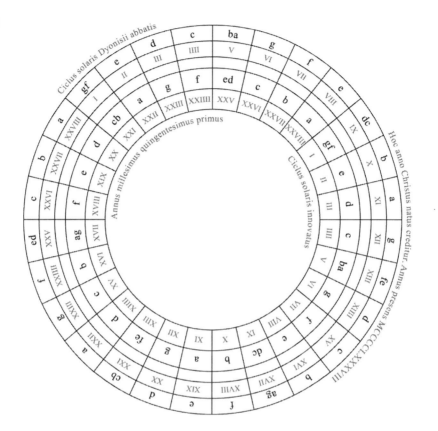

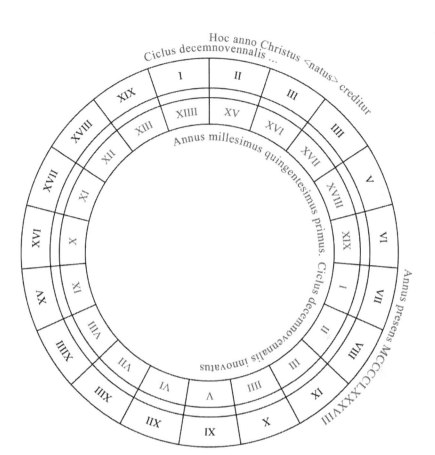

Anni servandi ut communes licet alias essent bissextiles

Annus millesimus octingentesimus quartus

Annus bis millesimus centesimus octavus

Annus bis millesimus quadringentesimus XII^{us}

Annus bis millesimus sextingentesimus XVI^{us}

Notes on the *Dyalogus de temporibus Christi*

Dyalogus, tr. 1, c. 3, ll. 84–92: In stating the time of mean opposition for the paschal lunations of AD 33 and 34, Peter tacitly relies on a table Roger Bacon had drawn up for his *Opus maius* (*c.*1267), which displays these times for March and April of AD 1–38. He confirms his use of Bacon later on in tr. 3, c. 1 (ll. 78–79, 127–128), where he repeats the data for March AD 34. Bacon's table shows the opposition of April AD 33 to have occurred after 2 days, 17 hours, and 16 minutes, and that of March AD 34 after 23 days, 2 hours, and 5 minutes.[1] Peter's times in tr. 1, c. 3, are nearly identical, save for him putting the opposition of April AD 33 after 2 days, 17 hours, and 15 minutes. If these 17 hours and 15 minutes are interpreted correctly as completed since the previous noon (i.e., noon on 2 April), it follows that the mean opposition in question occurred—approximately—during the last hour of the night (i.e., the hour *before* sunrise on 3 April), not the third hour of daylight, as Peter mistakenly states in l. 86. A misreading of *XVII horis* as *XX horis* may have been responsible for this internal contradiction.

Dyalogus, tr. 2, c. 1, ll. 131–132: Contrary to what is stated in this passage, the Alfonsine Tables placed the start of the Egyptian year in September.

Dyalogus, tr. 2, c. 2, ll. 120–121: Peter's dating of the First Council of Nicaea of AD 325 to "circa AD 322," which occurs both here and in tr. 2, c. 3, ll. 46–47, was probably derived from the famous fourth-century *Chronicle* of Eusebius of Caesarea. The Council of Nicaea is there assigned to the first year of the 275th Olympiad (*Chronicon*, ed. GCS 47, 230) and hence to the 322nd year (exclusive) since Christ's birth in the third year of the 194th Olympiad (*Chronicon*, ed. GCS 47, 169).

Dyalogus, tr. 2, c. 3, ll. 223–224: Eusebius's *Chronicle* assigns the beginning of King David's reign to the 940th year of Abraham (*Chronicon*, ed. GCS 47, 67a) and the birth of Jesus Christ to the 2015th year (*Chronicon*, ed. GCS 47, 169). It follows that the birth of Christ took place in the 1076th year (inclusive) from the beginning of David's reign. Peter, for unclear reasons, states that it was the 1104th year.

Dyalogus, tr. 3, c. 1, ll. 194–210: Gerland, the eleventh-century computist, is known for having dated the crucifixion to 23 March AD 42. Although this is eight years later than the conventional Passion date in AD 34, his total correction of the Dionysiac

---

[1] See Roger Bacon, *Opus maius*, lib. IV (ed. Jebb, 131 [facing]). Note that the table in the most recent critical edition of the *Opus maius* (ed. Bridges, 1:209 [facing]) features incorrect data for March AD 34 owing to the use of a garbled exemplar (MS London, British Library, Cotton Tiberius C.V, fol. 76r).

incarnation era amounted to only seven years, as he put the incarnation in AD 8. Johannes Jordaens's copy of the *Dyalogus* shows signs that either he or Peter was confused by this apparent inconsistency. Originally, Jordaens wrote—correctly— that Gerland subtracted seven years from the Dionysiac era (l. 194), but then made the mistake of applying the same seven years to the difference between AD 34 and 42 (l. 207). At a later stage, the word *septem* was in both passages changed to *8*, which effectively corrected the second statement, but rendered the first one false.

Dyalogus, tr. 3, c. 1, ll. 250–252: Peter here and elsewhere makes tacit use of the solar cycle according to Gerland, which is eleven years ahead of the conventional solar cycle associated with Dionysius Exiguus (see tr. 2, c. 1, ll. 159–162). According to the conventional cycle, AD 1471 was the 24th year, while AD 1 was the 10th year. On Gerland's count, AD 1471 was the 7th year and AD 1 was the 21st year, as correctly stated by *Paulus* in this passage. The same usage can be observed in tr. 2, c. 2, ll. 200–203, where the proposed reform turns the 21st year of Gerland's cycle into the 9th for AD 1. He also follows Gerland's count in tr. 3, c. 2, ll. 199–200, but not in ll. 189–192, where the years given in Peter's text conform to neither version of the cycle (see below).

Dyalogus, tr. 3, c. 2, l. 166: As preserved in Johannes Jordaens's manuscript, this passage equates the year of the crucifixion (in Christ's 34th year) with the 52nd year since the beginning of Caesar's reign, but this can hardly have been Peter's original intention. According to his reconstruction of Roman imperial chronology, as summarized in the tables appended to the *Dyalogus* (pp. 422–429 in the manuscript), the year of the crucifixion was the 80th year since the beginning of Caesar's reign. Like the 52nd year, the 80th would have been a bissextile year according to Caesar's original leap-year rule, so substituting *LXXX* for *LII* would not affect the subsequent remarks in ll. 166–168.

Dyalogus, tr. 3, c. 2, ll. 189–192: Peter here identifies AD 33 and 34 as the 17th and 18th year of the solar cycle as currently in use among computists. This is puzzling since these years would have been years 14 and 15 of the conventional cycle and years 25 and 26 of the Gerlandian variant (see above, the note on tr. 3, c. 1, ll. 250–252). The dominical letters associated with these years are D (for AD 33) and C (for AD 34), as correctly stated in the text. Why Peter would have associated these letters with the wrong years of the *cyclus solaris* remains unclear.

Dyalogus, tr. 3, c. 3, ll. 46–47: Peter here attributes to Bede the opinion that the interval of total years from the creation of the world to the incarnation of Christ was 5199 years. While it is true that Bede mentions this number in his work *De temporibus*

(703), he there presents it as the opinion of others (*iuxta alios*). Bede's own position was that Christ's birth took place in the 3952nd year since creation, as stated in both *De temporibus* and *De temporum ratione* (725).[2] The figure of 5199 years is instead rooted in the fourth-century world chronicle of Eusebius of Caesarea.[3]

Dyalogus, tr. 3, c. 3, ll. 75–81: The quoted passage in Pliny's *Natural History* refers to an old Babylonian convention of placing the equinoxes and solstices at the (end of the) 8th degree of the respective zodiacal sign. Pliny refers to degrees as *partes*, which occasioned a misunderstanding on Peter's part, making him believe that the equinoxes and solstices occurred after the first eighth of the respective sign, which is equivalent to the first 3;45°.

---

[2]   Bede, *De temporibus*, c. 22 (ed. CCSL 123C, 607); Bede, *De temporum ratione*, c. 66 (ed. CCSL 123B, 495).

[3]   For further details, see MacCarron, *Bede and Time*, 63–94.

NOTES ON THE *REFORMACIO KALENDARII ROMANI*

Reformacio, ll. 16–17: Peter here quotes Isidore of Seville as attributing the first ever Easter cycle to *Cirillus*, that is, to Cyril of Alexandria. Isidore indeed mentions Cyril in the cited part of the *Etymologies*, stating that he calculated a 95-year list of Easter dates. He does not, however, identify Cyril as a pioneer in this regard. Instead, he makes the same historical claim as Bede, according to whom to the first Easter cycle was the work of Hippolytus (ll. 17–18).

Reformacio, ll. 27–38: This paragraph uses the accession years of four popes recorded in Eusebius's *Chronicle* to establish the corresponding years of the *Anno Domini* era, the assumption being that Christ was born in the third year of the 194th Olympiad (or Ol. 194.3). This year historically overlapped with 2/1 BC, but Peter takes it for granted that Eusebius equated the year of Christ's birth with the first year of the *Anno Domini* era. He accordingly argues that the year AD of a given papal accession is found by counting four years for each Olympiad between Christ's birth and the pope in question. The year of Christ's birth itself must be included in this calculation, as Peter himself notes in l. 34. Based on this rule, Peter should have assigned the accession of Pope Pius I to AD 144, as the interval between Ol. 194.2 and 230.2 is $36 \times 4 = 144$ years. His own result of AD 143 betrays an exclusive count of years, whereas the years he assigns to the remaining three popes (Eleutherius in AD 179, Victor in AD 195, Silvester in AD 312) are all consistent with an inclusive count.

It is also worth noting that Eusebius dates Silvester's accession to Ol. 272.2 (*Chronicon*, ed. GCS 47, 229) and the Council of Nicaea to Ol. 275.1 (*Chronicon*, ed. GCS 47, 230), which implies that the Council took place in the 12th inclusive year of Silvester's reign. Peter, for unclear reasons, speaks of the 13th year (l. 19), which explains why he here assigns the Council to AD 324 (l. 38) rather than AD 323. An exclusive count of the years since Christ's birth would have justified dating the Council to AD 322, as Peter had done in his *Dyalogus* (tr. 2, c. 2, ll. 120–121; tr. 2, c. 3, ll. 46–47).

Reformacio, ll. 113–119, 125–131: Peter's text here again lacks consistency in the way it counts intervals between years. In ll. 117–118, AD 161 is identified as the 19th year before the coronation of Eleutherius (AD 179 according to l. 39) and the 19th year after the coronation of Pius (AD 143 according to l. 37), which in each case implies an inclusive count. It is different in ll. 129–130, where AD 285 is said to have been the 90th year since the coronation of Victor (AD 195 according to l. 37) and the 27th year before the coronation of Silvester (AD 312 according to l. 37). This time, the count is exclusive.

Reformacio, ll. 121–124, 131–138: In this section of the text, Peter cites the results of four different astronomical computations, viz. (i) the time of the vernal equinox in AD 1501; (ii) the time of the vernal equinox in AD 161; (iii) the time of the mean conjunction of Sun and Moon in AD 1501; (iv) the time of the mean conjunction of Sun and Moon in AD 285. When introducing (i), Peter notes that the computation is valid for the meridian of Rome. Although he does not repeat this statement for (ii)–(iv), consistency would dictate that all four computations pertained to the same meridian. Most astronomical computations in Peter's day would have been based, in one way or another, on the Alfonsine Tables, whose standard version places (iii) and (iv) 1 hour and 40 minutes earlier than does Peter.[4] This discrepancy indicates that the computations Peter cites in this section were carried out for a meridian 25° further east than the default meridian of the Alfonsine Tables, which is that of Toledo. For (i), the Alfonsine Tables yield a time of 11:03h from the previous noon, which is 1 hour and 48 minutes below Peter's result, suggesting that the meridian was shifted by 27°. In the case of (ii), the implied shift increases to 29°, since the Alfonsine time for the meridian of Toledo is 12:52h after the previous noon, 1 hour and 56 minutes earlier than Peter's result. This lack of congruence with his results for (iii) and (iv) is probably due to imprecisions in the way Peter or his informant applied the solar equation, which is the term needed to convert mean into true longitudes. Mean conjunctions were less difficult to compute than true solar longitudes, which is why the 25°-shift implicit in Peter's times for (iii) and (iv) is more dependable in revealing where he placed the meridian of Rome in relation to that of Toledo. This conclusion is also supported by medieval tables of geographic coordinates, in which the distance Toledo-Rome is typically given as 24;25°, only 0;35° below the shift implied by Peter's results.[5]

---

4   The Alfonsine results for (iii) and (iv) are 19 March AD 1501, 20:59h from the previous noon and 23 March AD 285, 18:55h from the previous noon. These have been obtained using the software *Deviations*, available at http://www.raymondm.co.uk/.

5   See *Toledan Tables*, ed. Pedersen, 4:1512–1513.

BIBLIOGRAPHY

1.   Manuscripts and Archival Material

Arras, Médiathèque Saint-Vaast
674 (722)
688 (748)

Augsburg, Universitätsbibliothek
II.1.4° 61

Averbode, Archief van de Abdij van Averbode
I, reg. 43

Bamberg, Staatsbibliothek
Msc. Astr. 4

Berlin, Staatsbibliothek
lat. fol. 753
Magdeburg 165* (lost)
Magdeburg 201
Magdeburg 220
Magdeburg 227

Bologna, Biblioteca Universitaria
1845 (957)

Brussels, Algemeen Rijksarchief (Comité van de Religiekas)
73/110

Brussels, KBR
129–130
733–741
5570
1022–1047
1382–1391
11750–11751
11752–11764
11915–11919
17320–17330

21874
II 1164
II 1185 (Volume 3)

Cambridge, University Library
Inc 3.F.2.9 [3294]

Erfurt, Universitäts- und Forschungsbibliothek
Dep. Erf., CA 4° 360
Dep. Erf., CA 4° 371

Ghent, Universiteitsbibliotheek
685
941

Glasgow, University Library,
Sp Coll Hunterian Bf.3.15

Greifswald, Bibliothek des Geistlichen Ministeriums
34.D.IX

Leuven, Maurits Sabbe Library (GBIB)
17

Leuven, Rijksarchief (Kerkelijk Archief Brabant)
726, no. 15076
726, no. 20437/2

Leuven, Universiteitsbibliotheek
1635

London, British Library
Cotton Tiberius C.V
Harley 2500
Harley 3675
Royal 12.C.XVII
Sloane 2509

Madrid, Biblioteca nacional de España
13250

Manchester, John Rylands Library
Latin 476

Milan, Biblioteca Ambrosiana
H 109 sup.

Munich, Bayerische Staatsbibliothek
Clm 18298

New York, Columbia University, Rare Book and Manuscript Library
Western MS 31

Oxford, Bodleian Library
Canon. Misc. 248
Rawlinson G.40

Paris, Bibliothèque Mazarine
300
567
3642

Paris, Bibliothèque nationale de France
lat. 3123
lat. 3658
lat. 15104
lat. 16404

Stuttgart, Württembergische Landesbibliothek
HB I 10

Vatican City, BAV
Ott. lat. 718
Ott. lat. 842
Vat. lat. 976
Vat. lat. 2580
Vat. lat. 5606

Vienna, Österreichische Nationalbibliothek
ser. nov. 12694
ser. nov. 12816
ser. nov. 12890

2. Early Printed Books (pre-1700)

Altercatio Synagogae et Ecclesiae. Frankfurt am Main: Melchior Novesianus, 1537.

Andreas, Valerius. *Bibliotheca belgica.* Leuven: Jacobus Zegers, 1643.

———. *Fasti academici studii generalis Lovaniensis, id est Origo & institutio: rectores, cancellarij, conservatores, doctores & professores, fundatores & benefactores, resque aliquot memorabiles ejusdem universitatis.* Leuven: Hieronymus Nempaeus, 1650.

Baluze, Étienne. *Nova collectio conciliorum.* Vol. 1. Paris: François Muguet, 1683.

Biblia sacra, cum Glossa ordinaria, primum quidem a Strabo Fuldensis monacho Benedictino collecta, nunc verò novis Patrum cum Graecorum, tum Latinorum explicationibus locupletata, Postilla Nicolai Lirani Franciscani, necnon additionibus Pauli Burgensis Episcopi, & Matthiae Thoringi replicis, opera et studio theologorum Duacensium diligentissime emendatis. 6 vols. Douai/Antwerp: Balthazar Bellère & Jan van Keerberghen, 1617.

John Chrysostom. *Opera.* Venice: Bernardino Stagnino, 1503.

Lucanus, Marcus Annaeus. *Pharsalia.* Edited by Giovanni Andrea Bussi. Rome: Conradus Sweynheym and Arnoldus Pannartz, 1469. ISTC: il00292000.

Macrobius. *In Somnium Scipionis expositio. Saturnalia.* Venice: Nicolaus Jenson, 1472. ISCT: im00008000.

Massaeus, Christian. *Chronicorum multiplicis historiae utriusque testamenti ... libri viginti.* Antwerp: Joannes Crinitus, 1540.

Nicholas of Cusa. *Opuscula theologica et mathematica.* 2 vols. Strasbourg: Martin Flach, [not after 13 Oct.] 1488. ISTC: in00095800.

Paul II, Pont. Max. *Bulla anni Jubilaei.* Rome: Sixtus Riessinger, [after 19 Apr.] 1470. ISCT: ip00156800.

Paul of Burgos. *Scrutinium scripturarum.* Strasbourg: Johann Mentelin, c.1474. ISTC: ip00203000.

Paul of Middelburg. *Prognosticon anni 1480.* Venice: Adam de Rottweil, 1479/80. ISTC: ip00184700.

Peter de Rivo. *Libellus quomodo omnia in meliorem partem sunt interpretanda.* Leiden: Jan Seversz, 1509.

Pierre d'Ailly. *Imago mundi et tractatus alii.* Leuven: Johannes de Westfalia, 1477/83. ISTC: ia00477000.

Ptolemy, Claudius. *Almagestum.* Venice: Petrus Liechtenstein, 1515.

Sanderus, Antonius. *Bibliotheca belgica manuscripta.* 2 vols. Lille: Tussanus le Clercq, 1641–1643.

———. *Lovaniense coenobium, S. Martini brevi historia ex domesticis potissimum ipsius et aliis fide dignis monumentis contexta.* Leuven: Petrus Sassenus, 1663.

Suetonius Tranquillus, Gaius. *Vitae XII Caesarum.* Edited by Giovanni Andrea Bussi. Rome: Conradus Sweynheym and Arnoldus Pannartz, [after 30 Aug.] 1470. ISTC: is00816000.

———. *Vitae XII Caesarum.* Edited by J. A. Campanus. Rome: Johannes Philippus de Lignamine, [Aug.] 1470. ISTC: is00815000.

Vincent of Beauvais. *Bibliotheca mundi seu Speculi maioris ... Tomus Quartus, qui Speculum historiale inscribitur.* Douai: Balthazar Bellère, 1624. Reprint, Graz: Akademische Druck- u. Verlagsanstalt, 1964–1965.

3.   Modern Source Editions

Alberic of Trois-Fontaines. *Chronica.* Edited by Paul Scheffer-Boichorst. In *MGH Scriptores*, vol. 23, edited by Georg Heinrich Pertz, 631–950. Hannover: Hahn, 1874.

Albertus Magnus. *Super Dionysii Epistulas.* Edited by Paulus Simon. Alberti Magni Opera Omnia 37.2. Münster: Aschendorff, 1978.

Alfonsi, Petrus. *Dialogue against the Jews.* Translated by Irven M. Resnick. The Fathers of the Church: Mediaeval Continuation 8. Washington, DC: Catholic University of America Press, 2006.

Aristoteles. *Metaphysica: Recensio et Translatio Guillelmi de Moerbeka.* Edited by Gudrun Vuillemin-Diem. 2 vols. Aristoteles Latinus 25.3. Leiden: Brill, 1995.

Bacon, Roger. *Opus Majus ad Clementem quartum pontificum Romanum.* Edited by Samuel Jebb. London: Bowyer, 1733.

———. *Opus Majus.* Edited by John Henry Bridges. 3 vols. Oxford: Clarendon Press, 1897–1900.

Baldi, Bernardino. *Le vite de' matematici.* Edited by Elio Nenci. Milan: Angeli, 1998.

Computus Gerlandi. Edited by Alfred Lohr. Sudhoffs Archiv: Beihefte 61. Stuttgart: Steiner, 2013.

Decretum magistri Gratiani. Edited by Emil Friedberg. Corpus Juris Canonici 1. Leipzig: Tauchnitz, 1879. Reprint, Graz: Akademische Druck- u. Verlagsanstalt, 1959.

Decretales pseudo-Isidorianae et Capitula Angilramni. Edited by Paul Hinschius. Leipzig: Tauchnitz, 1863.

Flavius Josephus. *Antiquitates Judaicae.* Edited by Franz Blatt. Acta Jutlandica: Aarsskrift for Aarhus Universitet 30.1. Copenhagen: Munksgaard, 1958.

Grosseteste, Robert. *Compotus.* Edited by Alfred Lohr and C. Philipp E. Nothaft. Oxford: Oxford University Press, 2019.

Isidore of Seville. *Etymologiae (V).* Edited by Valeriano Yarza Urquiola and Francisco Javier Andrés Santos. Auteurs latins du Moyen Âge 25. Paris: Les Belles Lettres, 2013.

———. *Etymologiae (VI).* Edited by César Chaparro-Gómez. Auteurs latins du Moyen Âge 23. Paris: Les Belles Lettres, 2012.

———. *Etymologiae (XV).* Edited by Jean-Yves Guillaumin. Auteurs latins du Moyen Âge 29. Paris: Les Belles Lettres, 2016.

Jacobus de Voragine. *The Golden Legend: Readings on the Saints.* Translated by
    William Granger Ryan. 2 vols. Princeton, NJ: Princeton University Press, 1993.
Jean des Murs and Firmin de Beauval. *Epistola super reformatione antiqui kalen-
    darii.* Edited by Chris Schabel, "John of Murs and Firmin of Beauval's Letter and
    Treatise on Calendar Reform for Clement VI: Text and Introduction," *Cahiers de
    l'Institut du Moyen-Âge Grec et Latin* 66 (1996): 187–215.
Jerome of Stridon. *De viris illustribus.* Edited by Aldo Ceresa-Gastaldo. Biblioteca
    patristica 12. Florence: Nardini, 1988.
pseudo-Jerome of Stridon. *Martyrologium Hieronymianum.* Edited by Giovanni
    Battista de Rossi and Louis Duchesne. In *Acta Sanctorum,* vol. 63 = *November,*
    vol. 2.1, [1]–[156]. Brussels: Apud Socios Bollandianos, 1894.
Lombard, Peter. *Sententiae in IV libris distinctae.* Edited by Ignatius Brady. 2 vols.
    3rd ed. Spicilegium Bonaventurianum 4–5. Grottaferrata: Editiones Collegii S.
    Bonaventurae ad Claras Aquas, 1971–1981.
Lucanus, Marcus Annaeus. *De bello civili libri X.* Edited by David R. Shackleton
    Bailey. 2nd ed. Stuttgart: Teubner, 1997.
Macrobius. *Saturnalia.* Edited by Robert A. Kaster. 3 vols. Loeb Classical Library
    510–512. Cambridge, MA: Harvard University Press, 2011.
Martin of Opava. *Chronicon pontificum et imperatorum.* Edited by Ludwig Wei-
    land. In *MGH Scriptores,* vol. 22, edited by Georg Heinrich Pertz, 377–475. Han-
    nover: Hahn, 1872.
Molanus, Joannes. *Historiae rerum lovaniensium libri XIV.* Edited by Petrus Fran-
    ciscus Xaverius De Ram (*Les quatorze livres sur l'histoire de la ville de Louvain
    du docteur et professeur en théologie Jean Molanus*). 2 vols. Brussels: Hayez, 1861.
Nicholas of Cusa. *De correctione kalendarii.* Edited by Viktor Stegemann. Heidel-
    berg: Kerle, 1955.
Orosius, Paulus. *Historia adversum paganos.* Edited by Marie-Pierre Arnaud-Lin-
    det. 3 vols. Paris: Les Belles Lettres, 1990–1991.
pseudo-Ovid. *De vetula.* Edited by Paul Klopsch. Mittellateinische Studien und
    Texte 2. Leiden: Brill, 1967.
Palmieri, Matteo. *Liber de temporibus.* Edited by Gino Scaramella. Rerum Italica-
    rum Scriptores 26.1. Città di Castello: Lapi, 1906–1915.
Pliny the Elder. *Naturalis historia (II).* Edited by Jean Beaujeu. Collection des uni-
    versités de France: série latine 133. Paris: Les Belles Lettres, 1950.
Sedulius, Coelius. *Carmen paschale.* Edited by Carl P. E. Springer. Writings from
    the Greco-Roman World 35. Atlanta, GA: Society of Biblical Literature, 2013.
Servius Honoratus, Maurus. *In Vergilii Bucolica et Georgica commentarii.* Edited
    by Georgius Thilo. Leipzig: Teubner, 1887.
Sigebert of Gembloux. *Catalogus de viris illustribus.* Edited by Robert Witte. Latei-
    nische Sprache und Literatur des Mittelalters 1. Bern: Lang, 1974.

Suetonius Tranquillus, Gaius. *De vita Caesarum*. Edited by Maximilian Ihm. Leipzig: Teubner 1907.

———. [*Lives of the Caesars:*] *Volume 1.* Translated by J. C. Rolfe. Rev. ed. Loeb Classical Library 31. Cambridge, MA: Harvard University Press, 1998.

Tabula Gerlandi. Edited by Fritz S. Pedersen. In *Petri Philomenae de Dacia et Petri de S. Audomaro Opera quadrivialia,* vol. 1, 399–402. Copenhagen: Gad, 1983.

Tabule astronomice illustrissimi Alfontii regis Castelle. Edited by Emmanuel Poulle (*Les Tables Alphonsines avec les canons de Jean de Saxe: édition, traduction et commentaire*). Paris: Éditions du CNRS, 1984.

Toledan Tables. Edited by Fritz S. Pedersen (*The Toledan Tables: A Review of the Manuscripts and the Textual Versions with an Edition,* 4 vols., Kongelige Danske Videnskabernes Selskab, historisk-filosofiske Skrifter, 24.1–4). Copenhagen: Reitzel, 2002.

Tertullian. *Adversus Iudaeos.* Edited by Hermann Tränkle. Wiesbaden: Steiner, 1964.

Thomas à Kempis. *Opera omnia.* Edited by Joseph Pohl. 7 vols. Freiburg im Breisgau: Herder, 1910–1922.

Tostado, Alfonso. *Opera omnia.* 27 vols. Venice: Typographia Balleoniana, 1728.

4. Other Literature

Andrei, Osvalda. "Cronologia di Cristo e cronologia di Gesù: un aspetto della ricerca storica su Gesù (molto) prima di Reimarus." *Annali di storia dell'esegesi* 30 (2013): 161–192.

Bartocci, Barbara, Serena Masolini, and Russell Friedman. "Reading Aristotle at the University of Louvain in the Fifteenth Century: A First Survey of Petrus de Rivo's Commentaries on Aristotle (I)." *Bulletin de philosophie médiévale* 55 (2013): 133–176.

Bartocci, Barbara, and Serena Masolini. "Reading Aristotle at the University of Louvain in the Fifteenth Century: A First Survey of Petrus de Rivo's Commentaries on Aristotle (II)." *Bulletin de philosophie médiévale* 56 (2014): 281–383.

Baudry, Léon. *La querelle des futurs contingents (Louvain 1465–1475).* Études de philosophie médiévale 38. Paris: Vrin, 1950.

———. *The Quarrel over Future Contingents (Louvain 1464–1475).* Translated by Rita Guerlac. Synthese Historical Library 36. Dordrecht: Kluwer, 1989.

Bentley, Jerry H. *Humanists and Holy Writ: New Testament Scholarship in the Renaissance.* Princeton, NJ: Princeton University Press, 1983.

Berbée, Paul. "Riet (Ryt, de Arundine), Johannes van." In *Die Bischöfe des Heiligen Römischen Reiches 1448 bis 1648: Ein biographisches Lexikon,* edited by Clemens Brodkorb and Erwin Gatz, 583–584. Berlin: Duncker & Humblot, 1996.

Best, Richard Irvine, and Hugh Jackson Lawlor, eds. *The Martyrology of Tallaght: From the Book of Leinster and MS. 5100–4 in the Royal Library, Brussels.* Henry Bradshaw Society 68. London: Harrison, 1931.

Bianchi, Luca. *Pour une histoire de la double verité.* Conférences Pierre Abélard. Paris: Vrin, 2008.

Blackburn, Bonnie J., and Leofranc Holford-Strevens. *The Oxford Companion to the Year: An Exploration of Calendar Customs and Time-Reckoning.* Oxford: Oxford University Press, 1999.

Blumenkranz, Bernhard, and Jean Châtillon. "De la polémique antijuive à la catéchèse chrétienne: l'objet, le contenu et les sources d'une anonyme *Altercatio Synagogae et Ecclesiae du XIIe siècle.*" *Recherches de Théologie ancienne et médiévale* 23 (1956): 40–60.

Boorman, Stanley. *Ottaviano Petrucci: Catalogue Raisonne.* Oxford: Oxford University Press, 2006.

Borst, Arno. *Die karolingische Kalenderreform.* MGH Schriften 46. Hannover: Hahn, 1998.

———, ed. *Der karolingische Reichskalender und seine Überlieferung bis ins 12. Jahrhundert.* 3 vols. MGH Antiquitates 3/Libri memoriales 2. Hannover: Hahn, 2001.

Bosmans, Griet. "De Pedagogie 'De Lelie' (1437–1560)." Diss. Lic., University of Leuven, 1958.

Brandis, Tilo. "Handschriften- und Buchproduktion im 15. und frühen 16. Jahrhundert." In *Literatur und Laienbildung im Spätmittelalter und in der Reformationszeit,* edited by Ludger Grenzmann and Karl Stackmann, 176–193. Germanistische Symposien-Berichtsbände 5. Stuttgart: Metzler, 1984.

Bresslau, Harry. *Handbuch der Urkundenlehre für Deutschland und Italien.* Vol. 2.2. 2nd ed. Berlin: de Gruyter, 1931.

Brown, Keith M. "Courtiers and Cavaliers: Service, Anglicization and Loyalty among the Royalist Nobility." In *The Scottish National Covenant in Its British Context,* edited by John Morrill, 155–192. Edinburgh: Edinburgh University Press, 1990.

Brown, Raymond E. *The Death of the Messiah: From Gethsemane to the Grave; A Commentary on the Passion Narratives in the Four Gospels.* 2 vols. New York: Doubleday, 1994.

Burke, Bernard. *A Genealogical and Heraldic History of the Landed Gentry of Great Britain and Ireland.* 3 vols. 9th ed. London: Harrison & sons, 1898.

Calis, Richard, Frederic Clark, Christian Flow, Anthony Grafton, Madeline McMahon, and Jennifer M. Rampling. "Passing the Book: Cultures of Reading in the Winthrop Family, 1580–1730." *Past and Present* 241 (2018): 69–141.

Caroti, Stefano. "La critica contro l'astrologia di Nicole Oresme e la sua influenza nel Medioevo e nel Rinascimento." *Atti della Accademia Nazionale dei Lincei,*

Memorie della Classe di Scienze morali, storiche e filologiche, 8th ser., 23 (1979): 545–685.

Castelli, Patrizia. "Gli astri e i Montefeltri." *Res Publica Litterarum* 6 (1983): 75–89.

———. "Magia, astrologia, divinazione e chiromanzia alla corte dei Montefeltro. Un caso particolare: Ottaviano Ubaldini della Carda." In *"Lo stato e 'l valore": i Montefeltro e i Della Rovere; assensi e conflitti nell'Italia tra '400 e '600*, edited by Patrizia Castelli and Salvatore Geruzzi, 29–65. Pisa: Giardini, 2005.

Chabás, José, and Bernard R. Goldstein. *The Alfonsine Tables of Toledo.* Archimedes 8. Dordrecht: Kluwer, 2003.

Champion, Matthew S. *The Fullness of Time: Temporalities of the Fifteenth-Century Low Countries.* Chicago: University of Chicago Press, 2017.

———. "The Presence of an Absence: Jews in Late-Medieval Louvain." In *A World Enchanted: Magic and the Margins; Essays Presented in Honour of Charles Zika*, edited by Julie Davies and Michael Pickering, 37–67. Parkville: Melbourne Historical Journal Research Collective, 2014.

———. "'To See beyond the Moment is Delightful': Devout Chronologies of the Late Medieval Low Countries." *Viator* 49, no. 3 (2018): 199–221.

Claes, Dirk. "Changes in the Educational Context of the Leuven Faculty of Theology in the Fifteenth and Sixteenth Centuries: Canon Law and Humanism." In *Schooling and Society: The Reordering of Knowledge in the Western Middle Ages*, edited by Alasdair A. MacDonald and Michael W. Twomey, 139–155. Groningen Studies in Cultural Change 6. Leuven: Peeters, 2004.

Coebergh-van den Braak, A. M. and Erika Rummel, eds. *The Works of Engelbertus Schut Leydensis (ca 1420–1530).* Supplementa Humanistica Lovaniensia 10. Leuven: Leuven University Press, 1997.

Coll, Emma, Isabelle de Conihout, Geneviève Grand, and Guy Lanoë. *Reliures médiévales et premières reliures à décor doré: 22 reliures choisies dans les collections de la Bibliothèque Mazarine.* Paris: CNRS—Institut de recherche et d'histoire des textes, 2003.

Connolly, Margaret. "A Manuscript Owned by William Scheves Now at Maynooth." *The Library*, 7th ser., 17, no. 3 (2016): 331–335.

Cordoliani, Alfred. "Abbon de Fleury, Hériger de Lobbes et Gerland de Besançon sur l'ère de l'incarnation de Denys le Petit." *Revue d'histoire ecclésiastique* 44 (1949): 463–487.

———. "Le comput ecclésiastique à l'abbaye du Mont-Cassin au XIe siècle." *Anuario de estudios medievales* 3 (1966): 65–89.

———. "Inventaire des manuscrits de comput ecclésiastique conservés dans les bibliothèques de Madrid (1e série)." *Hispania Sacra* 7 (1954): 111–143.

Cuppo, Luciana. "Felix of Squillace and the Dionysiac Computus II: Rome, Gaul, and the Insular World." In *Late Antique Calendrical Thought and its Reception in the Early Middle Ages: Proceedings from the 3rd International Conference on* *the Science of Computus in Ireland and Europe, Galway, 16–18 July, 2010,* edited by Immo Warntjes and Dáibhí Ó Cróinín, 138–181. Studia Traditionis Theologiae 26. Turnhout: Brepols, 2017.

D'Haenens, Albert. "Abbaye de Parc, à Heverlee." In *Monasticon Belge: Province de Brabant,* edited by Dom U. Berlière, 773–827. Liège: Centre national de recherches d'histoire religieuse, 1969.

D'Hoop, Alfred. *Inventaire général des Archives ecclesiastiques du Brabant.* 6 vols. Inventaires sommaires des Archives de l'État en Belgique. Brussels: E. Guyot, 1905–1932.

Dahan, Gilbert. "Critique et défense de la Vulgate au XIVᵉ siècle." In *Exégèse et critique des textes sacrés: judaïsme, christianisme, islam; hier et aujourd'hui,* edited by Danielle Delmaire and Geneviève Gobillot, 119–136. Paris: Geuthner, 2007.

de Ceuleneer, Adolf. "Paulus van Middelburg en de Kalenderhervorming." In *Handelingen van het eerste Vlaamsch Taal- en Geschiedkundig Congres,* 276–289. Antwerp: De Vos en Van der Groen, 1910.

de Jongh, Henri. *L'ancienne faculté de théologie de Louvain au premier siècle de son existence (1432–1540): ses débuts, son organisation, son enseignement, sa lutte contre Érasme et Luther.* Leuven: Bureaux de la Revue d'Histoire Ecclésiastique, 1911.

de Rossi, Giovanni Battista, and Antonio Ferrua, eds. *Inscriptiones Christianae urbis Romae septimo saeculo antiquiores.* Nova series, vol. 7, *Coemeteria Viae Tiburtinae.* Vatican City: Pont. Institutum Archaeologiae Christianae, 1980.

de Smet, Antoine. "Savants humanistes et astrologie." In *Acta Conventus Neo-Latini Lovaniensis: Proceedings of the First International Congress of Neo-Latin Studies, Louvain 23–28 August 1971,* edited by Jozef IJsewijn and Eckhard Kessler, 191–197. Humanistische Bibliothek, Reihe 1, Abhandlungen 20. Leuven: Leuven University Press, 1973.

De Visscher, Eva. *Reading the Rabbis: Christian Hebraism in the Works of Herbert of Bosham.* Commentaria 5. Leiden: Brill, 2014.

De Vocht, Henry. *History of the Foundations and the Rise of the Collegium trilingue Lovaniense, 1517–1550.* 4 vols. Leuven: Bibliothèque de l'Université, Bureaux du Recueil, 1951–1955.

Declercq, Georges. "Dionysius Exiguus and the Introduction of the Christian Era." *Sacris Erudiri* 41 (2002): 165–246.

Delisle, Léopold. "Fragments inédits de l'Histoire des Louis XI par Thomas Basin, tirés d'un manuscrit de Goettingue." *Notices et extraits des manuscrits de la Bibliothèque Nationale et autres bibliothèques* 34, no. 2 (1895): 89–117.

Demandt, Alexander. *Verformungstendenzen in der Überlieferung antiker Sonnen- und Mondfinsternisse.* Akademie der Wissenschaften und der Literatur: Abhandlungen der geistes- und sozialwissenschaftlichen Klasse, 1970.7. Wiesbaden: Steiner, 1970.

Derolez, Albert, Benjamin Victor, Lucien Reynhout, Wouter Bracke, Michel Ooster-
bosch, and Jan Willem Klein. *Corpus Catalogorum Belgii: The Medieval Booklists
of the Southern Low Countries.* 7 vols. Brussel: WLSK, 1994.

Dittmar, Hermann. *Die Handschriften und alten Drucke des Dom-Gymnasiums.*
Katalog der deutschen Bibliotheken 3. Magdeburg: Friese, 1878.

Dohrn-van Rossum, Gerhard. *History of the Hour: Clocks and Modern Temporal
Hours.* Translated by Thomas Dunlap. Chicago: University of Chicago Press,
1996.

Durkhan, John, and Anthoony Ross. *Early Scottish Libraries.* Glasgow: John S.
Burns & Sons, 1961.

Favaro, Antonio. "I lettori di matematiche nella Università di Padova dal principio
del secolo XIV alla fine del XVI." *Memorie e documenti per la storia della Università di Padova* 1 (1922): 3–70.

Federici Vescovini, Graziella. "Su un genere letterario astrologico: il pronostico
di Paolo di Middelburg, astrologo di Federico da Montefeltro." In *"Lo stato e 'l
valore": i Montefeltro e i Della Rovere; assensi e conflitti nell'Italia tra '400 e '600,*
edited by Patrizia Castelli and Salvatore Geruzzi, 67–84. Pisa: Giardini, 2005.

Filippoupoliti, Anastasia. "Spatializing the Private Collection: John Fiott Lee and
Hartwell House." In *Material Cultures, 1740–1920: The Meanings and Pleasures
of Collecting,* edited by John Potvin and Alla Myzelev, 53–69. Farnham: Ashgate,
2009.

Finegan, Jack. *Handbook of Biblical Chronology: Principles of Time Reckoning in the
Ancient World and Problems of Chronology in the Bible.* Rev. ed. Peabody, MA:
Hendrickson, 1998.

Foppens, Joannes Franciscus. *Bibliotheca Belgica, sive virorum in Belgio vitâ, scrip-
tisque illustrium catalogus.* 2 vols. Bruxelles: Petrus Foppens, 1739.

Gabriel, Astrik L. "Intellectual Relations between the University of Louvain and the
University of Paris in the 15th century." In *The Universities in the Late Middle
Ages,* edited by Jozef IJsewijn and Jacques Paquet, 82–132. Mediaevalia Lovanien-
sia, 1st ser., 6. Leuven: Leuven University Press, 1978.

Gamba, Enrico. *Le stelle sopra Urbino: storie di astrologi alla corte dei Montefeltro.*
Urbino: Centro Internazionale di Studi Urbino e la Prospettiva, 2011.

Gerrits, Gerard H. *Inter timorem et spem: A Study of the Theological Thought of
Gerard Zerbolt of Zutphen, 1367–1398.* Studies in Medieval and Reformation
Thought 37. Leiden: Brill, 1986.

Geudens, Christophe. "On the Logical Topics at the Eve of the Renaissance: A
Study of Saint-Omer, BA., Ms. 609 (c. 1502)." *Bulletin de philosophie médiévale*
59 (2018): 81–196.

———. "Louvain Theories of Topical Logic (c. 1450–1533): A Reassessment of the
Traditionalist Thesis." PhD Diss., KU Leuven, 2020.

Geudens, Christophe, and Serena Masolini. "Teaching Aristotle at the Louvain Faculty of Arts, 1425–1500: General Regulations and Handwritten Testimonies." *Rivista di Filosofia Neo-Scolastica* 108 (2016): 813–844.

Ginzel, Friedrich Karl. *Handbuch der mathematischen und technischen Chronologie: Das Zeitrechnungswesen der Völker.* 3 vols. Leipzig: Hinrichs, 1906–1914.

Grafton, Anthony. *Joseph Scaliger: A Study in the History of Classical Scholarship.* Vol. 2, *Historical Chronology.* Oxford: Clarendon Press, 1993.

———. "Mixed Messages: The Early Modern Reception of Eusebius as a Church Historian." *International Journal of the Classical Tradition* 27 (2020): 332–360.

Grafton, Anthony, and Joanna Weinberg. *"I have always loved the Holy Tongue": Isaac Casaubon, the Jews, and a Forgotten Chapter in Renaissance Scholarship.* Cambridge, MA: Belknap Press, 2011.

Guenée, Bernard. *Entre l'Église et l'État: quatre vies de prélats français à la fin du Moyen Âge (XIIIᵉ–XVᵉ siècle).* Paris: Gallimard, 1987.

Hallyn, Fernand. "Paul de Middelbourg, astrologue et astronome." In *Esculape et Dionysos: mélanges en l'honneur de Jean Céard,* edited by Jean Dupèbe, Franco Giacone, Emmanuel Naya, and Anne-Pascale Pouey-Mounou, 367–374. Geneva: Droz, 2008.

Hamilton, Alastair. "Gregory, John." *Oxford Dictionary of National Biography* (online). https://doi.org/10.1093/ref:odnb/11467.

Hamman, Adalbert, ed. *Patrologiae Latinae Supplementum.* Vol. 1. Paris: Garnier, 1958.

Heilen, Stephan. "Paul of Middelburg's *Prognosticum* for the Years 1484 to 1504." In *From Māshāʾallāh to Kepler: Theory and Practice in Medieval and Renaissance Astrology,* edited by Charles Burnett and Dorian Gieseler Greenbaum, 231–278. University of Wales, Trinity Saint David: Sophia Centre Press, 2015.

———. "Paul of Middelburg's Use of the *Mathesis* of Firmicus Maternus." In *Astrologers and their Clients in Medieval and Early Modern Europe,* edited by Wiebke Deimann and David Juste, 105–137. Beihefte zum Archiv für Kulturgeschichte 73. Cologne: Böhlau, 2015.

———. "Astrology at the Court of Urbino under Federico and Guidobaldo da Montefeltro." In *De Frédéric II à Rodolphe II: astrologie, divination et magie dans les cours (XIIIᵉ–XVIIᵉ siècle),* edited by Jean-Patrice Boudet, Martine Ostorero, and Agostino Paravicini Bagliani, 313–368. Micrologus Library 85. Florence: SISMEL, 2017.

Holford-Strevens, Leofranc. "Paschal Lunar Calendars up to Bede." *Peritia* 20 (2008): 165–208.

Humphreys, Colin J. *The Mystery of the Last Supper: Reconstructing the Final Days of Jesus.* Cambridge: Cambridge University Press, 2011.

IJsewijn, Jozef. "The Coming of Humanism to the Low Countries." In *Itinerarium Italicum: The Profile of the Italian Renaissance in the Mirror of its European Transformations,* edited by Heiko A. Oberman and Thomas A. Brady, 193–310. Studies in Medieval and Reformation Thought 14. Leiden: Brill, 1975.

Indestege, Luc. "New Light on Ludovicus Ravescot." *Quaerendo* 1 (1971): 16–18.

Jardine, Lisa, and Anthony Grafton. "'Studied for Action': How Gabriel Harvey Read his Livy." *Past and Present* 129 (1990): 30–78.

Jodogne, Pierre. "L'Umanesimo italiano nei Paesi Bassi sotto i duchi di Borgogna." *Rinascimento* 38 (1998): 317–335.

Jones, Charles W. *Bedae Opera de temporibus*. The Medieval Academy of America Publication No. 41. Cambridge, MA: The Medieval Academy of America, 1943.

Junyent i Subirà, Eduard. *Diplomatari i escrits literaris de l'abat i bisbe Oliba*. Edited by Anscari M. Mundó. Barcelona: Institut d'Estudis Catalans, 1992.

Kaltenbrunner, Ferdinand. "Die Vorgeschichte der gregorianischen Kalenderreform." *Sitzungsberichte der philosophisch-historischen Classe der kaiserlichen Akademie der Wissenschaften* [Vienna] 82 (1876): 289–414.

Kaster, Robert A. *Studies on the Text of Macrobius' Saturnalia*. Oxford: Oxford University Press, 2010.

Ker, Neil Ripley. "'For All That I may Clamp': Louvain Students and Lecture-Rooms in the Fifteenth Century." *Medium Ævum* 39 (1970): 32–33.

———. *Medieval Manuscripts in British Libraries*. Vol. 3. Oxford: Clarendon Press, 1983.

Kervyn de Lettenhove, Joseph Marie Bruno Constantin. *Chroniques relatives à l'histoire de la Belgique sous la domination des ducs de Bourgogne*. 3 vols. Brussels: F. Hayez, 1876.

Kock, Thomas. *Die Buchkultur der Devotio moderna: Handschriftproduktion, Literaturversorgung und Bibliotheksaufbau im Zeitalter der Medienwechsels*. 2nd ed. Tradition, Reform, Innovation: Studien zur Modernität des Mittelalters 2. Frankfurt am Maim: Lang, 2002.

———. "Lesen nach Vorschrift: Lektürepläne und Buchbestände devoter Gemeinschaften." In *Sources for the History of Medieval Books and Libraries*, edited by Rita Schlusemann, Jos. M. M. Hermans and Margriet Hoogvliet, 111–122. Boekhistorische reeks 2. Groningen: Egbert Forsten, 1999.

Kohl, Wilhelm, Ernest Persoons, and Anton G. Weiler, eds. *Monasticon Windeshemense*. Vol. 1. Brussels: Archives et Bibliothèques de Belgique, 1976.

Kotzor, Günther, ed. *Das altenglische Martyrologium*. 2 vols. Abhandlungen der Bayerischen Akademie der Wissenschaften, phil.-hist. Kl., Neue Folge, 88. Munich: Beck, 1981.

Kristeller, Paul Oskar. *Iter Italicum: A Finding List of Uncatalogued or Incompletely Catalogued Humanistic Manuscripts of the Renaissance in Italian and Other Libraries*. Vol. 5, *(Alia itinera III and Italy III) Sweden to Yugoslavia, Utopia, Supplement to Italy (A–F)*. London: University of London. Warburg Institute, 1990.

Krusch, Bruno. *Studien zur christlich-mittelalterlichen Chronologie: Der 84-jährige Osterzyklus und seine Quellen*. Leipzig: Von Veit, 1880.

——. *Studien zur christlich-mittelalterlichen Chronologie: Die Entstehung unserer heutigen Zeitrechnung.* Abhandlungen der Preußischen Akademie der Wissenschaften, Jg. 1937, phil.-hist. Kl., 8. Berlin: de Gruyter, 1938.

Kuithan, Rolf, and Joachim Wollasch. "Der Kalender des Chronisten Bernold." *Deutsches Archiv* 40 (1984): 478–531.

Künzle, Pius. *Heinrich Seuses Horologium Sapientiae.* Spicilegium Friburgense 23. Freiburg (Switzerland): Universitätsverlag Freiburg-Schweiz, 1977.

Labajos Alonso, José, ed. *Escritos académicos de Pedro de Osma.* Salamanca: Universidad Pontificia de Salamanca, 2010.

Lamberts, Emiel, and Jan Roegiers, eds. *Leuven University, 1425–1985.* Leuven: Leuven University Press, 1990.

Lazzarato, Damiano. *Chronologia Christi seu discordantium fontium concordantia ad juris normam.* Naples: M. d'Auria, 1952.

Lehmann, Paul. "Alte Vorläufer des Gesamtkatalogs." In *Erforschung des Mittelalters: Ausgewählte Abhandlungen und Aufsätze,* 5 vols, 4:172–183. Stuttgart: Anton Hiersemann, 1961.

Lejbowicz, Max. "Des tables pascales aux tables astronomiques et retour: formation et réception du comput patristique." *Methodos: Savoirs et textes* 6 (2006) (online), http://methodos.revues.org/documents538.html; doi:10.4000/methodos.538.

Lentes, Thomas. "Counting Piety in the Late Middle Ages." Translated by Pamela Selwyn. In *Ordering Medieval Society: Perspectives on Intellectual and Practical Modes of Shaping Social Relations,* edited by Bernhard Jussen, 55–91. Philadelphia: University of Pennsylvania Press, 2001.

Leonhard, Clement. *The Jewish Pesach and the Origins of the Christian Easter: Open Questions in Current Research.* Studia Judaica: Forschungen zur Wissenschaft des Judentums 35. Berlin: de Gruyter, 2006.

Linde, Cornelia. *How to Correct the Sacra Scriptura? Textual Criticism of the Latin Bible between the Twelfth and Fifteenth Century.* Oxford: Society for the Study of Medieval Languages and Literature, 2012.

Loi, Vincenzo. "Il 25 Marzo data pasquale e la cronologia giovannea della passione in età patristica." *Ephemerides Liturgicae* 85 (1971): 48–69.

Lourdaux, Willem. "De Sint-Maartensschool te Leuven: moderne devoten en onderwijs, een omstreden probleem." *Bijdragen: Tijdschrift voor Filosophie en Theologie* 37, no. 2 (1976): 172–211.

——. *Moderne devotie en Christelijk humanisme: de geschiedenis van Sint-Maarten te Leuven van 1433 tot het einde der XVIe eeuw.* KUL, Werken op het gebied van de geschiedenis en de filologie, Reeks 5, 1. Leuven: Universiteitsbibliotheek, 1967.

——. "Prieuré du Val-Saint-Martin, à Louvain." In *Monasticon Belge: Province de Brabant,* edited by Dom U. Berlière, 1137–1154. Liège: Centre national de recherches d'histoire religieuse, 1970.

Lourdaux, Willem, and Marcel Haverals. *Bibliotheca Vallis Sancti Martini in Lovanio: bijdrage tot de studie van het geesteleven in de Nederlanden (15de–18de eeuw)*. 2 vols. Leuven: Universitaire Pers, 1978–1982.

Lowe, Elias A. *Die ältesten Kalendarien aus Monte Cassino*. Quellen und Untersuchungen zur lateinischen Philologie des Mittelalters 3.3. Munich: Beck, 1908.

Lyall, R. J. "Scottish Students and Masters at the Universities of Cologne and Louvain in the Fifteenth Century." *Innes Review* 36 (1985): 55–73.

MacCarron, Máirín. *Bede and Time: Computus, Theology and History in the Early Medieval World*. Abingdon: Routledge 2020.

Macdougall, Norman. *James III*. Edinburgh: John Donald, 2009.

Marzi, Demetrio. "Nuovi studii e ricerche intorno alla questione del calendario durante i secoli XV e XVI." In *Atti del congresso internazionale di scienze storiche (Roma, 1–9 Aprile 1903)*, 12 vols., 3:637–650. Rome: Accademia dei Lincei, 1904–1907.

———. *La questione della riforma del calendario nel Quinto Concilio Lateranense (1512–1517)*. Florence: Carnesecchi, 1896.

Masolini, Serena. "Petrus de Rivo (ca. 1420–1499): Portrait(s) of a Louvain Master." PhD Diss., KU Leuven, 2016.

———. "How to Order Four into One: Harmonizing the Gospels at the Dawn of Biblical Humanism." In: *1516: Towards Erasmus and More*, edited by Anthony Dupont, Wim François, Andrea A. Robiglio, and Violet Soen. LECTIO: Studies in the Transmission of Texts & Ideas 10. Turnhout: Brepols, forthcoming.

Masolini, Serena, and Christopher Schabel. "Peter de Rivo." In: *Encyclopedia of Medieval Philosophy*, edited by Henrik Lagerlund, 1–7. Dordrecht: Springer, 2018.

McCluskey, Stephen C. *Astronomies and Cultures in Early Medieval Europe*. Cambridge: Cambridge University Press, 1998.

McConnell, "Lee [*formerly* Fiott], John." *Oxford Dictionary of National Biography* (online). https://doi.org/10.1093/ref:odnb/16297.

McEvoy, James. "The Historic Irish, Scots and English Colleges of Louvain, and the Irish Presence in other Colleges of the University." *Seanchas Ardmhacha: Journal of the Armagh Diocesan Historical Society* 23, no. 1 (2010): 57–90.

Mertens, Thom. "Lezen met de pen: Ontwikkelingen in het laatmiddeleeuws geestelijk proza." In *De studie van de Middelnederlandse letterkunde: stand en toekomst*, edited by Frits P. van Oostrom and Frank Willaert, 187–200. Middeleeuwse studies en bronnen 14. Hilversum: Verloren, 1989.

Meuten, Erich, and Hermann Hallauer, eds. *Acta Cusana. Quellen zur Lebensgeschichte des Nikolaus von Kues*. Vol. 1.3b. Hamburg: Meiner, 1996.

Monfasani, John. "Criticism of Biblical Humanists in Quattrocento Italy." In *Biblical Humanism and Scholasticism in the Age of Erasmus*, edited by Erika Rummel, 15–38. Leiden: Brill, 2008.

Morin, Germain, ed. *Sancti Augustini Sermones post Maurinos reperti*. Rome: Tipografia Poliglotta Vaticana, 1930.

Mosshammer, Alden A. *The Easter Computus and the Origins of the Christian Era*. Oxford: Oxford University Press, 2008.

——, ed. *The Prologues on Easter of Theophilus of Alexandria and [Cyril]*. Oxford: Oxford University Press, 2017.

Munding, Emmanuel, ed. *Die Kalendarien von St. Gallen: Aus 21 Handschriften, neuntes bis elftes Jahrhundert*. 2 vols. Texte und Arbeiten 1.36. Beuron in Hohenzollern: Beuroner Kunstverlag, 1948.

Naumowicz, Józef. "La date de naissance du Christ d'après Denys le Petit et les auteurs chrétiens antérieurs." *Studia Patristica* 34 (2001): 292–296.

Neugebauer, Otto Eduard. "On the 'Spanish Era'." *Chiron* 11 (1981): 371–380.

Nothaft, C. Philipp E. "Astronomy and Calendar Reform at the Curia of Pope Clement VI: A New Source." *Annals of Science* 74 (2017): 1–24.

——. "Between Crucifixion and Calendar Reform: Medieval Christian Perceptions of the Jewish Lunisolar Calendar." In *Living the Lunar Calendar*, edited by Jonathan Ben-Dov, Wayne Horowitz, and John M. Steele, 259–267. Oxford: Oxbow Books, 2012.

——. "Chronologically Confused: Claudius of Turin and the Date of Christ's Passion." In *Late Antique Calendrical Thought and its Reception in the Early Middle Ages: Proceedings from the 3rd International Conference on the Science of Computus in Ireland and Europe, Galway, 16–18 July, 2010*, edited by Immo Warntjes and Dáibhí Ó Cróinín, 265–292. Studia Traditionis Theologiae 26. Turnhout: Brepols, 2017.

——. "The Chronological Treatise *Autores Kalendarii* of 1317, Attributed to John of Murs: Text and Introduction." *Cahiers de l'Institut du Moyen-Âge Grec et Latin* 82 (2013): 1–89.

——. *Dating the Passion: The Life of Jesus and the Emergence of Scientific Chronology (200–1600)*. Time, Astronomy, and Calendars: Texts and Studies 1. Leiden: Brill, 2012.

——. "Duking it Out in the Arena of Time: Chronology and the Christian-Jewish Encounter (1100–1600)." *Medieval Encounters* 22 (2016): 213–235.

——. "Early Christian Chronology and the Origins of the Christmas Date." *Questions Liturgiques* 94 (2013): 247–265.

——. "An Eleventh-Century Chronologer at Work: Marianus Scottus and the Quest for the Missing 22 Years." *Speculum* 88 (2013): 457–482.

——. "John of Murs and the Treatise *Autores kalendarii* (1317): A Problem of Authorship." *Sudhoffs Archiv* 99 (2015): 209–229.

——. "The Mathematics of Calendar Reform in Medieval Europe." In *Ritual, Mathematics & Astral Sciences*, edited by Karine Chemla et al. (forthcoming).

———. *Medieval Latin Christian Texts on the Jewish Calendar: A Study with Five Editions and Translations*. Time, Astronomy, and Calendars: Texts and Studies 4. Leiden: Brill, 2014.

———. "Nicholas Trevet and the Chronology of the Crucifixion." *The Mediaeval Journal* 2 (2012): 55–76.

———. "Reforming the Calendar at the University of Salamanca ca. 1468: Pedro Martínez de Osma and his *Disputatio de anno...*" *eHumanista* 23 (2013): 522–556.

———. *Scandalous Error: Calendar Reform and Calendrical Astronomy in Medieval Europe*. Oxford: Oxford University Press, 2018.

———. "Strategic Skepticism: A Reappraisal of Nicholas of Cusa's Calendar Reform Treatise." In *Le temps des astronomes: l'astronomie et le décompte du temps de Pierre d'Ailly à Newton*, edited by Edouard Mehl and Nicolas Roudet, 65–102. Paris: Les Belles Lettres, 2017.

———. "Thomas Strzempiński, Hermann Zoest, and the Initial Stages of the Calendar Reform Project Attempted at the Council of Basel (1434–1437)." *Cahiers de l'Institut du Moyen-Âge Grec et Latin* 84 (2015): 164–303.

———. "*Vanitas vanitatum et super omnia vanitas*: The Astronomer Heinrich Selder and a Newly Discovered Fourteenth-Century Critique of Astrology." *Erudition and the Republic of Letters* 1 (2016): 261–304.

———. "Victorian Survival in High Medieval Chronography: The Strange Case of the Angevin Paschal Chronicle." In *Proceedings of the 4th Galway Computus Conference*, edited by Immo Warntjes and Dáibhí Ó Cróinín. Turnhout: Brepols (forthcoming).

———. "'With utmost certainty': Two Late Medieval Pioneers of Technical Chronology." *Journal of Medieval History* 46 (2020): 335–349.

Nothaft, C. Philipp E., and Justine Isserles. "Calendars Beyond Borders: Exchange of Calendrical Knowledge between Jews and Christians in Medieval Europe (12th–15th Century)." *Medieval Encounters* 20 (2014): 1–37.

Ó Cróinín, Dáibhí. "Archbishop James Ussher (1581–1656) and the History of the Easter Controversy." In *Late Antique Calendrical Thought and its Reception in the Early Middle Ages: Proceedings from the 3rd International Conference on the Science of Computus in Ireland and Europe, Galway, 16–18 July, 2010*, edited by Immo Warntjes and Dáibhí Ó Cróinín, 309–351. Studia Traditionis Theologiae 26. Turnhout: Brepols, 2017.

Ó Riain, Pádraig, ed. *Four Irish Martyrologies: Drummond, Turin, Cashel, York*. Henry Bradshaw Society 115. London: Boydell Press, 2002.

Oakley, Francis. "'Anxieties of Influence': Skinner, Figgis, Conciliarism and Early Modern Constitutionalism." *Past and Present* 151 (1996): 60–110.

———. "Constance, Basel and the Two Pisas: The Conciliarist Legacy in Sixteenth and Seventeenth-Century England." *Annuarium historiae conciliorum* 26, no. 1 (1994): 87–118.

Oates, John Claud Trewinard. *A Catalogue of the Fifteenth-Century Printed Books in the University Library Cambridge.* 2 vols. Cambridge: Cambridge University Press, 1954.

Obbema, Pieter F. J. "The Latin Classics in Monastic Libraries of the Low Countries in the Fifteenth Century." In *Medieval Manuscripts of the Latin Classics: Production and Use,* edited by Claudine A. Chavannes-Mazel and Margaret M. Smith, 150–165. Los Altos Hills, CA, and London: Anderson-Lovelace and the Red Gull Press, 1996.

———. "Problems in Editing the Rooklooster Register." In *Middeleeuwse bibliotheken en boekenlijsten in de Zuiderlijke Nederlanden,* edited by Wouter Bracke and Albert Derolez, 71–76. Brussels: Koninklijke Vlaamse academie van België, 2005.

———. "The Rooklooster Register Evaluated." *Quaerendo* 7 (1977): 326–352.

Offenberg, Adri K. "The First Use of Hebrew in a Book Printed in the Netherlands." *Quaerendo* 4 (1974): 44–54.

Ogg, George. *The Chronology of the Public Ministry of Jesus.* Cambridge: Cambridge University Press, 1940.

Ostorero, Martine. *Le diable au sabbat: littérature démonologique et sorcellerie (1440–1460).* Micrologus Library 38. Florence: SISMEL, 2011.

Palmer, W. M. "Landwade and the Cotton Family." *Proceedings of the Cambridge Antiquarian Society* 38 (1939): 1–49.

Paul, James Balfour. *The Scots Peerage.* Vol. 3. Edinburgh: David Douglas, 1906.

Peri, Vittorio. "La data della Pasqua: nota sull'origine e lo sviluppo della questione pasquale tra le Chiese cristiane." *Vetera Christianorum* 13 (1976): 319–348.

Persoons, Ernest. "De inkunabels van de priorij Bethleem te Herent." *Mededeelingen van de Geschied- en Oudheidkundige Kring voor Leuven en Omgeving* 1 (1961): 55–60, 151–169.

———. "Het intellectuele leven in het klooster Bethlehem in de 15de eeuw." *Archives et bibliothèques de Belgique / Archief- en bibliotheekwezen in België* 43 (1972): 47–84.

———. "Nikolaas van Cusa te Leuven en te Bethleem in 1452." *Mededelingen van de Geschied en Oudheidkundige Kring voor Leuven en Omgeving* 4 (1964): 63–69.

———. "Prieuré de Bethleem, à Herent." In *Monasticon Belge: Province de Brabant,* edited by Dom U. Berlière, 1005–1024. Liège: Centre national de recherches d'histoire religieuse, 1970.

Piper, Ferdinand. *Die Kalendarien und Martyrologien der Angelsachsen; so wie das Martyrologium und der Computus der Herrad von Landsperg.* Berlin: Verlag der Königlichen Geheimen Ober-Hofbuchdruckerei, 1862.

Pitre, Brant. *Jesus and the Last Supper.* Grand Rapids, MI: Eerdmans, 2015.

Pompeo Faracovi, Ornella. "Il tema dell'eclissi di sole alla morte di Cristo in alcuni testi del tardo quattrocento." *Micrologus* 12 (2004): 195–215.

Poole, Robert. *Time's Alteration: Calendar Reform in Early Modern England.* London: UCL Press, 1998.

Poulle, Emmanuel. "Les astronomes parisiens au XIVe siècle et l'astronomie al-phonsine." In *Histoire littéraire de la France*, vol. 43.1, 1–54. Paris: Boccard, 2005.

Price, Betsey Barker. "The Use of Astronomical Tables by Albertus Magnus." *Journal for the History of Astronomy* 22 (1991): 221–240.

Prims, Floris. "De Kloosterslot-beweging in Brabant in de XVde eeuw." *Mededeelingen van de Koninklijke Vlaamsche Academie voor Wetenschappen, Letteren en Schoone Kunsten van België* 6, no. 1 (1944): 1–34.

Quicherat, Jules. *Histoire des Règnes de Charles VII et de Louis XI par Thomas Basin.* 4 vols. Ouvrages publiés par la Société de l'histoire de France 29. Paris: Lahure, 1855–1859.

———. "Thomas Basin, sa vie et ses écrits." *Bibliothèque de l'École des Chartes* 3 (1841–1842): 313–376.

Renaud, Adam. "La circulation des incunables à Louvain au XVe siècles: étude sur la production du relieur Ludovicus Ravescot." In *Miscellanea in memoriam Pierre Cockshaw (1938–2008): aspects de la vie culturelle dans les Pays-Bas Méridionaux (XIVe–XVIIIe siècle)*, edited by Frank Daelemans and Ann Kelders, 2 vols., 1:1–21. Brussels: Archives et Bibliothèques de Belgique, 2009.

Reusens, Edmond, ed. "Testament de Maître Henri Wellens, par lequel il fonde l'abbaye de Saint-Martin à Louvain." *Analectes pour servir à l'histoire ecclésiastique de la Belgique* 7 (1870): 223–227.

———. "Chronique de la Chartreuse de Louvain depuis sa fondation, en 1498, jusqu'à l'année 1525." *Analectes pour servir à l'histoire ecclésiastique de la Belgique* 14 (1877): 228–299.

———. *Documents relatifs a l'histoire de l'Université de Louvain (1425–1797).* 5 vols. Leuven: Reusens, 1881–1903.

Reusens, Edmond, C.-B. de Ridder, and J. Barbier, eds. "Documents relatifs au monastère dit le Trône-de-Notre-Dame, à Grobbendonck (Anvers), et au prieuré du Val-Saint-Martin, à Louvain." *Analectes pour servir à l'histoire ecclésiastique de la Belgique* 12 (1875): 441–471; 13 (1876): 71–107.

Rice, Eugene F., Jr. *Saint Jerome in the Renaissance.* Baltimore, MD: Johns Hoplins University Press, 1985.

Ritter, Adolf Martin. "Dionysius Pseudo-Areopagites und die 'Sonnenfinsternis während der Kreuzigung des Erlösers'." In *"Stürmend auf finsterem Pfad...": Ein Symposion zur Sonnenfinsternis in der Antike*, edited by Helga Köhler, Herwig Görgemanns, and Manual Baumbach, 49–59. Heidelberger Forschungen 33. Heidelberg: Winter, 2000.

Robertson, Barry. *Royalists at War in Scotland and Ireland 1638–1650.* Farnham: Ashgate, 2014.

Rudy, Kathryn M. "Kissing Images, Unfurling Rolls, Measuring Wounds, Sewing Badges and Carrying Talismans: Considering Some Harley Manuscripts through the Physical Rituals They Reveal." *Electronic British Library Journal* (2011), Article 5: 1–56.

———. *Postcards on Parchment: The Social Lives of Medieval Books.* New Haven, CT: Yale University Press, 2015.

Rummel, Erika, ed., *Biblical Humanism and Scholasticism in the Age of Erasmus.* Leiden: Brill, 2008.

———. *The Humanist-Scholastic Debate in the Renaissance & Reformation.* Cambridge, MA: Harvard University Press, 1995.

Salembier, Louis. "Une page inédite de l'histoire de la Vulgate." *Revue des sciences ecclésiastiques* 56–62 (1887–1890).

Sambin, Paolo. "Il dottorato padovano in medicina di Paolo da Middelburgo (1480)." *Quaderni per la storia dell'Università di Padova* 9–10 (1976–1977): 252–256.

Saulnier, Stéphane. *Calendrical Variations in Second Temple Judaism: New Perspectives on the 'Date of the Last Supper' Debate.* Supplements to the Journal for the Study of Judaism 159. Leiden: Brill, 2012.

Schabel, Christopher. "Peter de Rivo and the Quarrel over Future Contingents at Louvain: New Evidence and New Perspectives. (Part I)." *Documenti e studi sulla tradizione filosofica medievale* 6 (1995): 363–473.

———."Peter de Rivo and the Quarrel over Future Contingents at Louvain: New Evidence and New Perspectives. (Part II)." *Documenti e studi sulla tradizione filosofica medievale* 7 (1996): 369–435.

———. *Theology at Paris, 1316–1345: Peter Auriol and the Problem of Divine Foreknowledge and Future Contingents.* Ashgate Studies in Medieval Philosophy. Aldershot: Ashgate, 2000.

Schmid, Joseph. *Die Osterfestberechnung in der abendländischen Kirche vom I. Allgemeinen Konzil zu Nicäa bis zum Ende des VIII. Jahrhunderts.* Freiburg im Breisgau: Herder, 1907.

Schmidlin, Joseph. *Geschichte der deutschen Nationalkirche in Rom: S. Maria dell'Anima.* Freiburg im Breisgau: Herder, 1906.

Schmidt, Thomas C. "Calculating December 25 as the Birth of Jesus in Hippolytus' *Canon* and *Chronicon.*" *Vigiliae Christianae* 69 (2015): 542–563.

Schwarz, Werner. *Principles and Problems of Biblical Translation: Some Reformation Controversies and their Background.* Cambridge: Cambridge University Press, 1955.

Scott, Hew. *Fasti ecclesiae scoticanae: The Succession of Ministers in the Church of Scotland from the Reformation to the Present.* Rev. ed. Edinburgh: Oliver and Boyd, 1915.

Sickel, Theodor. "Die Lunarbuchstaben in den Kalendarien des Mittelalters." *Sitzungsberichte der philosophisch-historischen Classe der kaiserlichen Akademie der Wissenschaften* [Vienna] 38 (1861): 153–201.

Silvestre, Hubert. "Le jour et l'heure de la nativité et de la résurrection pour Rupert de Deutz." In *Pascua Mediaevalia: Studies voor Prof. Dr. J. M. de Smet*, edited by Robrecht Lievens, Erik van Mingroot, and Werner Verbeke, 619–630. Mediaevalia Lovaniensia, 1ˢᵗ ser., 10. Leuven: University Press, 1983.

Solan, Olivier de. *La réforme du calendrier aux conciles de Constance et de Bâle.* Sources d'histoire médiévale 42. Paris: CNRS Éditions, 2016.

Spalding, John. *History of the Troubles and Memorable Transactions in Scotland, from the Year 1624 to 1645.* 2 vols. Bannatyne Club 25. Aberdeen: T. Evans, 1792.

Springsfeld, Kerstin. *Alkuins Einfluß auf die Komputistik zur Zeit Karls des Großen.* Sudhoffs Archiv: Beihefte 48. Stuttgart: Steiner, 2002.

Staubach, Nikolaus. "Der Codex als Ware: Wirtschaftliche Aspekte der Handschriftproduktion im Bereich der Devotio moderna." In *Der Codex im Gebrauch*, edited by Christel Meier, Dagmar Hüpper, and Hagen Keller, 143–162. Munich: Wilhelm Fink Verlag, 1996.

———. "*Diversa raptim undique collecta*: Das Rapiarium im geistlichen Reformprogramm der Devotio moderna." In *Literarische Formen des Mittelalters: Florilegien, Kompilationen, Kollektionen*, edited by Kaspar Elm, 115–147. Wiesbaden: Harrassowitz Verlag, 2000.

———. "*Memores pristinae perfectionis*: The Importance of the Church Fathers for the Devotio moderna." In *The Reception of the Church Fathers in the West: From the Carolingians to the Maurists*, edited by Irena Backus, 405–469. Leiden: Brill, 1997.

———. "Pragmatische Schriftlichkeit im Bereich der Devotio moderna." *Frühmittelalterliche Studien* 25 (1991): 418–461.

Steinmetz, Dirk. *Die Gregorianische Kalenderreform von 1582: Korrektur der christlichen Zeitrechnung in der Frühen Neuzeit.* Oftersheim: Steinmetz, 2011.

Stern, Sacha. *Calendars in Antiquity: Empires, States, and Societies.* Oxford: Oxford University Press, 2012.

Stevenson, David. "The King's Scottish Revenues and the Covenanters, 1625–1651." *Historical Journal* 17 (1974): 17–41.

Stokes, Whitley, ed. *Félire húi Gormáin: The Martyrology of Gorman.* Henry Bradshaw Society 9. London: Harrison, 1895.

———, ed. *Félire Óengusso Céli Dé: The Martyrology of Oengus the Culdee.* Henry Bradshaw Society 29. London: Harrison, 1905.

Strobel, August. *Texte zur Geschichte des frühchristlichen Osterkalenders.* Liturgiewissenschaftliche Quellen und Forschungen 64. Münster: Aschendorff, 1984.

Struik, Dirk Jan. "Paolo di Middelburg e il suo posto nella storia delle scienze esatte." *Periodico di Matematiche*, 4th ser., 5 (1925): 337–347.

———. "Paulus van Middelburg (1445–1533)." *Mededeelingen van het Nederlandsch Historisch Instituut te Rome* 5 (1925): 79–118.

Summit, Jennifer. *Memory's Library: Medieval Books in Early Modern England.* Chicago: University of Chicago Press, 2008.

van Aelst, José. "Het gebruik van beelden bij Suso's lijdensmeditatie." In *Geen povere schoonheid: laat-middeleeuwse kunst in verband met de moderne devotie*, edited by Kees Veelenturf, 86–110. Nijmegen: Valkhof, 2000.

Tournoy, Gilbert. "Gli umanisti italiani nell'Università di Lovanio nel Quattrocento." in *Rapporti e scambi tra umanesimo italiano ed umanesimo europeo: L'Europa è uno stato d'animo*, edited by Luisa Rotondi Secchi Tarugi, 39–50. Caleidoscopio 10. Milan: Nuovi orizzonti, 2001.

Van Belle, André. "La Faculté des Arts de Louvain: quelques aspects de son organisation au XVᵉ siècle." In *The Universities in the Late Middle Ages*, edited by Jozef IJsewijn and Jacques Paquet, 42–48. Mediaevalia Lovaniensia, 1ˢᵗ ser., 6. Leuven: Leuven University Press, 1978.

Van den Gheyn, J. *Catalogue des manuscrits de la Bibliothèque royale de Belgique*. 13 vols. Brussels: Lamertin, 1901–1948.

van der Essen, Léon. "Testament de Maître Guillaume de Varenacker (1478): un document pour l'histoire sociale du XVᵉ siècle." *Bulletin de la commission royale d'histoire* 93, no. 1 (1929): 1–31.

Van Eijl, Edmond J. M. et al., eds. *Facultas S. Theologiae Lovaniensis, 1432–1797: bijdragen tot haar geschiedenis*. Bibliotheca Ephemeridum Theologicarum Lovaniensium 45. Leuven: Leuven University Press, 1977.

Van Eijl, Edmond J. M. "Louvain's Faculty of Theology during the Fifteenth and Sixteenth Centuries." *Louvain Studies* 5, no. 3 (1975): 219–233.

———. "The Foundation of the University of Louvain." In *The Universities in the Late Middle Ages*, edited by Jozef IJsewijn and Jacques Paquet, 29–41. Mediaevalia Lovaniensia, 1ˢᵗ ser., 6. Leuven: Leuven University Press, 1978.

Van Engen, John. "A Brabantine Perspective on the Origins of the Modern Devotion: The First Book of Petrus Impens's *Compendium Decursus Temporum Monasterii Christifere Bethleemitice Puerpere*." In *Serta Devota in memoriam Guillelmi Lourdaux, Pars Prior: Devotio Windeshemensis*, edited by Werner Verbeke, Marcel Haverals, Rafaël De Keyser, and Jean Goossens, 3–78. Leuven: Leuven University Press, 1992.

———. "Multiple Options: The World of the Fifteenth-Century Church." *Church History* 77, no. 2 (2008): 257–284.

———. *Sisters and Brothers of the Common Life: The Devotio Moderna and the World of the Later Middle Ages*. Philadelphia: University of Pennsylvania Press, 2008.

van Leijenhorst, C. G. "Paul of Middelburg." In *Contemporaries of Erasmus: A Biographical Register of the Renaissance and Reformation*, edited by Peter G. Bietenholz and Thomas B. Deutscher, 3 vols., 3:57–58. Toronto: University of Toronto Press, 1987.

van Liere, Frans. "Gamaliel, Twelfth-Century Christian Scholars and the Attribution of the Talmud." *Medieval Perspectives* 17, no. 2 (2002): 93–104.

van Mierlo, Jozef. "De anonymi uit den katalogus van handschriften van Rooklooster." *Ons Geestelijk Erf* 4 (1930): 84–102, 316–357.

———. "Een katalogus van handschriften in Nederlandsche bibliotheken uit 1487." *Ons Geestelijk Erf* 2 (1928): 275–303.

van Mingroot, Erik. *Sapientie Immarcessibilis: A Diplomatic and Comparative Study of the Bull of Foundation of the University of Louvain (December 9, 1425)*. Translated by Angela Fritsen. Leuven: Leuven University Press, 1994.

Van Waefelghem, Raphaël. "Une élection abbatiale au XVᵉ siècle: Thierry de Thulden, abbé du Parc (1462)." In *Mélanges d'histoire offerts à Charles Moeller*, 2 vols., 1:671–682. Université de Louvain: Recueil de travaux publiés par les membres des conférences d'histoire et de philologie 40–41 Leuven: Bureau du Recueil, 1914.

Vanden Broecke, Steven. "Paulus van Middelburg, *Paulina. De recta paschae celebratione, et de die passionis domini nostri Iesu Christi*." In *De geleerde wereld van Keizer Karel*, edited by Tineke Padmos and Geerd Vanpaemel, 291–293. Leuven: Leuven University Press, 2000.

Vanderjagt, Arjo. "Classical Learning and the Building of Power at the Fifteenth-Century Burgundian Court." In *Centres of Learning: Learning and Location in Pre-Modern Europe and the Near East*, edited by Jan Willem Drijvers and Alasdair A. MacDonald, 267–277. Brill's Studies in Intellectual History 61. Leiden: Brill, 1995.

Venn, John. *Alumni Cantabrigienses: A Biographical List of All Known Students, Graduates, and Holders of Office at the University of Cambridge, from Earliest Times to 1900*. 10 vols. Nendeln: Krauz, 1974–1978.

Verbist, Peter. *Duelling with the Past: Medieval Authors and the Problem of the Christian Era, c. 990–1135*. Studies in the Early Middle Ages 21. Turnhout: Brepols, 2010.

———. "Een elfde-eeuwse dialoog tussen een leermeester en een leerling: het *Liber Decennalis* van Sigebert van Gembloux." In *In de voetsporen van Jacob van Maerlant: Liber amicorum Raf de Keyser*, edited by Raoul Bauer, Marjan de Smet, Brigitte Meijns, and Paul Trio, 101–113. Symbolae Facultatis Litterarum Lovaniensis, Ser. A, 30. Leuven: Leuven University Press, 2002.

———. "De Epistola ad Hugonem van Heriger van Lobbes († 1007): een belangrijk chronologisch traktaat." *Millennium: tijdschrift voor middeleeuwse studies* 12 (1998): 30–42.

———. "Reconstructing the Past: The Chronicle of Marianus Scottus (d. 1082)," *Peritia* 16 (2002): 284–334.

Vernarecci, Augusto. *Fossombrone dai tempi antichissimi ai nostri*. 2 vols. Fossombrone: Monacelli, 1907–1914.

Verweij, Michiel. *Adrianus VI (1459–1523): de tragische paus uit de Nederlanden*. Antwerp: Garant, 2010.

————. "Description and Interpretation of MS 17937 of the Royal Library of Belgium: A Case of Reception of Caesar's *Commentarii de bello Gallico*." In *Monte Artium: Journal of the Royal Library of Belgium* 6 (2013): 167–187.

Villanueva, Jaime. *Viage literario á las iglesias de España*. Vol. 8, *Viage á las iglesias de Vique y de Solsona, 1806 y 1807*. Valencia: Oliveres, 1821.

Vives, José. "Über Ursprung und Verbreitung der spanischen Ära." *Historisches Jahrbuch* 58 (1938): 97–108.

Wareham, Andrew F., and A. P. M. Wright. *A History of the County of Cambridge and the Isle of Ely*. Vol. 10, *Cheveley, Flendish, Staine and Staploe Hundreds (North-Eastern Cambridgeshire)*. London: Victoria County History, 2002.

Warntjes, Immo. *The Munich Computus: Text and Translation; Irish Computistics between Isidore of Seville and the Venerable Bede and its Reception in Carolingian Times*. Sudhoffs Archiv: Beihefte 59. Stuttgart: Steiner, 2010.

————. "A Newly Discovered Prologue of AD 699 to the Easter Table of Victorius of Aquitaine in an Unknown Sirmond Manuscript." *Peritia* 21 (2010): 255–284.

Weiler, Anton G. "Les relations entre l'université de Louvain et l'université de Cologne au XVᵉ siècle." In *The Universities in the Late Middle Ages*, edited by Jozef IJsewijn and Jacques Paquet, 49–81. Mediaevalia Lovaniensia, 1ˢᵗ ser., 6. Leuven: Leuven University Press, 1978.

Welker, Lorenz. "Ottaviano Petrucci and the Political-Cultural Elite of his Time: The 1513 Print of Paul of Middelburg's *Summa Paulina de Recta Paschae Celebratione*." In *Venezia 1501: Petrucci e la stampa musicale*, edited by Giulio Cattin and Patrizia Dalla Vecchia, 107–115. Venice: Edizioni Fondazione Levi, 2005.

Wiesenbach, Joachim, ed. *Sigebert von Gembloux: Liber decennalis*. MGH Quellen zur Geistesgeschichte des Mittelalters 12. Weimar: Böhlau, 1986.

Wilmart, André. *Analecta Reginensia: extraits des manuscrits latins de la reine Christine, conservés au Vatican*. Studi e testi 59. Vatican City: Biblioteca Apostolica Vaticana, 1933.

Wils, Joseph. *Matricule de l'Université de Louvain*. Vol. 2, *31 août 1453–31 août 1485*. Brussels: Palais des Académies, 1946.

Wilson, Henry A., ed. *The Calendar of St. Willibrord: From MS. Paris Lat. 10837*. Henry Bradshaw Society 55. London: Harrison, 1918. Reprint, Woodbridge: Boydell Press, 1998.

Wormald, Francis, ed. *English Benedictine Kalendars after A.D. 1100*. 2 vols. Henry Bradshaw Society 77 & 81. London: Harrison, 1939–1946.

————, ed. *English Kalendars before A.D. 1100*. Henry Bradshaw Society 72. London: Harrison, 1934. Reprint, Woodbridge: Boydell Press, 1988.

————. "A Liturgical Calendar from Guisborough Priory, with some Obits." *Yorkshire Archaeological Journal* 31 (1932): 5–35.

Yisraeli, Yosi. "From Christian Polemic to a Jewish-Converso Dialogue: Jewish Skepticism and the Rabbinic-Christian Traditions in the *Scrutinium Scripturarum*." *Medieval Encounters* 24 (2018): 160–196.

Source Index

GENERAL INDEX